The Political Economy of Bureaucracy

The Political Economy of Bureaucracy

P. M. Jackson

BARNES & NOBLE BOOKS
TOTOWA, NEW JERSEY

First published in the USA 1983 by
BARNES & NOBLE BOOKS
81 ADAMS DRIVE
TOTOWA, NEW JERSEY, 07512

Printed in Great Britain

Library of Congress Cataloging in Publication Data

Jackson, P. M. (Peter McLeod)
The political economy of bureaucracy.

1. Bureaucracy. I. Title.
HD38.4.J32 1983 350'.001 82-22674
ISBN 0-389-20352-1

Contents

Preface vii

1. **Why Study Bureaucracy?** 1
What is Bureaucracy?; Bureaucracy — The Early Writers; Some Modern Critiques of Bureaucracy; Bureaucracy, Resource Allocation and Political Economy; The Growth of the Public Sector and Bureaucracy

2. **Perspectives on Organisations** 14
The Organisation Theory Literature; What is an Organisation?; The Importance of Organisations; Approaches to the Analysis of Organisation; Scientific Management and Classical Administrative Theories; Classical Administrative Theories of Organisation; The Human Relations Approach to Organisational Analysis; Formal *versus* Informal Organisation; Recent Approaches to the Study of Organisations; Socio-Technic and Contingency Theories of Organisations; Contemporary Organisation Theory; Rational Model or Goal Paradigm; Crisis in Organisational Analysis — A Radical Critique

3. **Organisational Analysis: The Economist's Perspective** 46
The Traditional Theory of the Firm; The Existence of Firms; Managerial Theories of the Firm; The Economics of Internal Organisation; The Economic Theory of Teams; Organisations and the Distribution of Power; Williamson's Theory of Organisational Form; Public Sector Organisations; A Paradigmatic Crisis in Economics?; The Political Economy Paradigm of Organisations; Organisational Constitutions; The Internal Polity; The Behavioural Theory of the Firm; Critique of Behavioural Theory

4. **Decision Making Models** 86
Individual Decision Making; The Unbounded Rationality Model; The Bounded Rationality Model; Simon's Certainty Equivalent Theorem; Adaptive Behaviour; Individual Decision Making — Some Unresolved Problems; The Analysis of Goals; Collective Decision Making; Decision Making Under Conditions of Complexity and Uncertainty

5. **Bureaucracy: The Economist's Perspective** 121

Bureaucracy — The Analysis of Public Sector Supply; The Niskanen Model; Critique of the Niskanen Model; The Growth of Bureaucracy; Empirical Studies of Bureaucracy; Appendix 1

6. **Budgets and Bureaucrats** 143

Politics and the Budgetary Process; The Incremental Model of Budgeting; Empirical Tests of the Incremental Model; Critique of the Incremental Model; Incrementalism in the UK; The Political Economy of Budgeting — A Resource Dependence Perspective; Personal Influences in Budget/ Resource Allocation Decision Making

7. **Efficiency in Bureaucracy** 173

The Economist's Treatment of Efficiency; The Problem of Efficiency in the Public Sector; The Generalised Goal Model of Efficiency; Defining Output; Efficiency and Decision Making Costs; Control Loss and Efficiency; Empirical Studies of Public Sector Productivity; Efficiency and Organisational Structures; Efficiency, Complexity and Uncertainty; Incentives and Efficiency; Managerial Risks and Rewards in Public Bureaucracies; Efficiency and Decentralisation; Efficiency and Social Justice

8. **Accountability, and Control of Bureaucracy** 212

The Need for Control and Accountability; Accountability and Control; The Agency Relationship and the Professional Bureaucrat; Institutions of Accountability and Control — The Experience of the UK; Financial Accountability; Public Expenditure — The Case of Control; Post-Fulton Developments; Beyond Plowden and Fulton

9. **Organisational Limits: The Problems of Implementation** 252

Economists and the Implementation Process; A Framework — Organisational Failure; Models of the Implementation Process; Organisational Limits to Implementation; Organisational Limits and the Distribution of Information; Implementation, Efficiency and Control

Bibliography 273

Index 293

Preface

For many years economists suffered from analytical myopia produced by prolonged concentration upon the economics of the market place. In recent years the economist's field of vision has been widened to include non-market allocative processes. This shift in emphasis has resulted in economics incorporating much more of the social structure into its analysis, e.g. rights systems, structural constraints and the distribution of power. In this respect the economist has come much closer to other social scientists who attempt to, 'translate the acts of individuals into the regularities of social process' (Firth 1964, p.46).

Despite his increased interest in non-market decision making the economist continues to be misrepresented and misunderstood (see especially Self 1975; Barry 1970; and Wildavsky 1969). This book uses the concept of bureaucracy to build a number of bridges, especially between economists, political scientists, organisation theorists and public administrators. In writing this book I have become convinced that each of these disciplines has much to learn from the others. Unfortunately, modern developments in economics have caused economists to stand aloof from their neighbouring social scientists. For economists who are interested in the issues of structural adjustments, non-market decision making, and the wider questions of political economy, it is no longer meaningful to stand outside the arena of general social science. To do so would be to constrain their analysis of these topics so severely that their contribution would be minimal. In attempting to build bridges between subjects, there is a need to overcome the economist's automatic professional bias towards specialisation. I am only too aware that academics are rewarded for staying within their discipline and, moreover, for staying within a specific theoretical perspective within that discipline. Otherwise, they run the risk of severe criticism from colleagues, mild charges of being a 'theoretical dilettante' or an 'incredible eclectic', or worst of all 'theoretically inconsistent' (Argyris 1972). Whilst there are undoubtedly 'sunk costs' in the investment made in a particular theoretical framework and 'opportunity costs' involved in switching between frameworks, nevertheless I do take the view that such inter-theoretical linkages must be made if the fruits of scientific enquiry are to be reaped. My attempt at mixing together economics, organisation theory and political science is a modest one, far from complete, but hopefully sufficiently stimulating to encourage others to take up the challenge.

Although I have chosen to specialise as an economist, my original training included equal amounts of economics and organisation theory. This has assisted me in preparing this book. My thanks, therefore, go to Roy Wilkie, David Bradley and Peter Lawrence who, at Strathclyde University in the late 1960s, introduced me to the mysteries of organisation theory. My thanks must also go to another of my teachers, Dick Davies, also of Strathclyde University, who, as an economist, showed me the links between economics and organisation theory. I also owe a debt of gratitude to Brian Loasby of Stirling University whose writings and conversations stimulated many of my own thoughts and ideas. Royston Greenwood, of Birmingham University, gave me valuable assistance with Chapter 6. It should also be clear that I have benefited from the writings of Kenneth Arrow, James Buchanan, Herbert Simon, Aaron Wildavsky and Oliver Williamson.

Paul Boreham, Bob Borthwick, Justin Meadows and Ann Robinson have read drafts of a number of the chapters. Their comments were very helpful in preparing the final draft but, of course, all remaining errors are my own responsibility.

I would also like to thank my publisher, Philip Allan, who has been very patient with me as deadline after deadline has slipped past.

Finally, I must give a special word of thanks to Pat Greatorex, who not only typed her way through numerous drafts of the book, but also assisted with the preparation of the bibliography and the index, corrected my spelling and most important of all ensured that I kept to my final deadline.

P. M. Jackson
Public Sector Economics Research Centre
University of Leicester
Leicester LE1 7RH

March 1982

CHAPTER 1

Why Study Bureaucracy?

(Bureaucracy is) ... gigantic power set in motion by dwarfs ... a ponderous curtain hung between the service to be done and the man who orders it ... and as meddlesome as an old tradeswoman.

(Balzac: *Bureaucracy*)

... the Circumlocution Office went on mechanically, every day, keeping this wonderful, all sufficient wheel of statesmanship How Not to Do It *in motion. Because the Office was down upon any ill advised public servant who was going to do it, or who appeared to be by any surprising accident in remote danger of doing it with a minute or a memorandum, and a letter of instruction that extinguished him. It was this spirit of national efficiency in the Office that had gradually led to its having something to do with everything.*

(Dickens: *Little Dorrit*)

Introduction

During the last twenty years economists have been turning the tools of their trade to the investigation of political behaviour. Discarding the naive view that the public sector functions to promote the social welfare and further the 'public interest', economists have begun to examine the behaviour of utility maximising politicians, voters and bureaucrats. The study has focused upon the nature of the incentives and constraints which each group faces in an attempt to trace out the behavioural patterns implied by utility maximisation within a given environment. Within this 'political economy model', political behaviour is explained as a systematic response to a set of existing incentives as each group within the political arena acts in order to promote its own interests. This approach stands in distinction to the more traditional stance in economics which views political behaviour as a wholly altruistic act by political officials.

This new approach to the study of political economy grows out of the 'public choice school' founded by James Buchanan at the Virginia Polytechnic Institute. Rather than taking the existing set of fiscal institutions as given, theory must explain them. To understand the internal workings of the public sector it is necessary for the economist to turn attention to the dynamics of non-market decision making. The greater proportion of the economics literature has concentrated attention upon the workings of the market system. Public sector economics has traditionally been studied by examining the impact of taxes, subsidies and public expenditures upon market prices. The public choice approach examines the internal operations of the public sector itself. That is, it focuses attention on the institutions of the public sector and the decision making processes which produce the policies that determine the allocation and distribution of public services and the means of financing them.

Whilst the public choice school has concentrated attention upon collective choice mechanisms (such as voting systems), through which the demands of individual voters are aggregated into a single collective preference, it is only comparatively recently that the supply side of the equation (i.e. bureaucracy) has been subject to critical analysis. The economic analysis of bureaucracy is found in the seminal works of Downs (1965), Tullock (1965), Niskanen (1971) and Breton (1974).

In this book a number of different approaches to the study of bureaucracy will be examined. These alternatives will include those of the organisational sociologist, the political scientist, the public administration specialist and the economist. This review of alternative approaches is selective. It is written by an economist for economists which means that the cognitive filter through which this literature is reviewed will be distorted. The organising principle which has been used throughout this book is to introduce the economist to the issues, debates and controversies of bureaucracy which exist in other disciplines and which will, it is hoped, throw some light upon the questions which economists ask about bureaucracy. At the same time, the issues which have been drawn together in this book have been reformulated within the economist's framework. It is, therefore, hoped that those who are familiar with some of the well-worn debates will gain new insights from this perspective. The approach which has been adopted is not a simple review of the literature. An attempt has been made to put the elements of this mosaic into a fresh pattern; one which will be found to be useful for further developments of the subject. Specifically, two broadly based areas of study have been brought together. These are the sociology of organisations and the economics of non-market decision making. Both topics are comparatively recent developments within their subject areas and are as yet in the process of evolution. To bring them both together at this stage might be regarded by some to be a bit premature. Whilst the stitchwork in the mosaic is far from complete (only a start has been made here), it is believed that both disciplines have a contribution to make to each other's development.

Why Study Bureaucracy?

Today there is increasing concern about complex organisations, especially about the depersonalisation associated with them, their unresponsiveness to social needs, the nature of resource allocation within them and the power that they wield in society. One such set of complex organisations is the public sector bureaucracy. As the public sector grows in size relative to the rest of the economy, more and more activity is organised within the bureaucracy. More of the nation's wealth is allocated and distributed through decisions taken within the bureaucracy. In the post-war post-industrial society, the range of government activities has been rapidly extended to include an expansion of the welfare state, protection of the environment and consumers, regulation of industry and the military complex. Along with the extension of government powers, the number of civil servants servicing the public sector has also increased. Power has disappeared into the group and into the expert, which raises important questions about whose interests are being served by the bureaucracy. Does a representative democracy exist, or does the output supplied by the public sector serve the interests of the bureaucracy itself? 'Democracy inevitably comes into conflict with bureaucratic tendencies which democracy has produced' (Weber 1947, p. 226).

Elected politicians who head government departments are often thought of as conducting an orchestra without a score. The best that they can be expected to do is to have an impromptu rehearsal. Compared with the information held by their political masters the bureaucracy possesses much more technical information about the supply of public services. To the extent that information is power, there is a need for countervailing power to that of the bureaucracy.

Alongside the growth in government there has also been a rapid expansion in the quasi-nongovernmental sector (see Pifer 1967). This is the grey area which has come to be referred to as the QUANGOs, the 'contract state', the 'independent sector' or the 'mixed public private sector'. These organisations are not dependent upon continuing government appropriations for their existence, they do not report to a government department, and they obtain their authority directly from statute. They present a problem for control since they are managed by a non-elected board.

In the past politicians and administrators (bureaucrats) have been treated separately. There is, however, a great need to study the *relative* influence of these actors upon particular decisions. This has not been done in the UK to the same extent as it has in the USA. Very little is known about who makes the decisions in the policy making process or about how bureaucrats interact with one another and with politicians. Nor is much known about the consequences of interactions between politicians and bureaucrats. 'We do not know who governs; why and with what consequence,' (Greenwood and Hinings 1977).

What is Bureaucracy?

The early analysis of bureaucracy is found in the writings of Weber (1947), Marx (1970) and Michels (1911). These theories of bureaucracy tried to establish the formal position of the bureaucratic official in modern government, contrasting the concepts of bureaucracy and democracy. The concern of these writers was to demonstrate the ways in which public sector bureaucracies subverted democratic values and how this might be remedied. This is a theme which is continued in much of contemporary writings on bureaucracy in which the impact of large-scale bureaucracies on the power structure of society is examined (Jacob 1973, Bachrach 1969 and Pateman 1970).

There are several meanings of bureaucracy in modern usage. Albrow (1970) provides a useful classification:

(i) *Bureaucracy as rule by officials:* the bureaucracy is a powerful group which has considerable influence over the processes of government. Bureaucrats are employees of the State.
(ii) *Bureaucracy as rational organisation:* here bureaucracy refers to the nature of complex organisations and their structure. In particular bureaucracy is synonymous with hierarchy and refers to both public and private sector organisations.
(iii) *Bureaucracy as organisational inefficiency:* in this sense of the word bureaucracy is associated with red tape, complex organisational processes and inefficiency. Bureaucratic organisations are thought to be slow to respond to the demands of clients (customers) and employees.

Throughout this book we will have reason to make multiple use of the concept of bureaucracy. In particular, we will examine public sector bureaucracies which include those organisations of central and local government plus the public corporations and 'quangos'. Bureaucrats will be assumed to be civil servants and public sector employees who make executive decisions. At times the use of terminology will be loose and bureaucracy will simply refer to public sector organisations and bureaucrats will refer to public sector employees. For the purposes of our analysis a tighter language is not necessary. Bureaucracy is, therefore, a certain kind of formal organisation, characterised by a complex administrative hierarchy, specialisation of skills, and tasks, and prescribed limits on discretion set forth in a system of rules and impersonal behaviour with respect to clients. Examples of national public bureaucracies are the organisations that make up local and federal governments, the quangos and the public corporations. At the international level, NATO, OECD, and the EEC are public bureaucracies.

Bureaucracy: The Early Writers

Max Weber was one of the earlier writers to provide a systematic treatment of bureaucracy. The components of his bureaucratic model were:

(i) *Hierarchy of authority:* the locus of decision making is prestructured with decisions of varying types being made at different levels of the organisation. It is assumed that decision making ability and power are directly related to hierarchical position.
(ii) *Division of labour:* work tasks are subdivided into functional specialisation.
(iii) *Presence of rules:* the degree to which the behaviour of organisational members is subject to organisation control.
(iv) *Procedural Specification:* the extent to which organisational members must follow organisationally defined techniques in dealing with the variety of situations they face.
(v) *Impersonality:* describes the extent to which organisational members and outsiders are treated without regard to individual qualities (all people are treated the same way without consideration of individual differences).
(vi) *Technical competence:* the selection of personnel and promotion is based upon organisationally defined universal standards.

These elements of Weber's theory of bureaucracy formed the basis of an early analysis of organisations and were intended to maximise rational decision making. The systematic division of labour, rights and power was regarded by Weber as being essential for efficient organisation. Weber's analysis of bureaucratic organisations was not empirical. Having been brought up in a Prussian, legal and academic environment, he extrapolated from his German experience to describe a general set of organising principles. His analysis was, instead, normative and what he presented as a theory of bureaucracy was an 'ideal type' (see Mommsen 1974, for a discussion of the epistemological status of this approach).

Weber's analysis has not passed without criticism (see Albrow 1970). Merton (1957) argues that emphasis upon rule-bound behaviour can have undesirable consequences. Rules, which are a means of achieving organisational goals, can become ends in themselves (goal displacement). Selznick (1948, 1949), building on the work of Merton, identifies the dysfunctional consequences of bureaucracy. Whilst Weber had emphasised the formal structure of roles which define the internal society of the organisation, he had ignored the informal structure of relationships which characterise the reality of organisational life. The potential conflicts between the formal and the informal structures, along with the relationships between an organisation and its environment, can prevent the realisation of the organisation's goals. Parsons, in his editorial introduction to Weber (1947), draws attention to the possible conflict which might arise between a bureaucrat's authority derived from his position in the hierarchy, and that derived from technical expertise. To the extent that these do not match, other members of the organisation will not know who to obey — the person with the right to command or the person with the greater expertise. Gouldner (1952) and Bendix (1945) recognise that bureaucracies are part of a much wider social system which impinges upon bureaucracy through the values which individuals bring with them to the organisation. Finally, Weber's analysis is static. Blau (1963) examines the problems of rational administration in environments which are characterised by flux, change and uncertainty.

These points will be developed throughout the remainder of this book.

Marx, like Weber, characterised bureaucracy as an ideal type. The features of bureaucractic organisation were the division of functions and hierarchy. Although the analysis of bureaucracy was not central to Marx's thesis, as early as 1847 he had recognised it as one of the central phenomena of modern political and socio-economic life and of importance to the understanding of the modern state. The degree of bureaucratisation of any state would determine the degree of violence required by the proletariat to overthrow it. Bureaucracy was also viewed as a source of alienation. The power of the state, acting on behalf of the interests of capital, was concentrated in the hands of a bureaucratic elite.

The concept of bureaucracy has also been a source of interest for political scientists and sociologists who are keen to articulate the relationships between bureaucracy and democracy. Thus, Mosca (1958) characterised governments as being either feudal or bureaucratic. In feudal governments the ruling class was simple in structure, and functions (e.g. economic, administrative, judicial and military) were not clearly differentiated and might be performed by any one member at different times. The bureaucratic state, in contrast, was highly differentiated with functions being allocated to different groups within the ruling class. This distinction is of importance since bureaucrats are now viewed as being members of the ruling class, part of the power structure of society, rather than as servants of it. Whilst Mosca rejected the Marxian notion of a monolithic ruling class, in which there emerged an identity of interests among those in a similar class position, he did argue that liberty depended upon a clear differentiation of function among the ruling class.

Michels (1911) developed Mosca's work by attempting to explain why bureaucracy came to occupy a position in the ruling elite. The principal conclusion of Michel's analysis was that organisations which initially set out to be democratically controlled inevitably end up as oligarchies with control being in the hands of an elite. This is the basis of Michel's 'iron law of oligarchy'. True democratic control is possible only in small groups in which the members share the same interests and cultural values and operate through the collective choice mechanism of unanimity. As organisations become larger, rules become necessary and this breaks down self government. Moreover, speed in decision making requires that decisions be made by a small group within the larger organisation.

Much of modern public choice theory and the basis of the economic analysis of bureaucracy are contained in the works of Weber, Marx and Michels. It is, however, impossible to draw out the intellectual antecedents of the economic analysis here.

Some Modern Critiques of Bureaucracy

The conclusions of the earlier writers on bureaucracy give some clues about the development of modern criticisms of bureaucracy. Bureaucratic organisation is judged from a number of stances: (a) the relationship between bureaus and their clients; (b) the decision making processes within bureaus; (c) bureaucratic pathologies e.g. the alienation of bureau members; (d) the efficiency of bureaus; and (e) the control of bureaus. The relationship between bureaucracy and clients has taken up much attention. Kafka in many of his novels imagined the ultimate outcome of the bureaucratic way of life and Weber's original idea was to protect the client from the arbitrary decisions of the administrator.

However, the rule bound behaviour of bureaucrats (red tape) frequently frustrates clients who complain that simple requests are dealt with in a complex manner, that they are subjected to stupid procedures, and that they are forced to waste time dealing with the bureaucracy. Furthermore, clients are alienated since they frequently face a veil of secrecy and an obsession with format. These barriers to accessibility can result in the working classes being repelled and failing to make use of public services which are nominally available to them. Since the middle classes will tend to have both the resources (including access to information and time) and the energy to overcome these barriers, this has important implications for the question of who uses the public services and consequences for the distribution of welfare throughout society.

Sisson (1966) describes in a graphic way the heartlessness of the bureaucrat. Referring to Pontius Pilate as the archetypal administrator he says, 'the steps he took to still a particular local clamour were more or less what the service required, and he washed his hands with a civilising regret'.

Bureaucracy is also popularly viewed by citizens as being inefficient. Bureaucrats are regarded as being lazy, narrow-minded, power hungry, arrogant and Machiavellian. Bureaucracy is seen as: (a) too specialised; (b) bounded by rigid rules and procedures; (c) stupid and blundering; (d) slow and buck-passing; (e) empire building; (f) political favouritism; and (g) interfering with democratic rights (see Watson 1945).

There is undoubtedly an anti-bureaucratic movement (see Connell 1977, Wright 1972, Waldo 1971, Ostrom 1971 and Savage 1974). This focuses attention upon the extent and process of bureaucratic power. Public bureaucracies are undoubtedly powerful and yet, whilst those who study private sector organisations have emphasised the ramifications of large scale organisations for society, those who study public administration have been slow to research into the power of bureaucracy. This is surprising given the earlier realisation of the relationship between bureaucracy and democracy. One central issue is the power of the bureaucrat, the senior civil servant, *vis à vis* his Minister and Parliament (Parker 1976). The 19th century notion of ministerial accountability was appropriate when the scope of government was small and clearly defined. The party system, however, dominates parliament in the 20th century and this weakens a Minister's accountability to parliament, since an incompetent Minister can be protected by the party. Weakening ministerial responsibility weakens the link of bureaucratic responsibility, thereby weakening the bureaucracy's accountability to Parliament. Ministers often know nothing about many of the decisions made in their name by their bureaucratic officials. Issues are often presented to Ministers in a pre-digested form; problems are structured in a particular way, information has been filtered through the official system and options and alternatives are presented for consideration, (but what about those options which are not?). Senior civil servants play an important role in structuring the facts and the issues on which Ministers make decisions. This is stated clearly by Lord Armstrong (1976) who was for a time head of the UK civil service:

> Obviously I had great influence. The biggest and most pervasive influence is in setting the framework within which the questions of policy are raised. We, while I was in the Treasury, had a framework of the economy which was basically neo-Keynesian. We set the questions which we asked Ministers to decide arising out of that framework and it would have been enormously difficult for any Minister to change that framework, so to that extent we had great power. I don't think it was

> used maliciously or malignly. I think we chose that framework because we thought it was the best one going. We were very ready to explain it to anybody who was interested, but most Ministers were not interested, they were just prepared to take the questions as we offered them which came out of that framework without going back into the preconceptions of them.

Both Ministers and public servants have considerable power. The official's power originates in his contextual knowledge and sapiential authority, whereas the power of a Minister is weakened by the many claims on his time which prevent him being briefed by sources other than his officials. Even if a Minister has his own personal advisers, who act as a countervailing force to the bureaucracy, the pressures of office will constrain that power. Richard Crossman (1972) has made similar observations about the power of the Prime Minister. A Prime Minister has maximum power at the beginning of the term of office because all his Ministers are getting themselves organised and sorted out in their respective departments. Moreover, the Prime Minister can maintain his power by changing Ministers between departments every few years. The threat to a Prime Minister's power does not come from his cabinet colleagues, but comes instead from the civil servants, especially the cabinet secretariat. The Prime Minister's own personal staff at No. 10 is too small to counteract this power and changes in government and cabinet reshuffles increase the power of the civil service. Set against this, however, according to Crossman, is the problem that if a Minister spends too long with a department he will then tend to line himself up with that department's interests. The party manifesto, rather than the personality of any single Minister, is probably the principal countervailing force. Officials find it difficult to resist policies for which the incoming government has a strong mandate.

The problem facing democracy is, therefore, bureaucratic power. Ministers feel unable to institute single handed any programme for change. Barbara Castle (1973) who was Minister for Transport and also for Employment in a UK government, talks about the feeling of 'one person against the vast department'. This problem is not confined to any single country. The Report of the Royal Commission on Australian Government Administration pointed out that Ministers in Canberra exercise less power than their opposite numbers in Westminster. Hazelhurst and Nethercote (1977) quoting from the Coombs Report argue:

> Because ministers are frequently less skilled in administration than heads of departments and often lack comparable expertise, even in the policy aspects of their portfolios, they are sometimes content to allow their departmental heads to dominate both administrative and policy processes. This tends to make the political authority less effective.

The issue is, therefore, 'how accountable are civil servants and what powers does Parliament have over them?' It was once thought that certain policy questions were purely technical matters and were best left to the expert e.g. town planning, road building and water supplies. The general view was that political involvement would hamper decisions in these areas. But then there was the gradual realisation that there were important economic, social and environmental consequences of these decisions and that the cumulative effect of earlier decisions severely constrained current policy options. Having obtained these powers of decision making, do the institutional controls of Parliament, such as the Select Committees, have sufficient influence to call civil servants to account?

A politically motivated bureaucracy devalues Parliament and the democratic process and erodes individual freedom. In this respect the French refer to bureaucracy as *Seul le pouvoir arrête pouvoir.*

This view of the bureaucrat as a powerful agent stands in contradiction to the standard view in economic analysis. Rothenburg (1964, p. 252) wrote:

> Economists allowed themselves to be saddled with a Benthamite legislator whose own preference function played no role in the political decision making and whose adroit use of the felicific calculus enabled him to calculate that wondrous ambiguity 'the greatest good for the greatest number'. Pehaps even more astonishing than his ability to make this calculation was the assumption that he would in fact legislate accordingly

Mises (1944, p. 78) was similarly scathing in his remarks about this view of the bureaucrat:

> ... from the writings of the German estalists the civil servant emerges as a saintly being, a sort of monk who forsook all earthly pleasures and all personal happiness in order to serve ... The civil servant does not work for pay because no salary, however large, could be considered as an adequate reward for the invaluable priceless benefits that society derives from his self denying sacrifice.

Modern economic treatments of bureaucracy discard this romantic notion of a neutered bureaucrat and replace him with an individual who has his own preference function and who is motivated by a desire to promote his own self interests (see Chapters 5 and 6).

Bureaucracy, Resource Allocation and Political Economy

The subject of economics has often been described as an examination of the allocation of individually owned scarce resources. A considerable part of economic analysis, indeed the bulk of it, deals with the price mechanism, or market system, in solving the problems of production and allocation of resources among the members of society. The political process, however, also produces and distributes the products of jointly owned scarce resources. Thus, alongside the market processes of the price mechanism, there exist the non-market allocative processes of the political system.

There are many different institutional forms for the allocation and distribution of resources. These include: (a) the market and price system; (b) voting procedures; (c) bidding; (d) bargaining; (e) allocation by higher authority, fiat or dictatorship (allocation by fraud, force or deceit); (f) allocation by custom, including gifts and inheritance; and (g) allocation by chance (see Shubik 1970). Economists, however, have built up a grand theory of the price mechanism and have, until comparatively recently, ignored the importance of non-market systems, including the political processes of voting and bureaucracy. This, of course, is not a criticism which can be levelled at all economists and there are notable exceptions (see Arrow 1963, Downs 1965 and Buchanan 1979).

Alongside those economists who are interested in non-market allocation mechanisms, and who are also outside the mainstream of neoclassical economic analysis, are the institutional economists and modern political economists (see Myrdal 1957, 1968, 1978 and Kapp 1976).

One of the most popular institutional/political economists is J.K. Galbraith. In his *Economics and the Public Purpose* (1973), Galbraith divides the economy into the planning system and the market system. The planning system refers to the internal planning by individual firms and organisations which, although influenced by market signals, does not take place within a market context. One of the features of modern industrial societies is the capital intensive nature of the production process, the size of industrial organisation and hence the relative importance of the planning system over the market system. The planning system is served by the 'technostructure' i.e. groups of managers, lawyers, scientists etc. who control the activities of the large corporations and multinational companies. The technostructure exists to influence consumers in the market place and to obtain long-term government contracts. Resources are not allocated via competitive markets, but are instead allocated by bargains struck between the various groups *within* the corporations *between* the corporation and government purchasers.

Examination of the nature of the bargaining and exchange processes which take place in non-market institutions has resulted in the re-emergence of political economy. Institutional or political economists follow in the tradition of Smith, Marshall, Marx, List and more recently Veblen, Commons and Mitchell. These economists took into account factors other than the purely economic. 'I came to see that there are no economic, sociological or psychological problems, but just problems, and they are all mixed and composite' (Myrdal 1978, p. 772). When focusing upon specific problems political economists take into account the entire social system. In particular, they are interested in the distribution of power in society and the origin and locus of that power. This compares with the use of mathematical models by neoclassical economists in which the entire social system is kept out of sight.

Too often subject specialisation leads to demarcation disputes and bitter debates between sub-disciplines regarding the appropriate way in which to study a subject. Much of the intellectual effort which goes into these academic dog fights (methodological debates!) is misplaced. Once it is realised that the different sub-disciplines are asking different questions and studying different issues, we can then adopt a more rational perspective which will enable advances made in each part of the subject to complement each other. In Chapter 3 this theme is developed and there we compare the economist's equilibrium paradigm with the behavioural/political economy approach.

In recent years, partly as a response to the apparent failures of Keynesian macro-economic demand management, economic policy makers have turned to what has come to be referred to as *supply-side economics*. Low productivity, poor competitiveness (both at home and abroad), low rates of economic growth and bad industrial relations have deep rooted causes in the structural and institutional dimensions of an economy (i.e. its supply-side). In order to deal with these issues economists need to turn their attention to organisational processes and non-economic factors. It is, therefore, hoped that this book will make a contribution to that debate (see Chapter 2).

The Growth of the Public Sector and Bureaucracy

In 1851 the census showed that there were 75,000 public employees in the UK employed mainly in the Post Office and Customs and Excise. This compared with 932,000 in France at that time. Of the 75,000 UK public employees, only 1,628 were clerks and officials in the central departments of the civil government. By 1979, the UK civil service staff alone (non-industrial and industrial) numbered 733,176, with the majority working in defence (248,550), health and social security (97,650), and inland revenue (75,000). The total number of persons employed in the UK public sector in 1979 amounts to about $7\frac{1}{2}$ million; over half (about 55%) of these employees were females and about 25% of the total were employed on a part-time basis.

As can be seen from table 1.1, public sector employment has been growing in the major industrialised countries during the post-war period.

This growth in the public sector of OECD countries is accounted for in a number of ways. Demographic changes in the population, especially an increase in the absolute number of school age and dependent persons over 60 years, have caused public employment to rise. Expansions in the welfare

Table 1.1 Characteristics of Public Sector Employment

Country	*Share of Public Sector in Total Employment (%)* 1965	1977
Australia	22.2	25.3
Austria	12.0	17.9
Belgium	13.2	15.9
Canada	17.9	20.5
Denmark	13.3	24.1
Finland	n.a.*	17.4
France	15.9	17.4
W. Germany	9.8	14.3
Greece	3.8	5.2
Ireland	3.9	6.3
Italy	9.9	14.1
Japan	n.a.	6.5
Luxembourg	n.a.	10.8
Netherlands	11.5	14.3
Norway	13.8	20.0
Portugal	4.8	8.1
Sweden	15.3	27.5
United Kingdom	15.7	21.3
United States	16.7	17.1

Note: * n.a. = not available
Source: OECD National Accounts

state, along with an increase in the scope of the regulatory role of government (e.g. environmental and consumer protection), have resulted in an increase in the number of public sector employees (see Brown and Jackson 1978, Chapter 5).

A large public sector relative to the market or private sector of the economy has important consequences. Not only does the financing of public sector activities through taxes and borrowing have an impact upon market prices and allocations, but a large proportion of the nation's resources are allocated and distributed by non-market means through the bureaucracy. The economic analysis of bureaucracy is an examination of these allocative decisions and processes. How do bureaucrats make decisions; whose interests do they serve; what are the consequences of bureaucratic decisions; are public bureaucracies inefficient compared with market organisations; how effective is the public's control over bureaucracies; and what are the limits of bureaucracy's powers to implement the policies that will bring about the 'new society'? These are the principal questions which are considered throughout the remainder of this book.

CHAPTER 2

Perspectives on Organisations

Organisations are discrete, empirical units of action in our society. The better the language we have for understanding them the better will be the success of any discipline which aims to contribute more knowledge and understanding about our society.

(Bradley and Wilkie)

Introduction

Since the early 1960s there has been a rapid growth in the study of complex organisations. This development has given rise to what can only be described as a jungle of administrative and organisation theories. Different specialists have brought to the study of organisations their own particular analytic perspective. The economist is interested in organisational influences on resource allocation; the social psychologist in group behaviour; the decision theorist in how decisions should be made and how they are made; and the organisation theorist in the structure of organisations. Of all the disciplines which study organisations, the economist's perspective is probably the most deficient and limited. Economists, until very recently, have tended to ignore the importance of 'organisation' as a phenomenon to be explained and accounted for; internal organisational processes were instead treated as a 'black box' to be explained by someone else, whilst the economist concentrated on the organisation of the market system. Rather than contributing to any theory of organisation behaviour, economists concentrated upon the theory of price and output determination. Neither variations in organisational structures, nor other organisational features, entered into the economist's theory of supply. This chapter is, therefore, written specifically for economists who have not yet come to terms with the subject of 'organisation theory'. It is, moreover, written in the firm belief that economists, who wish to study the supply side of the economy, must have an appreciation of intra-organisational processes. This is the domain of any analysis of productivity and non-market resource allocation and distribution. Far too often in the past economists have, in their attempts to promote economic growth, made policy prescriptions which involve structural changes to existing organisations and institutions. These prescriptions, however, have been made in an intellectual vacuum with little understanding of the relationships which exist between changes in organisational structures and final outcomes. This chapter introduces the economist to the language and perspectives of the organisation theorist.

The Organisation Theory Literature

Any survey must be highly selective and open to the criticism of being superficial. It is hoped that the specialist in this field will find that a reasonably accurate interpretation has been provided and will not find that this subject has been misrepresented. To the newcomer to this literature there are a number of useful means of gaining a rapid entry to the principal themes and controversies of the subject. An excellent and thought-provoking introduction to the subject matter of organisation analysis is found in Bradley and Wilkie (1974) who, in a deceptively straightforward and short presentation, cover the foundations of organisation theory. Other texts which will be found to be useful introductions are Hill (1972), Dunsire (1973), Baker (1972), Silverman (1970), Perrow (1972) and Mouzelis (1967). Each of these texts provides useful presentations of the issues, and surveys of the *vast* literature on organisational analysis which the novice can then follow up in a selective way.

Anyone who ventures into the literature on organisation theory soon discovers that there is little unity. In an attempt to impose a structure on the literature, Kassem (1976) and Clegg and Dunkerley (1977) distinguish between the European tradition and the American tradition. The American tradition tends to stress 'people and goals' in organisations, whereas the European tradition concentrates on 'structure and technology and power'. The American theorists employ, in the main, the analytical perspective of the social psychologist taking a micro view of people within organisations and concentrating attention on individuals' needs and attitudes and what goes on within organisations in terms of functional processes. The underlying ideology of the American tradition develops out of a conservative, anti-Marxian school which emphasises consensus and harmony within intra-organisational relationships. Thus, American Business Schools prescribe job enrichment and participative management as techniques to be used in improving organisational performance.

The European tradition on the other hand is macro (structural) in its approach, uses the methodology of sociology and analyses the organisation as a whole, paying particular attention to what goes on between the organisation and its environment (however defined). Power relationships and conflict are principal components in European analysis of organisations, along with socio-technical systems and industrial democracy.

Whilst this schema helps to sort out the literature at a highly aggregated level, it should be kept in mind that within each tradition there is a good deal of disagreement. For example, within the European tradition there is the distinction between 'organisation theory' and the 'theory of organisations'. The former analyses the broad structural questions of society, whereas the latter incorporates questions about the structure of particular organisations within an examination of intra-organisational processes.

Finally, in recent years there has been a radical critique of organisation theory (see Burrell 1979, Clegg and Dunkerley 1977, Benson 1977 and Salaman 1978). This critique views much of the organisation theory literature as providing an intellectual foundation for control systems such as 'scientific management', 'welfare programmes' and 'incentive systems'. Boreham (1979) for example, writes:

> ... these techniques ... succeeded in establishing an extensive network of political, social and economic control over an increasingly homogeneous labour process ...

and

> theories of organisation and the practical prescriptions deriving from such theories, which have shaped the capitalist mode of production need to be viewed historically as aspects of control over the labour process.

What is an Organisation?

Clearly this is an important question to the organisation theorist. It is a question which has filled many pages in the literature; however, rather than becoming bogged down in definitional games[1] we will take as a useful working definition of organisations that they are 'discrete empirical units of action in our society'. Moreover, as units of action they are regarded as being purposeful systems which pursue objectives/goals. Like theories, however, organisations are creations of man and are examples of what Simon (1969) has called 'artifacts'.

One of the first things which students of organisation theory learn to realise is that there is a great variety of organisational forms and organisational types and much of the earlier literature was devoted to searching out the best taxonomy.[2] For example, the business firm, the service agency, the school, the mental hospital, the prison, the university and the church are all forms of organisation. What are their similarities and differences? Despite this recognition of different organisational types, until the late 1960s most of the theories of organisation had been developed for the industrial firm. This raises a number of interesting and problematical questions, e.g.: can the theories developed for the business firm be simply carried over and applied to other types of organisations; is there a general theory which applies to all organisations? Questions of this kind have not been satisfactorily answered and a good deal of empirical analysis of different organisation types must be done before that is possible.

Etzioni (1964) expresses this in terms of a hierarchy of approaches to any study. At the top level there is general theory (both *a priori* and empirical); at the bottom there are case studies. Middle range theories are a partial distillation of the common features of the case studies. In its current state, organisation theory is in a similar state of development as was natural science at the time of Lineas. Case study material produces the data which are then consolidated in middle range theories. However, the subject is a long way from producing any general theories of organisations.

The newcomer to organisation theory will frequently find the language of the subject difficult and confusing. Bradley and Wilkie (1974) caution about the language problem. The issue is how we think about an organisation. Take, for example, the statements, 'the organisation behaves in such a way to serve its needs', or 'the organisation made a decision to do something'. Such statements impart to an inanimate empirical entity the cognitive characteristics of an individual. Similar problems of reification are to be found in the literature of the nation state. Organisations do not have needs, nor do they have thoughts, neither do they behave. It is the individuals making up the organisation who possess such qualities; the problem then becomes that of studying how individuals' preferences are translated into the single decision of a collection of individuals.[3] For example, do the preferences of a single individual dominate all others, or is there some rule embodied in the constitution of the organisation which determines how individual preferences are to be treated in making a collective decision? Thinking in terms of individuals acting within an organisational setting reduces the possibility of treating organisations as if they were people. Thus, in order to understand individual behaviour, we need to understand the organisational context in which it takes place, '... a more accurate understanding of behaviour in organisations can be obtained if the organisational environment of that behaviour is precisely defined' (Child 1973, p. 16). This includes the notion that organisations embody power structures which order individual behaviour. Features of organisational life constrain the behaviour of the individual through a network of rules, roles and expectations. The ability of any individual to change the nature of these constraints depends upon the intra-organisational distribution of rights and where that individual exists in relation to the distribution.

The Importance of Organisations

Organisations are a ubiquitous feature of our lives. They are an integral part of the social structure and are themselves social systems. Organisations are social systems which are set up by individuals in order to meet, through coordinated actions, particular needs and to achieve certain goals. Thus organisations are collectivities which exist to serve the interests either of their members, or of other members of society, or both.[4] It is probably because organisations are ubiquitous that many of us do not give them much thought. There are, however, very good reasons for making organisations the focus of analysis. Organisations influence our behaviour and our welfare.

Since individuals spend most of their waking life in one organisation or another, one means of understanding individuals' behaviour is to examine the way in which the requirements of the organisation voluntarily or involuntarily, consciously or unconsciously, mould and direct it. Educational organisations engage in human capital formation and, through training in skills, modify individuals' potential behaviour; moreover, in less explicit ways the same organisations can influence an individual's value system and once again affect behaviour. More extreme ways of influencing an individual's behaviour are to be found in coercive organisations such as prisons and mental hospitals. In the case of these organisations, individuals do not necessarily voluntarily comply with the goals of the organisation nor with the means employed to achieve these objectives. However, the majority of organisations are voluntary associations of individuals who, when deciding to join the organisation, also agree to comply with the organisation's goals and the means of achieving them.[5] Thus, for coercive organisations, individuals' behaviour is modified by the application of threats and physical sanctions; individuals in such organisations have a highly negative intensity of involvement. In the case of the business firm or other economic organisations the individual's involvement is calculative, resulting from a balancing up of the material (economic) and social (non-economic) rewards obtained from entering into that particular association.[6] The individual's behaviour in this kind of organisation is controlled through the allocation of positions in a division of labour, the organisational coordination of which is determined by hierarchically allocated relations of power and authority.

Individuals' behaviour is, therefore, influenced in a formal sense by the means used to obtain compliance with the organisation's goal(s) and as members of an organisation individuals are expected to perform specific tasks in particular ways in return for their rewards. In this sense, organisations are frequently viewed as being a network of roles, with each role carrying with it an expected behaviour pattern.

Organisations also have an important influence over the welfare of individuals. As employees, their welfare is related in part to their ability to earn income and the level of income that they earn is dependent upon a set of decisions made within the organisation. Welfare is also dependent upon the extent to which individuals' rights are exploited,[7] e.g.: employees' welfare depends upon working conditions, including managements' attitudes to the labour force; decisions on product safety and quality affect consumers' welfare; and decisions on the treatment of the inmates of penal institutions affect welfare, just as much as decisions relating to the distribution of profit to shareholders.

Organisations are, therefore, significant features in our lives. They are important determinants of our behaviour and welfare and are sources of knowledge, belief and values; they therefore pose a number of interesting and perplexing questions. For example, given that some organisations are powerful, how can we control them and reallocate power?

Approaches to the Analysis of Organisation

Leaving aside, until the next chapter, the economist's treatment of organisations we will now review those approaches which are frequently identified and classified in the organisation theory literature as:

(a) scientific management and classical administrative theories of organisations;
(b) the human relations approach of social psychology;
(c) socio-technic and contingency theories of organisations.

Each approach will be outlined and the chapter will conclude with a discussion of the recent radical critique of these traditional approaches.

Scientific Management and Classical Administrative Theories

The school of scientific management is best known through the works of Frederick W. Taylor (1911) and Frank B. and Lillian M. Gilbreth (1917). The problem which they set themselves was to find the best way of organising work so as to obtain maximum efficiency from the labour force. The post industrial revolution brought with it complex production processes, in which labour and capital were combined in ever increasingly complex ways to produce the output of the manufacturing process which was in ever increasing demand. Owners/managers were faced with a variety of problems; not only did they need to supervise and control their labour force, but they had to have skills in dealing with finance, marketing and production technology. It was a rare person who was found to possess all the skills required to remain in control over all decisions in his own factory. These problems caused Taylor to conclude that in his day there was great inefficiency in industry. Inefficiency arose not only on the shop-floor amongst the work force, but also in the board rooms amongst the owners/managers. Given the prevailing values of his day, Taylor regarded inefficiency and the waste of resources to be a moral problem in need of a solution. Of the common worker he wrote:

> Underworking, that is, deliberately working slowly so as to avoid a full day's work, 'soldiering' as it is called in this country, is almost universal in industrial establishments, and prevails to a large extent in the building trades; and the writer asserts without fear of contradiction that this constitutes the greatest evil with which the working-people of both England and America are now afflicted.
>
> (Taylor 1911, pp. 13–14)

Taylor's solution was:

> It is the writer's judgement that while much can be done and should be done by writing and talking toward educating not only workmen, but all classes in the community, as to the importance of obtaining the maximum output of each man and each machine, it is only through the adoption of modern scientific management that this great problem can be finally solved.
>
> (Taylor 1911, p. 27)

The elements of scientific management were: (a) the making of recommendations about organisational structure and routine; (b) the measurement of work and the design of tasks; and (c) the management of incentives for workers in order to motivate them. These proposals formed the basis of the subjects of 'work study' and 'organisation and methods', which are part of the tool kit of modern production management. But Taylor also laid the basis of an early theory of organisations. His was a prescriptive theory of how organisations *ought* to be structured or designed in order to obtain maximum efficiency through the elimination of waste and by ensuring that workers earned a fair day's wage for a fair day's work.[8]

Many of Taylor's beliefs had been gained from his observations at the Bethlehem Steel Co.[9] By providing workers with the appropriate tools, by re-designing the task to be performed and by providing the appropriate economic incentives, their productivity could be increased dramatically. Economic incentives, it was argued, should be closely tied to output, through the mechanism of the 'differential piece-rate system'; that is, if workers did not produce a fair day's work they were punished via loss of earnings; if, on the other hand, the worker exceeded the production target then he was rewarded financially by being paid a bonus. Underlying Taylor's theory of organisation was an implicit social contract theory; both management and workers were assumed to be aiming for the same objective (material reward) and via cooperation both groups could achieve that objective. Effective management and productive labour would reap higher profits and higher real wages respectively.

Whilst a great number of the more naive current attitudes towards increasing labour productivity and improving the growth rates of economies are embodied in Taylor's ideas, it should be remembered that these ideas have met with a great deal of justified criticism. Rose (1975, p. 31) states the case strongly: 'the sheer silliness from a modern perspective of many of his ideas and the barbarities they led to when applied to industry, encourage ridicule and denunciation'. Whilst this might be regarded as an overstatement of the case against 'Taylorism', it should be remembered that Taylor's attitudes were such that he treated labour as an extension of the machine. Organisation methods and work-study timed labour against the clock; work was broken down (according to the Smithian principle of specialisation) into a large number of routine (and frequently monotonous) tasks, and incentive systems, especially the differential piece-rate system, placed great physical and emotional strains on workers as they tried to meet production targets. In Taylor's world there was no notion of important differences between individuals who had to perform the same tasks; no differences in skills or physical abilities. Labour was treated as a homogeneous input. Neither was there any concession to the fact that individuals become fatigued; that during long production runs their concentration lapses and that there may be a whole host of other 'reasonable' factors which would frustrate labour's attempts at beating the rate. Taylor's view was simple; those who cannot meet the output targets must be lazy and inefficient and should, therefore, be punished by loss of earnings. It was a mechanistic view of Man, who was assumed to be motivated purely by economic rewards. Any other motivating factors were seen as interferences which reduced the optimality of the system.

Clearly, Taylor's views are a demonstration of one of our earlier observations, namely that organisations can and do affect individual welfare. Moreover, as an approach to the design of organisations and work his views contain strong implicit value judgments about who possesses the rights to determine and implement the system of control over the work process. The worker is assumed to have few (any?) rights and is expected to respond passively to the structure of incentives which he faces.

Classical Administrative Theories of Organisation

The classical administrative theorists of organisations sought to establish a general set of principles or laws for designing organisational structures. Their design of organisations was intended to minimise the uncontrollable elements of the organisation and thus to minimise the amount of uncertainty *within* the organisation itself. The approach of the administrative theorists is best summarised by one of their principal proponents, Lyndall F. Urwick, a former Director of the International Management Institute in Geneva:

> There are principles which can be arrived at inductively from the study of human experience of organisation, which should govern arrangements for human association of any kind. These principles can be studied as a technical question, irrespective of purpose of the enterprise, the personnel composing it, or any constitutional, political or social theory underlying its creation. They are concerned with the method of subdividing and allocating to individuals all the various activities, duties and responsibilities essential to the purpose contemplated, the correlation of these activities and the continuous control of the work of the individuals so as to secure the most economical and the most effective realisation of the purpose.
>
> (Urwick 1957)

In setting down the principles of organisation and administration Urwick was following in the tradition of Fayol (1949), Follett (1918), Mooney (1947) and Taylor (1911). The division of labour arising from specialisation of task and function created a coordination or a management problem and the natural question was, 'how should this problem be solved?' The solution was to be found in a scientific approach to establishing immutable principles of organisation. For Gulick (1937) the functions of management were summarised as planning, organising, staffing, directing, coordinating, reporting and budgeting (POSDCORB). However, by distilling the essentials of the literature on the principles of administration we can present the five key elements to be:[10]

(i) *the scalar principle*: authority and responsibility should flow in a clear unbroken line from the highest executive to the lowest operative in the organisation. This is the basic principle of hierarchical organisation and gives rise to the familiar organisation charts which set out the formal lines of communication and authority.

(ii) *unity of command*: no person in an organisation should receive orders from more than one supervisor, see Fayol (1949).

(iii) *exception principle*: decisions that recur frequently should be reduced to a routine and delegated to subordinates, only those important non-recurring decisions should be referred to superiors.

(iv) *span of control*: this principle attempted to prescribe the number of subordinates that should report to a single supervisor (manager). It was generally held to be 5 or 6 and was based on the mathematical formulae developed by Graicunas (1937). Each supervisor has a limited number of subordinates he can effectively control, thus it is necessary to appoint a number of first line supervisors and the second line supervisors to control them. Each first line supervisor will have 5 or 6 workers reporting to him and every 6 first line supervisors and hence about every 40 workers report to a second line supervisor and so on. This results in a pyramid of control up to the top executive.

(v) *specialisation*: divide work into units with specialised activity in order to obtain efficiency gains. The problem then becomes that of deciding upon the basis of division. Should, for example, the specialisation be according to purpose, process, geographical area or clientele, or some combination of them all, see Etzioni (1964)?

The administrative theorists viewed any organisation as a rational instrument for implementing policies to achieve well specified objectives. This rationality of organisations was assumed to be enhanced and efficiency improved if organisations were structured along the lines suggested by the principles of administration.

The classical administrative theorists have been criticised on a number of counts. The principles of administration enunciated throughout their literature had no proper scientific status. They were not the result of empirical research which tried to establish the basis of organisational effectiveness (i.e. in terms of meeting its goals). Instead, the principles had emerged from the collected experience of practitioners of the 'art' of administration in both public and business organisations. For example, subsequent empirical evidence has shown that the span of control will vary from organisation to organisation, i.e. there is no *law* giving a specific number — it depends on the nature of the problem which the organisation has to solve.

One commentator has claimed that the principles of administration are no better than 'avuncular pontification' and Simon (1957) has put them on the same level as proverbs i.e. containing some element of truth and insight. The principles were derived from, and generally gave rise to, prescriptions for hierarchical forms of organisation. In other words, the hierarchical structure was regarded as being the 'best' and was unquestioningly prescribed for every kind of organisation. As we will see later in this chapter, there are organisation structures other than hierarchy. It becomes necessary, therefore, to state under what set of conditions hierarchical structures are considered to be best and also to enunciate the criteria against which 'best' is to be defined. Furthermore, do the principles carry over from private sector into public sector organisations and do they apply with equal force to organisations which have different goals and different environments? Classical administrative theory also suffers from the problem that it is a 'closed system' model (Thompson 1967), i.e. in all of its variants the theory attempts to reduce uncertainty to zero, since it is only variables *within* the organisation that are considered. The environment in which the organisation operates is ignored and along with it a major source of uncertainty. The theory is ultra-rational; each organisation is assumed to have a well specified set of non-conflicting objectives along with a well specified set of means of achieving those objectives. There is never discussion of the problems which might arise when objectives are ambiguous, or conflicting and when no clear means of achieving the objectives are known. Finally, the approach adopted by this group of writers is purely normative or prescriptive. Their lack of empiricism has already been noted, but here we draw attention to lack of understanding of how individuals behave in organisations. Individuals are assumed to behave in a blind mechanistic fashion within the prescribed organisation structure, almost like rats in a maze. They are assumed to obey the rules and fulfil their role expectations in their pursuit of the organisation's objective. Order is prescribed and designed, never predicted or explained.

Whilst formal administrative theory has been criticised, nevertheless Perrow (1970) points out that it was amongst the earliest attempts to recognise the importance of organisation structure and its impact upon efficiency in the allocation of resources within the organisation. This turned out, however, to be a more complex issue than many of the administrative theorists realised. Classical administrative theory tends to be embodied in modern management science literature; see for example, Brown (1970), Koontz and O'Donnell (1972) and Drucker (1954), to name but a few.

The Human Relations Approach to Organisational Analysis

During the 1950s, there emerged an alternative approach to classical organisation theory. This alternative literature has come to be referred to as the 'human relations school' and is a mixture of disciplines and approaches which includes sociologists, political scientists, industrial relations experts, and social-psychologists. The bond which unites this group of students of organisations is their distaste for the 'human engineering' approach of scientific management and its abuse and degradation of Man which, by treating him as a machine, ignores the impact of the organisation on individual welfare. Moreover, they were not sympathetic to the acceptance of the Weberian ideal of the hierarchy, nor to the unqualified pursuit of organisational efficiency without a proper regard to the effect that such efficiency requirements have upon individuals' welfare and behaviour.

The human relations school, which is exemplified in the work of Argyris (1957, 1960, 1964, 1972), McGregor (1960), Likert (1961, 1967), Maslow (1954), Herzberg (1959, 1968) and Vroom (1964), builds upon the earlier studies carried out by Mayo (1933, 1945) and Roethlisberger and Dickson (1939) and upon the insights provided in Chapter 1 of Barnard's now classic work *The Functions of the Executive* (1938). Classical organisation theory, by taking the ideal formal structure of the organisation as the unit of analysis and by concentrating upon economic incentives, ignored the actual determinants of individual behaviour, which include how individuals perceive and interpret their formal organisational roles and how they respond to non-economic incentives. The work of industrial psychologists and sociologists has revealed that this lack of understanding of human behaviour in organisation settings is the principal weakness in the models used by the classical theorists. 'Workers from two disciplines — one, largely sociological, concerned with demonstrating that Weber's formal model does not neatly fit the realities of organisational forms, the other, derived primarily from social psychology, concerned with showing how human behaviour will not readily fit into a formal organisational pattern — have been drawn together in the human relations approach to organisational behaviour' (Boreham 1976).

The human relations theory grew out of a set of studies called the 'Hawthorne Studies', carried out between 1926 and 1936 at the Hawthorne works of the Western Electric Company in Chicago, by F. J. Roethlisberger and W. J. Dickson under the supervision of Elton Mayo. Instead of concentrating upon individual behaviour in an isolated setting, it became recognised, through the Hawthorne studies, that to understand the behaviour of individuals they must be viewed as members of collectivities (groups) in which sanctions are brought to bear to make individual behaviour conform to that desired by the other members of the group. This discovery of the significance of 'social' and group factors as influences upon individuals' work behaviour was to be the major finding of the Hawthorne studies. It made problematical the relationship between the individual and the rest of the group — why for example should an individual surrender the complete fulfilment of his personal aspirations in order to satisfy the wishes of other members of his peer group; by what process are group decisions arrived at and how effective are group sanctions in making members comply? [11]

The major findings of the Hawthorne studies were:

(i) *social factors* play a significant part in influencing workers' levels of production (physiological factors also play a role, but are not as important as originally thought);
(ii) *non-economic rewards and sanctions*, are more important than economic incentives. Of particular significance were the friendliness and respect of co-workers and supervisors.
(iii) *the work group*, was an important constraint on workers' behaviour. Individuals did not tend to behave as individuals, but as members of groups.
(iv) *the informal leader* was found to play a key role in the group decision making process. The informal leader was so called to

distinguish him fom the person who occupied the leadership role in the formal organisation structure.

(v) *leadership style* was an important variable in explaining group behaviour. Those leaders who maximised the opportunities for communication and participation were found to be the more effective.

The findings of the Hawthorne studies opened up a whole new dimension for management. If management's task was to improve the motivation and efficiency of their employees in order to make them more productive, then what Roethlisberger and Dickson's findings suggested were that concentration upon formal principles of organisation structure (such as unity of command and span of control) and on the structure of economic incentives was wrong minded. Management should instead be concentrating upon the management of non-economic incentives, thereby increasing production by influencing group standards and improving leadership styles. In other words, emphasis is being placed upon an alternative system of control.

The human relations approach restored an amount of balance into the analysis of organisations. Likert (1967, pp. 98–9) has stated it as: 'reliance is not placed solely or fundamentally on the economic motive of buying a man's time and using control and authority as the organising and coordinating principles of the organisation.' Questions about the management of incentives had earlier been discussed by Barnard (1938) prior to the Hawthorne experiments. For Barnard there were positive and negative forces acting on individuals in any organisation; whether or not an individual joined or remained in an organisation depended upon how these combined forces attracting and repelling the individual netted out. Furthermore, Barnard saw it to be one of management's key functions to manage the *mix* of incentives in the organisation. Individuals make contributions to the organisation (e.g. supplying their labour and skills), but must be offered inducements to do so. These inducements (incentives) are provided, in the case of the business firm, out of the revenues obtained from selling the firm's products. In Barnard's framework the organisation grows and survives if it can continue to produce enough output to pay for the inducements.[12]

Following the Hawthorne studies there were numerous follow-up studies carried out by industrial psychologists and sociologists. A simple count of the number of papers and books published during the 1960s on the subject of organisation behaviour would have led to the reasonable conclusion that the research activity had reached epidemic proportions. Research was carried out into the factors which motivate individuals, the effects of leadership styles upon individual behaviour and relationships between the formal and informal organisation. Each study was to some degree implicitly concerned to show that improvements in human satisfaction, in the work place, brought about through manipulation of the physical and social environment, would improve worker productivity. Although the human relations school criticised the simplistic view of 'economic man' and minimised the role played by economic incentives, it is nevertheless important to note that, like the classical and scientific management approaches, it too was concerned to improve labour productivity and profit. The difference which the human relations approach offered was superficially a more humanising control system.

Social psychologists emphasised the role played by non-economic incentives; see Brown (1970) and Homans (1950). 'Social man' as compared to 'economic man' was assumed to value stable work groups and good social relations. These conditions were thought to be found (as in the Hawthorne studies) in small cohesive groups and so attention shifted towards organising work around such groups. Borrowing from the Durkeim tradition in sociology it was argued that individuals found a sense of belonging in the stable social relationships of their work group. For Durkheim, complex societies, based upon the division of labour and ordered into rational means-ends relationships, produced the conditions for irrational behaviour, a breakdown of norms and eventually anomie. Such a problem could be handled via the formation of informal relationships, hence the human relations school's emphasis on the primary work group and the informal organisation rather than on the rationality of the Weberian ideal. Finally, as the name suggests, the human relations approach was concerned with putting human beings back into the bloodless unpeopled organisations discussed by Weber and the classical administrative theorists; moreover, they had an implicit moral theory which treated individuals as human beings rather than as machines and which protected the individual's rights and dignity as a human being.

Further studies into human motivation revealed that social needs, like economic incentives, were only part of the picture. There are many factors which motivate individuals, for example: the desire to fulfil and to achieve ego motives, and to feel important; the need to feel secure; the need to be creative and to have new and worthwhile experiences; and finally, the basic economic motives. The "needs model' of human motivation was set out by Maslow (1954) in terms of a hierarchy of needs, in which individuals ordered the satisfaction of their needs from the most basic physiological needs of hunger and thirst to the highest of self actualisation. Followers of Maslow, especially Argyris (1957), Herzberg (1959, 1968), McGregor (1960) and Likert (1961), began to extend and apply the basic Maslow model to organisational behaviour. Their aim was to achieve both organisational efficiency and human satisfaction. Argyris considered that organisations made individuals passive, dependent and immature. Thus, by influencing the set of social relationships which individuals faced in the organisation, they could be provided with the potential for realising their higher order needs including that of self actualisation. The key to improving human relationships and increasing efficiency in organisations was to find the appropriate leadership style and then to train managers in these skills of leadership.[13]

Perhaps the clearest statement of the human relations school's 'needs model' is provided by Herzberg (1968). According to Herzberg, workers primarily receive non-monetary, vocational rewards from *industrial* work. It is only these rewards which provide positive motivation and job satisfaction (presumably the higher satisfaction and positive motivation increases worker productivity!). Good working conditions, job security and salary *are of secondary importance*; they are not sources of positive motivation or satisfaction and simply serve to reduce dissatisfaction to zero (note the lack of symmetry in this argument!). If workers do admit that they gain satisfaction from job security, good working conditions and salary, then they are classified by Herzberg as being 'maladjusted', 'neurotic', 'pathological' and 'immature'.[14]

Undoubtedly the human relations school was diagonally opposed to the teachings of the classical and scientific management theorists. McGregor (1960) set out these differences in approach in his Theory *X* and Theory *Y*. In Theory *X* Man is viewed as a recalcitrant who is opposed to change and who will respond only to the carrot and stick of economic incentives and denial of material rewards (the scientific management approach). Theory *Y* on the other hand views Man as a social being possessing a complex set of needs which can be satisfied in organisations, provided that the appropriate conditions to do so exist (the human relations school).

However, the human relations school was not free of methodological criticism; see Carey (1967, 1976) and Boreham and Dow (1979). First, many of the studies were carried out without proper regard to experimental design.[15] Essentially what each experiment or case study was aiming to do was to estimate empirically functions of the following kind:

$$\text{Individual productivity} = fn\ (\cdot)$$
$$\text{Individual satisfaction} = fn\ (\cdot)$$

in which the contents of the brackets $(\cdot)$ were the explanatory variables. The problem facing anyone in this area is to obtain suitable and sensible measures of magnitudes such as human satisfaction, leadership style, human needs and so on. Even if measures are obtainable there are further problems of combining cardinal and ordinal meaures into a single dimension.

Second, it was assumed in most of the human relations studies that the achievement of high morale/satisfaction would improve worker productivity. As early as 1960 McGregor had pointed out the fallacies in such an argument. Productivity was a much more complex subject than was realised and was also dependent upon the degree of capacity utilisation in the economy and technological change. Third, the approach was just as prescriptive as that of scientific management and classical administrative theory. The difference between the approaches was that the prescriptions differed. The human relations pursuit of a set of supportive social relationships as a desirable feature of modern complex organisations should have been regarded as an ethical proposition to be pursued in its own right. However, such propositions were dressed up in a pseudo-positive analysis, without always fully appreciating that there existed a genuine conflict between organisational efficiency and what is considered to be good for the individual. As Tannenbaum (1966) commented: '... the qualities of personality and motivation that we have discussed are *inconsistent* with the requirements of formal organisation'. This means, therefore, that there is a complex 'trade-off' to be made between the efficiency criteria (à la Taylorism etc.) and the effects that any efficiency procedures have upon human welfare. This trade-off, which was never fully articulated in the human relations literature, is developed in a subsequent chapter in this book.

Fourth, many of the propositions of the human relations school could not be formally tested. This arose either because the data were not readily available or because the propositions were ethical ones and hence not suitable for empirical testing. Many statements, especially those derived from the needs model, were tautologous — behaviour was defined in terms of actions aimed at achieving certain goals — and could not, therefore, be tested. Moreover, the needs model was highly rational, since it assumed that individuals' behaviour was always purposive and goal directed. It did not take into account the constraints which individuals faced nor the possibility that they might be misinformed both about their goals and about the means of achieving them. Nor were needs ever adequately defined; were they real and how could we test for their existence, or were they just a simple classification for rationalising what might be happening? It was never made clear why individuals expected to satisfy their needs in organisations such as the business firm. An alternative and just as reasonable view would be that individuals viewed work and the economic rewards it generated as a means to other ends which could be more appropriately satisfied outside the firm. Creating pleasant and meaningful working conditions was a desirable objective in terms of its effects on human welfare, but this did not make economic incentives and rewards insignificant factors in explaining human behaviour.

Fifth, there was no examination of conflict in organisations, nor of the importance of external factors as explanations of individual behaviour within organisations. Almost all of the literature on human relations is geared towards either ignoring the possibility of conflict, or of minimising it.

For Argyris the incompatibility between organisational efficiency and individual needs might have led to a gap which would be filled by conflict. However, by applying suitable management techniques (i.e. leadership styles etc.) such a gap could be minimised if not completely closed, thereby producing an optimal solution (note Argyris does not specify the properties of such an optimum or on what criteria such properties might be desirable). In this respect it is important to press the social-engineers of the human relations school to find out precisely what kind of set up they are aiming at, since what they seem to be advocating is some kind of utopian industrial order. Are they, for example, advocating complete industrial democracy, in which workers take a participative role in all decisions; or is it a pseudo-democracy that they intend, in which workers take a part in certain decision areas chosen by management? In that case management retains *power* over key areas.[16] Power relationships within organisations were completely ignored by the human relations school, especially when the locus of that power was external to the organisation. C. Wright Mills (1959, p. 93) has been critical of the emphasis of the human relations approach upon status and prestige in the primary work group setting, rather than upon more fundamental power relationships within the organisation, asking, 'why are class and power not only minimised and made subordinate to status, but even sponged up into it?' One possible answer to Mill's question is that, 'it is far easier and less politically portentous to make the worker feel that he belongs and is important than it is to tamper with the structure of industrial authority' (Blumberg 1968, p. 48). In designing their experiments the industrial sociologists have failed to note that status could be acting as an intervening variable, with power being the primary variable. An increase in power, it could be argued, increased the status of the worker, in which case the more interesting question becomes, 'what factors brought about this shift in power?' No satisfactory answer seems to have been provided so far.

Finally, the human relations school almost exclusively concentrated upon industrial organisations and industrial work behaviour. Moreover, it was blue collar workers and low level white collar workers who were the focus of attention. Whilst studies of non-industrial and public sector organisations do exist, these tend to be the exception rather than the rule.[17] This bias severely limits any claim by the human relations school of having a *general theory* of organisations. Despite these criticisms, the human relations approach did make a valuable contribution to organisation theory. It balanced up the formalism of the rational/efficiency approach of classical organisation theory by concentrating upon individual behaviour and individual welfare in an organisational setting.

Formal versus **Informal Organisation**

One of the recurring themes in much of the human relations literature is the distinction between the formal and the informal organisation charts and structure designed by the administrative theorists in the pursuit of efficiency objectives. These are compared to the actual set of social relationships, the actual lines of communication, and the explicit structure of authority within any given organisation. Individuals in the organisation do not carry out their roles in a purely mechanical way. Instead, individuals bring to the organisation their own attitudes, goals and motivations which do not always coincide with those of the organisation (Mouzelis 1967, pp. 57–8). 'Some factors assumed in the design may be lacking or so distorted in operational practice as to be meaningless, while unforseen embellishments dominate the organisational structure' (Katz and Kahn 1966, p. 16).

A number of writers have, however, made the point that such a dichotomy can be misleading, e.g. Hill (1972, Chapter 3). Whilst it is correct to point to the distinction between actual behaviour within the organisation[18] and the prescriptions (rules) which detail how things ought to happen, it is, however, a mistake to conclude that the informal organisation is in some sense deviant and should be made to conform to the blue-print. Rather, the emergence of a particular set of behaviour patterns becomes the subject to be explained and one of the explanatory factors might include the formal organisation structure itself. The value of the distinction is further reduced, since it assumes that the formal organisation structure is well defined and clearly articulated. This is frequently not the case for complex hierarchical organisations, and for flexible non-hierarchical organisations it is a contradiction. The formal structure is seldom completely specified in the sense that the goals and objectives are well known, or that all activities are predetermined, codified and set down in contracts.

If we wish to study the actual set of relationships which exists within an organisation in order to compare it with the formal relationships that ought to exist (according to the organisation chart), then we have in practice a severe identification problem. For example, if the problem is that of analysing formal and informal compliance relationships in the organisation, then we could take the formal statement of authority relationships from the organisation chart, but then if we try to establish the actual set authority relationships we are confronted with the problems that, the subjects of the study will be likely to be committed, emotionally as well as socially, to present a distorted view of their relationship with people (Hill 1972, p. 106). This leaves such ambiguous situations wide open to interpretation by the observer who cannot prevent his own ideological predispositions and value judgments from entering into the analysis. Finally, if we take this line of analysis one stage further, we can see quite clearly the underlying normative position of the human school. Advocating a consensus view of how organisations should behave in order to attain efficiency, they saw that any conflict between the formal and informal organisation could, and further more should, be reduced by good human relations management, i.e. by manipulating the social environment in which work took place.

Recent Approaches to the Study of Organisations

It would be well beyond the scope of this chapter to survey in detail all the different approaches which have been taken to the study of organisations; useful surveys are found in March (1965), Mouzelis (1967), Perrow (1972) and Silverman (1970). In this section we will concentrate upon some of the developments which arose partly out of particular sociological traditions to the study of social phenomena (including organisations) and partly from a reaction of dissatisfaction with the human relations approach. In an attempt to redress the balance, these approaches have in part turned attention back towards the questions of organisational design which were raised by the classical administrative theorists. However, rather than concentrating purely upon problems of leadership style, interpersonal relations, morale and productivity, the modern approaches return to questions of organisation structure. This is made clear by Perrow (1972, pp. 175–6): 'if organisations are to be studied rather than individuals or group processes then the structural view, characteristic of sociology, is superior ... designing and managing the structure of the organisation is the key'. A structural aproach to the study of organisations turns attention again to the rules, rewards and incentives, role prescriptions and lines of communication in an attempt to understand behaviour within organisations. If, for example, it is generally regarded that an organisation is not functioning efficiently (meeting its stated goals, for example), then we can either think in terms of changing people's attitudes, changing leadership styles etc., or we might think of changing the organisation's structure:

> Of course there are incompetent managers, and workers are sometimes not all that one would like them to be. But the immediate resort to explanations in terms of personality or human relations is not warranted; the first question to be asked is whether the structure of the organisation, or unit, or role is the appropriate one for the tasks being demanded.
>
> (Perrow 1972, p. 177)

Perrow has argued that the human relations' set of prescriptions can be an expensive way of solving organisational problems. Moreover, there is a limit to their effect upon organisational performance. In these circumstances changes in structure should be considered.

The *structural or systems approach* to the analysis or organisations has its theoretical foundations in the 'structural–functional' tradition of sociology.

Whilst there is always a problem of branding people with a particular label, it would not be too much of an injustice if the following contributors to the theory and analysis of organisations were grouped together as functionalists: Blau (1974), Litterer (1973), Blau and Scott (1963), Merton (1957), Etzioni (1964), Parsons (1951) and Selznick (1948).

Whilst each of the above has provided different emphases and drawn attention to different aspects of organisations, each has stressed the importance of the properties of organisation structures and in particular the formal *processes* through which organisations function (Selznick 1969, pp. 23–4).

The systems approach to organisations considers the relationship between the structure and processes of organisations and the society within which the organisations exist. This is seen clearly in Parson's (1956) attempt to construct a general theory of organisations. For Parsons the problem was to integrate the various levels or units of analysis (i.e. the individuals, groups and organisations) with that of society, in order to show the relationship between organisations and the society which they serve in the production of socially desirable services and functions. That is, organisations provide outputs which are necessary for the maintenance of the wider social system (society) which, in common with all social systems (including organisations), have to solve the problems of: (a) survival by adaptation to the environment; (b) survival by goal achievement; (c) coordination of effort, by integration of sub-units into the larger system; and (d) the maintenance of value patterns over time. It is clear from these problems, which social systems are supposed to solve, that structural functionalists are concerned with the question of the survival of the system (i.e. organisation or society) and the processes which are used to ensure that this goal is achieved. To model this problem they draw heavily upon analogies taken from physical and biological systems theory, in which homeostatic and other feedback mechanisms enable the system to adapt to any internal or external disturbance, thereby restoring equilibrium. Thus, certain parts and processes in the system are said to be *functional* if they contribute to the systems needs (but if, on the other hand, they act in the opposite direction they are dysfunctional). Functional analysis, therefore, examines the extent to which a process is concerned with goal attainment and the serving of organisation needs. The consequences of actions are evaluated in terms of their contributions to the goals of the system,[19] and explain the persistence of social systems and order in the face of external and internal pressures for change.

The approach is not, however, without its own logical difficulties. Discussion of the behaviour of organisations as if they were individuals possessing all the cognitive properties of individuals, plus needs and goals etc., leads to the problem of reification or anthropomorphism. Postulating organisational needs and then relating them to behaviour *might* provide some rudimentary *account* of what is going on within organisations, but certainly does not constitute an *explanation*, since the exercise is tautologous. It is always possible to postulate some need that will account for the observed behaviour. Second, by focusing upon equilibrium and consensus, the approach ignores the concept of social conflict and hence the role that it might play in providing a source of explanation for observed behaviour. Third, functionalists view organisations as highly purposive, goal directed systems, but it will be stated time and again throughout this book that in practice goals are frequently ambiguous and ill-defined.

There is, however, a sub-branch of the structural–functionalist school which has produced a more fruitful approach to the sociology of organisations than the pure Parsonian analysis has managed to date. This is the structural approach of Perrow (1972) and Selznick (1969) etc. *et al.*, which argues for a more systematic examination of the differences between organisations in an attempt to account for the distinctive characteristics of different organisations. The classical administration theorists and the human relations school had almost exclusively concentrated upon the industrial organisation, but where did other organisations fit into their models? What about, for example, the school, the hospital, the university, prisons, churches, or charities? Did the principles enunciated by organisation theorists apply with equal validity and relevance to these organisations? To understand the differences between organisations it was, therefore, necessary to think in terms of: how do members of the organisations perceive their task(s); how interdependent is the organisation system; how closely controlled is the system, and; what constraints does the system face from the environment? Moreover, such an approach broadens any attempts to improve the performance of an organisation, since we now might wish to: (a) change the techniques and processes used to produce the output of the organisation; (b) change the organisation structure, (c) change the control process; (d) change the personnel, or; (e) a combination of all the above. This approach opened up the organisation recognising the importance of the relationship between an organisation and its environment.[20] In *open systems theory* the organisation is viewed as being able to influence its environment rather then responding to it in a purely passive way as in Parson's theory. This complicates the feedback mechanisms which any organisation might be thought to employ, since there is now the choice of meeting a target by internal adjustments or external adjustments or a combination of the two.

Socio-Technic and Contingency Theories of Organisations

One line of analysis which has been developed is the way in which different organisation settings influence behaviour and in particular how different technological processes affect behaviour. Earlier work by Blauner (1964) argued that technology determined behaviour, since the technology determined the social organisation in the work place and this in turn determined behaviour. Moreover, worker productivity was determined by technology, since different technologies have different propensities to alienate the worker; assembly line working was the most alienating and craft industries were the most satisfying. Blauner, although his work was in the human relations tradition and was full of normative judgments and interpretations,[21] nevertheless did recognise the role which technology might play in a fuller explanation of behaviour. A more empirical approach to the connection between social relationships and the technological environment of the organisation was adopted by the *socio- technic-systems school* of the Tavistock Institute; see Trist (1959), Trist and Bamfort (1951) and Emery and Trist (1969). These studies showed that properties of the specific technology were important facts in judging the appropriateness of particular systems of economic reward, since in many situations it was impossible to measure an individual's work effort in the group situation. Furthermore, it was found that the social relations that develop in a work place are related to the technological character of the work, since technologies will, with varying degrees, act as a constraint upon social interaction. Woodward (1958) classified production processes according to whether or not they were: (a) batch or unit production; (b) mass production or; (c) complex process production. What she found was that organisations with similar production systems were organised similarly. For example, the levels of authority increase with technical complexity; in mass production systems there is a greater degree of bureaucratic structure than in organisations using other productive systems, and in organisations using mass production systems there is a greater degree of functional specialisation.

Organisations differ in terms of the environments they face. Economic organisations that produce and sell their output on the market face differing degrees of competition and differing degrees of uncertainty about future outcomes. They face different social and cultural influences in terms of individuals bringing their personal values to the organisation; and they face different political and legal constraints, e.g. anti-trust legislation or pollution laws. Thus the principles of organisation design, or the principles of organisation management, which are appropriate for one environment are not necessarily applicable to another. To understand organisation structure and hence behaviour within organisations it is necessary to recognise the importance of the environmental influences. This specification of the problem was recognised by Burns and Stalker (1961) who classified organisational structures along a continuum. At the extremes of the continuum they described two organisational types which were (a) the mechanistic model and (b) the organic model. Burns and Stalker argued that an organisation's structure is in part a function of the environment it faces. In particular, they were interested in the stability and degree of uncertainty associated with that environment. Thus organisations which had relatively stable and certain environments tended (empirically) to have hierarchical structures with stable lines of authority and communication and well defined roles. Such organisations went in for routinisation of operations and reaped the economies of a *stable* set of internal processes. This appeared to be appropriate, for example, for industrial firms confronted with stable markets (for inputs as well as outputs) and an unchanging technology. On the other hand, the organic model was more appropriate for those organisations which face relatively unstable and highly uncertain environments. In this case the organisation structure has no clearly defined hierarchy, being made up of decentralised quasi-autonomous units within the organisation. It is a highly fluid structure with frequent changes in the organisation of activities taking place, continual re-definition of roles and frequent meetings between managers or section leaders to coordinate the intra-organisational functions. This kind of organisation will clearly tend to have high overhead costs in terms of communication and change.

The approach adopted by Woodward, and by Burns and Stalker along with other contributors to this area, has made an extremely useful contribution in terms of supplying yet another element of that mosiac which constitutes our understanding of organisations. Organisations differ in the tasks they perform and in the nature of the environments they face. Thus it is not too surprising to postulate that such differences might be reflected in the organisations' structures and in the way in which they are 'managed'. In terms of organisational design, the best (most efficient) way of organising a set of activities will be a function of the task to be performed and the environment. No single organisation structure has inherent efficiency properties: these can only be evaluated once the task and the environment are specified. The organic model, whilst efficient for an unstable organisational environment is likely to be less efficient for one which is stable. Contrary to the conclusions of earlier approaches to organisation design, there is no one best way to organise. Rather, the most effective organisational form is contingent upon the nature of the environment in which the organisation operates; (Lawrence and Lorsch (1967) refer to this as the *contingency theory* of organisations).

Despite these insights offered by the systems school, too much should not be claimed for it. First, there remain the methodological problems which were pointed out in connection with Parson's general systems model of organisation; concepts such as system, structure technology and goals tend to become reified. For example, Imerschein (1977) argues that it is more useful to think in terms of technological knowledge, rather than the hardware which may be used to accomplish a given task:

> The crucial element in the structuring of an organisation is the knowledge of how to employ a technology, rather than the technology itself. It has been common in the organisational literature to speak of a change in structure. But if we distinguish between technology and the knowledge of how to employ a technology, then we can also clarify the nature of the change process.
>
> (Imerschein 1977, p. 35)

Second, the open systems model, whilst recognising the complexity of the environment, including its uncertainties, places emphasis upon the role played by organisational structures in handling the vagaries of alternative environmental states. But this is only part of the picture. If we consider the individual as the level of analysis, then we will wish to know how the individual makes decisions when faced with uncertainty and a complex environment. As we will subsequently demonstrate in greater detail, individual's cope with complexity by 'bounding' or partitioning their decision set into manageable parts. The relevant questions then become: (i) how do individuals go about bounding their environments; (ii) how do different individuals perceive identical environments; and (iii) what factors influence the individual's perception of the situation? Here the emphasis is placed upon the individual as a decision maker, either acting purely as an individual or as a member of a group, rather than examining the 'behaviour' of some contrived entity called an organisation, Katz and Kahn (1966, p. 453) put the point this way:

> Social organisations as contrived systems are sets of ... patterned behavioural events. They consist of events and have no anatomical structure analagous to that of physical and biological systems. In the most generic sense the structure of a social organisation is contained in its various functions. In small subsystems the functions might be directly observable in the human activities involved, in dealing with larger sectors of organisation activity the patterns and functions are inferred from observable events.

Placing the individual back into the centre of organisational analysis seems to be the main thrust of contemporary theories of organisations. Systems analysis, by concentrating upon the structural properties of organisations rather than upon the individual, has washed out of the analysis concepts such as values and ideologies and their impact on individual behaviour. Following on from the above quotation from Katz and Kahn, if we do infer the patterns and functions of organisations from observable events, then this places the perceptions of the observer and his interpretive apparatus in a strategic role in terms of knowledge about organisations and the way in which society is structured.

Contemporary Organisation Theory

The theory of complex organisation can be divided into two broadly defined groups: those who subscribe to structural approaches to the study of organisations and those who prefer an interactive perspective. As we have seen, the first group (e.g. Blau, Thompson, and Perrow *et al.*) view organisations as coherent systems; organisation members are passive, reactive and instrumentally oriented. The second group views organisations as aggregates and organisation members are considered to be proactive, self directing, and continuously negotiating organisational settings. Individuals are initiative taking, desiring a greater control and independence over their environment. This view is best summed up in the recent work by Argyris (1972).

Whilst the debates between the two groups have been going on within the confines of this recently developed sub-branch of sociology, Driggers (1977, p. 143) argues that is is not particularly new:

> The debates between these two very different views and sets of assumptions about Man and the social order are often a replay of the very ancient philosophical themes of realism, determinism, nominalism and free will.

But even whilst the two groups have been opposed to one another on such issues, it is now becoming fashionable to regard these views as being united in the same paradigm; namely the rational model or goal paradigm.

Rational Model or Goal Paradigm

This model has dominated organisation theory through to the 1970s (Benson 1977, p. 3) and has focused upon the administrative and technical concerns of organisation effectiveness. Organisational patterns and social structures are explained as the outcomes of the goal seeking and need fulfilling tendencies of organisations. The source of this conceptual schema is to be found in the key concept of Weber's rational model of bureaucracy. As we have already seen, this concept was modified with the introduction of variables such as technology and environmental uncertainty, but in each case the correlation between technological features and social structures was explained as the result of a rational goal seeking tendency of organisations which produces *effective combinations* of technology and structure. These concepts have been further developed by empirical analysis carried out by, amongst others, the Aston Management Centre. This approach attempts to find, through empirical study, optimal measures for organisational variables such as the span of control, or the degree of specialisation and centralisation.

Crisis in Organisational Analysis: A Radical Critique

The orthodox stance embodied in the rational model has come under severe attack in recent years. Benson (1977) argues that what appears to be happening is that the goal paradigm of the rational model is being challenged by competing paradigms, as current research begins to confront a series of new issues which stretch the established way of thinking about organisational problems. These new issues centre around the concepts of action and power, rendering problematic those features of organisations which conventional analysis had taken for granted. Moreover, by focusing upon these issues, the inadequacies, inconsistencies and omissions of the existing goal paradigm are revealed. The issues raised by the critics of the goal paradigm are, comparatively speaking, new and at this stage constitute a research agenda rather than a list of resolved problems. It will, therefore, be instructive to consider each issue in turn.

(a) *Action* The features and characteristics of organisations, e.g. structure (i.e. hierarchy and span control), technologies, and goals, are frequently taken as objective givens. Those variables are then empirically related to individual behaviour in a mechanistic fashion. Data on the independent (explanatory) variables are not treated critically, neither are the measures of individuals' actions and behaviour. What is ignored in the goal approach is:

(i) the process of measurement and recording through which data on dependent and independent variables pass;
(ii) the role of the investigator in producing the data through interaction with participants.

The importance of these omissions is that the standard approach to analysis:

> ... leads to an uncritical stance in which the investigator is unaware of the ways in which the viewpoints of (certain) participants are built into theoretical and empirical work. The investigator then unknowingly becomes an apologist for a particular construction of the social world.
> (Benson 1977, p. 6)

Whilst the physical scientist does not need to worry about how an electron defines its situation, the social scientist cannot ignore important sources of relevant data, since to do so would violate one of the basic canons of scientific enquiry. The 'action approach' focuses attention on the processes through which particular organisation patterns are generated and sustained. Thus, examination of history, sequences of events and contexts through which present arrangements have been manufactured are an integral part of this analysis. To take but one example of how this approach might constitute a problem, consider the question of organisation rules, goals etc. These are regarded as being a fiction or an illusion. Instead of there being consensus over rules and goals, there is continual negotiation between individuals in the organisation to decide upon how they are defined in each specific situation.

(b) *Power* One of the main problems with the majority of orthodox theories or organisations is that they fail to deal properly with the power dimensions in organisations (Hill 1972, McNeil 1978). Parsonian functionalist analysis, along with the teachings of the human relations school, minimised the role played by conflict, whilst stressing consensus and voluntary compliance with the existing control or authority system. This conservative bias, along with the emphasis placed upon organisational equilibrium, was criticised by Mills (1959) and Dahrendorf (1959).

Power is, however, an ill-defined concept, with many writers calling for a distinction to be made between power, influence, control and authority (Dahl 1957, 1961; Barnard 1938; Presthus 1962). Most people would agree that power does not exist independently of its use. Thus it is necessary to distinguish between power which is legitimised (i.e. *de jure*) and commonly referred to as authority (in which one individual forces another to comply with an instruction by rule of law), and the more extreme cases of interpersonal power relationships in which one individual forces another to comply with his wishes by means of physical threats. In their attempts to come to terms with the concept of power, different writers have used a variety of approaches. Some, following in the Weberian tradition, have sought to account for the origin of an individual's power,[22] whereas others, such as Etzioni (1961), have suggested that it is more useful to consider the concept of *compliance* i.e. why does one individual voluntarily or involuntarily comply with (i.e. obey) the instructions of another. In this case an individual's position of power is maintained because others allow it to happen through their voluntary compliance. The interesting question then becomes, why are individuals willing to comply, rather than why does an individual have power? Other writers such as Presthus (1962) and Goffman (1956) prefer to talk about deference rather than compliance. Whilst power forces us to take a 'top-down' view of the organisation, deference and compliance force a 'bottom-up' view.

Whilst the criticism of earlier studies' neglect of power can be sustained, this is not true of more recent organisational studies. 'Political economy' models of organisations (Zald 1970), strategic contingency theories (Crozier 1964, 1973(a) and (b) and Hickson *et al.* 1971) and resource dependence theories (Pfeffer and Salancik 1978) are all approaches which use power as a central variable. In the *political economy model*, power is seen as a principal determinant for the allocation and distribution of scarce resources and the economic rewards associated with them. This model is elaborated and developed in subsequent chapters. The *strategic contingencies theory*, which was enunciated in the work of Crozier (*op. cit.*), argues that the power of the individual (or a group of individuals) arises from his ability to control uncertainties within the system. Thus, suppliers of vital (strategic) inputs or maintenance crews possess power because of their ability to control important facets of the organisation's environment and thereby reduce uncertainty. The *resource dependence perspective* has similar logical origins to the strategic contingencies theory. In order to continue in operation an organisation requires resources and since organisations do not always have absolute control over resource supply, this creates an uncertainty and makes resource acquisition problematical. It also places those who have control over the supply of resources to organisations in a powerful position.[23]

Each of these theories, whilst it does provide some insight into the concept of power, normally implicitly assumes stability in the goals and structure of organisations. But what if the organisation's goals, functions and structures are a function of the distribution of intra-organisation power? Those theorists who ask this kind of question view organisations as social formations structured by power relationships. 'Power is no longer regarded as one among many factors: rather it is the essential core from which other organisational features proceed ... Through the exercise of power ... action premises are established, the relationship between components are arranged and environmental interchanges are negotiated' (Benson 1977, p. 8). In other words, coordination, which implies the sequencing of events for others and which is a central tenet or organisational analysis, requires power as the dominant influence. It is power which is the essential dynamic of real organisations.

> In order for conscious coordination to occur, power must be created to actively interconnect and synchronize salient objects, technology and action settings of others. Moreover, power is necessary in order to impose some socially constructed reality upon those being coordinated so as to create the needed sharing of 'land marks' in their conceptual maps. The scheduling of meetings, sequencing of job rotation and training sessions, the setting of target dates, establishing budget parameters and setting up manning charts are ready illustrations of conscious coordination within organisations.
>
> (Driggers 1977, p. 155)

The nature of human processes within organisations may, therefore, be best understood through analysis of the basic principal element of social life — the conflict resulting from the struggle of persons and groups to alter existing power distributions. Conflicts of class and race, along with conflicts of other interests and values, are ubiquitous as individuals attempt to extend or protect their rights. There is no single common value system in society as functionalism suggests, nor is there likely to be a common value system within any particular organisation. Consensus is an over-played concept. The controlling values are those of the elite who have control over key decisions within the organisation. These decisions have impacts upon the welfare of the organisation's members and the organisation's clients (see Perrow 1972, p. 194). This perspective forces many questions into the open; why does the power structure of the elite go unchallenged and whose interests are served by the control system? Thus, to understand organisational change and much of the behaviour which takes place within organisations, it is necessary to examine power/compliance/deference relationships and the process of conflict and its resolution.

Before leaving this discussion of power, a number of further observations are in order. First, the discussion of power as presented above was in terms of inter-personal and intra-organisational power i.e. traditional power relationships within the organisation (see Kahn and Boulding 1964). However, recent studies, especially those using the resource dependence perspective, have examined the question of inter-organisational power i.e. an organisation's relative power position within society. Just as those who have been interested in intra-organisational behaviour have neglected power relationships, so too have those who have studied the relationships between the organisation and its environment. The Parsonian framework considers how the organisation adapts to its environment, rather than how it seeks to control it. Clearly, an organisation will do both and different organisations will adapt and control with varying degrees of success. The question then is what determines its success? As Perrow (1972 p. 199) has suggested, powerful organisations are not necessarily those which are the largest. Powerful organisations are instead those which have control over their environment. An interesting example of an organisation's power is provided by McNeil (1978, p. 66): 'managerial elites must always make decisions as to whether to meet a goal, like greater profits, through more efficient internal adaptation or through power strategies such as influencing Congress to pass a favourable tax law'. Organisations have a range of means of exercising control over their environment e.g. increasing the price of their outputs, adopting take-over and merger policies, or trying to use any monopsony power to keep down the relative price of inputs. This raises the second of our questions: how can the power of organisations be controlled? There is more to this question than simply considering the techniques of control. First, it is necessary to know what is being controlled and this requires us to understand clearly the origins of organisational power. Second, it is necessary to know why the power of the organisation is being controlled. This forces out into the open a discussion of the normative issues involved and the criteria that are to be used to judge the distribution of power within society. Such debates lie in the province of the political scientist.

The Radical Critique

There is emerging in the organisation theory literature a group of theorists that opposes conventional treatments of the analysis of organisations. This group is broadly Marxist in its academic origins. Its contribution is not unified, but can be summed up broadly as follows. Conventional organisation theory has failed to identify the relationship between internal organisation structure and more general social structures within the wider society. Unwittingly, conventional theory, it is asserted, serves a particular ideology. In particular, it serves capitalist economic systems in which labour is forced to conform to the control mechanisms contained within organisations. These control mechanisms are legitimised in the wider socio-political system and are provided with academic validity by conventional organisation theorists. Such a system, it is asserted, is bad and is in need of radical reform. Representatives of this approach include Clegg and Dunkerley (1977), Benson (1977) and Salaman (1978). Employing a mixture of Marxian dialectics and radical sociology they build up their case.

This case is, however, flimsy, as Bradley and Wilkie (1979) have vigorously argued. Examining each contribution to the radical critique they have subjected each in turn to the basic principles of logic. None of the contributions emerges unscathed. They demonstated that, '... elemental truths about social life are being asserted — that nothing is ever perfect, that persons will always have to forego some things in order to enjoy others, and that invariably the pursuit of their interests leads them into conflict with others. These are quite unexceptional and universally acknowledged truths about social life' (p. 13). Furthermore, it is argued that many of the principles proffered by this approach are nothing other than, 'extravagant expressions of the mundane' (p. 15).

Conclusion

The theory of organisations remains an un-unified subject. Different perspectives of organisational life are subjected to analysis by different disciplines.

Each gives its own particular description from a specific perspective. There is not, as yet, a general theory of organisations and as Bradley and Wilkie (1979) argue, the new radical school does not provide a convincing foundation for such a general theory. Goffman's (1961) analysis of 'total institutions' does, however, reveal insights which are near universal.

To the economist who is interested in questions of resource allocation and distribution the theory of organisations provides many important insights, but he must be selective in his harvesting. Not all of the fruits of this literature are relevant to his interests. But as his interests in non-market decision making, productivity and structural adjustments grow, he will be unable to continue to ignore this literature.

Notes

1 This is not to be interpreted as implying that such definitional exercises are useless. Rather, they will not be dealt with here.

2 For example, the 'systems theorists' or 'structural functionalists' classified organisations according to the function they served in society e.g. see Katz and Kahn (1966). Blau and Scott (1963) used the question 'who benefits?' (as a means of classification), whereas Etzioni (1964) used the compliance structure to distinguish between coercive, remunerative and moral organisation forms.

3 Economists will recognise this as the problem of collective choice, or group decision making, which has been extensively studied by Arrow (1951), Black (1958) and Olson (1965).

4 This does not imply, however, that all collectivities should be regarded as organisations. Strictly speaking, collectivities may be nothing other than purely informal, loosely structured associations of individuals with no specific purpose in mind, e.g. a crowd. They may, on the other hand, be small groups which have a specific well-defined goal. The distinction between small groups and complex organisations is clearly problematical, but we will ignore this problem here.

5 The student of organisation theory will recognise this as a reference to Etzioni's (1964) taxonomy of organisations, which are classified according to their compliance structure and intensity of involvement. In this book we will not be concerned with the problems of classifying organisations, which are often reduced to a logical exercise in definition.

6 In Etzioni's taxonomy (*op. cit*) there is another form of organisation e.g. churches and charities, in which the individual's involvement is moral and highly intense. Individual behaviour in these organisations is controlled by means of controlling the allocation of symbolic rewards.

7 Frequently discussed in terms of alienation.

8 Taylor's emphasis on a 'scientific' approach to management, in which work is to be measured etc., reflects the Victorian's faith in science-based remedies and upon their objectivity. Moreover, Taylor's insistence that such measurements should be carried out by the trained engineer also reflects the value placed upon the role of the engineer in these days—see Bernard Shaw's *Man and Superman*.

9 There is the famous conversation between Taylor and a worker in the Bethlehem Steel Co. called Schmidt (see Taylor 1911, pp. 44–7). By re-designing Schmidt's task and increasing his day-rate, Taylor motivated him to move 47 tons of pig iron a day instead of the normal 12!

10 For an extensive review of this literature including an historical account of it, see Massies' chapter in the *Handbook of Organisations* by March (1965).

11 Unfortunately, most social and industrial psychologists and sociologists who took up the issue of group decision making did not quite articulate the quesions in this way. Instead, they became hung up on treating the group as if it were an individual which made decisions etc. For a well reasoned approach to the problems of group decision making, the reader should consult Olson (1965).

12 A complete analysis would also include the inducements paid to consumers and shareholders i.e. incentives paid to keep these groups participating in the firm's activities. Moreover, questions about the 'just' distribution of inducements would also be an interesting extension to the analysis.

13 A complete management education industry mushroomed, based primarily upon training managers in leadership skills and leadership styles; see Cartwright and Zander (1960) on 'group dynamics' and Likert's (1967) 'link pin' theory.

14 See Herzberg (1968 pp. 77–90 and 178–92). Carey (1967), in a severe critique of Herzberg's work, has pointed out that if industrial psychologists tell people who gain satisfaction from financial and material rewards that they are neurotic, sick etc., then through simple psycho-somatic mechanisms they might well begin to show such symptoms as Herzberg found.

15 See Bradley and Wilkie (1974) for an extended discussion of this and other methodological problems.

16 See Mouzelis (1967) pp. 116–7.

17 See the March (1965) *Handbook on Organisations* for a selection of non-industrial studies.

18 It is beyond the scope of this survey to discuss in any great detail the different approaches which have been used to study intra-organisational behaviour. The reader who is interested in this area should consult Homans (1950, 1961), Blau (1974) and Silverman (1970).

19 Some consequences of actions are intended whereas others are not. Merton (1957) distinguishes between manifest functions i.e. those which are intended and latent functions i.e. those which are unrecognised.

20 This approach is sometimes called the 'open systems approach' (in contrast to the closed systems approach of classical organisation theory and the human relations school). Clearly there is a problem in defining the organisation's boundaries with the environment; also, is there more than one dimension to an organisation's environment (see Starbuck 1965)?

21 For example, Blauner says: '... an industrial environment tends to breed a distinctive social type' (p. 166). He doesn't tell us how this happens, nor does he discuss other social environments in which the worker takes part. Neither does he explain how workers' attitudes towards technology are formed. His analysis is value-laden and interpretive.

22 Weber (1947) saw the origins of power as being: (a) in tradition; (b) in the charisma of the individual who is said to have power; (c) legally embodied in the role of the office holder; and (d) in the individual's expertise and knowledge. See also Presthus (1962) who examines the process through which authority is legitimated.

23 The contingency and resource dependency theories of organisation are in many respects similar to recent economic approaches to hierarchy; see Arrow (1975) and the next chapter.

CHAPTER 3

Organisational Analysis: The Economist's Perspective

Micro-economic theory and Organisational analysis ... (are) theoretical approaches which are closely related.

(Leibenstein)

Price systems have no special place and no general allocative superiority over centralisation, although they are analytically more tractible to the economist.

(McManus)

Introduction

For the most part economics does not have a general theory of organisations. Rather, economics has a theory of the business organisation (i.e. the firm) and a highly particularised theory at that. The economist's standard theory of the firm does not serve as an analysis of how firms behave, nor does it offer a description of the complex exchanges which take place between individuals within modern corporations. The theory of the firm has instead served as an integral part of the neoclassical theory of relative price determination. It has not been the analysis of the firm *per se* which has drawn the attention of the majority of economists, rather it is a highly abstract and bloodless creature which has been employed in the analysis of market behaviour.

Whilst other social scientists have studied the intra-organisational behaviour of a number of different types of organisations, economists for their part have, in the majority of cases, singled out one type of organisation, the business firm, analysing it in terms of an agent operating in the market place and thereby taking no interest in what goes on inside the organisation. A survey of the economists' perspective on organisational analysis is, therefore, not likely to be as wide ranging as that of the previous chapter. However, since the late 1960s there have been a number of significant developments which we can report upon and which, when taken together, show quite clearly that there is a strong link between micro-economic theory and organisational analysis; a link which will undoubtedly be the focus of much development in the near future.

The development of the economic analysis of organisations began with the publication of Cyert and March's extremely influential book on *The Behavioural Theory of the Firm* in 1964. Until then very few economists had concerned themselves with what went on inside the firm. Within the competitive model of the neoclassical micro-economic system there was a hypothetical construct called 'the firm' which was a single decision criterion (i.e. profit maximisation) and which had the ability to obtain information from an external word called 'the market'. The problem which economists had set themselves was not the analysis of the firm, but instead the conditions necessary to obtain an equilibrium set of market prices and quantities and the features of that equilibrium in terms of its uniqueness, stability, and existence and welfare characteristics.[1] The 'behaviour' of the firm (and it is only a limited form of behaviour that is discussed i.e. price and output behaviour) followed from the assumption of profit maximisation taken in conjunction with a specification of the external environment or market i.e. perfect competition, monopoly, oligopoly etc.

> None of the problems of real firms can find a home within this special construct. There are no organisational problems nor is there any room for analysis of the internal decision-making process. In fact, all of the empirical content of this neoclassical model lies in the description of the environment within which the firm must operate. Even the sole objective of the firm, profit maximisation, is determined by the environment because any other behaviour of the firm will lead to its extinction. The theory of the firm is *a priori* in the sense that its behaviour can be deduced from assumptions that describe the environment.
>
> (Cyert and Hedrick 1972, pp. 398–9)

What Cyert and March (1963) did was to depart from the then current practice of making the firm's environment more complex by making it more realistic and instead to specify *directly* some aspects of the firm's *internal* behaviour. In this respect they were part of the Simon or 'decision making theory' tradition of organisations (which are reviewed in the next chapter).

As we will see presently, Cyert and March's approach brings the economist's analysis of organisations much closer to that of other social scientists outlined in the previous chapter.

Other developments have also taken place. Some economists have turned their attention to the study of organisations other than that of the business firm, e.g. the hospital[2] has been studied by Reder (1965), Feldstein (1967), Newhouse (1970) and Pauly and Redisch (1973); and the public sector bureaucracy by Downs (1967), Tullock (1965), Niskanen (1971) and Breton (1974). Others have employed a particular development of the neoclassical model to study the 'economics of internal organisation' which is a fast growing and interesting branch of the micro-economics of information. One economist who has done much to develop the economist's analysis of organisational behaviour is Oliver Williamson. In 1964 Williamson presented his *Economics of Discretionary Behaviour* in which he replaced the traditional profit maximising objective for the firm with one in which managerial utility was maximised. Since then Williamson has paid particular attention to the effects that alternative organisational structures have upon the behaviour of the firm.

There have, therefore, been a number of interesting developments taking place in the economics of organisational behaviour. What this chapter will do is to pull together the findings of this literature in an attempt to find out (i) where is it leading us, (ii) does it in any sense fit together and (iii) how does it relate to the theories of organisation set out in the previous chapter? It will not be our intention to attempt a synthesis; this would be too ambitious and inappropriate at this stage. We begin with an examination of the traditional theory of the firm and work our way, almost chronologically, through to the present state of the subject.

The Traditional Theory of the Firm[3]

As was pointed out in the introduction above, the economist's standard theory of the firm represents a consistent body of generalisations that explain the behaviour of business enterprises. The modes of behaviour which are usually studied include decisions about pricing, production, innovation, employment and investment. Each of these decisions is analysed deductively employing the *a priori* assumption of profit maximisation.

The behaviour of the firm is studied as part of a more general analysis which sets out to establish the ideal form of economic organisation. As Marschak (1965, p. 423) argues, the main contribution of economic theorists to the study of organisation has been the examination of organisational design.[4] If we think of the economy as an organisation, then the market economy is probably the longest studied of all human organisations. The economist, from Adam Smith to the present day, is not only concerned with understanding and explaining the underlying economic behaviour of market organisation, he is also, in a large number of instances, more interested in the normative questions of establishing the principles of optimal design for the ideal organisation of the market economy. For Smith, the underlying organisational principle was the pursuit of self-interest by each individual; the reconciliation of conflicting individual goals via the market was assumed to promote what was best for society as a whole.

The organisational or institutional structure of the neoclassical, perfectly competitive economy is very simple and to all intents and purposes non-existent. Each individual produces his own product according to his comparative advantage, thereby giving rise to specialisation and the need for economic exchange. In the highly abstract analysis of the exchange economy (see for example Debreu 1959 and Arrow and Hahn 1971), there are no market organisers, there is not the institution of money, property rights are not specified and there are no combines of producers (i.e. firms). The firm is simply represented as a collection of technologically determined production possibilities (i.e. a collection of alternative bundles of goods each falling within the firm's production capabilities — in other words, its production function). Each vector (bundle) is defined as positive outputs and negative inputs and the problem facing the analyst is to choose that vector (i.e. combination of inputs and outputs) which will maximise profits for a given capability.

In this kind of analysis the problem is one of studying, at a highly abstract level, the interaction of households' preference orderings and firms' production possibilities in order to establish equilibrium prices. Thus the analysis proceeds according to the following kind of thought experiment; if the firm faces a particular set of demand and cost curves and if the objective is to maximise profit, then, given the specific characteristics of the market environment (i.e. perfect competition, monopoly, oligopoly etc.), what level of output will be chosen and at what price consistent with profit maximisation will that output be sold? Having solved that problem, other decisions can be deduced such as, what level of employment of capital and labour is required to produce that profit maximising output? This theory of the firm is also used to deduce the equilibrium conditions for an industry and for markets made up of many firms. The problems of establishing the conditions required to produce equilibrium under alternative specifications of the environment (perfect competition, monopoly, oligopoly etc.) then become the subject of analysis.

Of course, the analysis is more difficult than this simple characterisation might suggest. There are problems in defining profit, industry and market, and the complexity of the analysis is increased if more than a single time period is considered but, generally speaking, analysis has proceeded upon an *a priori* deductive basis. There is the added problem that, even at this level of abstraction and simplification, it requires rather a hefty battery of high-powered mathematics to solve for the equilibrium conditions and progress was halted until the 1950s because the appropriate mathematics did not exist. Empirical studies have examined the relationships between the firm's environment and its performance (usually measured in terms of profitability). The theory of the firm has, however, played a minor role in economic analysis (Arrow 1971), since most topics in economic analysis were developed around a theory of demand and a theory of prices and markets, thereby leaving production, supply and hence the theory of the firm comparatively ignored and underdeveloped. The main function of the entrepreneur, in the standard analysis, was to equalise profits in different sectors of the economy and in so doing to commit euthenasia (Marris 1974, p. 1).

The treatment of the firm as an integral part of the more general analysis of market behaviour is a continuation of Marshall's treatment of the 'representative firm' as a small scale replica of the supply curve of the industry as a whole.[5] Marshall was more concerned with industry analysis (it was later writers who became concerned with the firm) and the purpose of traditional theory was to explain the way in which resources were allocated by a price system through markets and not through other resource allocation systems such as (internal) hierarchical organisations or through planning or command economies. It is this earlier comparision of alternative allocative systems which was forgotten about in subsequent analysis and which has been recently rediscovered.[6]

In summary, therefore, the economist's treatment of the profit maximising firm was an integral part of price theory, in which the aggregate behaviour of firms acting in conjunction with one another in markets of varying structures influenced the determination of relative prices. It was not a theory of the behaviour, either internal or external, of any single firm and the individual firm's behaviour is not specified in any other terms than that of a production function or a production possibility set and a decision rule of profit maximisation under conditions of perfect information and complete certainty. The internal organisation of the firm (if indeed such an abstract entity can be thought of having structure) is assumed to have no effect upon its decisions; instead it is assumed that it is only the environmental factors or market conditions which affect behaviour.

The Existence of Firms

Whilst the abstract analysis of price theory required nothing other than the most rudimentary specification of a firm, other economists attempted to provide an economic rationale for the existence of firms. It would be an impossible task to account for the existence of every conceivable form of organisation. Indeed, such an exercise would first of all demand the supply of a satisfactory definition of organisation. As we saw in the previous chapter, formal organisations exist in a variety of forms: firms, universities, trades unions, hospitals, schools, and government. Organisations involve elaborate systems of communication and joint decision making and as such would include the price system of the economy. That is, the market system is a form of organisation and as we have already remarked has been extensively studied by economists for many years. The market system is an organisation or a social institution which is designed to allocate and distribute resources, but equally other organisations perform a similar function not through the mediation of prices, but through systems of authority and command. The purpose of any organisation is to exploit the fact that many (virtually all) decisions require the participation of many individuals for their effectiveness. Efficiency is increased by specialisation which results in the need for markets or systems of exchange. Furthermore, specialisation goes along with the division of labour and demands cooperation of labour units to work in association with one another. The cottage system, with the merchant acting as an intermediary, was one indirect form of association, but indivisibilities in the physical (capital) production process required the establishment of the factory system in which efficient production was carried out by labour and capital working in direct combination. This is a rudimentary account of the emergence of one type of organisation, but others remain. Why indeed do firms exist and why do they take the form which they do (e.g. partnership, limited liability etc.)? Knight (1921), for example, argued that the firm arose out of a response to an uncertain environment. The entrepreneur's role was to specialise in risk taking, i.e. the institution of the firm guarantees the incomes of the suppliers of inputs, whilst the entrepreneur takes the residual income and bears most of the risks arising from the uncertain future. But why organise production in this way? Would it not, as Coase (1952) and Alchian and Demsetz (1972) have argued, be just as valid to suppose that the entrepreneur could specialise in risk taking by making contractual arrangements in the market place rather than by managing the inputs? This, however, is an unreasonable criticism of Knight's position as McManus (1975) argues. Knight had recognised the transactions costs involved in enforcing such contractual arrangements made in the market: 'the fact which limits the application of the insurance principle to business risks generally ... is the peculiarly obstinate connection of a moral hazard with this sort of risk' (Knight 1921, p. 251). However, a more valid criticism of Knight would be that he hasn't so much provided an argument for the existence of firms, rather he has provided a rationale for the emergence of the entrepreneur, which is an entirely different argument. That firms can exist without entrepreneurs is witnessed by the presence of labour-managed firms, so that Knight's argument becomes ideological, based as a prop for the capitalist system of organisation.

Coase (1937) had earlier argued that any explanation of the existence of firms must rest upon the general notion of transactions costs i.e. the information gathering costs and decision making costs involved in any exchange process including that of market exchange.[7] In price theory it was assumed there were no costs of transacting in markets or, as one economist has put it, there was no answer to the question, 'who pays the auctioneer?' For Coase, by 'internalising' a number of transactions within the organisation of the business corporation or the firm, rather than in the market, the existence of the firm reduces transactions costs and supersedes the market as a means of allocating resources. Furthermore, the size of the firm would be limited by decreasing returns to management. Whilst Coase's theory provided both a rationale for the firm and a discussion of the limit on its size (i.e. questions not discussed by traditional price theory), it also left a number of questions unanswered; how do firms avoid transactions costs and why should transactions costs be lower in firms than in markets?[8] Since Coase assumes that the equilibrium level of output is the same in market organisation and in the firm organisation, there is, therefore, no discussion of the effect of the firm upon the equilibrium level of output.

The treatment of non-market forms of economic organisation, which include firms, public sector bureaucracies, and non-profit voluntary organisations such as charities, as arising from actions to reduce transactions costs, has been developed in recent years by, amongst others, Buchanan and Tullock (1962), Williamson (1967), Arrow (1969), Alchian and Demsetz (1972) and McManus (1975). This approach is developed in further detail below under the heading of the 'economics of internal organisation' and should be seen as growing out of the earlier work by Coase.[9]

Take as an example Alchian and Demsetz's (1972) analysis of the firm. Centralisation of productive activities within the firm amounts to a change in the production function which improves productivity and every individual's rewards. However, because much of the production process is organised on a work 'team', or primary work group basis, there exists a problem in monitoring the output of the team and apportioning payments in accordance with the productivity of individual members of the team. Alchian and Demsetz argue that if it is difficult to relate an individual's work effort to total output, it becomes rational for the individual to shirk, since he will obtain payment for less effort (i.e. he free rides). If, however, all members of the group did so, total output would fall. Hence there is a need to monitor team production. What Alchian and Demsetz (p. 192) argue is that specialisation (by a firm) in monitoring is economical; the entrepreneur is the monitor and earns residual income:

> ... through the reduction in shirking that he brings about, not only by the prices he agrees to pay the owners of the inputs, but also by observing and directing the actions or use of these inputs.

Whilst this attempt by Alchian and Demsetz is a stab in the direction of providing a rationale for the existence of the firm, one does get the feeling that they are describing some primitive type of firm and not the production processes of modern firms in which, as we saw in the previous chapter, monitoring is incomplete because in many cases it is the primary work group members who direct and control the actions of the inputs, thereby working against the monitors. In other words, the monitoring problem arises not so much because of team production *per se*, but because of the problems of identifying at low cost the relationship of the contributions made by individual members to total output. The interesting question then is, when monitoring by an external agent is too expensive, how do the members of the primary work group regulate output and productivity and sanction these shirkers? Alchian and Demsetz, therefore, do not provide anything like a complete analysis of the existence of firms and what we are left with are incomplete impressions that there are economies to be gained from an association between workers working in conjunction with indivisible units of capital.

Managerial Theories of the Firm

Earlier criticisms of the degree of abstraction used in price theory and the logical games played by economists were made by J. H. Clapham (1922) in his celebrated article on 'empty boxes'. Clapham's argument was that crucial concepts in economic theory were devoid of meaning because they did not describe actual empirical relationships. The firm as used in price theory was one such empty box. Pigou's (1922) critical reply to Clapham took the traditional line that these boxes or concepts employed by economic analysts are part of an economic framework and are full of meaning if considered within that framework. It will be recalled from the introductory remarks in this chapter that the essential thing to remember about the traditional marginalist or price theory of the firm is that it was and remains an *a priori* deductive approach. By setting up a set of axioms the analyst then proceeds to test the internal logical consistency of his theory. Whether or not the theory has real world counterparts is of no interest.

What Clapham was demanding from economics, however, was an empirically based theory of the firm and he was joined in the fullness of time by others such as Hall and Hitch (1939), Andrews (1949, 1964) and Wiles (1956). The firm of traditional theory did not have any of the problems or face any of the complexities of real firms. The result was the development of alternative theories of the firm which posited alternative objective functions to that of profit maximisation.[10]

Empirical studies of the behaviour of firms by the Oxford group in the 1930s[11] demonstrated that firms cannot be thought of as maximising profits. Management simply did not have sufficient information to do so. In order to maximise profits, it would have been necessary for managers to have knowledge of their demand curve, marginal revenues and marginal costs.

Furthermore, what does the statement 'to maximise profits' mean? Is it the profits of a single accounting period or of an average of periods and is it accounting profit or economic profit that is to be maximised? Because of the technical difficulties and the cost of obtaining this information, management used simple rules of thumb such as 'mark up' pricing to determine their price and output levels and moreover used simple rules of thumb in managing inventories.

Furthermore, why should managers in the modern corporation set out to maximise profits; is this a meaningful objective for them to strive to attain? To answer this question it becomes important to take account of institutional arrangements which did not feature in the abstractions of price theory. Whilst profit maximisation might seem a reasonable objective for the owner-manager of a firm, it was thought to be less reasonable for the managers of modern corporations in which management was separated from control and ownership[12]. Williamson (1964, p. 55) argues that profit maximisation by management:

> ... would appear to require an unusual variety of rationality — and one not widely found in human affairs — namely a complete detachment of individuals' interest from occupational decision making.

What Williamson is suggesting is that it is more reasonable to assume that non owner-managers will pursue objectives other than that of maximising profit and the most likely candidate as an alternative to profit maximisation is that of the maximisation of the manager's own utility. Managerial utility is assumed to depend upon salary, perquisites, expenditure on staff, on-the-job leisure etc. That is, management is assumed to gain increased satisfaction from higher financial rewards, including expense accounts, company cars, and international trips. Since a manager's salary and status are frequently associated with the size of his department he will go in for empire building.[13] The extent to which management is able to pursue its own utility maximisation depends upon the degree of control which the owners of the firm have over managerial actions, i.e. the pressures from the capital markets and also the pressure of competition in product markets. Management does, however, have much discretion over its own actions since shareholders (owners) are insufficiently informed. Thus management can pursue its own objectives provided that it produces a satisfactory, i.e. acceptable, level of profits.[14] Therefore, where there is scope for discretion, business behaviour is more likely to be explained in terms which reflect the interests of the manager-decision makers.

Whilst Williamson has concentrated upon the scope for discretionary behaviour by non owner-managers it is also pertinent when analysing decision making and the implementation of decisions to consider the amount of discretion possessed by lower level personnel in the organisation. Thompson and Bates (1957), for example, argue that the more non-routine the tasks, the more discretion must be left to lower level personnel. This question of the amount of discretionary behaviour possessed by organisational members will be examined in greater detail in Chapter 8.

Loasby (1968) has provided another view of the relationship between the goals of the individual manager and those of the organisation which complements that of Williamson. First, there is the problem of giving meaning to the idea of an organisation having goals, since it is individuals who have goals. If, however, we assume that there is a corporate or a collectively agreed goal, say profit maximisation, the second problem is, will any individual manager subscribe to the collective goal? Any individual manager is one amongst many and as such he might rightly assume that his activities will only make a small contribution to the achievement of the collective goal. It would be rational for him to assume that the others are contributing to the goal, thereby allowing him to serve his own goals and to become a 'free-rider' in the group. This is, as Loasby suggests, similar to the problems of collective choice and it 'demonstrates the fallacy in the argument that members of an organisation should share a common purpose. It is not that a common purpose is unnecessary as a rational incentive; it is actually worthless' (Loasby 1968, p. 356). Whether or not management has the discretion and the freedom to pursue its own goals does not only depend upon the amount of control which shareholders possess, but the extent to which any single manager can pursue his own self interest depends upon whether or not other members of the organisation will allow him to do so. As in any collective choice problem, whether or not the free riders can be identified and sanctioned depends upon the size of the group and the costs of monitoring individual members' actions (see Wiseman 1978).

Marris (1966) has also provided a theory of the firm based on managerial behaviour similar in essence to that of Williamson. In this case management once again seeks to promote its own self-interest by increasing its salary perquisites, expenses, staff etc..., but Marris argues that this is achieved by maximising the growth of the firm. Managerial utility is in Marris' model a function of the size and growth of the firm, since large faster growing firms provide the necessary resources which are required to finance managerial salaries, perquisites etc.[15]

Managerial theories of the firm, such as the discretionary behaviour of management (Williamson), growth maximisation (Marris 1966) or sales revenue maximisation (Baumol 1959) depend upon the assumption of the existence of imperfections in either input or output markets. For the traditional firm facing perfectly competitive markets, profit maximisation is necessary if the firm is to continue to trade; it follows from the fundamental goal of survival. When there is market imperfection, however, the goal of profit maximisation becomes an explicit *assumption*. What the managerial theories of the firm are doing, however, is modifying that assumption in an attempt to construct more empirically appealing theories of the firm. If profit, the excess of revenues over costs, is regarded as representing discretionary resources, then we have a distributional problem. Should these resources (rents) be allocated to the shareholders in the form of higher dividends, to the employees as higher wages, to management in higher salaries and perquisites, or to meet sales revenue maximisation or growth maximisation objectives? Clearly this is a normative question which can only be answered in the context of welfare economics by appealing to criteria of distributive justice. However, the empirical question, 'how *are* the rents distributed' becomes a matter of setting out the data, including that pertaining to the existing distribution of rights within the system. 'The existence of market imperfections introduces the possibility of discretionary resources and gives us the first hint that the internal structure and processes of organisations may affect the pattern of resource allocation in ways not completely dictated by external markets' (Pondy 1970, p. 277).

Moreover, the maximisation of discretionary resources becomes a more general concept than that of profit maximisation which then reduces to a special case. This more general case then applies not only to business organisations but to non-business organisations also.

The Economics of Internal Organisation

Earlier managerial theories of the firm asked the question, 'what do firms really maximise?'. The question was interesting, but did not turn out to have a compelling answer. Indeed, one likely candidate as an answer to the question was that firms did not maximise anything at all. 'The failure to find an objective function is symptomatic of the diversity and complexity of the environment within which firms operate and of the decisions they make'. (Spence 1975, p. 163). Moreover, 'all firms do not behave in the same way in similar circumstances and a theory which helps to explain why they do not is perhaps preferred to one which asserts that they should' (Loasby 1967, p. 167).

In recent years a number of writers on the theory of economic organisation have addressed themselves to the following set of questions: 'what are the factors which induce a shift of transactions from markets to internal organisation, and within internal organisation, how do we explain the types of hierarchical relations that predictably emerge?'. The pioneer of this particular approach is Oliver Williamson, who also developed the 'managerial discretion' theory of the firm. Williamson's obvious intellectual debt is found in the earlier work of Coase's theory of the existence of firms, but Williamson's own efforts in this field have transcended these earlier ideas of Coase.

The economics of internal organisation is a relatively new approach to the study of firms and utilises the results of the economics of information and of uncertainty. As a topic it embraces an enormous range of subject matter, with no particular unifying theme other than that writers in this area try to account for the particular institutional arrangements which are found and appraise and evaluate such arrangements through comparisons of alternative forms.[16] The approach, therefore, closely follows Coase (1960) insofar as it emphasises that the problem of efficient economic organisation needs to be examined by comparing institutions, rather than by means of comparing real world institutions to some unattainable ideal. Emphasis has, in the past, been placed upon market failures arising from frictions e.g. transactions costs. However, Williamson (1971) has pushed forward the idea that the concept of market failure should be more widely expanded to include 'institutional failure', since it is the same factors which are responsible for market failures which also explain the failures of internal organisations. Thus it would seem to be more appropriate to think in more general terms of 'systems failure' and this is the topic of Chapter 9.

Economic exchanges, whether or not they are made through markets, are exchanges of contracts; contracts to deliver goods of a certain specification on a certain day, and contracts to supply labour services or capital services under certain specified conditions. Economic activity and economic structure can, therefore, be thought of as a network of contractual arrangements. There are an infinite number of possible contractual arrangements, but for one reason or another only a limited number of contractual arrangements seem to be feasible and of that latter set only a few are chosen. The interesting questions which arise from this line of enquiry are: what factors determine the feasible set of contracts and what determines the choice of one set of contracts compared to another? In other words, can we explain and account for the specific contractual arrangements which exist in the economy and evaluate their efficiency? The contractual arrangements which the economics of internal organisation have tended to concentrate upon are labour service contracts and capital service contracts.

Another line of inquiry is to view the organisation (in this case the firm) as a non-market institution whose function is to deal with resource allocation in the presence of informational constraints. The economics of internal organisation from this viewpoint are part of the more general problem of information-constrained resource allocation. Non-market procedures such as internal organisations might be superior to markets as resource allocation systems for a number of reasons. The theory of public goods, externalities and economies of scale are all examples of non-convexities which are frequently associated with the failure or the elimination of a market. If, however, we argue that there are increasing returns to the acquisition and use of information by organisations, we introduce yet another non-convexity which reduces the superiority of markets over other non-market allocative systems. Moreover, earlier theories of the firm had employed the concept of economies of scale in the technology of physical production or a Marris type managerial theory of the firm to argue for increased scale of operations by firms. However, even if there are no such managerial motives nor economies of scale in the technology of physical production, there is still a reason for expanding the firm's scale of operations if there are economies of scale in the acquisition of information (Wilson 1975).

The economics of information opens up a new dimension to the study of the firm. This is clearly seen in Arrow's (1975) examination of the motives for vertical integration. Building upon an earlier study by Williamson (1971) it is argued that any uncertainty in supply from upstream firms generates a need for information by the downstream firm. This creates an incentive for the downstream firms to purchase the upstream firms in order to reduce their uncertainty of supply. The result is that market transactions in intermediate outputs between upstream and downstream firms become internalised within the organisation following vertical integration. In other words, the internal system of resource allocation is regarded as being superior to that of the market and the interesting result which emerges is that, if we assume uncertainty, then no competitive equilibrium with many firms can survive.

Information problems exist in all contractual arrangements. Generally speaking information is incomplete either because it does not exist, or because it is costly to obtain and process. Information problems do, however, give some insights into the structuring of incentives within the firm. For example, if the personnel of an organisation knows more about the job than does the supervisor, then it could be argued that it would be more efficient to structure incentives so that information is wholly or even partially revealed in the performance of the job (Mirrlees 1976 and Stiglitz 1975). This argument is often countered by labour which points out that if the piece rate system is in operation and if it is 'bust', then the piece rate is revised downwards. Whilst economists might have discovered the importance of structuring incentives, or choosing one set of contractual arrangements rather than another in order to promote the generation of information to improve efficiency, these problems have been recognised by industrial sociologists and industrial relations experts for some time. Barnard (1938), it will be recalled, laid great stress upon management's task of managing incentives and studies of work group behaviour, beginning with the Hawthorne studies of Roethlisberger and Dickson, have shown that members of primary work groups sanction those members who are rate busters i.e. the group acts to withhold information from management in order to safeguard members' interests.

Information problems also arise in the training and promotion of a firm's personnel. For example, should a firm train personnel if this improves their occupational mobility and they leave to join another firm? Does or should the firm have any property rights to appropriate the benefits provided through training? What is the most appropriate promotion system that a firm should follow, and are some promotion systems more efficient than others? For example, we can imagine a number of alternative rules or procedures that a firm could adopt in promoting personnel; it could employ a seniority system in which it is the longest serving members who are promoted, or it could ignore age and promote on ability and performance, or it could use a system which combines age and performance. If, for the present argument, we ignore questions of justice and fair play and concentrate purely upon questions of efficiency, what can be said about the alternative systems of promotion? Older members in the organisation who have been long serving will have gained a great deal of personal experience (i.e. information) about their job. If the promotion system is not geared to seniority, then this could create a disincentive for longer serving members passing on job-specific information (via some training system) to younger recruits who serve as a threat to the more senior person's promotion prospects. In other words the choice of promotion system can reduce efficiency in the organisation by distorting the free flow of information.

There are other problems which exist in this area of personnel promotion. Promotion is a method of sorting out personnel in an organisation and the method used for screening is of importance to the allocation of human resources within the firm and hence for the efficiency of the organisation, i.e. ensuring that labour in the organisation is allocated optimally. The problem with all screening systems is that they are imperfect, because information is not readily available at low costs. In this example, individual capabilities are not well known, individual's performance is not well known and the rewarding of certain activities that do signal (at low cost) abilities in certain dimensions may produce incentives that distort the individual's allocation of time and effort with respect to attaining organisational objectives. For example, if performance is judged in terms of results and outcomes, then this can produce very conservative risk averse activity, in which individuals, rather than face the penalties of disaster, will minimise failure probability rather than take reasonable risks. But to judge performance in any other terms under conditions of uncertainty would require detailed information which is costly to obtain.

Finally, the economics of internal organisation has also examined the firm's capital markets. Should firms use retained earnings to invest in new plant and machinery, or should they use the resources to expand by merger? The outcome of decisions of this kind taken by management is likely to be different from the outcome of a similar decision taken by investors in the capital market. The retained earnings of the company are internal funds and can be thought of as representing an internal capital market compared to the external funds of the new issues market. Investors in internal markets (i.e. management) have access to different amounts of information and information of different qualities as compared to investors in the external capital market. Furthermore, given different preference functions for internal and external investors, this can produce different allocations of capital resources. For example, stockholders and managers are likely to produce different evaluations of the probability of failure and bankruptcy, or management might allocate funds to low productivity investments within their particular firm, whereas external investors would have invested in a different firm offering a higher productive investment with a greater return.

The Economic Theory of Teams[17]

Economics has, in conjunction with mathematical statistics and some branches of psychology, articulated a well defined theory of individual decision making or individual choice: e.g. the analysis of consumer choices, choices over a set of current goods and services, choices between current and future consumption and the individual's choice between work and leisure. These theories have been well developed and are the stock in trade of all undergraduate economics courses. The theory has not only been set out in static terms for conditions of complete certainty, but has also been developed for conditions of uncertainty, as embodied, for example, in the expected utility theorem. Moreover, it has been developed in the form of sequential decision making to take account of decisions made over time.

Recently, attention has been directed to the problem of decision making when several persons are involved. Compared to the single person decision problem, a number of new elements must be taken into account: (a) there are differences among the members of the organisation with respect to possibilities of action, preferences, and information, and this means that different individuals will have different beliefs (subjective probabilities) about events and different preferences for the alternative consequences of actions; (b) when there are many persons involved there is an added element of uncertainty introduced arising from other members' actions; and (c) there is the problem of defining optimality for a group/organisation when individual preferences differ.

Information structures lie at the centre of much of the analyses of the economics of internal organisation. This is especially true in the economic analysis of *teams* (Marschak 1955) which is a highly abstract mathematical examination of the performance of different 'information structures' i.e. different allocations of the organisation's total knowledge amongst its members. A team has a specific technical definition. Following Marschak (*op. cit.*), a team is a specific type of *theoretical* organisation. In any organisation, individuals differ with respect to: (i) the extent of their control over different action variables; (ii) the amount and quality of information on which they base their decision; and (iii) their preferences (i.e. tastes and beliefs). A team, however, is a particular type of organisation in which the members of the organisation (team) have identical preferences in the sense that there is single pay-off function reflecting the common goals of the members. The basic questions to which the theory of teams addresses itself are: (a) for a given structure of information what is the optimal decision function; and (b) what are the relative values of alternative structures of information? In the search for optimal decision functions and information structures in a team, we are dealing with highly abstract statistical decision theory to examine optimal decision strategies. These models are not descriptive. Each individual is assumed to respond instantaneously to environmental changes and to choose that decision rule which maximises his expected pay-off. The expected pay-off rule is taken as a measure of gross performance.

This general approach is best seen in the work of Radner (1961, 1962) who has analysed and demonstrated the relative gross performances of different information structures for differing assumptions about the pay-off function and probability distribution. The different information structures refer to different amounts of centralisation and decentralisation and in this sense the theory of teams can be thought of as a systematic examination of the logical properties of the classical administrative theories as set out in the previous chapter.

Parallel developments to the theory of teams are found in Arrow, Hurwecz and Uzawa (1958) and Arrow and Hurwecz (1962). These writers examine the decision processes within the firm from the point of view of determining the equilibrium values of the processes, i.e. values which once attained cause the process to stop. This analysis sets up pseudo-price mechanisms for decision making within the organisation and then proceeds to find those processes which converge to an equilibrium and whose equilibrium values maximise the firm's pay-off function. The studies are applied to the problems found in firms with multi-branch plants, to multi-national firms and to national planning agencies. The major problem is to discover the conditions under which the ideal competitive mechanism is organisationally superior to alternative schemes i.e. under what conditions are decentralised decision processes superior to alternative processes?

Both the theory of teams and the comparison of alternative decision processes can easily be criticised by anyone who is looking for an empirical analysis of decision processes. However, that would be an unfair criticism of an approach which does not purport to be descriptive but is instead normative. These information theories are similar to the abstract analyses of the price system; both are systems studies and both set as their problem the examination of the logical properties of the artificial systems.

Whether or not these abstract studies provide any useful insights for either the study of actual decision processes or for prescriptions of how organisations should be designed is a question that we are a long way off answering. Before we can answer such a question, a number of the features of reality would need to be incorporated into the analysis in an attempt to find out if the results which currently exist stand up to change in the conditions. For example, it would be necessary to consider: (i) the costs of decision making; (ii) the factors affecting the speed of decision making; (iii) scope for learning and feed back; (iv) factors influencing individuals' perception of the environment and problem definition (rather than treating individuals as passive and mechanical reactors to an environment); and (v) analysing in greater detail the role played by the individual in choosing a decision rule, in promoting the individual's self-interest etc.

In other words, once organisations or decision making systems are peopled by self-interested individuals who bring to the organisation their own value systems and perceptions etc. we need to start examining the interactive relationships between individuals and the system.

Moreover, it is necessary to think more critically about the present status and methodology of the economics of internal organisation. To what extent does it represent a renewed plea for returning to the more traditional approach of economics in which problems of efficiency become a matter of getting the organisation structure correct and of finding the appropriate control system? Also, to what extent does the new approach offer insight and to what extent does it simply assume away the real problems from the analysis by fixing upon a suitable set of assumptions regarding institutions. It is doubtful if anyone would deny that organisational structure is a necessary condition of achieving improvements in efficiency, but it is of itself an insufficient condition, as was emphasised repeatedly in the previous chapter.

Organisations and the Distribution of Power

We have already noted that the economists' standard theory of the firm has very little to say about organisational structure or institutional form and has, therefore, very little light to shed upon empirical questions of how alternative organisational structures might influence the distribution of power, the distribution of rights, or the distribution of resources within a society. Instead, the theory of the firm sets out to analyse the allocation of resources by means of decisions made using the information contained in relative prices in a decentralised system of markets. To make this task simpler it ignores institutional detail.

It would, however, be a mistake to conclude that the economist's striving for analytical tractability means that he regards institutional details to be of little or no consequence for the way in which resources are allocated in practice, although given the way in which many economic discussions are conducted the external observer could be forgiven such a conclusion. Many economists' dissatisfaction with the neoclassical profit maximising theory of the firm is found in the development of alternative approaches which we have already referred to as 'managerial' theories of the firm.

However, one economist who has reacted more than most to the standard neoclassical theory of the firm and who goes beyond the alternative approaches offered by the managerial theories of the firm is J.K. Galbraith who is well known through his books, *American Capitalism, The Affluent Society, The New Industrial State,* and his most recent *Economics and the Public Purpose*. Galbraith argues that the structure of modern organisations plays an important role in determining the distribution of power, of rights and of economic resources. The simple notion of text book economics, that the individual is all powerful (consumer sovereignty) and that the modern corporation is an automaton, subordinate to the market, is a dangerous myth that must be falsified.[18]

In *Economics and the Public Purpose,* Galbraith distinguishes between the market system and the planning system. Agriculture, the service industries, and those industries which are not susceptible to large-scale organisation exist in the market system of the economy and to a greater or lesser extent conform to the text book model of the market system. But organisations such as General Motors and General Electric, i.e. the world of corporate giants, are different. They are located in the planning system rather than the market system. These corporations command resources. Resource use is not exclusively determined by consumer choice. It is influenced very strongly by producer power, i.e. by the power: to persuade the consumer to buy; to persuade the state to lend support; to command earnings for re-investment; to stabilise prices and costs; and to plan resource use. Moreover, those public services which are aimed at assisting the large corporations tend to grow faster than other parts of the public sector i.e. industrial subsidies and where the products of the planning system are purchased e.g. weapons. The firms which Galbraith locates in the planning system do, of course, sell their products through markets. His argument is, however, that the super large national firms and multi-nationals are not subjected to the controls of the market place as is commonly supposed. Instead, they have considerable control/influence over prices and costs; they go beyond prices to influence the responses of consumers and the state; and they organise supply so that they no longer rely on the market determination of resource use. A market system exists when the allocation of resources to the production of different commodities and the distribution of these commodities for final consumption is impersonally determined by the decisions of consumers. A planning system, on the other hand, exists when resource decisions are made by producers.

There is, therefore, reason to suspect that large powerful business organisations, which are comparatively recent phenomena and which control a large proportion of the Nation's assets, hire a significant proportion of the society's highly trained personnel and represent sources of employment opportunities upon which millions depend, may not be entirely sensitive to the dictates of the market or the political process (see also Boulding 1953 and Presthus 1962). To the extent that we regard the proper use of society's scarce resources to be an important problem, then the allocation of resources *within* large organisations through administrative mechanisms (i.e. the planning system) becomes an important topic for critical analysis.

Having identified the power of the large corporation in the process of allocating and distributing resources, Galbraith also recognises the importance of power relationships *within* the firm as a source for explaining how certain decision outcomes are arrived at. In *The New Industrial State* (1967) Galbraith coined the term 'technostructure' to refer to the power which is associated with knowledge. The development of the corporation brings with it the transmission of power from the shareholders to the management and thereafter to functional groups possessing specialist knowledge within the organisation. Since the shareholder does not possess this information and knowledge he becomes increasingly powerless and so also to an increasing extent do top executives. 'The power of substantive decisions passes into the technostructure' (Galbraith 1967).

Galbraith is not setting down a general theory of organisation behaviour. Indeed, he regards it as a common error to carry the search for a single solution into the world of the big corporation. Each corporation is different in terms of its degree of power, its control over its environment and the extent to which it is technically oriented. To understand the behaviour of such firms requires the approach of detailed case studies to be adopted. Rather, what Galbraith is doing is to draw attention to broad and general trends within society and to incorporate into economics the language and the perspectives of the political scientist and the social philosopher. In doing so he re-introduces to economics the institutional parameters which neoclassical analysis has left out. Especially by introducing the power of the large corporation, he focuses attention upon real allocative processes and draws attention to where public policies should be directed if the objectives of such policies are to improve upon the existing performances of allocative systems.

Another interesting observation that we can make is that if Galbraith is correct and the planning system, which characterises the large corporations, is a widespread feature of the market economy, then the economics of market decision making has less widespread applicability than is commonly supposed. Decisions made within firms (i.e. within the planning system) become essentially non-market; decisions made within the household (i.e. the family) are non-market decisions; likewise are decisions made in committees, in charitable organisations, in non-profit making organisations and finally, of course, in the public sector itself. Except for the few organisations which operate in markets approximating the conditions of the neoclassical system of decentralised markets, the majority of allocative and distributional decisions are made in non-market settings. Yet economics is only beginning to recognise the importance of non-market decision making and requires a body of theory to study it.

Williamson's Theory of Organisational Form

Whilst Galbraith's writings have tended to be more polemic than analytic, Williamson (1970, 1971, 1973, 1976) has developed a theory of the development of internal organisational forms in the modern diversified corporation. For Williamson, questions about organisation form (i.e. structure) have important implications for business behaviour, especially the consideration of efficiency in the organisation. However, as he points out, such considerations have not had a noticeable impact upon the theory of the firm. This is probably:

> ... attributable to a failure to regard organisation form seriously. This neglect of organisation form is partly to be accounted for by a common tendency to involve the standard behavioural assumption (profit maximisation) without regard for circumstances.
>
> (Williamson 1971, p. 354)

In Williamson's view, business behaviour (i.e. decisions on pricing, production, investment, employment and R&D etc.) is a function of: market circumstances, internal efficiency, the strategic decision process, and the internal compliance process, the latter three being in turn affected by organisational form. Thus any explanation of business behaviour must make use of organisational form as an independent variable.

There are two organisation structures which are distinguished — the unitary form (i.e. U-form) and the multi-divisional form (i.e. M-form):

(a) *the U-form* Each operating unit in the U-form organisation performs a specialised function (i.e. sales, finance, production, R&D, personnel etc.) for *all* product lines of the firm;
(b) *the M-form* This is composed of operating divisions or quasi-firms which perform all the specialised functions for a *single* product. Each quasi-firm is responsible to a head office, which allocates resources amongst them.

These alternative forms are illustrated by means of organisation charts in figures 3.1 and 3.2. The full implications of these alternative organisation structures will be realised as we proceed.

What problems does a firm (organisation) experience when it expands in the U-form? First, there is a cumulative control loss, with consequences for

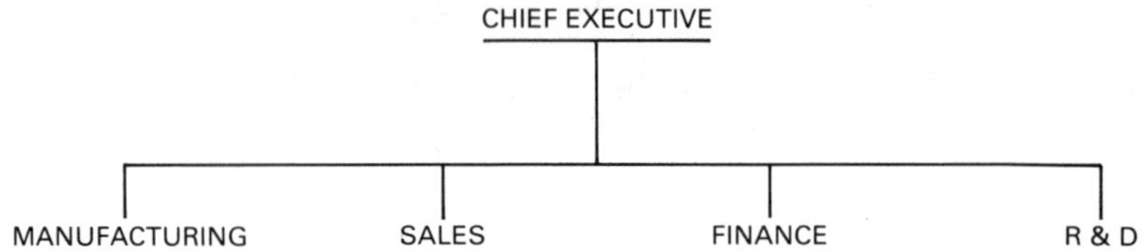

Figure 3.1 *U-Form*

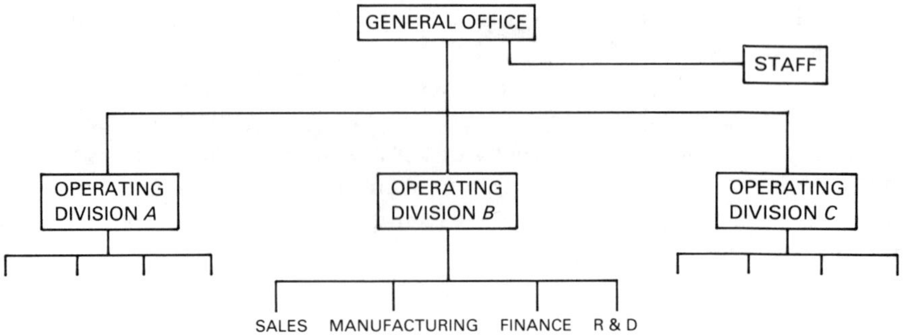

Figure 3.2 *M-Form*

efficiency of internal operations. Second, it alters the character of the strategic decision making process. Because the span of control of any office within the organisation's hierarchy is finite, then as the organisation grows in size in the U-form, levels are added to the hierarchical structure. This results in effective loss of control through incomplete and inaccurate transmission of information both up and down the organisation and also from side to side, i.e. in terms of the transmission of information from one remote part of the hierarchy to another on the same level.[19] Information is summarised, processed, and interpreted as it flows through the organisation, thereby changing its message content. Such changes are frequently unintentional, however, 'cumulative losses of these types stand eventually as an efficiency bar to the further expansion of the firm' (Williamson 1971, p. 346).

The role of the chief executive is to draw together/coordinate the functional executives in providing information to take long-term strategic decisions. However, if each functional executive advocates the partisan interests of his own specialist group and perceives his role as that of representing his group's interests, then the wider and more general organisational interests become submerged.[20] The result is that there is a more favourable allocation of resources (i.e. more expenditure) for those specialist divisions headed by stronger and more powerful executives. This result can then be tied to Williamson's earlier thesis concerning managerial discretionary behaviour. If an executive's performance is judged by his divisional employees in terms of his success in obtaining additional resources then more powerful and more successful executives have more resources to allocate to staff, perquisites, staff expenditure etc. These rents, as we have already noted, allow the development of a permissive attitude towards efficiency and organisational slack.

As the U-form organisation develops and grows in size, decisions tend to depend increasingly upon the relative power of the functional executives, there are increasing problems of making comparisons between the relative performances of the various divisions, and management, unable to see or to identify the global objectives of the organisation, concentrate upon the localised goals of their own division or province. There comes a point when functional executives become overloaded and unable to perform operating (i.e. day-to-day or short-term) tasks and at the same time to coordinate, appraise and go for long-term policy formation. The complexity and demands of the situation simply become overwhelming. 'The difficulties that the large U-form enterprise become subject to ... can be expressed in terms of indecomposability, incommensurability, non-operational goals and confounding of strategic and operating decisions' (Williamson 1971, p. 349).

The confounding of strategic and operating decisions, and the displacement of operational by non-operational goals we have already noted; but what about indecomposability and incommensurability? *Indecomposability* refers to lack of co-ordination and loss of control. Given the specification of an overall objective, the problem is one of decomposing it into a number of specialist tasks, each of which will contribute to the global objective. The decision making problem, therefore, is to find an optimal set of decomposition rules that will ensure the attainment of the objective by efficient means. Examples of simple decomposition rules are: specialisation according to function, or product, or geographical area etc. Specialisation or decomposition can, however, result in loss of control if each specialist functional group or component which is part of the overall global objective decides to sub-optimise i.e. go for its own objective. Sub-optimisation by each specialist group produces spillover effects (costs) for other parts of the organisation, in the sense that if groups use as inputs to their activities the outputs from other parts of the organisation, then their effectiveness is constrained by the decision of the proceeding group in the activity chain to sub-optimise.[21]

In addition to the intra-organisational externalities which one part of the organisation might impose upon others, there is the problem of *incommensurability,* or the logical problem of specifying the goals of the functional divisions in ways which clearly contribute to global goals. At the moment we do nothing other than state this as a problem and will develop it further in a subsequent chapter.

Given the problems which the growing U-form organisation is likely to face, one solution is to change the organisation structure in an attempt to improve efficiency through greater internal control. This kind of statement is clearly similar to the approach adopted by the structuralists of the previous chapter (see especially Perrow).

The alternative form of hierarchical structure which is considered by Williamson is what he calls the M-form; see figure 3.2. Organisational tasks in this case are in the first instance decomposed according to product into operating divisions, with each division being responsible for the manufacture of a single specific product. Thereafter, the operating division is organised on functional lines as in the U-form. The corporation is then a mixture of organisational forms. On the first decomposition it is an M-form made up of quasi-firms, whereas on the second decomposition it is found that each quasi-firm is organised on the U-form.

The superior efficiency of the M-form is due to the removal of executives from operational decisions to long-term strategic planning. This gives them time to deal with strategic decision making, planning, appraisal, control and resource allocation between the divisions. Moreover, because they are not attached to any single division, they do not necessarily represent parochial interests. Finally, the executives in the general office are served by specialist staff whose function it is to provide management information of a kind suitable for long-range planning.

In addition to distinguishing between the day-to-day operating decisions in the organisation and the long-run strategic decisions, the M-form also provides relatively more information about the performance of each division. Each division becomes a 'profit centre' and hence each operating division can be judged by the head office on its relative efficiency e.g. its expansion plans can be judged in terms of its relative return on capital. There is less scope for the pursuit of managerial discretion in the M-form than there is in the U-form *ceteris paribus*.

It can be seen, therefore, from this account that Williamson, amongst all economists, has made the major contribution in bringing organisational parameters to the forefront of our analysis. Rather than comparing organisational form to some ideal, as have market economists when they compare market structures to the unattainable ideal of perfect competition, Williamson prefers to compare the relative peformances of actual forms. They are compared in the dimension of 'the differential capacities for superior peformance'. But clearly there are other ways in which organisations could be compared and Williamson is not blind to this obvious fact.

Public Sector Organisations

Whilst Williamson's analysis is directed specifically towards the organisation structure of the modern business corporation, there is no reason to suppose that his results do not have wider and more general applicability to other types of organisations. It was noted in an earlier chapter that the concept of bureaucracy as an organisational form is not particular to public sector organisations, despite the popular usage of the term. Organisation principles, enunciated by economists, such as the relative performances of centralised *versus* decentralised organisational forms as discussed in the economics of internal organisation, or U- and M-forms as analysed by Williamson, have general applicability to public sector as well as private sector organisations. The problems of incentive management, contract specification, internal labour market management, indecomposability, incommensurability, non-operational goals and the confounding of strategic and operating decisions are also found in public sector bureaucracies. It is, however, the case that economics has concentrated in the main upon public sector organisations, rather than spreading the analytic net more widely to incorporate other organisational types.

A Paradigmatic Crisis in Economics?

It must be clear by now that it is only comparatively recently that a few economists have recognised the importance of organisation structure as an explanatory variable and hence the need to carry out both normative and empirical discussions of resource allocation and distribution and efficiency in terms of *organisation space*.[22] The firm of neoclassical theory is, as Boulding has said, a 'bloodless creature' and, moreover, the firm of general equilibrium theory has neither body nor any rationale for existence.

In the previous chapter we noted that since the later 1960s there has been a feeling of crisis amongst organisation theorists; existing paradigms have been found wanting in their ability to handle questions about conflict and power. A paradigm is like a frame of reference — it defines the relationships to be investigated and the methods and abstractions which are to be regarded as being legitimate. Problems to be solved are defined within the terms of reference circumscribed by the paradigm and hypothesis testing is an exercise of filling in the empty boxes defined by the paradigm. A paradigm itself is neither right nor wrong in the sense that it can be tested by appealing to facts or reality. Instead, a paradigm is judged in terms of its heuristic value, a useful paradigm being one which leaves many questions unanswered whilst at the same time providing the means for beginning to answer them.

A paradigm begins to break down and lose its heuristic value when either it can no longer generate new questions to ask, or when new questions cannot be formulated within it. The classical example of a shift in paradigm is found in physics, when we compare the paradigm of classical Newtonian mechanics with the paradigm of quantum mechanics as set out in Einstein's theory of relativity. Empirical observations such as the constancy of the speed of light and the periodic motion of the planets, in addition to the paradoxes laid bare by Einstein, could not be reconciled with the framework of standard physics; a new framework was demanded to handle *these* questions. But there was no question of one paradigm displacing or replacing the other. Theorems, propositions and results derived from the old paradigm did not suddenly become redundant and wrong. They remain valid within their own terms of reference i.e. those of their own paradigm. They could be re-formulated, if that was logically possible, within the new paradigm, in the hope that the new paradigm would provide further insights and developments.

In many subjects at any moment in time there is likely to be more than one paradigm. The analyst is then faced with choosing between them. Which paradigm is more likely to be most useful in analysing this problem or that? But for most scientists the choice is not a real one. There are high fixed costs involved in learning the methods of one paradigm rather than another. Such costs invariably limit the mind of the scientist, forcing him into a commitment to use one paradigm rather than another. But there is a price to be paid. The exclusion of important problems from consideration is the price paid for using one paradigm rather than another. Moreover, bringing a set of problems or questions within a particular paradigm determines the characteristic virtues and defects of the results.

Our interest in paradigms arises because both economics and organisation theory appear to be confronting paradigm crises. In both subjects questions are being asked which cannot be handled within the existing frames of reference.[23] Leontieff (1971), a Nobel Laureate in economics, drew attention in his Presidential Address to the American Economics Association to:

> an uneasy feeling about the present state of our discipline ... . This concern seems to be shared even by those who are themselves contributing successfuly to the present boom (in the subject). They play the game with professional skill but have serious doubts about its rules.

In other words, they are highly skilled technicians who are able to operate within the existing paradigm, whilst at the same time having doubts about the relevance and the ability of that paradigm to handle new problems, especially the relevant problems of the real world. Hutchinson (1977) refers to this as the 'crisis of abstraction'.

Loasby (1971) has done much to draw fellow economists' attention to the inadequacies of the neoclassical paradigm of profit maximisation. By regarding profit maximisation as a paradigm, rather than as a hypothesis, Loasby is able to distinguish between the logical status of those theories of the firm which employ the working assumption of profit maximisation from those which do not, such as the managerial theories discussed above. Thus, whether or not we employ the profit maximisation theory of the firm is no longer an empirical question or a question of introducing realism into the analysis; instead, it becomes a problem in choosing a particular paradigm. The appropriate question is, does the profit maximising theory of the firm prove to be useful in formulating and answering specific questions and in solving a particular problem? This is very similar in essence to the approach used by Machlup (1967) who argued that the value of the profit maximising model is to be found in the qualitative results that it provides. If we ask what is the likely effect of a marginal *change* in the firm's costs or a tax paid by the firm or a subsidy received by the firm, then the neoclassical marginalist analysis of the profit maximising firm will give an answer in terms of the *direction of change*. To answer the question *by how much* will it change, requires that we undertake empirical measurements.

There is an associated view which argues that for qualitative analysis it does not really matter what firms maximise, be it profit, growth rates or managerial rents. This view is held by Solow (1971, p. 319) who argues that:

> ... it may not matter very much exactly what firms maximise. It is perhaps more important to know how firms respond to changes in data, like tax rates, interest rates, wages, investment subsidies and the like. It is possible that the answer to this practical question is pretty much the same, regardless of what the firms are assumed to maximise. Firms with different objectives are unlikely to respond in exactly the same way to changes in data. But if their qualitative response is more or less insensitive within limits, to the precise nature of their objectives, then it is at least possible to get on with research without first answering the much more difficult question about what they wish to accomplish.

Solow then proceeds to carry out a comparative qualitative analysis of profit maximising and growth maximising firms. His conclusion is that an observer would find it difficult (in qualitative terms) to distinguish one kind of firm from another. If the objective is to predict or to control the firm's behaviour, then the realism of the objective function is an unnecessary requirement. There will, of couse, be *quantitative* differences between the types of firm, but these become interesting empirical rather than analytic questions.

The choice of framework depends upon the questions to be answered and the problems to be solved. Whilst the profit maximising paradigm and its associated variants (e.g. growth maximisation) can handle a wide variety of qualitative questions, such as those posed above, and can solve problems about price determination and the existence of uniqueness and stability of the equilibrium of price systems, it cannot handle many empirical questions and problems of the decision making process.

In order to answer questions about the decision making process economists have searched for an alternative to the profit maximising paradigm. Joan Robinson, as early as 1933 in her *The Economics of Imperfect Competition*, demanded that the analysis of price and output be based upon the study of individual decisions. Commenting upon this development, Loasby (1971, p. 879) points out that, 'Mrs. Robinson for the first time appeared to bring decision making by the competitive firm within the ambit of research'. This was followed up in 1939 by the famous Oxford Studies conducted by Hall and Hitch (1939) which demonstrated empirically that businessmen do not necessariy behave as maximisers. Many of these results were developed by Andrews (1949, 1964). However, whilst that notion of decision making had been introduced to economics, Loasby argues that Robinson's analysis was not really about individual equilibrium. Thus for Loasby (1971, p. 880), 'it is the concept of equilibrium that is at the centre of the crisis ... the abandonment of equilibrium is a much more fundamental change'.

We have already noted on a number of occasions throughout this chapter that equilibrium models or the equilibrium paradigm are useful for studying the internal logical consistency of theories and for predicting the qualitative changes in a firms's reaction to a change in some parameter. However, alternative 'expositions and explanations which conflict with micro-equilibrium theory have met with vigorous onslaughts'. This conflict has been described by Maclup (1967) in terms of a war which ensued between those who employed marginalist analysis (i.e. the equilibrium paradigm) and those who preferred to flirt with the teachings of other Gods. But the war, as both Maclup and Loasby have clearly demonstrated, was the result of misunderstandings on both sides. Paradigms, as we have suggested, are not judged in terms of their realism, but rather in terms of their relative heuristic values. That is, by their ability to formulate and solve particular problems. So what problems were those who rejected marginalist analysis trying to solve?

Essentially the problems studied were those relating to the internal decision making processes *within* the firm. How did managers go about making decisions about prices, production, investment and location? Questions about internalised decision making had been identified earlier by Coase (1937) in his analysis of the firm, but had not been followed up and developed by economists. Instead it was sociologists, political scientists, accountants and the new decision making theorists using operations research techniques etc. who had developed theories of the decision making process.

The positive analysis of decision making processes had a number of features which set it apart from the equilibrium paradigm, First, it was behavioural. Rather than *a priori* theorising about 'representative firms', case studies of actual decision processes were recorded. Because the case studies were specific cases, generalisations of the kind made in equilibrium analysis were not possible, nor was much of the technical superstructure of equilibrium analysis applicable. Second, the decision processes studied were more general than those of equilibrium or marginal analysis, in the sense that they were not confined to maximisation of the traditional objective functions containing arguments such as profits, utility or growth. Instead, what is to be maximised becomes part of the object of study, which leaves open the possibility that there are decision processes that have no definable objective (for one reason or another). In such cases optimisation techniques break down. Hence the lack of determinate solutions arising from the positive analysis of decision making. Loasby (1971, p. 882) argues that:

> It had no answer to the questions of efficiency or stability as those questions are traditionally posed. It had no use for traditional basic concepts: optimisation has no usable meaning: economist's heavy investment in calculus becomes redundant; equilibrium is not defined and there are no general analytic solutions.

Third, the decision making approach brings together a number of different disciplines and ways of studying organisations. But such an approach is not without its costs. There is the time and the effort involved in making the link between paradigms or approaches. Since each paradigm has relatively high fixed costs which act as formidable barriers to entry, specialism and parochialism are rife.

Having made this digression into methodology and having made the distinction between the equilibrium paradigm and a decision making or behavioural paradigm (as yet unspecified), we can now sort out the economic theories of the firm (organisations) reviewed hitherto. Essentially, all of the models examined above belong to the equilibrium paradigm. The maximisation of objective functions, irrespective of their arguments, and the normative study of internal organisation and organisation structure are of the equilibrium paradigm. They are powerful theories which are usefully employed in the analysis of a wide range of problems. However, they are less useful in the analysis of actual *processes* which take place within specific organisations. It is to the examination of these processes which we now turn.

In analysing *intra*-organisation processes and behaviour we will set out the elements of what we choose to call the political economy paradigm.

The Political Economy Paradigm of Organisations

The general approach to the study of organisations embodied in the political economy paradigm has been suggested either implicitly or explicitly in the writings of a number of disciplines e.g. Lasswell (1936), Boulding (1953),

Krupp (1961), Cyert and March (1963) and Zald (1970). One of the values of the political economy paradigm is that it integrates a number of alternative approaches by concentrating upon both internal and external determinants of organisational activities.

'Political economy is the study of the interplay of power, the goals of power wielders and the productive exchange system' (Zald 1970, p. 233). As a framework, political economy does not concentrate exclusively upon *market* exchanges. Rather, it first of all analyses exchanges in whatever institutional framework they occur and second, analyses the relationships between social institutions, such as government, law and property rights, each fortified by power and the economy i.e. the system of producing and exchanging goods and services.

The political economy paradigm is integrative in the sense that it provides a useful watershed for the confluence of many of the alternative approaches to the study of organisations which have been suggested earlier in this chapter and the previous one. Specifically, it focuses attention upon resource allocations and decision making *within* an organisation, irrespective of the organisation type. Economics has too often been identified as the study of resource allocation via the price mechanism, to the exclusion of other allocative institutions within society. Also, economics has been thought of as being the only social science interested in questions of resource allocation. That the questions asked by economists are also of interest to political scientists was demonstrated by Lasswell (1936) in his book, *Who Gets What, When and How?* Whereas economists focused upon relative prices to explain resource allocations in markets, Laswell concentrated upon differences in power. Focus upon the internal *processes* of decision making and resource allocation brings together political and economic dimensions of the same problems e.g.:

(a) the goals and objectives served by collectivities such as organisations are the product of a political process in which bargaining takes place over *whose* goals are to be served, in what order and with what consequence;

(b) the means through which bargaining and political struggles over goal determination can take place. This is the study of organisational *constitutions* (Buchanan and Tullock 1962, Arrow 1951, Zald 1970);

(c) an examination of the power and control relationships in the organisation, which includes both the constitutional and the actual or *ex ante* set of relationships (i.e. see formal/informal organisation p.31 above). This is described as the *internal polity*, i.e. the system of transforming raw materials into finished products.

Let us now examine the concept of organisational constitutions and the internal polity in greater detail.

Organisational Constitutions

According to Zald (1970, p. 225), 'the constitution of an organisation is its fundamental normative structure ... a set of agreements and understandings which define the limits and goals of the group (collectivity) as well as the responsibilities and rights of participants standing in different relations to it'. Constitutions are either written or unwritten. They regulate behaviour in a number of ways which are frequently backed up by the power of legally enforcing the elements of the constitution, as in the case of contractual relationships. Regulation of behaviour takes the form of:

(a) the incentives exchanged within the definition of the constitution. Contracts and terms of exchange between individual members of the organisation and the legal or corporate entity of the organisation determine what other members (usually upper management) *expect* of the individual. Moreover, since rights are defined within the contract, it determines the amount of discretion which an organisation (defined in terms of the roles of other members) has over an individual's behaviour.

(b) the constitution's specification of how individuals' preferences are combined into collective actions or goals. This is the familiar problem of defining any collective choice rule which is both efficient and 'just' and has been studied at considerable length by economists and political scientists alike; see Arrow (1951), Buchanan and Tullock (1962), Coleman (1974) and Sen (1970).

(c) the constitution's specification of the organisation's relationship with the rest of society, especially to whom the organisation is accountable. This is often an area which is defined clearly only in periods of crisis when certain implicit rights are challenged.

By specifying the procedures, rules and mechanisms for carrying out the process of allocating resources within organisations, the organisational constitution becomes an important object for analysis. However, as we have already seen in the previous chapter, taking the constitution as a clearly defined set of rules which regulates and directs individual's behaviour would be a mistake. Like any other object of organisational reality, the constitution is likely to be perceived and interpreted differently by different groups and individuals in the organisation. Thus, the establishment and the implementation of changes in the organisational constitution become problematical and the focus of study becomes the internal polity. How are interpersonal relationships within organisations defined by the organisational constitution and how do these inter-relationships bring about changes to the constitution?

The Internal Polity

If all members of the organisation had the same preferences and goals and if information costs were zero, then it would be possible to treat the firm as a single decision maker as in the traditional theory of the equilibrium paradigm. Treatment of individuals 'as if' they had identical preferences is implicit in those models in which goal consensus has been established by purchasing compliance as part of the employment contract, or by selective recruitment, or by persuasion as in human relations techniques. Given goal consensus (i.e. the single decision unit of the firm) then, for any specified production function, resource allocation is determinate and takes place so as to maximise the objective function.

If the assumptions of goal consensus and costless information are dropped, then we can no longer treat the firm (organisation) as if it is a single decision maker (Feldman and Kanter 1965). The result is that individual members and groups in the organisation will wish to pursue their own goals and attempt (as in a zero sum game) to gain additional organisational resources at the expense of others. The organisation is then viewed as a political arena or a political system in which the distribution of power and the process of conflict resolution are as important determinants of the allocation and distribution of resources as are relative prices. Power struggles (i.e. the process of change) over rewards and rights are features of all allocative systems including that of markets.

Resource allocation within organisations is a function of traditional rules, inter-group bargaining, mechanisms for resolving conflict and perceptions of new areas for growth and change. Thus, it is the organisational structure, the constitution, and the organisational rules used to reach decisions for allocating resources which become the focus of study, i.e. the mechanisms of allocating resources such as capital for investment and major facility change, the accounting and allocating rules, and the consequences of different allocative and accounting procedures in terms of 'who benefits'.

From the point of view of cooperative integration, hierarchy is a necessary adjunct of organisation and is justified as a means of obtaining coordination. However, implicit within hierarchy is a structure of rights, authority, differentiated rank and control. Social structure within the organisation is not completely divorced from the social structure outside. It is seldom the case that the person who is at the top of the social ladder outside the organisation is found in a menial role at the bottom of the social order within the organisation. This relationship between the social orders of different institutions within society has given rise to a number of studies which examine the socio-economic backgrounds of top executives and civil servants. Recognising this relationship, Krupp (1961, p. 169) argues that, 'the detail of internal relationships is shaped by the broader environmental forces in society. The internal relations in organisations, however, also create the structural qualities that organisation theorists usually number as 'given' for their problem. Within the organisation, groups are moulded by the structural properties ... But groups also reinforce, rearrange, or dissolve the structural conditions'.

Economics, by focusing upon internal resource allocation decisions and how internal processes and external events influence such decisions, has a major contribution to make to the study of organisations. Moreover, by concentrating upon internal processes economists, in their attempt to understand how resource allocation decisions are made in practice, must begin to integrate into their corpus of knowledge the contributions which have been made by political scientists and organisation sociologists.

The organisational constitution and the formal hierarchical or command system of authority has been regarded by many to be sufficient to explain how resources are allocated within administrative structures or systems such as organisations. This, however, denies the realities of the internal polity. The structural conditions are subject to continual re-interpretation and bargaining. Thus the stability of structures becomes problematic. 'Authority ... can be viewed as a property right. It is a matter to be bargained over and a subject of continual redistribution ... Power concerns redistribution of authority. Power reflects the ability to change authority' (Krupp 1961, p. 174). Thus, whilst the political scientist or organisation theorist is interested in the processes through which authority is redistributed, including the factors which give rise to power differentials, the economist analysing resource allocation processes cannot ignore the explanatory power provided by the incorporation of variables such as power and authority. 'Within the firm, the structure of authority, the relationships of power, the arena of conflict and the allocation of resources are all highly inter-dependent' (Krupp 1961, p. 177).

The Behavioural Theory of the Firm

To date the most sophisticated model presented within the political economy paradigm is Cyert and March's, *A Behavioural Theory of the Firm*, which was published in 1963. The behavioural theory, which builds upon the work of H.A. Simon, rejects the deductive approach of the marginalist or equilibrium theory of the firm as a useful paradigm for solving problems associated with the *decision making process* within firms. Instead, it emphasises an inductive approach which relies upon the observation and description of decision and other intra-organisational processes which are recorded and presented as a series of case studies. Thus, rather than being a general theory of aggregate resource allocation, the results of any behavioural case study are specific to a particular organisation and to a particular period of time.

Since the behavioural theory is not regarded by Cyert and March as a competitor to the traditional marginalist theory of the firm, but instead as a supplement, we now consider the questions and problems to which behavioural theory addresses itself.[24] Essentially, these are the questions of resource allocation decision making which we have already said are not readily answered by marginalist analysis e.g.: how are organisational goals determined and how are they changed over time; how are investment, pricing, employment and location decisions made; how do decision makers cope with complexity and uncertainty? To answer these questions, behavioural theory sets out to discover the rules of thumb and other administrative procedures which are used by decision makers. These routines are in some cases simulated upon a computer to show the internal logic and the consequences of following rules of thumb. By changing the circumstances under which the decision is made and re-running the simulation it is then possible to predict the outcome of decisions if the rules are adhered to.

Cyert and March view the firm or any organisation as a coalition of interacting groups. An organisation is, therefore, a political as well as a resource allocating system, in which each group of individuals within the firm has parochial interests which they fight to preserve. Goals play a key feature in the behavioural theory. Rather than reifying the concept of organisational goals, Cyert and March prefer to recognise that it is individuals who have goals and that an individual's self-interest is frequently best served in association with other individuals i.e. through groups. At any moment in time within an organisation, these various groups are competing with one another to increase their share of the organisation's resources.

The 'Simon, Cyert and March view' of organisations as made up of coalitions explicitly rejects the notion that organisations operate as if they were individuals, resolving conflicts with the use of economic incentives, in an attempt to create an ordering of preferences that is shared by all organisational participants. Instead, the coalition view of organisations exphasises the differences in objectives and preferences of the sub-groups that go to make up the organisation and then proceeds to describe the processes through which conflicting preferences and beliefs are resolved. When there are differences and uncertainties about the appropriateness of actions, then judgment, negotiation, trading and compromise become necessary to reach a decision.

In the classical theory of the firm, the owner-managers were assumed to determine the goals that the activities within the firm were designed to serve. By a suitable set of side-payments (e.g. wages, bonuses etc.), the members of the organisation were assumed to conform to the overall goal of the owner and thereby any potential conflicts of goals were resolved; i.e. in return for suitable payments, the employees contract to perform whatever is required of them. 'For a price the employee adopts the organisation goal'. This, as was pointed out above, is equivalent to treating the organisation as a single decision making unit and is implicit in managerial theories of the firm also. What Cyert and March, however, are arguing is that in practice, organisations are coalitions of sub-groups whose individual goals and objectives can be and are frequently contradictory.

The different goals which are identified by Cyert and March are:

a) *inventory goals* i.e. target levels for stocks;
b) *production goals* i.e. smoothing-out production and achieving output targets;
c) *sales goals* i.e. meeting volume and value targets;
d) *market share goals* i.e. maintaining or improving upon the relative share of output markets;
e) *profit goals* i.e. capital investment targets and distribution of dividends.

Since the achievement of one of these broad goals often depends upon whether or not another group achieves its objectives, there is potential conflict between groups. Which goal is dominant depends upon the relative power and strength of that group within the internal polity. The maintenance of the dominant position of any particular goal over time depends upon that group's ability to preserve its rights over the authority structure and this in turn, as we have already seen, depends upon it holding onto its relative power position. Goal displacement follows after a re-distribution of the authority rights within the organisation, brought about by a power struggle in which the dominant group loses.

Closely associated with the notion of goals is the concept of *aspiration levels*. This concept, which is borrowed from psychology, refers to the targets set on the various goals e.g. a production level target. Aspiration levels therefore influence and regulate the behaviour of the various organisational activities. For example, if the actual performance is below the aspiration level, as is likely to be the case during a depression, then in the next decision period the target will be revised down. The reverse will occur in boom times when aspiration levels are revised up. In steady state the performance and aspiration levels coincide with one another. It should be clear that the process of setting aspiration levels, including the process of feedback and learning about actual performance, is extremely important in explaining decisions about hiring labour and capital etc. That is, explanations of behaviour in the input markets and explanations of labour shortages or excess supply of labour are made relative to the aspiration levels of the decision maker. This, however, is not dissimilar to the notion of '*ex ante*' decisions in standard economic analysis and forms the basis of adjustment models such as that of the cobweb model of inter-temporal market disequilibrium.

The stability of the inherently stressful, conflicting, and continually changing system is aided by what Cyert and March refer to as *organisational slack*. We have already seen in the previous chapter that incentives are paid to organisation members in order to induce them to stay; Barnard (1938). Moreover, in terms of the different coalitions' competition for organisational resources it would be possible to allocate resources to meet coalitions' demands during years of plenty, i.e. the demands of the various coalitions can be 'bought off' out of the proceeds of growth. Slack is, therefore, defined as payments (i.e. financial and non-financial resources) made to coalition members in excess of what is required to maintain the organisation. Organisational slack is an economic rent paid to organisation members and is built up during years of plenty, thereby providing a cushion or a contingency reserve during lean years. Slack, therefore, absorbs variability in the organisation's environment. As the environment becomes more hostile and as resources become less plentiful, conflicts between groups increase. Intra-organisational activities are then directed towards conflict and performance declines.

Cyert and March also set out to study the way in which businessmen make decisions under conditions of uncertainty. In this respect they were building upon the tradition established by H.A. Simon and the earlier work of Tintner (1941 (a) and (b), 1942) and Alchian (1950), who had identified the problem of using classical marginalist analysis to study such problems.

The first point to realise in all behavioural models of the decision making process is that decisions are made in real time which has a direction or flow. Thus decision processes are sequential and not simultaneous as is often implied from equilibrium analysis; see Steiner (1974). The sequential nature of decision making has a number of important consequences. First, not only do objectives or goals conflict and change with relative bargaining powers/strengths, but the dominant goal might also change as a result of changes in experience and learning. This is different from saying that the aspiration or target level changes as a result of learning. Instead, the nature or definition of the goal being aimed at changes as more information becomes available as a result of experience and learning.

Another feature of sequential decisions is that not all objectives or activities will receive the same attention from decision makers at the same time. Objectives are attended to in sequence and the decision problem then becomes one of deciding upon the sequence. One factor determining the sequence is the urgency of dealing with certain activities first; what Radner (1975) refers to as 'putting out fires management'. However, devoting all efforts to tackling short-term or immediate problems diverts attention from seeking long-term solutions. The ordering of objectives in the decision sequence is also a means of resolving conflict. The simultaneous maximisation of conflicting objectives intensifies the conflict by juxtaposing them in time. If potentially conflicting objectives are dealt with sequentially and separated by a long time interval then conflict can be reduced.

The environment facing decision makers is highly uncertain. In order to cope with this uncertainty they use a number of routines. For example, one means of avoiding uncertainty is to use standard operating procedures or decision rules of thumb and to modify decisions in response to feedback from the outcome of earlier decisions. If goals are satisfactorily achieved then it becomes possible to cruise along with organisational slack in the system. If the goals are not satisfied then search procedures are activated. In looking for a solution it is generally found that simple solutions are preferred to complex ones and that complex solutions are only adopted once it is found that simple ones fail.

The general finding that decision makers tend to use simple rules of thumb has been emphasised by a number of economists; see Baumol and Quandt (1964), Day (1967) and Day and Tinney (1968). Simple rules of thumb are used rather than complex and refined decision procedures, in part because of the costs of obtaining the necessary information for the complex decision rules and because of the relative performance of simple rules over complex ones. Baumol and Quandt (1964) simulated different rules of thumb comparing their relative performances. The results of the simulations were that in terms of the profits earned the simple rules performed well.[25]

Critique of Behavioural Theory

The behavioural theory of the firm has received misplaced and wrong-minded criticism from those who have regarded it as a competitor to the models of the equilibrium paradigm. We have already said sufficient about this matter to indicate to the reader that we must judge the behavioural model in terms of its success or otherwise in answering the questions which it set out to answer.

Cyert and March's behavioural model attempts to explain repetitive decisions within a stable organisation i.e. an organisation which faces a relatively stable environment and one in which major structural reorganisations are not taking place. Thus they are interested in standard solutions and 'organisational' learning. It is important to re-emphasise this because if situations repeat themselves only infrequently, then standard solutions for these situations are unlikely to exist. This means that organic organisations of the kind analysed by Burns and Stalker (*op. cit.*) become a special group for behavioural analysis i.e. if standard solutions are not available to such organisations, how are decisions made in organisations which face unstable environments?

It is not organisations that learn, but individual organisation members who do. This means that additions to the stock of knowledge obtained through learning resides with individuals and is, therefore, located within particular coalitions in the organisation. To the extent that knowledge is power, the learning process becomes an important factor in the power struggle within the internal polity.

Because learning is an individual activity, rapid changes in the incumbents of key decision making roles within the organisation have consequences for the speed of decision making, especially in those instances in which the situations for action repeat themselves only infrequently. Loasby (1968) points out that since it is long-term strategic decisions that tend to be made infrequently, then the Cyert and March model is more appropriate for explaining short-run repetitive decisions.

One of the basic weaknesses in the behavioural theory is that it fails to explain how the rules of thumb are determined and how they change and develop over time. Clearly, a straightforward answer would suggest that those rules which consistently perform best and are inexpensive to operate will have a greater chance of survival. However, even that leaves out questions of how decisions are taken about relative performance and how performance criteria are determined.

However, the full value of the behavioural model has yet to be demonstrated. In a recent survey article by Cyert and Hedrick (1972) the authors point out that economists have been altogether too coy in adopting the behavioural approach of studying decision processes in real organisations and have on the whole tended to stick with marginalist analysis. This means that until more behavioural studies have been carried out it is too early to judge the heuristic value of this approach.

Conclusions

Economics has been described as the study of the allocation and distribution of scarce resources. To the extent that all organisations face the task of allocating scarce resources, then economics must include the study of organisations. The economies of the Western world, and to an increasing extent those of the emerging nations also, are dominated by large organisations. The romantic ideal of perfectly atomistic markets is a will-o'-the-wisp which Liberal economists long for. The decisions of multi-national corporations and similarly large organisations increasingly affect the distribution of a society's resources. Pondy (1970, p. 272) has noted that: 'to the extent that the social sciences regard the proper use of society's resources as an important problem, the allocation of resources within large organisations through administrative mechanisms becomes an important sub-problem'.

Notes

1 That is, whether or not the equilibrium was Pareto-optimal. Standard theory demonstrated that the general competitive equilibrium was Pareto-optimal i.e. at the equilibrium set of prices it was not possible to make one individual better off, by rearranging production or consumption of outputs, without making another individual worse off.

2 It should, however, be noted that in some instances, especially in US studies, the hospital is treated simply as another form of the profit maximising firm. This is not true in the case of Feldstein (1967) and Newhouse (1970) who deal with 'not for profit' hospitals.

3 In this group we include the work by Robinson (1933) on imperfect competition and by Chamberlin (1933) on monpolistic competition. These, along with various theories of oligopoly and monopoly, constitute equilibrium theories of the firm which represent the bulk of the undergraduate's diet of price theory.

4 By organisational design in this context we mean the inherent belief found in most Paretian welfare economics that resource allocation via perfectly competitive markets is best and hence economic organisation should be designed along these lines.

5 Marshall set off a whole set of subsequent studies of the relationship between long-run and short-run industry equilibria, which occupied a good deal of the work of micro-economics in the 1920s and 30s; see Kaldor (1938). Once again these were exercises in price theory, rather than in the study of the behaviour of the firm.

6 This is picked up below in Coase's analysis of the rationale of the firm and later in Chapter 9 on the limits of organisation.

7 Transactions costs are now an important concept in modern micro-economics. Transactions costs refer to the costs paid by an individual engaging in any kind of exchange and include: (a) the costs of enforcing contracts e.g. legal and policy costs; (b) the measurement and information gathering costs e.g. checking on the weight of goods purchased, use of punch time clocks in labour markets, inspecting a used car before purchase; and (c) information processing or decision-making costs including the costs of time it takes to arrive at an outcome to the decision. No social system or set of institutions or organisations is costless to operate and so by identifying transactions costs we can begin to discuss the costs of different social systems.

8 Malngren (1961) has argued that the advantage of the firm is its capacity to control information and achieve plan consistency between interdependent activities i.e. the firm has information processing advantages over markets.

9 This approach includes the work of economists such as Spence (1974) and Akerloff (1970) who are interested in the economics of information.

10 At this point it is worthwhile reminding the reader of quite a forceful tradition in economic methodology following on from the work of Friedman (1953). His argument is that since the purpose of formal economic analysis is that of drawing implications, it does not matter how unrealistic the description of the assumptions is, provided that the theory generates *predictions* that fit reality.

11 See Hall and Hitch (1939) and Andrews (1949, 1964).

12 See Berle and Means (1934) and Furubotn and Pejovich (1972) for extended discussions of these interesting questions of the role played by property rights in defining the system.

13 This is, of course, a generalised concept and different individual managers will choose different amounts and different combinations of the arguments in the managerial utility function. This is consistent with the view that the managers extract rents from the firm.

14 That is, maximisation of the managerial utility function subject to a minimum profit constraint. If managers are maximising their utility functions, then shareholders can be 'satisficing'. This situation arises because of the flows of information in the system. Shareholders it is assumed face high costs of being informed.

15 In Marris' model, not only does management maximise its own utility subject to a minimum profit constraint, but it also maximises the growth of the firm subject to the constraint that successful fast growing firms might be taken over and merged with others, thereby offering a threat to existing management's freedoms.

16 Once the topic has developed sufficiently, it might seem less appropriate to include all such studies under the heading of the 'economics of internal organisation'. For a representation of these studies, see the report of a recent symposium which is published in *The Bell Journal of Economics*, Spring 1975.

17 Much of this section is based on Radner (1975).

18 Galbraith and his followers would go further by pointing out the ideological basis of neoclassical economics. They would argue that economics, as it is frequently taught, is part of the process which persuades people to accept the power structure of society and is a vital part of the conditioning process which disguises that power. Whilst being in sympathy with Galbraith's overall thesis, I would, however, wish to qualify it by saying that we must distinguish between the purpose of the abstract analysis of decentralised price systems and the appraisal of economic power distributions in real economics. A confusion between these two aspects has resulted in students abandoning abstract theory for the wrong reasons.

19 This interesting idea of side-ways communication problems in an organisation is emphasised by Dunsire (1978) in his House of Babel model. Remote parts of an organisation are those which have little day-to-day contact and interaction. Information is filtered through neighbouring offices in the organisation. When one office makes use of information originally produced by a remote office and subsequently filtered through the transmission process, the logical basis of that information is unknown. These ideas are developed in Chapter 9.

20 This should not be interpreted as a reification of organisational goals. It is simply a statement that the specialist groups have sub-goals that contribute to the overall objectives of the organisation. There are problems involved with any discussion of goals and objectives.

21 Dunsire (1978) argues that the extent of this problem will depend upon whether or not, '... the nature of a succeeding step is uniquely determined by the proceeding step' (p. 121) or, 'getting something done is seen as a matter of putting together a number of discrete units ...' (p. 125). These ideas are developed further in Chapter 9.

22 The phrase *organisation space* needs some explanation. It refers to discussions of economic problems in terms of the nature, structure, and principles of

organisation and organisation theory, rather than in terms of economic exchanges i.e. in which institutional and organisational specifications are ignored.

23 The sense of crisis is to be found in MacDougal (1974), Heller (1975), Leontieff (1971), Worswick (1972) and Kaldor (1972). These authors provide examples of economists who are frustrated with the lack of realism in much of current advanced economic theory. More especially they argue that most economic theory is irrelevant and incapable of answering the pressing problems of economics. In the language which we are adopting in this chapter, these authors are confronting a crisis in the paradigm of neoclassical *equilibrium* economics. That paradigm is unable to answer their questions.

24 For the purposes of the equilibrium paradigm of neoclassical economics, it is generally regarded that it is simpler to stick with the assumption of profit maximisation because it is 'applicable with less detailed information'.

25 The behavioural theory is not regarded by Cyert and March as being a competitor to the traditional marginalist theory. Instead, they are two different paradigms which deal with different questions.

CHAPTER 4

Decision Making Models

... the first principle of Economics is that every agent is actuated by self interest
(F.Y. Edgeworth)

Administrative theory is peculiarly the theory of intended and bounded rationality of the behaviour of human beings who satisfice because they do not have the wit to maximise.
(H.A. Simon)

Introduction

Decision making and choice lie at the heart of much of the discussion of human behaviour. How are decisions made; what influences the choices made by individuals; what performance criteria are to be used when judging between good and bad decisions? These are but a small sample of the questions studied by those who make the act of decision making or the decision making process their focus of interest. Applewhite (1965, p. 54) points out that:

> Social scientists are interested in how individuals and groups reach a decision; how much information is necessary, who influences the outcome the most, how disagreements are resolved, what procedures are used and how choices are made.

The economist's interest in the allocative process is at the same time an interest in decision making processes. The allocation of resources and the distribution of welfare result from decisions about how much to produce, what mix of goods to produce and when and how they will be produced. These decisions in turn depend upon other decisions made by, for example, consumers when they choose a consumption plan. However, traditional partial and general equilibrium analysis in economics has essentially washed the decision making process out of discussions of resource allocation. It will be recalled, from an earlier discussion, that neoclassical economics is concerned either with establishing the necessary and sufficient conditions for equilibrium, or with identifying the likely consequences which follow from a marginal change in one of the system's variables. Behavioural specifications of the economic agents are, therefore, kept to a minimum in this kind of analysis for the sake of parsimony. In the neoclassical system, economic agents are treated as if they are mindless automata who respond in a fully programmed fashion to external stimuli such as price and quantity signals. Defining an individual as a preference ordering (i.e. the programme), each decision maker is assumed to compute that set of activities (i.e. production and consumption plans) which will maximise his utility. This view of the decision maker is simplistic in its image of Man the decision maker and demanding of his powers and capabilities.[1]

Analysis of organisations from the perspective of decision making is well established.[2] Decisions are made by individuals within the context of organisations, committees, and other group settings. As in much organisational analysis there is always a temptation to reify the organisation and talk in terms of organisational decision making or group decision making. Organisations do not make decisions, but individuals do. Thus, we will be interested in questions such as, who are the decision makers, or as Applewhite (*op. cit.*) asked, 'who influences the outcome the most?'. Our attention will concentrate not only upon the act of decision making or choice as performed by an individual. We will, in addition, analyse the problems involved when individuals are brought together to make a collective decision, as in the case of a committee, or a group setting, or a constellation of groups such as a complex organisation. Here, individuals acting *jointly* are asked to produce a single decision outcome which will then be binding for all. The problems posed by collective choice are extremely interesting and testing and include questions such as: how might the preferences and values of the different individual members of the collectivity be combined in producing a single decision; how are disagreements and conflicts between individual members resolved; and what procedures are adopted when making collective choices?

As in all types of analysis it is important to distinguish between normative and positive questions. This has already been seen in the earlier discussion of behavioural theories. When it comes to a discussion of the literature on decision making, the same distinctions apply and a blurring of these distinctions has, in the past, caused much confusion and pointless debate between those who have taken prescription as their purpose rather than description. Moreover, the analysis of decision making does not constitute a unified body of thought. The common thread which runs through each theory is the problem of making decisions either under conditions of certainty or under conditions of uncertainty, in which case, individual decision makers face complex and often ambiguous environments. Thus, statistical decision making analysis and much of the work by economists on topics such as investment appraisal (including cost-benefit analysis) and efficiency criteria are not to be regarded as descriptions of how decisions are made or how decision-makers do behave. They are instead normative theories, insofar as they are aimed at establishing a set of techniques which will assist in the making of 'good' decisions judged against some set of performance criteria determined outside the analysis.[3] On the other hand, there are studies of how decisions are actually made and descriptions of decision making processes in a number of different contexts. These different approaches are not in competition with one another as is often mistakenly thought. Rather, they address themselves to different questions and should, in principle at least, be complementary, insofar as once having identified and described a set of decisions it is then possible to judge them as being either good or bad and then proceed to make suggestions as to how they might be improved.

To understand how resources are allocated and how the benefits of economic activity are distributed it is, therefore, necessary to look more closely at decision making processes. Given the prevalence of allocative decisions, which take place within organisations, this means that we will consider the problems of organisational decision making. In this chapter we will look at the issues of individual decision making and the question of collective decision making will also be explored. Here, the interesting problems are the processes through which individuals express their own values and preferences, how individuals relate to the process, and how consensus is achieved if at all. The concepts of power and conflict, already identified as important explanatory variables, are then introduced into the analysis. Finally, decision making costs will be discussed and the problems of decision making under uncertainty will be reviewed.

Individual Decision Making

The two principal approaches to the study of individual decision-making are: (a) the *unbounded rationality model* of 'economic man'; and (b) the *behavioural or bounded rationality model* of the decision process. These two models will now be examined.

The Unbounded Rationality Model

The rational model has been presented in the literature under a variety of labels. It can either be called the bureaucratic model, the synoptic model, or the normative model. This approach to decision making considers how a fully informed individual, who possesses far reaching powers of computational ability and who knows what (s)he is aiming at, will make rational choices between alternatives by comparing benefits and costs at the margin. It is the basic behavioural postulate which underlies all the optimising models of the economist's equilibrium paradigm, whilst at the same time it is within the Weberian tradition of the analysis of bureaucratic organisations i.e. organisations are viewed as being goal directed and the decisions made within organisations are intended to find the most efficient means of achieving these goals. The basic axioms of the rational model are, therefore, that all behaviour is goal directed and that individuals, when making rational choices between competing goals, or between competing means of achieving these goals, will always choose that alternative which best serves the individual's own self-interests.[4] In the language of the economist, rational choice is a question of an individual choosing, in accordance with his own preferences, from a set of alternatives so as to maximise his utility, whilst being subjected to external constraints. Moreover, rational choice is deliberate. The maximisation of some objective function has been the hallmark and basic premise of standard micro-economics since the time or Cournot. Alternative theories differ with respect to the arguments of the objective function, but on one thing they do agree; individuals, be they consumers, producers, manager bureaucrats, or workers, maximise something, be it called personal utility, profits, budget size, revenue (sales) rate of growth of assets, probability of survival etc. ... In other words, decision makers are assumed to act *as if* they maximise the value of a utility function.

The maximising postulate has played a central role in the development of the optimality model of the economist's equilibrium paradigm. Without the concept of constrained maximisation, the technical apparatus of partial and general equilibrium theory and the decision making algorithms of linear/non-linear and dynamic programming could not have been developed with the elegance and determinateness that they have. But such an approach is obviously behaviourally naive and this, as we shall see presently, leads to a number of problems, not least of which is a disagreement amongst economists as to the importance of optimality. In the meantime let us pursue the uses to which this model has been put.

Apart from computing equilibria, the rational model has been used prescriptively (or normatively) to establish the ground rules for 'good' decision making or how decisions *ought* to be made. This approach is to be found in the literature on statistical decision theory (including operations research), project appraisal and cost-benefit analysis, and most of the works of public and business administration. In each case techniques and routines are established which should help a completely rational decision maker to arrive at a *best* decision. One of the implications of the maximisation premise is that alternatives must be compared with one another. That is, search for the maximal requires testing and evaluating alternatives. If comparisons are not made, then the decision maker cannot be said to be maximising anything. The general approach assumes a highly structured situation which can be summarised in the following decision process:

(a) *Problem identification*: decision making is a particular form of problem solving and the first thing to be done is to identify the nature of the problem. Signals either from inside or outside the organisation indicate the existence of a problem and the need for action. This is usually performed by comparing the actual state of affairs with some ideal, as in all standard cybernetic feedback control systems. The presence of a gap between the actual and the ideal suggests the need for action either to close the gap or to reduce it to within acceptable limits.

(b) *Search for solution*: alternative feasible means of solving the problem are listed; the consequences of each alternative are set out; these consequences are then evaluated.

(c) *Choice of solution*: the data for each alternative solution to the problem are presented to the decision maker, who then tests each alternative in terms of acceptability and feasibility. Those solutions which bring the system closest to the desired state are preferred over those which do not. There are a number of different ways of conceptualising this selection procedure. Much of economic analysis uses the method of maximisation of a social welfare function to solve for the best outcome.[5] Such a procedure is appropriate for analysis where we are interested in searching for an equilibrium solution, but it begs too many questions about the details of *how* the outcome of the decision is established. The choice of solution might be made by a single decision maker who pays no regard to the other members of the organisation, or the solution chosen might need to be negotiated with different sub-sets of the organisation. In the latter case, the solution has to be discussed at a number of levels in the organisation i.e. *consultation*. Then the views expressed in the consultation process are collated and examined for conflict of interests. The original proposal is then judged as to whether or not it is feasible. Feasibility can be thought of in a number of dimensions. There is first the question of technical feasibility, i.e. is the technology available to perform the necessary activities to achieve the objective? Second, there is budget feasibility; is it possible to perform the task etc. with the resources (budget) available? Thirdly, is the solution politically feasible, in the sense that once all negotiations are completed the relevant parties to the decision process find the outcome acceptable? In searching for a feasible solution to a decision or a problem, the unintended consequences and side effects will, to the extent that they can, be identified in discussion and negotiation. Once the feasible solution[6] is found, a clearance decision is made before proceeding to authorisation.

(d) *Implementation*: once a solution has been found and authorisation has been obtained there then follows a series of procedures in which the activities required to solve the problem are implemented. Much decision theory and decision analysis stops short at the point of authorisation, thereby ignoring completely the nature of and the problems involved with the implementation process. It is because of this neglect of the implementation process that much will be said about it later in Chapter 9.

(e) *Monitoring*: once the authorisation has been implemented, the monitoring process compares the actual state of the system with the planned or desired state. In order to find out how a system is behaving over time, the monitoring process will require a sophisticated set of measurement and computational techniques. A monitoring system essentially judges and appraises the performance of the behaviour of the system. To do this adequately, rather than on an *ad hoc* basis, requires some *a priori* reasoning about the expected behaviour of the system, some judgment about the reasonableness of the expectations and hence an articulated set of criteria for establishing the system's norms. In some cases, however, monitoring is not considered as being evaluative, but simply a recording of how policy worked out in practice.

The stylised set of points set out in (a)–(e) above characterises the model of optimal decision making which is frequently presented in economics. This is a normative approach, since it considers how decisions should be made if the intention is to maximise some objective function (usually utility) at least resource cost i.e. in the most efficient manner. The unbounded rationality model is, however, based upon a number of implicit assumptions around which a great deal of controversy exists. This controversy is best introduced by considering the question 'what is meant by rationality in the context of decision making?'

Rationality in Decision Making

There are two questions that we need to consider. First, what is rationality and secondly, in what sense is it unbounded? To the economist the notion of rationality is more than that which is normally thought of in everyday speech, where rationality is usually regarded as something which is intelligent or sensible. However, when the economist uses the concept of rationality and applies it to the making of choices or decisions, he wishes it to mean more than intelligence or sensibility. In particular, the economist regards a rational choice as one which is deliberate, internally consistent and which maximises the decision maker's objective function. Thus rational decision making is purposeful and goal directed. But is all goal directed decision making rational? This question will be answered as we proceed through this chapter.

Rationality in decision making or choice, therefore, involves internal consistency. 'A person's choices are considered rational in this approach if, and only if, these choices can all be explained in terms of some preference relation consistent with the revealed preference definition, that is, if all his choices can be explained as the choosing of the "most preferred" alternatives with respect to a postulated preference relation' (Sen 1976, p. 323). Thus, from an observation of the choices made by an individual (i.e. his revealed preferences) we can deduce the individual's preference ordering, since he is assumed to be always acting to maximise his utility. Clearly there are logical problems with this line of analysis. First, there is circularity and tautology, since behaviour is to be explained in terms of preferences which are in turn defined only by behaviour.[7] However, Samuelson (1955, p. 90) has argued that the theory of revealed preference is not technically meaningless. Internal consistency in the making of choices (decisions) can be refuted by observation. This raises the second problem; how to distinguish empirically between inconsistencies and changes in tastes. Whilst these problems are bothersome for the analysis of choice, they do not constitute a problem for the definition of rationality which only requires that the choices made be consistent.

Looking at the notion of consistency in more detail it would be possible to set out a complete set of axioms as is frequently done in choice theory. This, however, would be quite laborious and would not serve much purpose in this context. Instead, we look at two basic principles of consistency. First, there is the '*sure thing principle*', as set out by Savage (1954), which embodies the basic requirements of consistency and reflexivity in the choice situation. If, of two actions, the consequences of the first action in each state of the world are at least as highly valued as the corresponding consequences of the second action, then the first action is considered to be as good as the second action. Second, there is the '*independence of tastes and beliefs*' as expounded by Marschak (1955). Tastes refer to the ordering of consequences of states of the world according to the individual's preferences; beliefs refer to the ordering of states of the world by subjective likelihood. This principle requires an individual to rank consequences independent of the states of the world in which they might occur and the ranking of likelihoods of states to be independent of consequences associated with them. This, therefore, frees the individual from wishful thinking, thereby making choices rational. Whether or not, however, an individual's beliefs need to be rational (i.e. intelligent and sensible) for his behaviour to be rational, or whether all that is required is that an individual acts consistently given any set of beliefs, irrespective of their status, is a question which has been actively pursued by philosophers.[8]

Thus a rational choice (decision) is one which is deliberate and consistent, but it is also one in which the individual chooses so as to maximise his utility. Maximisation is, therefore, a defining characteristic of rationality. This point is brought out by Simon (1978) and by Machlup (1969):

> Economics tends to emphasise a particular form of rationality — maximising behaviour — as its preferred engine of explanation ...
>
> (Simon 1978, p. 6)

> The fundamental assumption — whether it be regarded as a conventional postulate, a useful fiction or a well known fact of experience — of maximizing behaviour, that is of utility maximizing reactions of households and firms, is recognised as a useful and probably indispensible part of the theoretical system of economics. The assumption has frequently been hypostatised into the symbolic figure or personal 'ideal type', the Economic Man.
>
> (Machlup 1969, p. 117)

That is, Economic Man will settle for nothing but the best that his constrained resources will provide for him. Differences between the benefits and the costs of various alternatives are compared *at the margin* and the best choice (or decision) is that which equates benefits and costs at the margin.

Having considered the meaning attached to the notion of rationality, in what sense is it to be regarded as unbounded? Models of unbounded rationality assume that economic agents know all their alternative choices and all the relevant consequences that follow from each alternative. That is, individuals are assumed to be omniscient. It is models of unbounded rationality which underlie most general equilibrium theories of the economy. Information is assumed to be complete in the sense that individuals are able to obtain the data about the best choice. Individuals choose their most preferred alternative from the set of available alternatives and face no barriers such as search and calculating costs in discovering it.

In models of unbounded rationality there are no surprises, nor are individuals, in retrospect, disappointed by their choice. Models of unbounded rationality are clearly unrealistic and behaviourally naive, a point which will be developed at greater length later in this chapter. Does this, therefore, mean that they should be discarded and abandoned? Some economists, such as Milton Friedman (1953), would argue that if the theory predicts well, then for some purposes it does not matter that the assumptions on which the theory is founded are not satisfied in reality.

The lack of realism in the unbounded model does not matter too much provided that the objective of the analysis is to: (a) work out the conditions required for an equlibrium; and (b) to use the model to make qualitative predictions. However, where such approaches are weakest is that prediction is not sufficient to provide explanation and understanding of *how* choices are made i.e. about the decision *process*; see Shackle (1972).

The critiques of the unbounded rationality model, of which there are many, can be set out summarily as follows:

(i) It has been argued by Tisdell (1975) that theories of unbounded rationality make stronger assumptions than are necessary to secure choice of the most preferred alternative. For example, a complete and transitive preference ordering is not necessary. If intransivities exist in a non-feasible sub-set of the total choice set, or if inconsistency and incompleteness exist over a sub-set of alternatives which are inferior, then such problems of the preference ordering do not influence the final choice and allow a weakening of the conditions.

(ii) In the case of business decisions businessmen do not maximise well-defined profit or growth functions. This point, which is similar to that raised previously in Chapter 3 where alternative theories of the firm were considered, was advanced at an early stage by Cyert, Simon and Trow (1956) and by Cyert, Dill and March (1958). They argued that business decisions were not made solely on the basis of profitability and that expectations and forecasts were generally developed to *justify* the decision which was desired. These studies were the precursors of a completely new school of decision making which we will examine in greater detail in the next section. Essentially they were unhappy with the normative or unbounded rationality decision model, because it did not help to account for or to explain many of the features of decision making in reality. They argued that real decision making situations are seldom well structured; the lack of complete information and the constraint of time prevent decision makers from taking a structured/comprehensive view; rational decision making is time consuming and would paralyse an organisation. Finally, Simon (1957) made the point that ends and goals are pure values and difficult to define. Final ends are empty and meaningless e.g. what does it mean to say that the objective of a policy is to provide 'good housing' or 'good health'? These ends cannot provide guidance for decision making and rational choice, since we need to know something of the value system which accepts one policy as promoting good housing say, as compared to another which does not.

(iii) The final point of criticism of the unbounded rationality model strikes a blow at the heart of much of traditional general equilibrium analysis. As was pointed out above and previously in Chapter 3, economists have associated rational choice with the attainment of equilibrium/optimisation. However, the attainment of such an equilibrium is possible only if economic agents are unbounded rational decision

> makers. This point has been articulated by Shackle (1972). According to Shackle, rational choice is impossible if the decision maker's knowledge is incomplete. 'Rational choice, choice which can demonstrate its own attainment of maximum objectively possible advantage, must be fully informed choice. But there can be no full information except about what is past, or else what is exempt from the world of time altogether. The paradox of rationality is that it must concern itself with choosing amongst things fully known; but in the world of time, only *that* is fully known which is beyond the reach of choice, having already become actual and thus knowable'. (Shackle 1972, pp. 245–6).

Shackle's argument is that rationality is incompatible with unpredictable changes which *in practice* occur with the passage of time. Thus, if a decision maker having made, as he thought at the time, the best choice with the information available, then discovers after the decision has been implemented that there was a better choice, that decision, according to Shackle, was not rational.

On definitional grounds Shackle's concept of rationality can be regarded as being rather specific, since it fuses rationality and perfect knowledge.[9] However, as other writers such as Kornai (1971) and Loasby (1976) have argued, the use of the unbounded rationality model does have implications for the logical status of most of equilibrium economics and hence for the bulk of economics itself. If we are to *understand* the behaviour of economic decision makers, and if we are to account for the emergence of specific forms of economic organisation and institutional structure, then the highly restricted model of unbounded rational Economic Man must give way to one which incorporates the features of a reality in which information is incomplete, time is racing, decisions are urgent, and the future is uncertain and often unknowable — in other words, a world in which there is both surprise and disappointment when plans are not realised. This is the world of 'bounded rationality' and it is to its description that we now turn.

The Bounded Rationality Model

One person who has done most to criticise the economist's model of unbounded rationality is Herbert Simon. 'Traditional Economic Man, however attractive he is to the economic theorist, has little or no place in the theory of organisation ...' (Simon 1957, p. 198). Simon's critique is specific. He is not arguing that the model of unbounded rationality is inappropriate for the abstract analysis of economic equilibrium, rather he attacks the presumption that such models have much to say about the processes which take place in the economy, especially decision making processes. The unbounded rationality model is behavioural and seeks to understand and explain how decisions come to be made. Theories of unbounded rationality do not help an understanding of these issues, not just because they are unrealistic, but because they assume out of existence most of the interesting and problematic features of reality.

Individuals, as decision makers, do not have the capacity or the capability to store all the information and perform all the calculations which the unbounded rationality model presumes. According to Simon, individuals do not maximise because they do not have the wit to do so.

There are two principal concepts which are used by Simon in his analysis of the decision making process. These are (a) bounded rationality and (b) satisficing. Both concepts will be examined in turn. The insights provided by these concepts will then be evaluated.

(a) *Bounded Rationality*

This takes as its starting point: (i) the obvious observation that the real world is a highly complex and uncertain place; and (ii) the individual's limited ability to deal with and to comprehend the ambiguities and complexities of his environment. Bounded rationality arises out of necessity because the information processing and computational powers of decision makers are limited relative to the complexities of the environment. In practice the individual decision maker, compared to the decision maker embodied in the concept of Economic Man, does not have full information about the consequences of his decisions; does not have an unambiguous specification of the nature of the problem; and frequently does not have a well defined set of objectives. Compared with the decision maker of the unbounded rationality model, the decision maker of bounded rationality is constrained by his understanding of the complexity of the situation which in turn is either due to his own personal limitations and/or to the fact that he cannot know the unknowable i.e. knowledge of the future, which means knowledge of the consequences of his decisions and the influence of unknowable future events upon the outcome of his decision.

Simon, throughout his writings on decision making and problem solving, uses examples drawn from chess playing. The game of chess is one in which the individual player has to determine a strategy drawn from a large number of alternative possible moves. In developing a robust strategy and in playing out the game, the player has to anticipate his opponent's moves. Thus the game of chess is an excellent model in which to think about problem solving and decision making, since all the essential elements are there, i.e.: problem identification; search for a solution (considering the moves); implementation of solution (play); and monitoring and feedback (evaluation and anticipation). Using the chess game example to think of bounded rationality, each player has a very large number of strategies and the possible games of chess could be in the order of 10^{120}. Players do not, however, think their games right through. Instead, they explore a limited number of moves at any given stage in the game. The game is played on the basis of incomplete information, because the players do not have the time and capacity to consider all possible alternatives. For 'chess player' now read decision maker or problem solver.

The decisions of Economic Man are, in comparison, made in a world in which all complexity has been washed away; indeed, it would be stretching language to the point of abuse to claim that the unbounded rationality model has a theory of decision making. Take for example the classic Arrow and Debreu model of general economic equilibrium. In this model individuals have a preference ordering over all possible states of the world from now until the end of time. This preference ordering is known to them as too is the vector of all states of the world. Individuals then contract with one another to buy and to sell (i.e. exchange) goods and services, not only today but for all future time periods. What we have to imagine is that on the first day of the economy, individual plans are made with respect to how much labour to supply to which firm(s) for all time periods, along with the quantities of the various goods that will be consumed (including leisure) for all future time periods. Likewise, all firms[10] will have production plans which specify which goods will be produced and when, and to whom they will be delivered. Hence the derived demand for the inputs to the production process will also be specified. Combining the demand side and the supply side of the system along with the specification of initial endowments (i.e. property rights), the final equilibrium specifies the distribution of welfare. A compatible or equilibrium set of plans is established by changing the prices of the various goods and asking individuals to re-compute their plans, bearing in mind that the decision maker is seeking to maximise his own utility (this is the familar Walrasian process of price adjustment and atonement). In equilibrium, individual plans are compatible with respect to a particular set of equilibrium prices and initial endowments. All that then remains is for the individual to live out the plan. Life in an Arrow–Debreu world would be extremely boring!

However, lest the reader jumps to the wrong conclusions the following points are stressed. First, the Arrow–Debreu model is extremely simple and behaviourally naive. It assumes the existence of perfect future markets, the non-existence of externality and uncertainty and any other non-convexities, and grants powers of foresight and speed of computation to individuals well beyond those dreamed of by science fiction writers. Second, the Arrow–Debreu model is *not* a description of any reality and no reputable general equilibrium theorist would claim it to be. What the model does is to show the extreme conditions that are necessary before one can compute an equilibrium for the economy (and at the technical level this is not a trivial task!). If the world of reality is not like that of the Arrow–Debreu world (and of course it is not), then we gain a better understanding of why the real economy might not be in equilibrium i.e. we are able to understand more clearly the implications for the attainment of an equilibrium of increasing returns to scale, transactions costs, uncertainty and externality etc.

Having set out the stylistic general equilibrium model and thought about the unbounded rationality model within that system, we can now make an important point. The unbounded and bounded rationality models are not, as is frequently thought, competing models of the decision making process. They are instead differing paradigms and are used to study different problems. The unbounded rationality model is appropriate for the equilibrium paradigm, insofar as the problem to be solved is the technical one of establishing the necessary and sufficient conditions for an equilibrium. To simplify the technical problems of computing an equilibrium, the decision maker is made as simple as possible, which means that he is unconstrained, i.e. unbounded. In comparison, the bounded rationality model is best thought of in terms of the behavioural paradigm, where the problem is one of analysing the decision making *process* i.e. how decisions are made and especially the constraints placed on decision makers.

But the world of the analyst is not as clear cut as the two paradigms might suggest. There is an expanding grey area between the two. Modern equilibrium analysis, as it relaxes its assumptions, is moving in the direction of bounded rationality. The introduction of uncertainty into the analysis and a deeper regard for the constraints facing decision makers have brought the equilibrium and behavioural paradigm closer together[11]; see Hahn (1973) and Radner (1968, 1970, 1974). However, the purposes of the two paradigms are and continue to be distinct and must be recognised to be so, otherwise wrong minded criticism of the two models will be perpetuated.

As a behavioural concept, bounded rationality draws heavily upon Gestalt psychology. The insights which this perspective brings to the analysis of decision making and problem solving are quite considerable. It will be recalled from the schema set out above that one of the first problems any decision maker faces is that of problem identification. Organisations will have developed routines which assist with the recognition of problems, especially recurrent problems. However, problems are recognised and solved by individuals not by organisations. Individuals with different specialisms and backgrounds will identify different problems, or see a different facet of the same problem, or they will give a different definition of a similar problem; see Dearborn and Simon (1958). Problems are structured in line with individuals' values, prejudices and beliefs. Moreover, experience gained in solving previous problems is used in solving current problems; that which worked satisfactorily in the past is tried again. Also, there is in some sense a 'collective experience' insofar as an organisation's history and experiences are found in files, records, rules, precedents etc. and can be referred to by current decision makers. This produces efficiency in effort, because decisions/problems do not have to be thought out from scratch on each occasion. However, it does tend to bias the results, since it pushes the decision in a particular direction by filtering out alternative considerations. Thus, in identifying the nature of a complex problem an individual will decompose it or factor it into a small number of key features which are readily identifiable; this is his means of dealing with complexity and is the basis of the Gestalt school of perception. Perception is highly selective and the way in which a complex problem is decomposed and hence identified will reflect the individual's specialism, background, values etc. As we will demonstrate in Chapter 9, the fact that different decision makers, located at different positions in the same organisation, have different perceptions of common problems can result in considerable difficulties for the implementation and coordination of policies.

Economic Man in the unbounded rationality model is able to deal with all the complexities of the real world. All alternatives and their consequences are known to him and if he is thought to face an uncertain future then he simply evaluates these futures, by placing probabilities on their occurrence and calculates their expected values.[12] Administrative Man of the bounded rationality model is more modest in his ability to deal with complexity. He needs to simplify, he does not have the ability to think about all possible alternatives and he has a limited capacity to calculate the consequences of all the alternative courses of action. Moreover, he seldom has sufficient information gained from experience to calculate the prior probabilities of the occurrence of future events. His experiences of the past are selective and his current experience of the continuous present is too recent to be incorporated in any evaluation. Administrative Man acts rationally only with respect to his simple model of reality and in terms of his limited knowledge; this is bounded rationality and is summed up by Simon (1957, p. 198) as:

> The capacity of the human mind for formulating and solving complex problems is very small compared with the size of the problems whose solution is required for objectively rational behaviour in the real world — or even for a reasonable approximation to such objective rationality.[13]

(b) *Satisficing*

This is the second main concept put forward by Simon in his bounded rationality model. The elements of the concept of satisficing can be illustrated by means of a simple example. Suppose an individual is considering the purchase of a house. When deciding upon which of a large number of alternative houses he could purchase he weighs up a number of decision variables, e.g. price, location, age, size, access to other services. The scope or range of choice is narrowed considerably once the constraints on choice are specified — especially the budget constraint — but nevertheless the individual is still left with the problem of weighing up and comparing the benefits of a number of alternatives. Given his limited capacity and capabilities of calculating the net benefits of each alternative, in his attempt to maximise his utility, the individual decision maker uses the simplifying device of 'satisficing' i.e. the individual satisfices because he does not have the wit to maximise:

> ... the key to the simplification of the choice process ... is the replacement of the goal of maximising with the goal of satisficing, of finding a course of action that is 'good enough'.[13]
>
> (Simon 1957, p. 204)

The concept of satisficing is similar to that of an 'aspiration level', a concept borrowed from psychology and used by Cyert and March (1963) in their behavioural theory of the firm. An individual behaves and makes choices and decisions on the basis of aspiration levels, which are revised in the light of his success or failure in attaining them. When an individual finds a solution that meets his aspiration level (*at the time*), he chooses it as being good enough or satisfactory rather than necessarily the best i.e. that which maximises his utility function. Thus, satisficing and maximising behaviours are distinct, with the former recognising the need for the decision maker to simplify in order to cope with the complexity of reality within the confines of his own personal limitations.

Simon provides a number of graphic illustrations of the satisficing principle. Two of them are worthwhile recounting here. First, there is the example of an individual searching for a needle in a haystack. In the haystack there are many needles scattered randomly. To proceed the individual must specify the problem. For example, is he (a) searching for the sharpest needle, i.e. the maximisation process, or is he (b) searching for a needle which is sharp enough, i.e. the satisficing process? Simon argues that different search procedures are required for the two different problems. Broadly speaking, we can distinguish between algorithmic search and heuristic search procedures.

An algorithmic search procedure represents a full and systematic search via an algorithm in order to find the right or the best solution. Such a search can take a long time. Examples of algorithmic search are found in equilibrium economics. Scarf's algorithm (1967) for computing a general equilibrium is a good illustration, because even for the most simple specification of an economy it requires a good deal of computer capacity and computer time to search for the equilibrium solution. Likewise, linear programmes are algorithms which are used to search for the solution which maximises the objective function.

A heuristic search procedure is more pragmatic, recognising that a solution to the problem must be found within other constraints which include the costs of the search procedure (i.e. computing costs and decision costs) and also the time constraint, i.e. the decision has to be made according to some specified timetable. It makes use of the clues that are readily available and readily accessible; it makes use of previous solutions and previous searches, trying out first a repertory of responses that have been used in the past; see March and Simon (1958, p. 164). The decision process then becomes one in which a feasible region becomes defined by a set of acceptability constraints (e.g. profit must be sufficiently high to prevent a shareholder's revolt or a takeover). The decision process or search procedure for a solution involves setting out a *limited* number of alternative solutions (the limitation being determined by the decision and time constraints in producing them and the computational limitations of the decision maker in comparing them). These solutions are usually based upon experience and *a priori* reasoning and are not laid alongside one another and compared. Rather, they are laid alongside the acceptability constraint and the first one which passes the acceptability test is adopted. Clearly this means that a better solution to the one finally adopted might exist. Moreover, the order in which the alternatives are considerd affects the chances of any alternative's adoption.[14]

Simon's second example of the generality of the satisficing principle over the maximising principle is drawn from chess. Recently, computers have been programmed to play chess. However, nowhere in the programming is there a maximisation routine or procedure which takes all the alternative moves and computes the best. Rather, the programme undertakes a limited search over the set of possible alternatives and chooses that play which is good enough. Satisficing is a procedure for finding the good, rather than the best.

Simon's Certainty Equivalent Theorem

A number of economists have attacked the behavioural paradigm as represented by the bounded rationality model on the grounds that it is insufficiently general and fails to provide universally applicable insights. That this criticism is misplaced can best be demonstrated by referring to Simon's 'certainty equivalent theorem' (see Simon 1957).

The problem is how to decide upon inventories, production and work force levels when demand is fluctuating and uncertain. One means of tackling the problem is to employ the use of a dynamic programming algorithm. Information about future sales is summarised by means of a joint probability distribution and the cost function, no matter how complex, is assumed to be known. The dynamic programming algorithm solves the problem by minimising expected cost, subject to the probability distribution of sales, the relation between production and labour (i.e. the production function) and the accounting identity that sales plus inventories must equal output (i.e. production). In practice, however, such dynamic programming models are difficult to solve, even with the aid of a computer. Ando (1979, p. 85) has put it this way:

> The decision maker could not have obtained a straight maximising solution even if he had tried ... he would not have been able to write out the exact cost function and the exact description of constraints (probability distribution of all future sales). Secondly, even if he succeeded in writing out the 'true' problem the maximisation of the 'true' problem would have been beyond his computational capacity however augmented by, say, the most powerful computer that may become available in the foreseeable future.

In order to make a decision or to find a solution to this problem the decision maker requires a *decision rule* which will translate the initial conditions, including the sales forecast, into employment and production data. Moreover, the rule must be inexpensive to operate and must also be quick (the dynamic programme does not meet these criteria). Simon's solution to the problem was to approximate the cost function by a quadratic function and to replace the probability distribution of future sales by its first moments. This provides a simple solution called the 'certainty equivalent theorem', in which the cost function is minimised subject to constraints. At first sight the specification of the problem appears to be in the standard maximisation mould but not so. It is a genuinely satisficing type solution because:

(i) the choice of a quadratic to approximate the cost function (which is not known) involves judgment on the part of the decision maker;
(ii) there are many different quadratics that could be chosen. The precise functional which is actually chosen by the decision maker is that which is satisfactory/acceptable, not necessarily the best;
(iii) the decision maker keeps checking to find out how satisfactory/acceptable the decision rule is.

Simon's certainty equivalent theorem does, therefore, clearly demonstrate the power of the bounded rationality model.

Adaptive Behaviour

Finally, within the bounded rationality model we will consider a few of the problems raised when we look at processes of dynamic adjustments or adaptive behaviour. According to Simon, the study of Man's adaptation to a very complex environment is the central issue in the social sciences. Economists have for some time now talked about dynamic adjustment processes, but with little foundation to the analysis. Their approach has typically been one in which the speed of adjustment is to be maximised and the costs of adjustment are to be minimised. Ando (1979, p. 86) has pointed out that such a theory of adjustment is muted:

> If the capability of individuals and organisations to comprehend, describe and respond to their environment is without limit, then their behaviour reflects nothing but their goals and the characteristics of their environment. If any change occurs in the environment, such a change will be instantaneously and completely reflected in the behaviour of the decision makers concerned.

Most of micro-economics depends upon this approach. But what if there is no response from the individual following a change in the environment? How do we explain that? Here the bounded rationality model has much to offer. First, the individual might simply be unable to comprehend the complex reality and the changes taking place in it. Thus, the individual is paralysed into doing nothing. Second, in an attempt to deal with uncertain signals arising from the environment, the individual may decide that it is better to do nothing i.e. minimise the risks. Third, the computation of the maximising response, for all the reasons we have given above, may be beyond the abilities of the individual.

Individual Decision Making: Some Unresolved Problems

Two models of individual decision making have been reviewed. These models, it was emphasised, are not to be thought of as competing with one another but should instead be considered as alternative paradigms, which are used to solve different problems/questions. However, some economists, especially Baumol and Quandt (1964), have argued that the differences between the two models are not quite as stark as has been suggested in this Chapter. They argue that if information is costly and if other decision making costs are taken into account then satisficing is nothing other than optimally imperfect decision making. However, optimally imperfect decisions are not quite the same as those decisions which are the result of satisficing. An optimally imperfect decision is the product of a maximising process in which information and decision costs are constraints, whereas the satisficing decision outcome is the first which is found to be satisfactory or good enough. Clearly, the decision produced by these two processes need not be the same.

There is, however, another point which is emphasised by Baumol and Quandt (1964), that is, optimising models can perform well when predicting behaviour within acceptable margins of error. Given the limited and costly information available to businessmen, they showed that many of the rules of thumb, decision rules, conventions and routines frequently used by businessmen result in optimal choices. For example, the simple 'cost plus mark-up' rule for determining prices is roughly optimal insofar as the extra costs of using a more sophisticated pricing rule will outweigh the marginal benefits. Whether or not decision rules are consciously chosen to achieve optimal results, or whether they are employed to attain satisfactory results, remains an open question; see Margolis (1958).

The unbounded rationality model is rich in insights for the analysis of the way in which decisions are actually made. However, there are a number of problem areas which are not adequately considered. For example, how are the criteria determined against which solutions are judged to be satisfactory or acceptable? In some respects this is equivalent to asking the question, how are the decision makers' aspiration levels established and what causes these to change over time? March and Simon (1958) and Cyert and March (1963) have all emphasised that decision makers use a repertory of well-established standard operating procedures and rely heavily upon precedent to solve problems. But what happens when they face a radically new situation for which the standard procedures are not valid; how are decisions made then?

Before concluding this section, which has extended the notion of rationality to include that of bounded rationality, it is worthwhile considering for a moment Leibenstein's (1975) contribution to this debate and his concept of *selective rationality*. Leibenstein's use of this concept focuses attention more sharply upon the constraints faced by the indivual decision maker.

Leibenstein distinguishes between individuals who behave (i) as they like to, i.e. assuming no constraints of obligation or other influences and (ii) as they feel they must, i.e. according to duty. Somewhere between these two extreme positions an individual will strike a compromise and the extent of the compromise will vary from individual to individual depending upon the characteristics of the situation he faces. These differences are called the 'constraint concern', which can be explained as follows. An individual has a set of personality traits. These help him cope with his environment and include: (a) a sense of obligation to commitments; (b) a degree of calculatedness used in decisions and transactions; (c) a degree of sensitivity to differences in magnitude; (d) a degree of satisfaction with established routines of performance; and (e) a degree of perserverence with which people pursue goals. Each component of the vector of traits has an intensity value ranging from 0 to 1. If the intensity value equals unity then this implies maximising behaviour. Individuals who score low on constraint concern 'don't give a damn' and hence have a low sense of obligation to commitments etc. In Leibenstein's system, one of the behavioural assumptions is that individuals trade off constraint concern against pressures from outside, i.e. sanctions etc. The weaker the sanctions and incentives, then the lesser are the demands to be constraint concerned.

Leibenstein's concept of selective rationality throws light on a number of related topics. As an extension of his earlier work on *X*-efficiency (see Chapter 7) it gives another dimension to the concept of efficiency. Individuals low on constraint concern are likely to be less committed to honouring contracts and meeting production targets etc. Their productivity is likely to be lower than those who score high on constraint concern.

Constraint concern is also related to the concept of managerial discretion in particular and employee discretion in general. The greater the degree of discretion, the less likely will employees be constraint concerned. These issues are taken up again and developed in Chapter 5.

The Analysis of Goals

Goals are an integral part of any theory of decision making or problem solving. Both the bounded and unbounded rationality models assume that the decision maker is aiming at something; that his behaviour is purposeful. For the most part in economics, as in the other social sciences, goals are not regarded as being problematical. The individual is assumed to take as his goal the pursuit of his own utility and the owner/manager of a firm is regarded to be interested in maximising profit or productivity etc. There does, however, exist a literature on goal analysis which takes goals as problematic. Some of this literature was touched upon in Chapter 3. Economists such as Baumol, Williamson, Marris, and Cyert and March questioned whether or not profit maximisation was a realistic specification of the goal of the modern business corporation. In its place they put a modified specification of the non-owner/manager's objective function, which included sales revenue maximisation, growth maximisation and the personal utility of management. Whether or not organisations have a single collective goal or a multiple of different goals remains an empirical question. In the case of multiple goals there is the additional problem of weighing up the different goals. There is also the problem of how individuals joining a group or organisation accept the collective goals of the group (see Barnard 1938) and whether or not their own personal goals conflict with those of the collectivity. But how are the goals of the collectivity established; are they fixed or do they change over time and what factors cause them to change? Although goals are freqently taken as given, it can be seen from these question that they present problems which decison making theory and hence economics cannot ignore.

In practice, goals are frequently not as precise as theory would suppose. It is for this reason that decision makers find it extremely difficult to make use of many of the decision making algorithms. In the public sector bureaucracy the objectives of policies are usually vague e.g. the goal of policy *X* is to make provisions for 'good housing' or the goal of policy *Y* is to ensure that we have a 'healthy population'. These policy goals are ill-defined, extremely ambiguous and not very informative. To find out what the goals of a collectivity are, researchers frequently consult documents such as the organisation charter or an Act of Parliament. However, these simply provide information about the formal goals or objectives and not necessarily about the actual goals which are being pursued. Either there is a problem of perceiving and interpreting the formal goals, or individuals have, for some reason or another, found that it is possible to pursue other goals whilst to some degree or another minimally satisfying the formal objectives. The origin and nature of this discretion, which is available to decision makers within the organisation, and the problems of interpreting official goals become the interesting questions for analysis. Some would argue that the ambiguity is deliberate because it then offers maximum scope for almost any set of activities to achieve the objective. This, however, opens up a number of problems for efficiency studies, which will be developed in greater detail in Chapter 7. If goals are not clearly specified, then it becomes difficult to judge the efficiency and effectiveness of means/ends relationships. In policy analysis it is, therefore, a mistake to assume that policy goals/objectives are unambiguous and clearly defined. They are not. It is also a mistake to assume that objectives can be worked out or revealed from observing the implementation of decisions. The role of the observer in imputing the goals by interpreting behaviour opens up such a technique to the criticism of bias.

There is also the question 'what is the distinction between means and ends?' As Simon (1965) pointed out, means/ends relationships are abstractions, but in practice means and ends are not distinct. The end product or output for one individual frequently represents an input or a means to another.[15] Thus Simon talked about organisations as 'means/ends hierarchies', since the ends produced by one part of the organisation are then used as the means of achieving a higher order goal elsewhere in the organisation. Ends or goals are, therefore, 'nested'. To ask one group in the organisation what its goals or ends are does not by itself provide information about the overall goal of the organisation or about the goals pursued in other parts of the organisation.

It has already been pointed out in an earlier chapter that individuals have goals, but organisations do not. However, there is a sense in which we can talk about an organisational, or more precisely, a collective goal, by which we mean individuals contract or agree to recognise a common goal and act *as if* it were their own. The interesting question which then emerges is, how do collective goals become established? One answer is that individuals recognise that, by pursuing a common goal, each is made better off than would otherwise be the case if they acted independently. This is what is probably referred to by Gestalt social psychologists who argue that a group is more than the sum of its constituent elements (see Olson 1965). It does, however, require a 'political entrepreneur' to organise the group and to absorb the transactions costs involved (see Frohlich and Oppenheimer 1978). Another alternative, but not necessarily competing, answer is that proposed by the 'social contract theorists'. The collective goal emerges either as a result of voluntary trading and contracting between individuals who have different personal goals, as in the case of a social contract (see Buchanan and Tullock 1965), or as a result of a conflict in which one of the personal goals is imposed upon the rest. Goals will then change as individuals see scope for improving their collective benefits by means of a goal change, or if the dominant goal is toppled in the power struggle.

The analysis of goal changes occupies a large part of the literature on the sociology of organisations (see Merton 1957, Sills 1957 and Perrow 1961). The collective goals of an organisation evolve over time (i.e. called 'goal succession'), an observation which was made as early as 1911 by Robert Michels when he wrote about the evolving character of European political and trade-union movements. Once one goal is successfully achieved, then the organisation will either cease to exist, or will search for a new purpose, a new goal; e.g. compare the activities of the Red Cross when it was set up during war with its peacetime activities of disaster relief. Changes in goals may be dramatic, or they can, and usually do, take place gradually.

Goal displacement is another concept frequently examined; see Merton (1957) and Blau and Scott (1963). In this case, means frequently become ends, thereby making the means/ends distinction meaningless. For example, in the bureaucracy, the practice of good drafting of bills is a means to the end of efficient administration and justice, and fairness in the implementation of policy. However, it is frequently remarked that good drafting becomes an end in itself, so that the bureaucrat becomes more concerned about the 'nit picking' details of grammar and punctuation, rather than about the substantive content of the bill itself.[16] The maintenance of stability of the organisation is a means, but can become an end at the expense of the primary objectives of the organisation.

It is frequently argued that the economist is more interested in the outcome of a decision than in the decision making process. But this is to argue that outcomes are independent of the processes that produce them and that is patently not so. This digression into the analysis of goals highlights the dynamic of the decision process. If we are to understand decision making processes, if we are to appreciate the limitations on decision making and therefore the difference between the expected outcome of a decision and the actual outcome, then we cannot take goals as being an unproblematic element of the analysis. Whose goals are being served; what goals should be served; how have the goals changed over time and why? These are all basic questions which must be carefully considered.

In their critique of the unbounded rationality model of decision making, Braybrooke and Lindblom (1963) argue that right from the start practical decision making is fraught with difficulties. What precisely is the problem to be solved? What is the objective that is to be satisfied? Different parties to the decision bring with them different perspectives and different interests. This is where politics enter into the analysis. The problem to be solved and the operational goal (objective) to be served emerge from a bargaining process. This is a significant departure from the view which assumes that the goals or preference orderings are given, having been imposed authoritatively by the leadership. Of course, once a problem is defined and once a dominant set of goals emerges, then decision making techniques come into play to find an acceptable solution (outcome).

The political or interactive elements in the decision making process were explored in the political economy model of Chapter 3. One means of minimising the amount of conflict in an organisation is to space out conflicting goals through time and to attain them sequentially rather than simultaneously. The sequential nature of real decision making, rather than the heuristic fiction of the simultaneous attainment of goals, as is characteristic of general equilibrium models, illustrates what Shackle (1974) has referred to as the 'human predicament':

> In order to secure its ends, choice must apply a knowledge of what will be the consequence of what. But the sequel of an action chosen by one man will be shaped by circumstance, and its circumstances will include the actions chosen now and actions to be chosen in time to come by other men. If, therefore, choice is effective, it is unpredictable and thus defeats, in some degree, the power of choice itself to secure exact ends. This is the human predicament.

Collective Decision Making

The problems raised when we move from quesions of individual decision making to collective decision making or social choice are quite considerable. It is well beyond the scope of this section to consider all of these problems. All that can be done here is to identify some key problem areas and sketch out some possible solutions. The reader who is interested in following up these problems should consult Brown and Jackson (1978), Mayston (1974) and Sen (1970).

Given that individuals make decisions and organisations do not, and given that individuals frequently as members of large or small groups make decisions collectively, then the questions which follow are: (i) how are individual preference orderings aggregated so as to produce a collective preference ordering (i.e. the positive question); and (ii) what rule should be used to aggregate individual preferences into a collective ordering (i.e. the normative question)? The basic thing to remember throughout the following discussion is that a collective decision has the characteristic that, once it is made, it affects all members of the collectivity, who are therefore bound to it, so that the minority, who may disagree with the outcome, have to go along with the wishes of the majority.

The *normative* question of finding an ethically acceptably means (i.e. rule) of adding together the preference orderings of individuals over alternative states of the world[17] was analysed in considerable depth by Arrow (1959, 1963) and by Black (1948). Arrow set out a number of basic weak axioms which any social ordering, derived from a set of individual orderings, should conform to. What Arrow showed analytically was that there does not exist a collective choice rule or a social ordering which obeys his basic axioms. This result has come to be known as *Arrow's Possibility Theorem*, stated as, 'if we exclude the possibility of interpersonal comparisons of utility, then the only methods of passing from individual tastes to social preferences which will be defined for a wide range of individual orderings are either imposed or dictatorial' (Arrow 1963, p. 59).

Arrow's result generated a vast literature which sought to find logical flaws in the analysis (none has been found), or to weaken the axioms and find what results thereby follow (see Sen 1970 and Mueller 1979 for excellent surveys). For our purposes, however, we are more interested in the *positive* question of, 'how *are* individual preferences aggregated into a collective choice'; in other words, what are the collective decision rules which are frequently used in practice?

The most prevalent collective choice rule used is that of majority voting or some variant thereof. Other rules include more authoritarian principles e.g. 'it is the will of God, all must obey' or 'the word of the ruler is law, all must obey'. In these authoritarian cases, the choice is made on behalf of the collectivity with or without regard to the interests or preferences of the individuals who make up the collectivity. Such an imposed solution is only in the weakest sense a collective choice. The problems of collective choice in practice emerge in an environment of liberal democracy. Some of these problems can be summarised as follows: (i) the majority outcome is imposed upon the minority who did not vote for the eventual outcome i.e. the tyranny of the majority; (ii) under simple majority voting it is possible to express the intensity of preference felt for the alternatives against which votes are cast; and (iii) majority voting outcomes are unstable since the outcome depends upon the order in which the issues are voted, i.e. cyclical majorities. Many of these problems are minimised as soon as the possibility of vote trading and exchange is introduced. Thus, if we think of a universe of different issues on which different decisions have to be taken at different times, then individuals can engage in voting strategies in which they arrange to trade their votes with one another in an attempt to secure the outcomes that they most favour (see Buchanan and Tullock 1965). Moreover, if the number of voters is large relative to the number of issues, then the instability of cyclicity is reduced.

Collective decision making presents to the analyst many of the most difficult problems of decision making. Take, for example the issue of whether or not an individual will decide voluntarily to join a group (organisation). This is the question which Olson (1965) considered in his now classic study of collective action. Individuals are most likely to join small groups in order to secure jointly collective or common interests. For large groups, however, the propensity for individuals to act jointly is greatly reduced. This arises from the problem of the 'free-rider' which recognises that individuals can obtain the benefits of acting jointly or collectively, but might at the same time distort their preferences in order to reduce the costs of their membership in the group. Thus, on this basis, large groups whose membership is based on voluntary self-interest are likely to be unstable and in the limit might not exist. However, it is an empirical fact that large groups (organisations) do exist and so the question to be asked is, why? Olson argues that the reasons for the existence of large groups are:

(i) membership is compulsory and not voluntary as in the case of joining a trades union in a closed shop;
(ii) the organisation has a pool of discretionary resources which can be used to offer individuals selective incentives to induce participation (see also Barnard 1938 and Simon 1965); and
(iii) a 'political entrepreneur' will bear the costs, provide the good and collect payments from each individual member (see also Frohlich and Oppenheimer 1978).

Olson's analysis therefore provides a basis for dicussing the rationale and existence of larger groups and transcends the more limited analyses which either concentrate upon small voluntary groups, or which define away the problems by concentrating upon the anthropomorphic life of groups or individuals' group instincts. However, Olson's approach is partial. Large groups and organisations which do exist are those which are allowed to continue to exist, either in the sense that they serve the interests of the ruling elites in society, or that they are tolerated. Thus, group (organisational) existence cannot be separated from the processes which legitimate these collective activities.

Whilst economists have long studied the interaction of individuals in markets and barter exchange, the examination of the behaviour of individuals in non-market situations is a relatively new departure for economists (see Downs 1967, Olson 1965 and Buchanan and Tullock 1962). This was noted in Chapter 3, where it was also pointed out that in groups, goal conflicts are often the general rule. Thus the natural question which follows is, 'what effect does goal conflict have upon resource allocations?' One possible answer is that, in making decisions about how resources shall be allocated amongst the interest groups that make up the organisation, the dominant coalition automatically makes the decision which favours it, with or without concessions being made to the other groups within the organisation. The amount of discretion which it has to serve its own interests and the extent to which it is constrained to take into account the interests of other groups depend upon the prescriptions set out in the constitution and the extent to which any constitution (if it exists) is effective i.e. adhered to in practice. Since the constitution, in principle at least, legitimises the actions of the various constituent members of the organisation, it is an important element of any study of collective decision making, because it sets out the normative rules and mechanisms through which resources *should* be allocated. This is not, however, to suggest that a study of resource allocation would proceed from an examination of the written records or the constitution of an organisation. Indeed not — the pitfalls of such an approach are well known, since the public records of the organisation can present a story or a picture for a purpose other than that which is of interest to the organisation theorist. Instead, the constitution provides the analyst with information which in the first instances gives some clues as to some of the relevant constraints on individual behaviour. If from further examination it turns out that these constraints are ineffective, then that raises another set of empirical questions about the system of control within the organisation.

Despite recent theoretical interest by economists in the subject matter of collective/non-market decision making, relatively few empirical studies have been carried out on the comparative performance characteristics of different group decision rules. This can also be extended to studies of the internal dynamics of communication, persuasion and the exercise of personal power (see Bower 1965, Wheeler 1967 and Pondy 1970). Some of these points are picked up and developed again in Chapter 6 when we examine resource allocation and budgeting within bureaucracies.

As soon as the possibility of trade or exchange is introduced into the collective decision making process, then power relationships become vital. Power, it will be recalled from the discussions in earlier chapters, is defined as the ability of one individual to influence another individual with respect to some set of activities (see Dahl 1957). Within the rules of the game, as defined by a constitution, power relationships are delineated. Thus, within the confines set by the majority decision rule, individuals (voters) have equal power to influence the outcome. However, once voting strategies are opened up as a possibility, then the power of individuals to influence the outcome, by virtue of their power over individual voters, becomes an integral part of the analysis, as does the basis of this power and the means of influence.

Thus the concept of power has explanatory value in determining the final outcome of any relationship of exchange or negotiation, be it at the level of the individual or the collectivity. The public sector is an obvious example of collective decision making. Within this system of collective choice there is much exchange and there is scope for influencing the final outcome. The relevant questions then become: just how representative are democracies; who is it that has the power to influence decisions; is it voters, if so which voters; is it politicians, if so whose interests are they serving; or is it the bureaucrats? What is the basis of the power and influence in public collective decision making? These questions are explored in greater detail in Chapters 6 and 8.

Decision Making Under Conditions of Complexity and Uncertainty

Recently, economic theorists and organisation theorists have started to incorporate notions such as complexity and uncertainty into their standard analyses, which have generally been formulated for conditions of perfect knowledge and perfect foresight (Arrow 1971, McGuire and Radner 1972, and Pfeffer, Salancik and Leblebici 1976). Prior to such developments, decision theory proceeded on the assumptions of certainty, well defined goals, and well specified technologies. There is not, however, such a well developed theory of decision making under conditions of uncertainty and ambiguous objectives.

Uncertainty exists when there is a lack of consensus about purposes and the means of achieving them, when the results of an action are indeterminate, or when future events are unpredictable, either because these future events are unknowable or the individual decision maker is incapable of processing information, which would allow him to make a number of estimates about the likelihood of future states of the world occurring. In statistical decision theory the distinction is frequently made between situations of uncertainty and those of risk. An uncertain situation is one in which the individual does not know what future state of the world will exist, but does have a description of the future states which *could* exist. He then assigns probabilities to each of these future states, thereby forming some *expectation* of which state is most likely to occur. The origins of these probabilities are either *objective*, having been calculated from the frequency of the occurrence of these events in the past, or they may be *subjective*, in which case they depend upon the decision maker's guesses and hunches. A situation of risk is one in which no information is available about the future states of the world. It places the decision maker in a position of complete ignorance.

Uncertainty is also used less precisely as a catch-all for a number of characterisations of the environment, including stability, differentiation, complexity, resourcefulness, and competitiveness. In each of these cases the decision maker is faced with an information processing problem; see Pfeffer and Leblebici (1973) and Pennings (1975). Uncertainty originating outside the organisation can result in uncertainty inside, to the extent that individuals lack knowledge of what to do, which problem solving tasks to engage in, and how their individual activities relate to one another.

One view of the reaction to uncertainty is to think about gaining control over the source of the uncertainty. A producer will, therefore, buy over or merge with suppliers of vital inputs if the supply of these inputs is subject to an intolerable amount of uncertainty. Another associated view is to set up buffers within the organisation in the form of routines to deal with unforeseen contingencies. However, such buffers can be expensive to maintain and are unlikely to be complete in their capability to deal with all possible contingencies. A cost minimiser would, therefore, choose to cover those contingencies which have the greatest probability of occurring. Both of these views of decision making under uncertainty concentrate upon the allocation of activities and resources to the avoidance and reduction of uncertainty.

One approach to the study of uncertainty is that of the 'contingency theorists', a name coined by Lawrence and Lorsch (1967) for an approach to organisational design based on the empirical observations of Woodward (1958) and Burns and Stalker (1961). These studies suggested that effectively functioning organisations have structural characteristics which 'fit' the characteristics of the environments in which they operate.[18] Stable and certain environments tend to be associatied with 'mechanistic' or hierarchical organisation structures, in which pre-programmed decision making routines exist to deal with a well known set of standard problems, whereas, highly uncertain and frequently changing environments are empirically associated with highly fluid or 'organic' structures. In each environment, the appropriate organisation structure proves to be effective when judged by a number of performance criteria. Thus there is no one best way to organise. Instead, the most effective organisational form is contingent upon the nature of the environment in which the organisation operates.

This amounts to saying that, when faced with ambiguity, uncertainty and complexity, those organisations which are based upon a rigid and well defined set of decision routines, will tend to be paralysed, if the problems being presented to the decision makers do not conform to the standard package of routines. On the other hand, those organisations which are less rigidly organised can quickly mobilise and reorganise resources in order to *search* for a solution. In such 'fluid' organisations there is a greater de-emphasis of rules and procedures; see Becker and Gordon (1966), Perrow (1972) and Hinings *et al.* (1974)

Whilst the contingency theorist's approach has a certain amount of intuitive appeal, especially as an account of the constraints which different organisation structures place upon the ease of initiating search procedures, it has been severely criticised (Pennings 1975). Current empirical studies provide no conclusive evidence of structural correlates between environment and technology. This arises in part from conceptual and empirical problems of defining and measurimg environmental characteristics, technology and organisation structure.[19]

Organisation *per se* assists decision making, whether it be under conditions of certainty or uncertainty. Decision making and problem solving are exercises in searching for a solution through the collection and processing of information, and organisation enables the existence of specialisation, division of labour and the pooling of information and expertise. In the absence of organisation, each individual would need to contract with others (via exchange) to receive the information required for decision making. This would be an expensive operation. Thus organisation is a means of minimising the transaction costs and decision costs involved in information collection and processing (Alchian and Demsetz 1972).

Organisations develop routines and channels for communication — a message that does not fit in cannot be communicated. However, this does not of itself imply rigidity and inflexibility in the design of organisation structures. As was pointed out above, management (decision makers) have to cope with complexity and ignorance. Decision makers must, therefore, learn to tolerate ambiguity and in order to help them to do so they require structures, definitions and abstractions (in sum, a paradigm). However, as Loasby (1976, p. 135) points out, 'the types of abstractions to be used instead of being decided in advance, are left entirely for definition by the changing needs of the situation'. If a complex organisation is to cope successfully with uncertainty and change, its decision making systems must remain incompletely specified. This means that many parts of the organisation's structure will remain incompletely specified. One way of viewing the set of relationships within an organisation and between an organisation and the external agents within its environment is as a set of contracts. If all contracts are rigidly specified in advance and are contingent upon specific states of the world occurring with certainty, then such contracts will tend to be inappropriate and inefficient for those environments which are rapidly changing. There are a number of ways of dealing with this. Contracts could be specified in such a way that they contain a variety of clauses which become activated when certain pre-specified states of the world prevail. In such a case a single contract would be equivalent to a set of individually specified contingent contracts. In either case the negotiations prior to the signing of the contract(s) would revolve around the conditions pertaining to the contingencies. Whilst decision costs might appear to be high for this form of contract, they are also high for traditional, rigidly fixed contracts. As conditions change, the rigidly specified contract increasingly becomes less appropriate and has to be re-negotiated, a process which takes time and can involve costs of lost opportunities through delay.

The *costs of decision making*, which are also referred to as transactions costs, are illustrated in figure 4.1. This analysis follows from the initial work of Buchanan and Tullock (1962). The total costs of decision making are divided into (a) information processing costs and (b) external costs. As the total number of sub-units within the organisation increases, then the number of individual contracts increases also. This presents a coordination problem for the central decision maker, who is presented with an increasing number of data points which have to be collated and processed. Hence information processing costs are shown to increase with the total number of sub-units in the organisation. However, these are not the only costs which increase. Embodied in the information processing costs are the costs of delay and lost opportunities. As the number of individual agents (contracts) increases, the process of coordination takes time and meanwhile there is the opportunity cost of foregone or lost advantages arising through delay in not seizing the opportunity. Offset against these costs are 'external costs'.[20] As

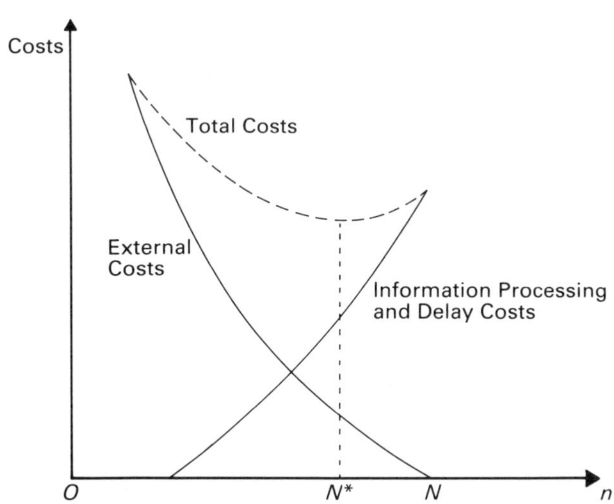

n = size of coordination unit
N = total number of sub-units (contracts) within the organisation
N^* = optimal size of coordination unit for minimum total cost

Figure 4.1 *Costs of Decision Making*

the decision maker draws more and more individuals into the decision making process and establishes agreement with them, then the costs of imposing an unwelcome solution on these individuals diminishes. But of course, such negotiations take time and as agreement is sought, information processing costs and delay costs rise. Total costs are the sum of these two sets of costs and are minimised at the point where marginal information processing costs equal marginal external costs, (i.e. at N^* in figure 4.1).

If we were being prescriptive and considering the question, 'how much coordination should management attempt', then this framework illustrates the relevant issues that have to be taken into account. Close supervision and coordination are costly activities, but at the same time there are other external costs arising from a lack of coordination, especially in highly interdependent and non-separable systems. Thus, the contingency theorists (like Burns and Stalker (*op. cit.*)) can, in part, be recast in this mould. In order to cope successfully with uncertainty and minimise decision costs, decision making systems and contracts must remain incompletely specified.

Complexity is not, therefore, necessarily best handled by a rigid bureaucratic organisational structure. Moreover, there is much to be said in favour of *not* taking positive decisions when the decision making environment is complex and uncertain. On first reflection this might seem to be a naive view — surely some kind of decision must be made. There is almost a complusion by some bureaucrats to take decisions. Unless bureaucrats are taking decisions there is a feeling that they will be criticised for not doing a proper job. An example of this problem is illustrated by Dunphy (1978). At a conference, a senior government official who had been involved in a decision to drop tariffs in the electronics industry by 23% in one year remarked; 'You know when we dropped tariffs by 23% we had no idea it would affect employment in the electronics industry'. There was a stunned silence and Dunphy looked at the face of one manager to whom he had been talking earlier in the day and who in the previous week had fired 600 of his employees as a result of that decision. In an uncertain, complex and ambiguous environment, the decision not to act is one means of coping with uncertainty.

Whilst environments are uncertain, complex and ambiguous, the way in which organisations are structured and the interactions between organisational members can give the impression that the situation is less uncertain, less complex and more precisely defined than in fact it is. March and Simon (1958, p. 165) refer to this as *uncertainty absorption*. Each part of the organisation when preparing a statement or presenting a departmental view, as some input to the policy decision process, goes in for much guessing and approximation. Information is edited and summarised as it passes through the organisation and becomes more structured and simplified the further away it gets from its point of origin. As a consequence, information which started off as being ambiguous and uncertain is processed and re-defined and there is then a tendency to treat such processed information as if it were more precise than it is. The informational output of one part of the organisation which is subsequently used as an input to the decisions and deliberations of another part of the organisation is treated as a given. Those who use the information tend not to question too closely its source, status, or the assumptions upon which it is predicated. To do so would be time-consuming and frequently the information is technical and the user of the information does not possess the contextual knowledge required to question its validity. The role played by the process of uncertainty absorption is illustrated by the following;

> ... the boilings down and snap judgements which if you knew about them would enable you to make your own estimate of the reliability of the information as evidence are mopped up out of sight in the tidy 'official' presentation. The same thing occurs when a technical expert 'simplifies' something for the layman, in any form of averaging and when a mass of original survey data, for example, is presented in classified tables.
>
> (Dunsire 1978a, p. 199)

> ... great power is wielded by those at the point where the greatest amount of uncertainty is absorbed, since they can considerably influence the decisions that will finally be made by others. Such a position may be filled by an 'expert' who is nominally quite junior in the hierarchy or by an 'adviser' who can be appealed to on matters of difficulty that cannot be resolved by rational analysis.
>
> (Brown 1970, p. 148)

The relationship between power and control over information is clearly similar to that approach in organisational sociology adopted by Crozier (1964, 1970). An interesting series of case studies of decision making under conditions of ambiguity and uncertainty is contained in a recent book by March and Olsen *et al.* (1976). It is more a search for a theory of how things are done, rather than how they should be. Collectively these case studies can be referred to as *the garbage-can model of choice*. Essentially the 'garbage-can model' argues that individuals face situations over which they often have only modest control. These are usually complex situations which are ambiguously defined because individuals possessed very little cognitive understanding of them. The components of any decision process are problem specifications and possible solutions. These components are thought of as being thrown into a garbage-can and mixed around. Solutions and problems are not matched up, but are instead thrown together independently. This view of the search for solutions is overlaid with a theory of social structure within organisations. The social structure of the organisation influences the decision process, since the structure of property rights within the organisation influences who has and has not access to the decision process. Thus the particular structure will determine which skills, expertise, background (values), norms, etc. will be brought to bear on searching for a solution.

Decision making under conditions of uncertainty adds another dimension to the discussion of the theory of choice. When uncertainty is high, the ability of decision makers to use universalistic decision criteria is difficult. To the extent that a field is paradigmatically well developed, uncertainty in decision making concerning that field is much reduced (Lodahl and Gordon 1972). This could account for many of the present problems in macro-economic management today. If standards and criteria for decision making are well-defined and agreed upon, then decisions based upon such criteria will not depend upon the particular persons making the decisions. It is in those situations in which uncertainty is high that personal influence has greatest effect (Pfeffer, Salancik and Leblebici 1976). In those situations there are few standards agreed upon and decision outcomes depend more upon the particular social relationships between individual decision makers.

Finally, complexity and uncertainty cannot be totally separated. Any large modern organisation, such as the public sector bureaucracy, is an incoherent system. An organisation is a system because its activities constitute a non-random pattern. But for participants the pattern of events is generally unpredictable. This is one of the elements of uncertainty. 'The complexity of events is too great for them to grasp what is going on and they do not know how they themselves are going to act' (Cornford 1974, p. 239). Actors involved in decision making are frequently unable to assess the significance of what it is they are doing. This is partly due to the problem of predicting the future and of dealing with uncertainty, but it is also due to the difficulty of understanding what is going on now. 'Some officials do not deal with complexity at all; they are just overwhelmed and never quite recover' (Wildavsky 1964, p. 11).

Conclusions

In this chapter a variety of topics have been reviewed. The limitations of the rational model of decision making have been set out against the organisational process model of decision making, which emphasises the imperfections of information, complexity, uncertainty, the costs of resources for decision making, the pressures of time, the attainment of satisfactory outcomes rather than the best, and the sequential rather than the simultaneous nature of decision making. The internal politics of decision making has also been stressed. Decisions do not necessarily emerge from reflection, but are instead the result of argument and conflict within and between organisations, partly over who shall do what and who should be a net beneficiary, and partly because of different perspectives about problems and the means to deal with them.

Whilst a behavioural perspective to decision making offers many insights and is considered by many to be more realistic, it must nevertheless be balanced against the view that the historical account of 'what really happened' is fiction, an imposition of order, coherence, and purpose remote from the experience of participants. With hindsight we can discern a pattern in events unperceived by the actors; but we may also falsify or distort the nature of the events by divorcing them from the experience and understanding of the participants.

But is decision making a real process which is a subject for analysis? Do individuals make decisions? Is choice real or is it an illusion? If decision making involves an element of chance, then choices are often illusory. The questions raised above do, however, go deeper than that. Who are the individuals who make decisions of any substance within organisations? Are all members of the organisation decision makers, or are the choices of the majority of organisational members already pre-determined, leaving them no discretionary decision making powers? Throughout this chapter it has been the decision making process which has been studied rather than the question, 'who are the decision makers?'. By asking ourselves this question we remind ourselves that the *distribution* of resources within the organisation is not independent of the allocation of rights to make decisions, which is itself in turn determined by the structure of rights within the wider socio-economic system. Thus, for many individuals, their set of choices is so severely constrained that decision making and choice have little or no meaning. Whilst these questions are of relevance to a wider analysis of decision making within organisations, we have chosen to ignore them and have instead concentrated upon alternative views of the decision making process, when such an event is a meaningful activity.

Notes

1 For an extremely stimulating critique of the conventional neoclassical treatment of decision making as it is treated in economics, see Loasby (1976).

2 It would be impossible and impractical to give a complete list. However, those organisational writers who have made most use of the decision making perspective include: Simon (1965), March and Simon (1958), Brown (1970) and Perrow (1972). For a critique of this approach, see Storing (1962).

3 The questions of 'what is a good decision' and 'what is an efficient decision' (the two questions not necessarily referring to the same concept) are not trivial and straightforward to answer. Correctness, good/bad, and efficient/inefficient are all concepts which can only be established by appealing to value judgments. Thus value judgments will, in addition to evaluating the ends/goals of the decision process, also evaluate the means through which the attainment of these ends are effected. This crucial question of what constitutes good decision making is found in Simon's early work (1957).

4 As soon as we mention 'self-interest' we open a hornet's nest concerning whether or not individuals are selfish and amoral, in the sense that they do not have any altruistic motives. For a discussion of these problems, see Sen (1976) and Collard (1978).

5 This is found in the optimising approach to macro-economics as embodied in the Theil/Teinbergen fixed targets approach and is, moreover, the basis of all social policy analysis based on a strict neoclassical approach to the problem.

6 It might be too strong to suggest that a single feasible solution is found. Given the various dimensions to feasibility, a zone of feasibility is more likely to emerge within which a number of feasible solutions could exist. There is then a higher order problem involved in making that choice within the feasible set.

7 Sen (1976) points out that this approach assumes that there is no means other than the use of revealed preference to understand someone's attitudes towards alternatives. Moreover, this approach presumes too little and too much, insofar as there are other sources of information (apart from those obtained from choices) on preferences and welfares and because actual choices might reflect a compromise among a variety of considerations of which personal welfare may be just one.

8 The interested reader should consult Oppenheim (1953) on this point.

9 This point was made by Newman (1974).

10 General equilibrium theorists will realise that strictly speaking the concept of a firm does not exist in such models.

11 Modern general equilibrium theory does, of course, relax many of the earlier assumptions and does make attempts at incorporating features such as uncertainty, externality, and increasing returns; see Arrow and Hahn (1971).

12 On this point, see Shackle p. 2, quoted above.

13 This is not to imply that Simon is arguing that Man is irrational. Simon is not subscribing to the Freudian psychiatrist's view of Man as essentially irrational by nature. Instead, Simon is looking at the constraints placed on rationality (see H.A. Simon *Administrative Behaviour* second edition 1957, p. xxiii).

14 This point is not generally emphasised in the literature on bounded rationality. It is similar to that result in the social choice literature which demonstrates that because of intransitivities in the social ordering over a set of alternatives, the adoption of an alternative by means of the majority decision rule depends upon the order in which the issues are voted.

15 The economist does of course recognise this as the distinction frequently made between final and intermediate outputs.

16 A similar charge can be made against many academics when they mark students' assignments! Of course, grammar and punctuation are important, but not of sole importance.

17 A social state is a complete description of reality defining the quantities of goods and services produced and their qualities, the distribution of welfares, the level of unemployment, rate of inflation and so on. Each individual is assumed to have a preference ordering over all possible states.

18 This approach belongs to that group of organisation theorists who relate organisation structure to environmental characteristics e.g. Dill (1958), Katz and Khan (1966) and Thompson (1967). See Chapter 2.

19 For an attack on contingency theory from the perspective of organisational psychology, see Argyris (1972).

20 External costs, as used in this context by economists, are similar to the concept of 'interdependence' as employed by Thompson (1967).

CHAPTER 5

Bureaucracy: The Economist's Perspective

Bureaucrats as individuals are neither more or less efficient, honest, hardworking, thorough, public spirited and generally worthy of admiration than non-bureaucrats
(Downs 1967, p. 26)

It is not from the benevolence of the bureaucrat that we expect our research grant or our welfare check, but out of his regard to his own, not the public, interest.
(Tullock)

Introduction

Previous chapters have now considered the concept of bureaucracy and some of the issues which interest students of bureaucracy. In addition, different perspectives to the study of organisations have been examined. In this chapter some of these strands will be drawn together. Particular attention will be directed to the economist's current treatment of bureaucracy. The models which will be reviewed are set within the equilibrium paradigm of neoclassical economics which was set out earlier in Chapter 3.

The analysis which follows is based upon a simple and straightforward definition of bureaucracy. A bureaucracy is a particular form of organisation comprised of a set of bureaus or agencies, such that the overall bureaucracy is a system of consciously coordinated activities which has been explicitly created to achieve specific ends.

This definition is sufficiently general that it will apply to any bureaucracy, whether or not it lies within the public or the private sectors of the economy. One means of separating out organisations is to do so according to their source of finance. Thus, in the first instance profit-making and non profit-making organisations are distinguished from each other, the latter being financed, '... at least in part, from a periodic appropriation or grant' (Niskanen 1971, p. 8). Public sector non profit-making organisations differ from those in the private sector, because they are financed in part from a grant which originates from tax revenue. Public sector bureaucracies are, therefore, non profit-making organisations which do not market the major proportion of their outputs and which depend upon tax revenues as their principal source of finance.

Bureaucracy: The Analysis of Public Sector Supply

The analysis of public sector bureaus is a comparatively recent addition to the economic literature. The 'new political economy' which stems from the pioneering work of Downs (1957) and Buchanan and Tullock (1962) concentrated upon the demand side of the equation. Thus the early 1960s saw the application of the economist's maximising calculus to the behaviour of voters, politicians, pressure groups etc. Within this framework, attention concentrated upon alternative systems of demand articulation, voting mechanisms etc. through which the voters expressed their demand for publicly provided goods and services. The public sector bureaucracy which produced and/or supplied the public sector was, in these demand models, regarded as a passive agent which responded in a neutral and efficient way to the demands of the electorate. Bureaucrats were passionless, grey figures who served the 'public interest'. They were portrayed as administrative eunuchs, devoid of personal ambition. Such a view of the bureaucrat could not be sustained from casual empiricism and could not be squared with other parts of the literature, especially that which saw the activities of the bureaucrat as a threat to the functioning of democracy. Rather, the neutral bureaucrat was more a fiction derived from classical normative public administration theory e.g. Weber (1947) and Wilson (1887).

In response to this unrealistic approach to bureaucratic behaviour, a number of economists began to model bureaucratic decision making explicitly. Specifically, they modelled the bureaucrat as a maximising agent, just as the consumer, the producer, the voter and the politician had been modelled earlier. The pioneers of this approach were Downs (1967) and Tullock (1965), although an implicit theory of bureaucratic behaviour had been suggested many years earlier by the German economist, von Mises (1944). Their analysis of the supply side of the public sector provided the basis of two recent syntheses: Breton (1974, 1978) and Niskanen (1971). This chapter will set out the details of these models in an attempt to find out what stage of development the economic analysis of bureaucratic supply has reached and where it is leading.

Basic Concepts

A working definition of bureaucracy has already been supplied in this chapter. Any economic discussion of the nature of bureaucracy is to a great extent a continuation of the discussion of the 'firm' or of economic organisation. Some of these topics were discussed in Chapter 3 where questions of the following kind were asked, 'why should a set of productive resources (including labour) be united through a rigid organisation (the firm), when cooperation via such resources across markets is conceivable?' This question, which was originally posed by Coase (1937), was developed by Alchian and Demsetz (1972) who stressed compliance by the cooperating factors (see also Stiglitz 1975). In these models of economic organisation, hierarchy and bureaucracy are seen as mechanisms for enforcing agreements and contracts and for securing compliance. Other models, such as the theory of teams (Marshak and Radner 1972), view bureaucracy as a group of individuals committed to the same goals. The information flows used in decision making processes become the focus of analysis in these models.

In this chapter we will look at a different class of models. We will abstract from the processes which take place within the 'black box' of the bureaucracy (organisation), leaving discussions of budgeting and resource allocation decision making to subsequent chapters. The approach adopted here will discuss a number of issues in the context of the equilibrium paradigm. In particular, a partial equilibrium approach will be used.

The Niskanen Model

To Niskanen, the public sector bureaucracy is a non profit making monopoly supplier which is financed wholly or in part from a periodic appropriation or grant. His specific interest in the study of bureaucracy is to find out how bureaucrats influence the efficiency of resource allocation and how bureaucracy compares, in efficiency terms, relative to other forms of economic organisation such as the *market* structures of perfect competition or monopoly.

Niskanen's starting point is to recognise the relevance of the personal preferences of the bureaucrats. 'Any theory of the behaviour of bureaus that does not incorporate the personal preferences of bureaucrats ... will be relevant only in the most rigidly authoritarian environments' (Niskanen 1971, p. 5). What, if anything, is it that motivates the bureaucrat; or to ask the same question as the economist does, what is it that the bureaucrat attempts to maximise? What are the arguments of his objective function? The initial response to this question is that the bureaucrat, like any other economic agent, will seek to maximise his personal utility. 'By itself this is not very helpful, but it does suggest that a bureaucrat will engage in purposive behaviour and that there are probably some elements in his utility *other than* the general welfare and interests of the state' (Niskanen 1971, p. 37).

By focusing upon the behaviour of bureaucrats, Niskanen is bringing together some of the earlier work of Downs (*op. cit.*) and Tullock (*op. cit.*). For Downs, bureaucrats are personal utility maximisers. Bureaucrats, 'in general have a complex set of goals, including the following elements: power, income, prestige, security, convenience, loyalty (to an idea, an institution, or the nation), pride in excellent work, and desire to serve the public interest (as the individual official conceives of it). However, different types of officials focus on smaller sets of these goals' (Downs 1967, p. 441). In particular, Downs (*op. cit.*) proceeded to identify the following groups of bureaucrats:

(a) *self interested officials:* are motivated by goals which benefit themselves rather than their bureaus or society at large. For example, 'climbers' maximise their own power, income, prestige etc. by engaging in strategies that will enhance their chances of promotion within the hierarchy. On the other hand, there are 'conserves' who promote the status quo and hence their existing prerogatives, income, power etc. Being more risk averse than the climbers, they fear that change will threaten their present income etc.

(b) *mixed motive officials:* combine self-interest and altruistic loyalty to larger values. 'Zealots' are loyal to narrow policies or concepts whereas 'advocates' are loyal to a broader set of policies or to a broader organisation. The advocates are impartial in judging the merits of various proposals within the organisation to which they are loyal. The 'statesmen' are loyal to the nation or society as a whole. This last group of bureaucrats are like those of the classical public administration text book, but still seek power and prestige, since they are assumed to enjoy having influence upon important policies.

Thus, the bureaucrat's utility function contains a large number of arguments which include: salary, perquisites of the office, public reputation, power, patronage, ease of managing the bureau and ease of making change. This formulation of the bureaucrat's utility function is identical to Williamson's (1964) theory of managerial discretion which was reviewed earlier in Chapter 3. Rather than working with such a complex specification of the bureaucrat's utility function, Niskanen collapses the whole analysis into the simple assumption that all the variables in the bureaucrat's utility function are a positive monotonic function of the total budget of the bureau. Two variables which are not, are the ease of managing the bureau and the ease of making change. These variables are reduced by increases in the budget.

Bureaucratic behaviour and the internal structure of bureaucracy cannot be explained without reference to the relationships between bureaucrats and their environment. The bureaucrat, like any maximising agent, behaves subject to a number of constraints. What are the constraints which are placed upon the size of budget which bureaucrats can secure? To answer this question we need to consider a bureau's relations with its sponsor organisation i.e. the agency which provides it with its funds.

The sponsoring organisation which finances public sector bureaus is a single collective organisation which is financed by tax revenues, borrowing and/or money creation. Examples of sponsors are the legislature or the government, with the Treasury being a special kind of bureau which acts as an intermediary that allocates funds to the other bureaus, whilst also facing them in a control relationship. Decisions to allocate funds are made by the elected representatives in the legislature i.e. Parliament in the UK, or Congress in the USA. The precise institutional details of this sponsor/bureau relationship will not detain us here. Suffice it to say that the sponsoring organisation is dependent upon a specific bureau supplying a given service, (but there might be some minor private sector alternative source of supply). The bureau on the other hand usually does not have an alternative source of finance to that provided by the sponsor. Given this two way dependency, the relationship which exists between the sponsor and bureau is best described as one of bilateral monopoly. For example, the Department of Education and Science is in this context a bureau and is more or less a monopoly supplier of its services. The sponsor is central government whose budget to the DES is approved by Parliament. The central government is a monopsonist in terms of purchasing education output.

A bilateral monopoly relationship is one of exchange. What is it, therefore, which is being exchanged between sponsor and the bureau? 'A bureau offers a promised set of activities and the expected output(s) of these activities for a budget. The primary difference between the exchange relation of a bureau and that of a market organisation is that a bureau offers a total output in exchange for a budget, whereas a market organisation offers units of output at a price' (Niskanen 1971, p. 25).

In any bilateral monopoly relationship the final outcome is indeterminate, since it depends upon the relative power and bargaining strengths of the two sides. On the one hand the sponsor does not have an alternative means of supply and on the other the bureau is dependent upon the sponsor for its budget. Who wins the game? A number of writers have suggested a variety of reasons why the bureau might come off best (see Downs 1967, Wildavsky 1964 and Niskanen 1971).

The world in which decisions are made differs sharply from the perfectly informed world of traditional economic theory. This is developed at some length in Chapter 4. Information is costly. It takes time and effort to obtain, process and comprehend data. Decision makers are constrained by their abilities to consider a large number of alternatives simultaneously. They are also limited in their computational facilities and their abilities to comprehend ('bounded rationality'). Given these constraints upon the decision making of the sponsor and given that the bureaucrat is often responsible for supplying the data for decision making, then the sponsor is often unaware of the finer details of what the budget he is supplying to the bureaucrat actually purchases in terms of services provided. In other words, the sponsor is unlikely to have sufficient information about the bureaus' cost function which will enable it to exercise effective administrative control. The sponsor will generally cope with this state of affairs by checking whether or not the outputs from the budget are 'good enough' i.e. 'satisficing' in terms of not losing too many votes. Thus, whilst bureau activities must meet the sponsor's minimal expectations, the informational constraints which are placed upon decision making grant a good deal of discretion to the bureaucrats.

The similarities between Niskanen's theory of bureaucratic behaviour and Williamson's theory of managerial discretion have been noted. Both theories grant discretionary powers to managers (bureaucrats) to allocate organisational resources to activities which will increase their personal utilities. This freedom or discretion depends upon the competitiveness of the environment and upon the constraints which managers face. A number of questions follow once managerial discretion is introduced into the analysis:

(i) what volume of the organisation's (bureaucracies') resources are available to the manager (bureaucrat) for such allocation?

(ii) how are these resources allocated and what are the effects upon the equilibrium level of output?

To answer these questions we will use Niskanen's explicit analysis. The elements of the analysis are as follows:

(a) *the Budget–Output Function* This is depicted in figure 5.1(a) and represents the maximum budget which the sponsor is willing to grant to the bureau for a given level of output, i.e.,

$$B = aQ - bQ^2; \qquad 0 \leqq Q < a/2b$$

where B = maximum budget the sponsor is willing to grant the bureau during a specific time period

Q = expected level of output.

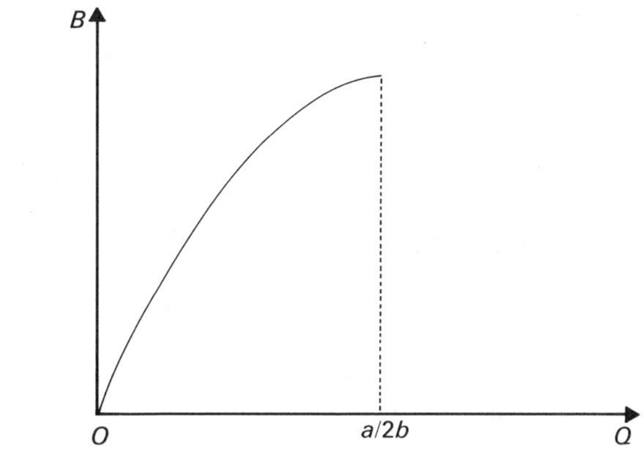

Figure 5.1(a) *Budget–Output Function*

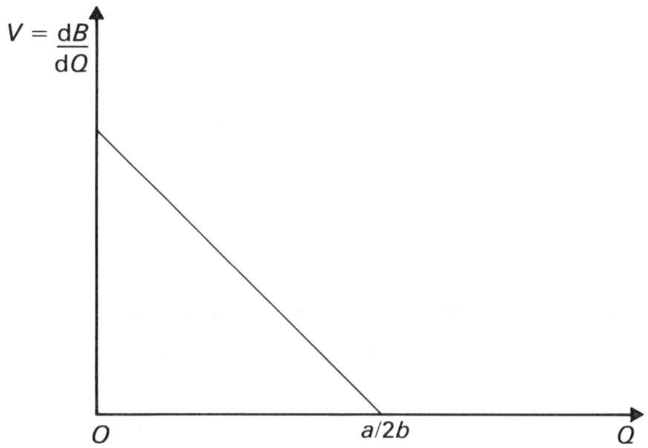

Figure 5.1(b) *Marginal Value Function*

(b) *the Marginal Valuation Function* This is shown in figure 5.1(b) and corresponds to the standard concept of demands i.e.

$$V = a - 2bQ\ , \qquad 0 \leqq Q < a/2b$$

where V = maximum 'price' per unit that the sponsor is willing to pay.

Since the preferences of governing politicians (i.e. the sponsors) are assumed to reflect accurately the preferences of all citizens/voters, the marginal valuation curve is taken to represent the *sum* of the citizens' marginal valuations of the bureaus' services.

Care should be taken when placing operational significance on these concepts. The marginal valuation function has no operational significance, since the bureau does not actually offer its services at a price. However, the function is relevant to the sponsor as a control device, especially if he can compare the supply price of the bureau with that of other market (private sector) firms. It should, however, be clear that there would be enormous problems involved in calculating a marginal valuation function in practice, since outputs are not tangible and alternative sources of supply are generally not available. The marginal valuation function is, therefore, a concept which has greater analytical than practical significance. This is especially true when we compare (analytically) the behaviour of a budget maximising bureau with the behaviour of profit maximising organisations. The budget–output function has greater practical significance since the bureau receives a *total* budget in exchange for a promise to produce an expected level of output. The sponsor does not purchase a specified number of units of output. Instead, the bureau receives the budget and then has discretion to allocate it to a number of activities over which the sponsor has little control.

(c) *Cost–Output Function* This function, which is shown in figure 5.2(a), represents the minimum payment to factor inputs necessary to produce a given output, assuming given input prices and level of technology, i.e.,

$$C = cQ + dQ^2, \qquad 0 \leqq Q$$

where C = minimum total payment (cost) to factors during a specific period.

(d) *Marginal Cost Function* This is simply the additions to total cost of producing one more unit of output and is shown in figure 5.2(b), i.e.,

$$\frac{\mathrm{d}C}{\mathrm{d}Q} = c + 2\mathrm{d}Q, \qquad 0 \leqq Q$$

where $\mathrm{d}C/\mathrm{d}Q$ is marginal cost.

The bureau's cost function is clearly sensitive to the factors which determine the prices of its inputs. Since bureaus are monopoly suppliers of services, they also tend to be the monopoly buyers of certain types of labour (skills) e.g. doctors, dentists, nurses, social workers, teachers, policemen, soldiers etc. In addition, the public sector bureaucracy can use its monopoly power to acquisition certain inputs at zero or near zero costs, e.g. compulsory purchase of inner city development land. This is shown in figures 5.2(a) and (b). If the bureau faces conditions of perfect competition in input markets, which means that by definition it cannot influence input prices, then the cost functions shown by the continuous line in figures 5.2(a) and (b) are relevant. For the case in which the bureau acts as a monopsonist the hatched lines are relevant.

The elements of Niskanen's model have now been set out. The next step is to put them all together and introduce the constraints. Bureaucrats maximise the total budget of their bureau, subject to the constraint that the

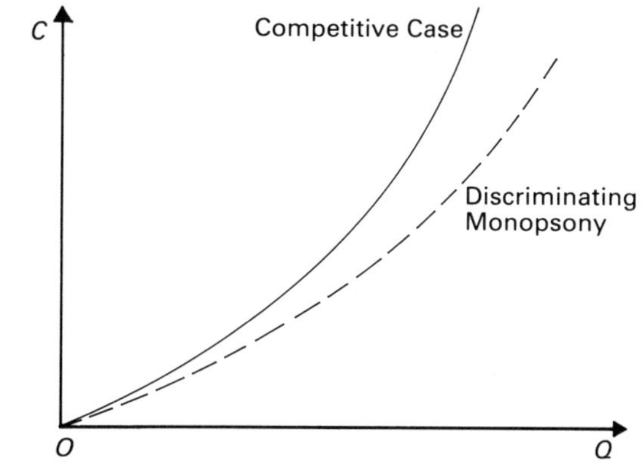

Figure 5.2(a) *Cost–Output Function*

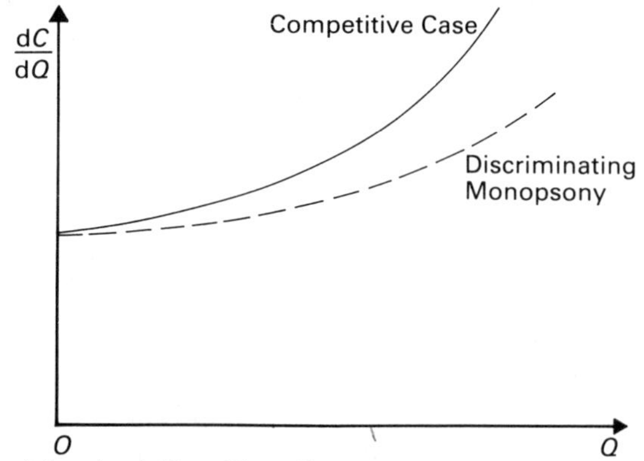

Figure 5.2(b) *Marginal Cost Function*

budget must be greater than or equal to the minimum total costs at the equilibrium output. That is,

$$B \geqq C$$

It will be recalled that,

$$B = aQ - bQ^2 \tag{1}$$

$$C = cQ + dQ^2 \tag{2}$$

Thus the maximum value of B is given by setting $\frac{dB}{dQ} = 0$

i.e. $\frac{dB}{dQ} = a - 2bQ = 0;$

therefore, $Q = \frac{a}{2b}$

This gives an upper bound on the value of $Q = a/2b$. To find the lower bound set $B = C$.

$$aQ - bQ^2 = cQ + dQ^2.$$

Divide throughout by Q. Then, after collecting terms:

$$a - c = Q(b + d)$$

Hence

$$Q = \frac{a - c}{b + d}$$

Thus, for an elementary bureau which buys factors in competitive markets, the equilibrium level of Q exists where:

$$Q \begin{cases} = \dfrac{a-c}{b+d} & \text{for } a < \dfrac{2bc}{b-d} \\ = \dfrac{a}{2b} & \text{for } a \geqq \dfrac{2bc}{b-c} \end{cases}$$

This is shown diagramatically in figure 5.3. The line V_1 represents the marginal valuation curve of the sponsors (i.e. demand curve) and the marginal cost curve is shown. What is the equlibrium size of the bureau? Equilibrium will occur at the point h, i.e. where $B = C$ and where $Q = (a_1 - c)/(b+d)$. The equilibrium output of the bureau is in the 'budget constrained' region. At this point the area $ea_1gh = ecfh$, i.e. the budget received equals total costs. There is no 'fat' in this budget and no *cost-effectiveness* analysis would reveal inefficiency.

The level of output is, however, greater than that which corresponds to the social optimum. In the latter case, the optimal level of output is k i.e. where marginal valuation = marginal costs. Thus it is readily seen that the equilibrium budget output h exceeds the socially optimal output k. At h, marginal costs (fh) exceed the marginal valuation (gh) of producing that level of output.

This analysis enables us to make a distinction between efficiency and optimality, a distinction which is developed in much greater depth in Chapter 7. In the budget-constrained equilibrium, a bureaus' behaviour is efficient since it produces outputs at minimum feasible costs and a cost effectiveness analysis would not reveal any inefficiency. The bureaus' behaviour is not, however, optimal, since the marginal costs of producing the equilibrium output exceed its marginal valuation. Consumer surplus ca_1m is used to expand output to h ($a_1cm = mfg$).

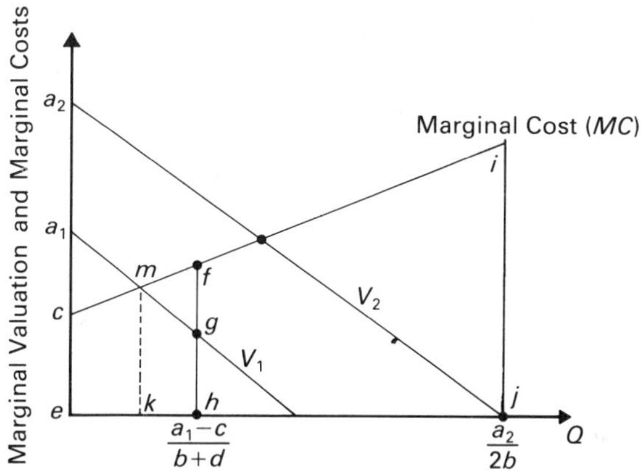

Figure 5.3 *The Equilibrium level of Q*

Consider now an increase in demand which moves the marginal valuation curve from V_1 to V_2. The maximum equilibrium output attainable for this budget is j (i.e. $a_2/2b$). In this case the output lies within the demand constrained region and $B > C$, i.e. $ea_2j > ecij$.

The budget received (i.e. the area under the demand curve) exceeds the costs of producing the level of output (j), which implies that there is 'fat' in the budget which could be eliminated through cost effective means. This 'fat' in the budget is consumed by the bureaucrat in the form of a large number of employees, higher salaries and perquisites etc.

In other words, there is a transfer of consumers' surplus to the bureaucrat in the form of an increase in output and a larger budget. This loss in consumer surplus is 'paid' to the bureaucrat as economic rent. Niskanen demonstrates that a bureau can supply an output which is up to two times as large as the rate of output of a competitive firm facing the same demand and cost conditions. Since all bureaus are assumed to behave in the same way, it follows that the size of the public sector and hence the amount of taxes paid will be up to *twice* the social optimum (see Appendix 1).

In summarising the Niskanen model the following are the essential points:

(a) bureaucrats obtain utility from larger budgets;
(b) bureaucrats possess both discretionary and monopoly powers;
(c) bureau outputs are greater than those which are socially optimal i.e. bureaus over-produce.

Critique of the Niskanen Model[1]

The basic conclusion derived from Niskanen's model that bureaucrats are free to choose the level of output, provided that total costs are covered by total revenues, must be looked at more closely. This result is derived from the assertion that bureaucrats have superior bargaining abilities relative to the sponsors who act as the trustees of the customers' interests. Superior bargaining abilities in turn arise from technical information superiority of the bureaucrats. However, technical information superiority 'has nothing to do with who gets to choose the output and the price in a transaction (Thompson 1973, p. 951). Rather, this factor determines the price *limits* in the bargaining relation. What then does determine who chooses the ruling prices and outputs in a bilateral monopoly relation? The answer is the relative power strengths of the two parties and this, in turn, depends upon the distribution of the decision making rights. A bureau deals with a single set of sponsors, whereas the sponsoring agency has to deal with a large number of bureaus. Thus, the relative costs to the sponsoring agency are likely to be great. But against this must be balanced the power of the sponsoring agency to replace any bureaucrat who refuses to comply with its demands and also the sponsor's power to fix the size of the budget at whatever level it requires.

Whilst the sponsor can fix the budget size, the bureau can adjust quantity and the quality of output by misrepresenting the costs of producing outputs. This situation, however, exists only if the sponsor has relatively little information about the production and cost functions of bureaus. This is an empirical question and in many democracies the legislature has review committees which monitor the activities of the various parts of the bureaucracy and carry out cost reviews etc. Whether or not the activities of review committees are effective in returning control over the choice of output to the legislature is an open question and is considered in more detail later in Chapters 7 and 8. The essential point to be made here is that Niskanen has granted too much power to the bureaus, without considering fully the nature of the constraints which they face.

From the above argument one can easily sense that the bureaucrat in the Niskanen model is all powerful. The sponsor is assumed to have very little power. However, this approach tends to wash out politics from the analysis and the influence of interest groups etc. on the choice of policies (i.e. outputs etc.). The politicians (sponsors) in the model are, in practice, under continuous pressure from sectional interests to change policies, improve services, reduce taxes etc. Are these decisions made by politicians or bureaucrats? Niskanen's model tends to pre-judge the issue. This specific question of where the decision making power lies is also considered later in Chapter 8. Having ignored the demand side and played up the supply side, Niskanen has unbalanced his theory. The upper limit to the budget implies an output where marginal valuation equals zero. At this point the median voter (assuming it is the median voter's demand curve which counts) would just as soon have no government spending, since he gets no surplus from the existence of government.

Since the bureau is producing twice as much output as the social optimum, consumer voters are in disequilibrium and will press for changes in the budget, via their elected representatives, provided that the marginal costs of such actions are less than the marginal benefits. Politicians interested in their re-election must pay attention to these demands for a smaller budget. This reduces the monopoly power of the bureaucrat in Niskanen's model and focuses attention onto the relative power strengths of the two sets of agents (politicians and bureaucrats) and the means of control which are available to politicians.

The analysis of bureaucracy and bureaucratic behaviour involves studying the objectives, incentives and constraints which influence bureaucrats. Niskanen has played up those arguments which expand the budget that bureaucrats demand. However, it should be remembered that there are other items in the bureaucrat's utility function which are inversely related to budget size. For example, the ease of administration and the amount of 'on the job leisure'. These factors are enhanced through smaller rather than larger budgets. Thus, there is a trade-off to be made by the bureaucrat. Should he strive for a larger budget which will increase his salary and his psychic income, or should he increase his ease of administration and his leisure through a smaller budget? Again, Niskanen has tended to pre-judge the issue in order to generate his desired result, namely that bureaus tend to over-produce. This result is, therefore, not general, but depends (amongst other things) upon the trade-offs of the arguments in the bureaucrat's utility function.

If one concentrates upon the incentives and constraints faced by bureaucrats, then this forces one to recognise the ethnocentricity of Niskanen's analysis. His model is the product of his own introspection and experiences as a bureaucrat operating within a particular institutional environment and within a specific culture at a single moment in time. Variations in the cultural and institutional settings, along with changes in the time period, will provide different conclusions. For example, it would appear from casual observation that the US bureaucrat of Niskanen's model is much more dynamic than his UK counterpart, who is more willing to forego increases in power at the margin (in terms of budget size) and to go more for a quiet life (i.e. on-the-job leisure). Moreover, if, as in the UK, the bureaucrat's salary, perquisites etc. are not related to budget size, then wherein lies the incentive for the bureaucrat to increase the size of his bureau? This question again requires us to know more about the trade-offs which the bureaucrat makes between the arguments within his utility function.

Thus the key elements to understanding the behaviour of bureaucrats in different cultural settings and in different time periods is to specify the objectives, incentives and constraints which they face. Niskanen has pointed us in the correct direction but has not through his partial equilibrium analysis framework, taken us far enough. The next stage of development must be to examine alternative incentive systems and constraints and to model more explicitly the demand side as an integral element of the analysis.

Finally, the economist's model of bureaucratic behaviour as embodied in Niskanen's analysis has come under attack from some political scientists, especially those in the UK tradition (see Kogan 1973). Kogan's criticisms can be paraphrased as follows:

(i) the economist's model has empirically unacceptable assumptions;
(ii) complex organisational patterns are left out of the economist's simple behavioural model. It ignores the non-economic factors which affect organisational behaviour e.g. values, technologies and organisational structures;
(iii) top UK civil servants, unlike many of their US counterparts, are not dependent upon politicians for their appointment or promotion;
(iv) economic motivation is secondary to understanding the behaviour of bureaucrats — budget maximisation does not make bureaucrats in the UK tick. Instead, UK civil servants are to be thought of as promoting their careers and this means aiming to be appointed to a senior position, either in the Treasury or the Cabinet Office. That is, they are aiming for departments where 'control rather than expansion is the ethic'.

Some of Kogan's criticisms have already been noted and amount to saying that an understanding of the effects of alternative incentive structures are important for any explanation of bureaucratic behaviour. Like Breton and Wintrobe (1975), Kogan's criticisms call into question the assumption that bureaucrats are budget maximisers. Niskanen (1971, p. 38) argued that such a maximand can only be used if, 'salary, perquisites of the office, public reputation, power, patronage, output of the bureau ... are a positive monotonic function of the total budget of the bureau during the bureaucrat's tenure in office'. However, this is clearly not the case in the UK. Moreover, Breton and Wintrobe have argued (1975, p. 204) that the salaries of bureaucrats are in many instances greater in smaller bureaus. Also, some bureaucrats are promoted because they are budget cutters. The US Secretary of Defence, James Schlesinger, made his reputation, while Head of the CIA, by substantially reducing the agency's personnel.[2] Again, this amounts to saying that to understand the behaviour of bureaucrats we need to understand the incentives that they face.

However, when criticising the economist's approach to the analysis of bureaucracy, many political scientists made the error of attacking the equilibrium paradigm for its lack of realism etc. without fully understanding the questions/issues which such an analysis seeks to answer. This general problem was noted in Chapter 3. Niskanen's analysis had the specific objective of comparing the equilibrium outputs of alternative organisational forms. He did not set out to provide a behavioural model of bureaucracy. Behavioural models are reviewed in the next chapter.

The Growth of Bureaucracy

In Chapter 1 it was noted that the public sectors of the major industrial powers had grown rapidly over the post-war period. Many explanations have been proposed to account for these trends.[3] How does the theory of bureaucracy fit into the existing set of explanations of public expenditure growth? Do we have, as yet, a sufficiently well-developed dynamic theory of bureaucratic behaviour? The straight answer is that our current knowledge does not permit us to make any firm conclusions. There are a number of factors which influence the demand for public services e.g. increases in real incomes and increases in the client group (population), whilst changes on the supply side include increases in factor input costs and increases in factor inputs due to deteriorating service environments, such as an increase in the crime rate in the case of police expenditure.

Whilst Niskanen's model concludes that bureau outputs might be up to twice those that would be produced under perfectly competitive conditions, it does not offer an explanation of *changes*. Outputs will rise if the marginal valuation curve shifts to the right, as in figure 5.3, or if there is an upward shift in the marginal cost curve. These explanations do not, however, depend upon any particular theory of bureaucracy.

A number of hypotheses about public expenditure growth can be advanced which assign an active role to bureaucrats:

(i) Bureaucrats may lobby for salary increases for public sector employees. Assuming no staff reductions following the pay award, budgets will rise.
(ii) Bureaucrats might join forces with specific pressure groups which advocate an expansion in the bureau's activities and hence its budget. Given the specialised information available to bureaucrats, they make valuable allies for pressure groups.
(iii) Bureaucrats as voters might support expansionary policies.

It should, however, be emphasised that the above are nothing other than hypotheses which remain to be tested. Further empirical analysis will hopefully provide some insights into how bureaucrats might influence the public expenditure growth process.

Empirical Studies of Bureaucracy

In this section a number of examples are provided which illustrate the economist's analysis of bureaucracy.

(a) *Serving the Elderly*

Sterne, Rabushka, and Scott (1972) argue that budget maximising bureaucrats will ensure that this year's budget is fully spent. This ensures an increase in next year's budget, but can also result in inefficient spending patterns. In their study of an agency which provided low cost meals for the elderly in Miami, Sterne, Rabushka and Scott (*op. cit.*) showed that the most needy were not the most important clients of the agency. Instead, the actual clients were those who allowed the bureaucrats to spend their allocated funds.

The *stated* purpose of the meal centres was to fulfil certain social service needs through the provision of low cost, dietically balanced hot lunches for aged persons. These needs were (a) economic assistance, (b) increase in health and (c) reduction in emotional distress. The *unstated* purpose in terms of the Niskanen model of bureaucracy is the maintenance, survival and expansion of the centres themselves. To achieve this objective, the lunch centres might provide lunch services to clients whether or not they are 'needy'.[4]

After a detailed analysis in a sample of the centres of those clients who were served with meals, the researchers concluded (p. 90) that 'there is no relationship ... between the serving of low cost meals and the designated social needs of the target clients. The stated purpose justifies the continuation of the centres and their funding, while the unstated but real purpose is the continution of the organisation by staff members whose chief concern is that the facilities be used. As a result, clients that do not need those services aid and abet the professional staff members (who apparently need their jobs)'.

If budgets are tied to the size of the client group and if bureaucrats have control over the eligibility of members of the population to join the client group, then budget maximising bureaucrats can promote public expenditure growth. The issue is that of designing the appropriate set of incentives.

(b) *Utility Maximisation at University*

One non-profit/non-market institution which will be well known to many readers is that of the university. In a recent study, Culyer (1970) has applied to universities a utility maximising model. State and public universities are not 'owned' by anyone in particular, thus the allocation of property rights is a complex issue, as too is the question of control over the allocation of resources inside the university. Culyer identifies three groups of utility maximising agents within the university. They are:

(a) administrators:
(b) teachers; and
(c) students.

At the same time, he also discusses the conflicts which result from the interactions of each set of utility maximising agents:

(a) conflict between administrators and teachers;
(b) conflict between teachers and students; and
(c) conflict between administrators and students.

To understand the basis of the conflicts it is worthwhile reminding ourselves of the basic purpose of a university, which is to produce (jointly) research output and instruction to graduate and undergraduate students. Each group of agents is assumed to engage in activities which will maximise its respective utility. However, since UK universities are not constrained to make profits, there exists a great deal of discretion for university 'managers' to obtain 'on-the-job sources of utility', since the costs of doing so are lower than they would be if the university faced a profit constraint. It is, therefore, predicted that there will be an increase in the consumption of such components of their utility functions:

> Pretty secretaries tend to be substituted for efficient ones, solid mahogany desks for veneered, and so on ... Some of the testable implications of this theory are ... far more sinister, as for example when inefficient white employees are substituted for efficient black ones. In universities similar behaviour is predicted: the office furnishings of administrators will tend, on average, to be luxurious compared with those of academics; labour intensive teaching techniques are retained though in many cases productivity could be increased with more capital intensive methods, especially of lecturing.
>
> (Culyer 1970, p. 353)

The conflicts arise because, '... in the absence of institutional constraints on the utility maximising controllers of higher educational resources which compel them to economise on certain sources of utility (which may be disutilities to others such as students), they will impose non-price taxes on students which are not subject to the negotiability of prices via usual exchange procedures' (Culyer 1970, p. 366).

In this paper Culyer does not provide empirical evidence in support of his interesting hypotheses. Casual empiricism does, however, tend to support some of his claims, whilst at the same time it challenges others. There is no doubt that cost savings (i.e. costs per student) could be effected by employing less labour-intensive teaching methods. The effects upon quality of output and upon productivity are, however, more debatable. It is not clear that there is such a strict division between academics and administrators as Culyer supposes. Frequently, resource allocation and budgeting decisions are made in universities by committees made up entirely of academics, with administrators playing a minor role. This issue of budgeting and the politics involved is discussed again in Chapter 6.

(c) *The Regulation of Public Sector Sources of Pollution*

In the literature relating to externalities and environmental pollution, economists have for many years argued the case for a heavy reliance of pricing incentives for environmental protection. Applying the 'polluter pays' principle forces producers to internalise the costs which they impose on society. The imposition of effluent charges, fees, prices etc. adjusts the set of relative prices, thereby allowing the system to move towards the optimum (i.e. achieve the target pollution standard) at minimum costs. Using price adjustment is preferred to adopting and trying to enforce a system of regulations which polluters will then try to circumvent. This analysis is, however, based upon the assumption of profit maximising firms and is weakened when the analysis is extended to the behaviour of public sector agencies which are themselves polluters.

The issue of the public sector as a major source of pollution is one which has been recently analysed by Oates and Strassman (1978). They show that many public sector agencies in the USA have been resistant to the public sector's own regulatory activities regarding pollution abatement and set out to answer the question, 'could the extension of effluent fees to public agencies prove more effective than direct controls in inducing pollution abatement efforts?' To answer their question Oates and Strassman use the Niskanen model of bureaucracy to predict the likely response of bureaucrats to a system of effluent fees.

In figure 5.4, the output of the bureau is shown along the horizontal axis. The curve MC_1 is the bureau's marginal cost curve. Suppose that the production activities of the bureau involve a negative externality and that a unit fee is imposed upon such spill-over costs. The fee shifts the bureau's marginal cost curve from MC_1 to MC_2 and the bureau's output falls from OB to OC (in both cases the bureau is operating in the cost constrained region). Oates and Strassman then suppose that there exists a less polluting technology such that abatement costs are less than the effluent charge, given by MC_3. The bureaucrat will shift to the alternative technology because the

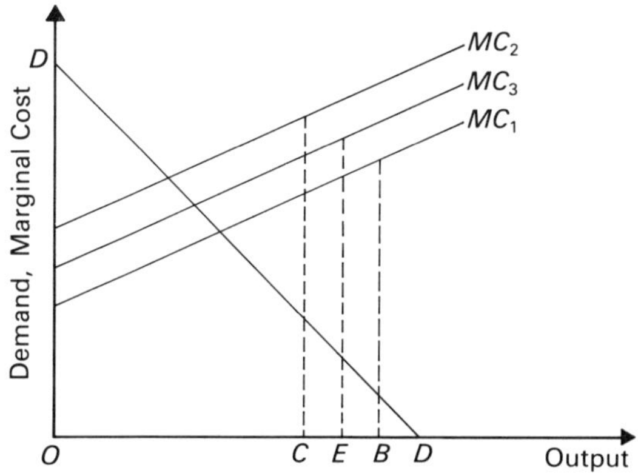

Figure 5.4 *Response of Bureaucrats to a System of Effluent Fees*

savings in the costs of effluents will allow an expansion in output from *OC* to *OE*.

The above results assume a cost constrained bureau which acts in the same way as a cost minimising firm i.e. the bureau will save on fees by adopting less polluting methods of production. What are the results for a demand constrained bureaucrat? In this case the results are not unambiguous. For example, the bureau might absorb the fees within some of its 'fat', in which case the fees, as a cost, are substituted for other cost elements and the effluent fees will be unable to induce a reduction in bureau output. On the other hand, the bureaucrat might have an incentive to economise on fees in order to allocate the 'fat' in the budget to utility increasing items, rather than to effluent fees. In this case output will fall as a result of the effluent fee.

The effect of effluent fees on the behaviour of bureaus depends, therefore, upon whether or not the bureau is cost or demand constrained and then if it is demand constrained, upon whether or not the bureaucrat responds by substituting items of fat in the budget for the effluent fee costs.

It has, however, already been noted that the simple discriminating monopoly model of the bureaucrat is probably misleading to the extent that bureaucrats are not as powerful as the Niskanen model suggests (Breton and Wintrobe 1975). Moreover, Migue and Belanger (1974) have argued that utility maximising bureaucrats are not, as Niskanen supposed, necessarily budget maximising if, for example, the increase in budget size comes at the expense of other utility enhancing items such as a quiet life. Developing this argument, Oates and Strassman employ a bureaucratic utility function which includes the bureau's output (Q) and the level of perks (P), derived from the 'fat' in the bureau's budget. Thus:

$$U = u(Q, P) \tag{1}$$

The bureau has a straightforward production function:

$$Q = Q(L, E) \tag{2}$$

where L = labour inputs and
E = waste emissions.

If output is held constant, then emissions can be reduced only if more labour is employed to recycle wastes. The bureau's budget constraint is given by:

$$B = wL + fE + cP \tag{3}$$

where B = bureaus' budget;
w = competitive wage rate;
f = effluent charge per unit of waste; and
c = cost of a 'unit' of perks.

The straightforward optimising solution would be to maximise equation (1), the utility function, subject to the constraints in equations (2) and (3). This, however, leaves out of the analysis the process of budget determination. Oates and Strassman assume that the bureau makes an agreement with the legislature to produce some specified level of output over the short term (Q_0) for some fixed level of budget funding (B_0). This means that for the budgetary period, Q_0 and B_0 can be assumed to be fixed. Having specified the problem in this form the bureaucrat's problem then becomes one of maximising his perks subject to the production and budget constraints. This is solved by forming the Lagrangian:

$$M = P + \lambda_1[Q_0 - Q(L,E)] + \lambda_2[B_0 - wL - fE - cP] \tag{4}$$

where λ_1 and λ_2 are the Lagrangian multipliers. From this it follows that

$$\frac{MP_E}{MP_L} = \frac{f}{w}$$

i.e. utility maximising bureaucrats behave in the same way as a cost minimising firm and will use a combination of factor inputs, such that the ratio of marginal products is equal to the ratio of factor prices. After the budget and output levels have been determined by the legislature, the bureaucrat maximises his perks by searching out the least-cost method of producing Q_0. The utility maximising bureaucrat is a cost minimiser with respect to pollution abatement activities and behaves in the same way as does the cost minimising firm. Within the specific context of their analysis this result allows Oates and Strassman to extend the 'Baumol–Oates cost minimisation theorem' to a system composed of both cost minimising firms and public agencies.

> In an economy consisting of cost minimising firms and utility maximising bureaus, the selection of the appropriate unit tax on waste emissions applicable both to firms and bureaus will lead to the achievement of the designated standard of environmental quality (necessary reduction in aggregate waste emissions) at the least cost to society.
>
> (Oates and Strassman 1978, p. 289).

Conclusions

In this chapter we have reviewed the economist's equilibrium paradigm as it has been applied to the analysis of bureaucratic decision making. The analysis is relatively new and speculative, and awaits exhaustive empirical testing. Despite these qualifications, the approach has already demonstrated that it can be usefully employed to analyse *a priori* issues such as whether or not effluent taxes might be more or less efficient compared to regulatory policies as a means of reducing polluting activities by public bureaus. As was noted in Chapter 3, the equilibrium paradigm allows the analyst to make qualitative predictions, whilst at the same time it structures the problem in such a way that the relevant *economic* issues are highlighted.

The Niskanen model of bureaucracy is founded on two basic premises. First, that the objective of the bureaucrat is to maximise the size of his budget. Second, that the bureau exchanges some agreed level of output for a budget which equals the total value of the output to the public. It follows that the bureau is in essence a perfectly discriminating monopolist, since whatever level of output it provides the bureau will appropriate all of the consumer's surplus. This original simple model has been questioned by Thompson (1973), Migue and Belanger (1974) and Breton and Wintrobe (1975). Given the bilateral monopoly relationship between the bureau and its sponsor it is clear that any results of this type of analysis will be sensitive to the specification of how budgets are actually made and how much effective discretion bureaucrats have in practice. These issues are developed in greater detail in the chapters which follow.

Appendix 1

Following the approach set out in the text of the chapter

$$C = cQ + dQ^2$$

and $$B = aQ - bQ^2$$

when $C = B$ (i.e. the budget constrained region)

$$\text{then } Q = \frac{a - c}{b + d}$$

The social optimum occurs when marginal valuation equals marginal costs, i.e. where:

$$\frac{\mathrm{d}B}{\mathrm{d}Q} = \frac{\mathrm{d}C}{\mathrm{d}Q}$$

i.e. $$\frac{\mathrm{d}B}{\mathrm{d}Q} = a - 2bQ$$

and $$\frac{\mathrm{d}C}{\mathrm{d}Q} = C + 2dQ$$

Thus, at the social optimum:

$$a - 2bQ = c + 2\,dQ$$

or $$Q = \frac{1}{2}\,\frac{a - c}{b + d}$$

This is half the output of the maximum equilibrium budget.

Notes

1 This critique is gleaned from a number of sources including Thompson (1973), Migue and Belanger (1974), Hettich (1975), Breton (1974) and Breton and Wintrobe (1975). In addition, I have benefited from a seminar on the 'Economics of Bureaucracy' provided by Alan Peacock at the University of Leicester 1978.

2 See Breton and Wintrobe (1975) page 205.

3 See Brown and Jackson (1978) for a summary of the alternative theories of public expenditure growth.

4 Stated in this way the approach is similar to that of the functionalists who argue that the set of activities is directed at system maintenance.

CHAPTER 6

Budgets and Bureaucrats

If politics is regarded in part as conflict over whose preferences shall prevail in the determination of national policy, then the budget records the outcome of this struggle. If one asks, 'who gets what the government has to give?' then the answers for a moment in time are recorded in the budget. If one looks at politics as a process by which the government mobilises resources to meet pressing problems, then the budget is a focus of these efforts.

(Wildavsky 1964, p. 4)

Introduction

A budget is more than a financial statement. It is instead a record of how real resources (expressed in money terms) will be or have been allocated to different activities. If organisations are viewed as political coalitions, budgets are mechanisms through which subunits bargain over conflicting goals, make side payments and try to motivate one another to accomplish their objectives.[1] Thus, a budget records, for example, a society's preference for peace over war, for the elimination of poverty and ill health and the pursuit of cultural activities such as education and the arts. Budgets are the translation of policies (outputs) into financial terms. Hence, to a political scientist, budgets are a useful means of studying policy formation.

Throughout earlier chapters it has been emphasised that there are a number of different issues associated with the allocation and distribution of scarce resources. If a particular allocation and distribution of resources is to be explained and accounted for, then a number of purely economic factors such as the relative price and income elasticities of demand for the different commodites will be relevant in the account provided. However, other elements of the decision making or allocation *process* will also be of relevance and interest. For example, there is the question of how much information about the relative benefits and costs was available to the decision maker at the time the decision was made. Then there is the nature of the decision and allocation process itself. If individuals are competing with one another for scarce resources their ability to succeed in such competitions will depend upon their relative strengths, as reflected in their purchasing power, and their command over information and key organisations variables, (i.e. general power).

The concept of the budget and the budgeting process enables us to bring together many of the ideas that have been built up in the earlier chapters. Resource allocation is *not* the passive mechanical response of economic agents to external stimuli as is frequently depicted in the economists' 'black box' models. Rather, resource allocation and budgeting are replete with drama and excitement as competitors vie with one another for scarce resources. To understand who gets what and why they get what they do, requires that we adopt both a positive and a behavioural perspective to the analysis of budgets.

Moreover, just as the 'market', as a social institution for allocating resources, has served to focus the attention of much of economics, so too does the 'budget' act in a similar way by concentrating the attention of those interested in *non-market resource allocation mechanisms*. The questions we ask are: where do budgets come from; how are they formed; what is the relationship between a budgetary intention (*ex ante*) and the final budget outcome (*ex post*);[2] what budgetary rules do decision makers follow and where did these rules originate; why do they follow one set of rules rather than another; how do decision makers perceive and interpret budgetary rules? This is a selection of the questions which help us to open up the 'black box' of the non-market resource allocating processes which lie behind budgets. It should, however, be realised that such an approach complements the more traditional approach of the applied economist and is not in competition with it as a radical alternative. The economist is typically interested in equilibrium, the relationships between a limited number of specific variables such as prices and quantities, and wishes to say something about long-run general tendencies. The behavioural approach, however, is more concerned with the short-run relationships which exist between agents who make decisions about budgets.

In this chapter the short-run behavioural approach to the study of budget determination will be explored. The longer-run equilibrium approach of the economist is reviewed in Chapter 3. Throughout this chapter we will maintain a theme which runs right through the whole book, namely that to understand how resources are allocated and distributed in non-market settings requires that we pay particular attention to concepts such as power distribution, information distribution and process.

Politics and the Budgetary Process

Politics is defined as conflict over whose preferences are to count in the determination of public policies. An examination of the composition of the public budgets of any country will reveal that, within the total budget, expansion in spending has not been uniform between programmes. The questions which are forced out of this observation are: what factors determine the relative expansion of different programmes, and who (or what) determines national priorities? To answer questions of this kind political scientists have taken the budgetary process as the object of analysis, since 'the budgetary process, the most important "action forcing" mechanism in government, reflects the aspirations and controversies which cause some programmes to be favoured over others' (Natchez and Bupp 1973, p. 951). Within the budgetary process, clashes of interest and priorities are expressed in financial terms. There are many individuals who can influence the budgetary outcome: e.g. voters (clients), politicians and bureaucrats.

Different writers focus upon different facets of the budgetary process. For example, Wildavsky and those of the 'incremental budgeting school' are interested in exploring the way in which bureaucratic chiefs and politicians interact in determining budgets. The early writings of Buchanan and Tullock, and Downs, on the other hand, tend to concentrate upon the interactions between voters and politicians, leaving bureaucrats out of the picture. Another literature, essentially cost–benefit analysis, explores decision making techniques and leaves all behavioural aspects out of the analysis. Each of these approaches is partial, which means that on its own the conclusions may not be of universal applicability.

A more general approach to the analysis of the politics of budgeting is, therefore, likely to take into account the interactions of all of the agents who play a role in the process, i.e. voters, politicians, pressure groups and bureaucrats.

A political approach to the budgetary process raises a number of questions: (a) who holds the power to influence decisions about resource allocation; (b) how do individuals gain property rights to that power; (c) which group has effective power[3] to influence budgetary outcomes — is it voters, politicians or bureaucrats; (d) is power normatively allocated in the system i.e. how effective is the system of control? All of these questions will not be answered in this chapter. Issues raised about control of the budgetary process are reviewed in Chapter 8.

Studies of the politics of the budgetary process have been produced by Dahl (1961) and Sayre and Kaufman (1960). Dahl's study examined budget decision making in New Haven, Connecticut. He found that few people in the external community had sufficient power to influence budget decisions and that a power elite, within the organisation, exerted power in almost all decision areas. In their study, Sayre and Kaufman (1960) viewed decision making as a conflict process between politicians, bureaucrats and pressure groups, with the latter including client groups as well as public sector employees. Whilst general case studies of this kind abound in the literature, more recent studies have tended to concentrate upon the formulation of budget requests by bureaus and the legitimisation of such requests by the legislature. These studies are found in the incremental model of budgeting.

The Incremental Model of Budgeting

Incrementalism refers to a particular view of the budget decision making process. That view can be stated simply: in the end what happens during any given period determines what will happen in future periods. In budgetary terms it is expressed as, 'this year's budget is a function of the amount spent last year i.e. last year's budget'. Incrementalism, therefore, refers to a simple budgetary rule and is derived from the observation that, 'once enacted a budget becomes a precedent: the fact that something has been done before vastly increases the chances that it will be done again' (Wildavsky 1975, p. 4). Budgets are not written from scratch each year and it would be foolish to think that they were. However, such observations are by themselves of limited interest. The deeper question is, why do decision makers follow an incremental rule rather than others? It is this question which will occupy our attention. The intellectual basis of the incremental model of budgeting is to be found in the works of Dewey (1933), Barnard (1938) and Simon (1965). It is an application of the satisficing and bounded rationality decision models reviewed in Chapter 4. As a theory of budgeting, incrementalism is often thought to stand in contra-distinction to that of the economist's 'means–ends model' of unbounded rationality. The incrementalist model has been popularised and developed in the works of Lindblom (1959), Wildavsky (1964, 1968, 1975), Dahl (1961), Dye (1966), Fenno (1966) and Braybrooke and Lindblom (1963). Empirical studies of incrementalism are to be found in Davis, Dempster and Wildavsky (1966, 1974), Crecine (1970), Heclo and Wildavsky (1974) and Sharkansky and Hofferbert (1969).

Incrementalism, as a model of public sector budget decision making, grew out of the related topics of political science, decision analysis and the analysis of policy making. Discontented with the prescriptive approach to budgeting contained in the economists' synoptic[4] or unbounded rationality models, writers within the incrementalist tradition set out to establish a positive and behavioural model of budget decision making. This led them to a behavioural view of budget decision making as an intra-organisational *process* characterised by conflict and competition over scarce resources. Such an approach emphasises the politics of the budgetary process, identifies the principal actors and the strategies they adopt, and regards the budget as an outcome of the interplay of these forces. In other words, the incrementalist or behavioural framework used in the study of budget decision making belongs to the political economy paradigm of non-market decision making, which was discussed in earlier chapters. A budget is thus the outcome of a bargaining process between a large number of economic agents, which include politicians, voters and bureaucrats. One way of studying and hence understanding how resources come to be allocated and distributed to competing activities is to study these bargaining/political processes.

It will be recalled that the unbounded rationality/satisficing model of decision making assumes that individuals do not consider the full range of possible alternatives, do not possess complete information, do not have well defined objectives and tend to accept solutions to problems which are found to be acceptable, defined in terms of their aspiration levels. Lindblom (1959) in his classic study of decision making, or 'muddling through' as he prefers to call it, described the process of making choices as a set of 'disjointed incremental' strategies which are decided upon the basis of comparing a limited number of alternatives without any attempt at total comprehensiveness. Lindblom believes that it is the strategy of disjointed incrementalism which characterises the behaviour of the policy making process of all the major political institutions in democratic polyarchal systems, in which the decision maker faces complexity and ambiguity. By 'muddling through' as best they can, administrators make only marginal changes to what they are doing. They rarely depart significantly from what they are doing, with the result that budgets are extremely stable from one year to the next.

The first problem which has to be solved is, given the large number of semi-autonomous decision points within the system (i.e. the disjointedness), how are these decisions coordinated? The second pertinent question is, why do decision makers use the incremental rule?

Lindblom (1965) and Braybrooke and Lindblom (1963) address themselves to the issue of the coordination individuals, by using the notion of *partisan mutual adjustment* (PMA), which is defined as an adaptive or manipulative process through which partisan decision makers can coordinate with one another 'without anyone coordinating them, with a common dominant purpose, and without rules which fully prescribed their relations to each other' (Lindblom 1965, p. 3). The features of PMA are, therefore, the absence of cooperation between decision makers, the absence of agreed-upon criteria to govern mutual adjustment. PMA is compared with 'centrality' in which there exists a set of decision makers, such that one of the decision makers has a symmetric, dominating control relationship with all others. The central decision maker uses this relationship to adapt and coordinate the total set of decisions in order to achieve some common objective.

In the fluid pluralistic system of PMA, policy makers advocate and pursue their own specialised interests in a disjointed fashion such that, 'adverse consequences of any one decision for other decisions in the set are to a degree and in some cases frequently avoided, reduced, counterbalanced or outweighted' (Braybrooke and Lindblom 1963, p. 154). Disjointed incrementalism and PMA are not confined to the literature on public sector budgeting. Similar approaches have been used in the area of economic development by Hirshman and Lindblom (1961) who tie together Lindblom's notion of disjointed incrementalism to Hirshman's ideas of unbalanced growth in economic development.

Why do decision makers use incrementalism as a decision rule? To answer this question, the following facets of the problem will be discussed: (a) complexity, (b) objectives and motives and (c) aids to calculation.

Complexity

The real world is complex and decision makers are frequently at a loss as to how to handle the complexity of the phenomena that they have to deal with.[5] This point was emphasised in Chapter 4. Decision makers often tend to find themselves either with too much data, or too little data, or with imprecise and ambiguous data. If they have too much data they have the problem of sorting the data out into that which is relevant and that which is irrelevant for the decisions to be made. The social system in which decision makers operate is, moreover, subject to change, so that it is conceivable that in some instances, by the time it takes the decision maker to understand and model the system, it will have changed so much as to make the model redundant and inappropriate for the problem that has to be solved.

In the face of this complexity, decision makers simplify and employ aids in order to understand the complexity — a point which we will return to presently.

Objectives and Motives

As in behavioural models of decision making, which were reviewed in Chapter 4, the incremental model assumes that budget decision makers satisfice rather than maximise. Given the pressure of demand on their time and other resources, decision makers set up standards of 'good enough' and accept the first alternative which satisfies that criterion. This choice rule is easier to follow, since it does not require the decision maker to set up and search out all alternatives.

Aid to Calculation

The limited capacity of individuals to comprehend complexity leads them to simplify. They bound their rationality, satisfice and use simple aids to calculation. One such aid is incrementalism, i.e. budgets are seldom reviewed as a whole. Budgets are not prepared on the basis of comparing on-going programmes with all possible alternatives, as would be the case, for example, in zero base budgeting. Incrementalism is history dependent and budgetary decisions proceed from an existing base. The base is not actively reviewed each year. It is, instead, deviations from the base (i.e. marginal increases or decreases) which are reviewed.

In order to appreciate why decision makers employ aids to calculation, we will extend the analysis of decision making which was set out earlier in Chapter 4. Complexity arises from a number of sources: (a) problems of incomplete data and information; (b) problems of uncertainty; and (c) problems of valuation.

If we regard the definition of data and information in the widest possible sense, then information will include the contextual knowledge of decision makers. That is, information on the relationships between key instrumental variables and information about the consequences of alternative courses of action. The problem which faces a decision maker, who is confronted by complexity, is that by definition either the data are not readily available, or the data could only be made available at a very high cost. The raw data for decision making and model building come from two principal sources. First, there is the logical or analytical *a priori* data generated by the individual himself. Second, there is the empirical data fed into the *a priori* model, which allows the decision maker to determine the appropriate values of the parameters in his system.

The description so far has been that of the standard decision making model. But the reality of most decision making situations places severe constraints upon the standard model. First, the decision maker has a limited capacity for computation. His logical and deductive powers are often limited, relative to the nature of the complex environment which he has to cope with. Thus, his *a priori* models are a pale reflection of the reality which they are supposed to represent. Second, given any *a priori* model, no matter how good it is, the choice of a preferred strategy requires computation. Moreover, the implementation of a preferred strategy requires computation. Computation requires the expenditure of real resources in terms of man-hours working on the problem and calculating machines and computers. These computation costs are an element of the more general decision costs desribed in Chapter 4. Given these costs, ideal search and choice procedures are seldom feasible. In terms of the language introduced in Chapter 4, the decision makers' rationality is bounded.

In order to cope with the problems created by uncertainty, the decision maker adopts 'aids to calculation' such as rules of thumb. The decision maker simplifies, ignores complicated parts of the problem and deals only with those parts of the problem with which he is familiar. He will tend to go for 'experiential budgeting', if the problem is of great magnitude, making only the roughest of guesses while he lets experience accumulate. Moreover, he depends upon feedback from his decisions to gauge their consequences.

Problems of complexity are compounded by uncertainty or total ignorance of future events, which will include the consequences of present decisions. This in turn presents problems for the evaluation of alternatives.

In summary, the behavioural perspective upon which incrementalism is based assumes that the decision maker is, 'a man with limited information and limited cognitive ability making a policy choice in an uncertain world by drastically simplifying the problem and making marginal adjustments in past successful policies to formulate current policies' (Crecine 1969, p. 11).

Given this background, which is drawn from the analysis of decision making, how are public budgets determined and what is the decision making process underlying them? These questions are now considered.

A large number of individuals and groups of individuals, all of whom represent different interests, participate in budgetary decision making which is a multi-stage process. At some time during the annual budget cycle, bureaucrats advocate their budget for the next year by making a budget request. These requests are scrutinised and discussed by the legislature (politicians), who may consider the requests with or without the consultative guidance of the executive or the financial control bureau of the executive (e.g. the Treasury or its equivalent). It is generally recognised that the full-time members of the bureaucracy possess more contextual knowledge about the substantive content of the budget requests than do the members of the legislature who serve on the sub-committee(s) which scrutinise and ultimately sanction the request. Why should this be so? Essentially, it arises because the bureaucrat has, first, a working knowledge of the relationships which exist between the expenditures contained in the budget and the policy outcomes which these expenditures will purchase; second, the bureaucrat has an understanding (no matter how incomplete) of the relationships between the activities performed by his department and the ultimate policy outcomes. In other words, the bureaucrat has a greater understanding of his departments' production function. For the majority of cases, the members of the legislature do not have the specialist knowledge required to challenge the information contained in the budget request. This implies that a great deal of trust[6] exists between bureaucratic chiefs who are making budget requests, and those in the legislature who grant them their budgets. Clearly, such a relationship can produce problems for the control of public spending, problems that are considered in greater detail in Chapter 8.

Having studied the way in which the legislature cope with the problems created by complexity, the lack of specialised information and uncertainty, Wildavsky (1964), Braybrooke and Lindblom (1963) *et al.* conclude that the prime aid to calculation is that of incrementalism:

> Budgets are almost never actively reviewed as a whole in the sense of considering at once the value of all existing programmes as compared with all possible alternatives. Instead, this year's budget is based on last year's budget with special attention given to a narrow range of increase or decrease.
>
> (Davis, Dempster and Wildavsky 1966, p. 529)

Thus incrementalism suggests that the greatest part of any budget is a product of previous decisions. This is similar in essence to Cyert and March's (1963) notion that the budgetary process is 'history dependent'. Incrementalism is more than an aid to calculation. Ultimately it becomes a theory of the way in which budgets are determined:

> because most of the budget is a product of previous decisions the largest determining factor of the size and content of this year's budget is last year's budget ... The budget is thus like an iceberg. By far the largest part of it is below the surface, outside the control of anyone.
>
> (Wildavsky 1973, p. 89)

The conclusion, that budgets in any particular year are dependent upon decisions taken in previous periods, is not surprising. Long-range commitments have financial or resource consequences for future budgets as the budget plan unfolds. The bulk of expenditures and resources are allocated to the maintenance of the existing system. Thus, public sector employees' contracts are not re-negotiated each year; schools, hospitals and other public buildings are maintained and will continue to be from one year to the next. The budgetary decision does not begin with a *tabula rasa*. It is not comprehensive. In other words, budgeting is incremental; existing programmes and commitments are in the main continued and are expanded (or contracted) in both real and monetary terms; and new programmes are introduced slowly. By concentrating on the margin (the increment) and what goes into the margin by way of resources, decision makers reduce the size of the problem which comprehensive zero based budgeting would present. Moreover, it is easier to think in terms of percentages than in terms of absolute amounts. Typically, the kind of question asked is, 'by what percentage has this year's budget increased or decreased on last year's?'

What evidence exists to support the notion of incrementalism? If the budget rules of different countries are examined, then it would appear that they conform to the incrementalist's rule of thumb. Since 1955 France has had what is referred to as the 'service vote'. That is, all past expenditures are treated as a continuing commitment. The French parliament only votes on additions to and subtractions from past totals. In Japan, the Ministry of Finance imposes a 125% ceiling on the previous year's expenditures and when voting on next year's budget plans past expenditures are never challenged or questioned. Finally, in the UK, the Public Expenditure Survey Committee (PESC) in drawing up the medium term public expenditure plan, which is presented to Cabinet and finally to Parliament in the form of a public expenditure White Paper, would find it difficult to enable an individual department to include in its budget request new items which will cause large increases in the size of its budget over a five year period.

There are, of course, many other aids to calculation at lower levels in the decision making process, which try to ensure that future expenditure will only marginally deviate from that of the past. These include the imposition of cash limits, which were introduced in the UK in 1976 as an attempt to obtain greater control of public spending, the scrutiny of tax rate increases, and the control dates on which capital projects will start.

Incrementalism also recognises that decision making is usually sequential rather than simultaneous.[7] This compares with the neoclassical models of economics and much of decision theory in which a general solution to a problem is found by solving all parts of the system simultaneously. Problem solving, however, in reality tends to be serial and decision making tends to be incremental. Lindblom (1965), in his discussion of the coordination of non-market systems, adds another dimension which follows from the serial nature of problem solving. That is, decision making tends to be fragmented, by which he means, prior decisions and those which follow are, in some systems, regarded as if they were independent of one another. For example, a set of decisions is made on a new housebuilding programme on the outskirts of a city. That decision will have important implications for decisions made in other parts of the system, such as street lighting, road building, water services and sewage services, plus the siting of schools, health centres and fire stations etc. If the decisions are indeed fragmented and uncoordinated, as Lindblom suggests they are, then it follows that one set of decisions could act as a severe constraint upon subsequent decisions. It follows, therefore, that the *order* in which decisions are made and implemented will be important in determining the nature of the final outcome of a series of inter-related decisions and also the transactions and decision costs involved in the implementation process.[8]

Organisations are frequently thought of as complex structures of roles. These roles, it was argued in Chapter 2, are sets of expectations about the behaviour of the role occupant. Whilst the role occupant will, as in a theatrical production, interpret the role and play it out in his own way, there are limits to this,[9] so that the essential expectations associated with each role are independent of the role occupant. Within an organisation certain expectations exist with respect to the budgetary process, especially expectations about the rules which budget makers will follow when making budget decisions. These expectations are over and above those such as that 'the level of expenditure granted in previous years will be maintained next year and will probably be increased'. Expectations about budgetary rules are part of the folklore or mythology which surround the budget. For example, it may be an implicit expectation that those who make budget requests will not ask for too much, because if they do they will expect to get less than if they had made a moderate request. This is contrasted with the rule, 'if you don't ask for enough then it is assumed that you don't need the funds (resources)'. Departments within an organisation are the advocates of their own expenditures, but those drawing up the budget request come under pressure from a number of quarters. First, there are the internal expectations from lower rank executives that their chief executive will argue, on their behalf, for increased funds to enable them to carry out their activities adequately and to increase their salaries and the non-financial arguments of their managerial utility function. Lower level executives' views are that their department's expenditure is only a small part of the total budget, so that any substantial increase in their budget will have an insignificant impact upon the total. The chief executive, however, will have his own set of expectations and these will often relate to external factors. For example, one decision rule which the chief executive might follow is, 'come in a little high (padding) but not too high (loss of confidence)'. In this case, when deciding what might be too high, the departmental chief will pay particular attention to signals in the organisational environment, e.g. last year's experience, legislative votes, executive policy statements, the actions of client groups, etc.[10] The problem which the chief executive faces in drawing up his budget request is to find that budget which is 'acceptable' to a group of people who have diverse preferences. In such a case, the budget is unlikely to be 'optimal' to all who have an interest in the budget size and its composition.

In summarising this section, it should be remembered that budgets are the expression of expectations or aspirations of activity. The concept of the budget that we are using is *ex ante* rather than *ex post*, so that the budget is the financial counterpart of the public sector output plan. The budget requested by a department and the actual budget granted to it is the result of a process of sequential, fragmented and incremental decision making, based upon simple rules that form the expectations of organisational members. There are two principal parties to any budgetary process: those who make the request (i.e. departmental chief executives/bureaucrats) and those who grant the budget and legitimise it (i.e. members of the legislature). Both sets of agents face complex and uncertain environments and use aids to calculation. Moreover, bureaucrats and members of the legislature are assumed to satisfice rather than maximise. The serial nature of the problems which bureaus tackle means that one year's budget will not diverge appreciably from that of the previous year. Faced with complexity and uncertainty and the high costs of acquiring contextual and empirical data, decision makers prefer simplification of problems and prefer to make decisions over a small range of alternatives. These problems are aptly summed up by Bismark who remarked:

> At the end of a lifetime devoted wholly to public affairs, and with the experience I now possess, I think I can see one year ahead of me ... The rest is outside my competence.[11]

Empirical Tests of the Incremental Model

Bureaucratic behaviour, and the budgets that result from it, is reduced to a simple set of rules which, it is argued, are extremely stable. The question which naturally follows from this kind of statement is, can it be supported by the facts? Davis, Dempster and Wildavsky (1966 (a) and (b)), hereafter DDW, were the first to subject the budgetary rules of incrementalism to stringent empirical testing.

DDW modelled the budgetary decision making process in the following way. An agency (i.e. a department/bureau) draws up a budget and makes a request to be granted that budget by the legislature. In the case of the US, it is a Congressional appropriations committee which grants the budget. Thus, to understand the outcome, it is important to know the decision making rules which the agencies and Congress follow. DDW proposed a number of alternative decision rules, which were compared with one another by appealing to the facts. For example, the alternative agency decision rules were:

Agency Behaviour

(1) $$x_t = \beta_0 \, y_{t-1} + \xi_t$$

i.e., the agency request for a certain year (x_t) is a fixed mean percentage (β_0) of the Congressional appropriation for that agency in the previous year (y_{t-1}) plus a random variable (ξ_t), which is normally distributed with mean zero and unknown but finite variance.

(2) $$x_t = \beta_1 y_{t-1} + \beta_2 (y_{t-1} - x_{t-1}) + \chi_t$$

i.e., this rule expands upon that in equation (1) by taking into account the difference between the previous appropriation (y_{t-1}) and the previous request (x_{t-1}) which is roughly a fixed proportion of the previous year's appropriation, but in addition it tries to smooth out its stream of appropriations by taking into account the difference between its request and appropriation for the previous year. That is, if there had been a large cut in the agency's request for the previous year, it will in the current year submit a 'padded' estimate to make up for the loss in expected funds. This equation incorporates strategic decision making on the part of the agency. χ_t is a stochastic disturbance.

(3) $$x_t = \beta_3 x_{t-1} + \rho_t$$

i.e., the agency request for a certain year is a fixed mean percentage of the agency's request for the previous year. This rule reflects the agency's undying and unquestioning faith in the worth of its programmes. It makes requests without regard to previous Congressional action. Also, ρ_t is a stochastic disturbance.

In addition to the decision rules set out above, DDW considered alternative gaming strategies in which the agency might engage (see DDW 1966(b), p. 534).

Congress Behaviour

(4) $$y_t = \alpha_0 x_t + \eta_t$$

i.e., the Congressional appropriation for an agency in a certain year is a fixed mean percentage of the agency's request in that year plus a stochastic disturbance (η_t). Congress trusts the agency to make reasonable requests that are relatively stable indices of the expenditures required to carry out its programmes.

(5) $$y_t = \alpha_1 x_t + \alpha_2 \nu_{t-1} + \varepsilon_t$$

i.e., the Congressional appropriation for an agency is a fixed mean percentage of the agency's request for that year, plus a stochastic disturbance ($\alpha_2 \nu_{t-1}$) representing a deviation from the usual relationship between Congress and the agency in the previous year, plus a random variable in the present year.

(6) $$y_t = \alpha_3 x_t + \alpha_4 \lambda_t + \nu_t$$

i.e., the Congressional appropriation for an agency is a fixed mean percentage of the agency's request, plus a dummy variable λ_t which represents Congress' learning of the agency decision rule and hence Congress' adjustment.

Having set out the system of equations, DDW then tested them against

Table 6.1 Summary of Decision Equations

Agency Equations		1	2	3
	4	44	1	8
Congress Equations	5	1	0	0
	6	12	0	0

time series data on requests and appropriations over the period 1947–1963 for 56 non-defence agencies of the US government. Table 6.1 represents a summary of the combinations of Agency and Congressional decision equations which were supported by evidence.

Thus the combination of equations (1) and (4) was the most popular according to empirical testing being supported on 44 occasions, as compared to combinations (3) and (6), which was never supported.[12]

(1) $$x_t = \beta_0 y_{t-1} + \xi_t$$

(4) $$y_t = \alpha_0 x_t + \eta_t$$

Combining equations (1) and (4) gives

$$y_t = \alpha_0 (\beta_0 y_{t-1} + \xi_t) + \eta_t$$

i.e. $$y_t = \alpha_0 \beta_0 y_{t-1} + (\alpha_0 \xi_t + \eta_t)$$

or $$y_t = \alpha y_{t-1} + \mu_t \qquad (\text{where } \alpha = \alpha_0 \beta_0 \text{ and } \mu_t = \alpha_0 \xi_t + \eta_t)$$

This is the simplest of all behavioural rules i.e. this year's current appropriation is a linear function of last year's appropriation (budget). This is the incremental decision rule. Empirical evidence, therefore, confirms that this year's budget is a function of last year's, plus or minus some stochastic factors.

The next question to answer is, 'are these simple decision rules stable?' That is, are the parameter values of the equations constant over time? Many important events took place over the period 1947–1963, so that it might be reasonable to suppose that the appropriations structures would be altered. If this was so, then values of the co-efficients (i.e. the year on year average percentage requests) would change from one period to the next. The equations would be stable for a short period, but would show changes over a longer period of time. DDW then tested for the presence of 'shift points' i.e. years in which the value of a co-efficient of an equation changes value. Segmenting the time series into two parts they tested for temporal stability and found that, of the Congress equations, 6 equations were temporally very stable, 12 were stable, 12 were not stable and 28 were unstable. Of the agency equations, 18 were stable, 18 were not stable and 18 were unstable. It is, therefore, clear from these results that whilst the process was temporally not stable in the majority of cases, for the whole period it was stable for short periods.

Numerical Example

To obtain an understanding of what this conveys, consider the following example. Suppose the education department's budgets have been examined over the period 1960–1979 and it is found by means of statistical estimation that the budget decision rule for that department is represented by the equation:

$$y_t^E = 1.15\, y_{t-1}^E + \mu_t$$

If last year's budget was £1000m (i.e. y_{t-1}^E), then

$$y_t^E = 1.15(1000) + \mu_t = £1150\text{m} + \mu_t$$

i.e., this year's budget is 15% up on last year's (plus the stochastic term μ). Moreover, if this 15% 'mark up' is stable, then we have in essence a simple forecasting model for departmental expenditure.

In summary, DDW 1966(b) concluded that 'evidence from over half of the non-defence agencies indicates that the behaviour of the budgetary process of the United States government results in aggregate decisions similar to those produced by a set of simple decision rules that are linear and temporally stable' (p. 529). Their decision rules fit the data; the results are very good in the sense that they leave very little of the variance statistically unexplained. Moreover, their analysis squares up with other research which suggests that the budgetary process has become an institutionalised series of actions sanctioned by an elaborate set of norms and behaviours.

Critique of the Incremental Model

Despite its apparent simplicity and its appeal to empirical evidence, the incremental model has been the subject of a good deal of criticism.[13]

(a) *The Importance of Exogenous Factors*

Since we know that departmental expenditures are related to objective factors within their environments such as, for example, the rate of inflation, changes in the size of client groups, the level of unemployment etc., an obvious limitation of the similar linear equations outlined above is that these exogenous factors are washed out of the system and do not appear as explanands of the trend in expenditures. In response to this critism DDW (1974) extended their analysis to include exogenous variables.

By including exogenous variables they also hoped to find out if the original temporal instability which they had identified was in fact caused by mis-specification, by not including the effects of important events in the equation. The omission of these variables would cause what appear to be shifts in the underlying relationship. To test if they had included some of these missing variables in their new model, DDW compared the extended model against the original over the period 1964–1968. DDW found that war, armed forces overseas, and the ratio of young persons in the population were important. War was found to reduce domestic Congressional appropriations, but the ratio of young persons increases them. Of the economic variables that they examined, the GNP deflator and the unemployment rate were the most influential. Changes in political parties in office had the expected effects. In summarising their work, which is one of the latest statments from the incrementalists, they say:

> ... an examination of exogenous variables shows that when they do exert an influence, it is over the most vulnerable agencies. Outside influences affect an agency when it performs a routine service, readily pushed forward or held back as circumstances suggest or when it is an object of dispute, so that its fortune depends upon the growth of friends or the decline of foes. For the most part, however, our agencies live in worlds of their own, worlds which are fully comprehensible to them but not yet to us. When and if we can better the model of the executive side of the budgetary process, we shall have largely solved the problem of prediction. Even so, we have shown that our models now predict better than known alternatives.
>
> (DDW 1974)

Despite the inclusion of general exogenous factors DDW have not proceeded to draw up agency specific demand and supply functions for agency outputs which would then relate these objective factors to agency expenditures. This point will be picked up again below.

(b) *Political and Organisational Forces*

'In politics the budgetary process, while certainly responding to the requirements of administrative life, is also a battlefield for conflicting priorities and alternative policies' (Natchez and Bupp 1973, p. 955). The incrementalist analysis established by Wildavsky *et al.* does give insights into the behaviour of decision makers and the way in which they try to solve problems. But it washes out of the analysis many of the other dimensions of behaviour. In terms of our earlier discussion their approach is partial. Of equal interest is the dynamic of political bargaining which sets priorities and which determines the activities that become the continuing policies of government, while others fade and are discarded. 'It is this variation in the *competitive* success of alternative programmes, rather than the cognitive processes of decision makers, which is central to the politics of public administration. It is this aspect of government that the "problem solving" perspective is inherently unable to explain' (Natchez and Bupp *op. cit.*).

Political choices and the budgetary process are completely intertwined. What needs to be done is to separate out:

(a) changes in expenditures from one year to the next; and
(b) changes in policy outputs purchased by a budget.

By concentrating first upon the stability of the decision making process and second upon the idea that this year's budget is a function of last year's gives the false impression that the policy *outputs* are stable and unchanging. This ignores the *cumulative* effects of changes made at the margin and the consequences of these changes for the character of final public outputs. What goes into the margins of each agency and the way in which agency services develop is a matter of politics and bargaining both inside and outside of the agency. Concentrating upon budget expenditures rather than upon what these expenditures buy, means that a great deal has been lost from the analysis. Let total planned expenditure for some agency (i.e. its budget) be denoted by E and let the expenditure on each component (i.e. programme) be denoted by e; then,

$$E = \Sigma e_i$$

Suppose there are two activities $e_1$and e_2, such that $e_1 = e_2$ in financial terms in year t. The decision is that expenditure on e_1 will be reduced by 10%, whereas expenditure on e_2 will be raised by 15%. If in year t, $e_1 = e_2 =$ £100, then $E_t =$ £200. In year $(t + 1)$, $E_{t+1} = 90 + 115 =$ £205. In other words, the whole budget has increased by an increment of $2\frac{1}{2}$% in expenditure terms, but the composition of the budget has changed. An examination of the composition of public outlays and agency programme outputs requires that we operate at a different level of aggregation from that normally used in incremental studies. (See Natchez and Bupp 1973 and Danziger 1976.)

Bureaucracy is not necessarily inherently inert, continuing to do what it did yesterday without responding to changing political pressures (preferences). Natchez and Bupp (*op. cit.*), Danziger (1976), and Greenwood, Hinings, and Ranson (1977) prefer to use a political economy model in which the budgetary process involves public policies in a continuous struggle for scarce resources. The normal state of affairs in the policy process is one of extreme competition between programmes for public funds. Competition exists for those programmes which wish to do nothing other than to continue doing what they did last year. 'There is nothing simple or automatic about continuing'.

(c) *Lack of a Theoretical Basis*

Danziger (1976) and Greenwood, Hinings and Ranson (1977) *et al.* have drawn attention to the lack of theoretical foundation to the incremental model:

> ... incrementalism as a theory of budgeting ... is depressingly weak as an explanatory theory despite its considerable predictive force. There is no convincing narrative contained in the literature ... that can explain either why incrementalism occurs at all or why some systems are less incremental than others
>
> (Greenwood, Hinings & Ranson 1977, p. 26)

In this section we will consider more deeply the methodological basis of the incrementalists' empiricism. At the same time we shall raise a number of questions which are not easily answered within the incrementalist framework e.g. why does the size of the increment vary from one agency to another? Although DDW (1974) have related agency expenditures to exogenous variables (see above), the whole system is statistically estimated by a set of reduced form equations. As with all macro-reduced form systems, the micro foundations providing a theoretical account of why the variables which appear in the equations are relevant, are missing. This ties up with the observation made in the previous section.

In their most recent contribution to the debate, DDW (1974 p. 452) taunt the economist by claiming that their approach to the study of budgeting is superior:

> Our methodological contribution is not so obvious, but we think it will be of interest to economists, whose traditional methods are found wanting, and to political scientists, whose procedures are found superior — a nice reversal of the usual line of criticism ... Economists are used to working from axioms, applying them to data and ending up with predictions. Political scientists are used to providing theories, or at least descriptions, based on an understanding of how political processes actually work. As political economists we have sought to combine the model building propensities of economists with the process orientation of political scientists. ... For economists the present work should provide encouragement to go deeper into the step-by-step operations of economic processes. For political scientists it should suggest that if they can find even approximate quantitative indicators, their model can be made to work.

The distinction between the usefulness of the equilibrium and behavioural paradigm was set out at great length in Chapter 3 above. Like many attacks upon the economist's approach, DDW are hitting out at straw men, whilst at the same time laying thmselves open to criticism. The economic models that they are referring to are within the equilibrium paradigm. Of course they are not descriptively realistic, but economists operating within that paradigm would not argue that their models are describing actual processes. Instead they employ 'as if'[14] models (as do the incrementalists also) and ignore many important institutional features so as to concentrate upon one relationship. It is of course necessary to simplify in order to get *analysis* going and pure theory set out within the equilibrium paradigm has the attraction that it concentrates upon rational action in the face of intrinsic constraints and may therefore point to underlying long-run tendencies. The economist's models are heuristic devices which are intended to assist in the *understanding* (as opposed to the description) of complex phenomena. This is well known to anyone who has thought seriously about scientific method. Einstein (1950) made the point 'now we realise, with special clarity, how much in error are those theorists who believe that theory comes inductively from experience'.

The error which Wildavsky *et al.* continually make is that they fail to distinguish between the purposes of alternative paradigms. They do not consider carefully enough the questions which the different approaches to budgeting are attempting to answer. Their approach is inductive rather than deductive, which poses problems when it comes to empirical tests of their model, since they are testing their propositions against the same data that gave rise to the propositions in the first place. Throughout their papers, DDW are at pains to demonstrate the predictive powers of their theory. However, given their inductive approach to modelling, all that can be said is that the properties of their model are consistent with the facts. In no sense have they set out, in a Popperian way, to refute their propositions. Nor did they set down alongside each other the predictions generated by their incremental model and those generated by the economists and then compare them. If they had done so, then they might have seen the obvious differences which exist between them. For a start, they would have been forced to consider the predictions which the two sets of models are capable of generating.

Prediction is not equivalent to explanation. It is possible to predict successfully without understanding the inter-relationships between the forces that determine the objective reality. As Greenwood, Hinings and Ranson (*op cit.*) argued, incrementalism is 'depressingly weak as an explanatory theory'. It is interesting to draw attention to another literature which addresses a similar issue i.e. the use of rules of thumb by managers in private firms. Papandreou (1955, p. 395) argued '... the advocates of the non-rational approach must be in a position ... to predict *which* rule of thumb will be employed in *what* firms and at *what* time and place. The attempt to do so, I am convinced, will make it necessary for them to fall back upon a rational-action model'.

What determines the size of an agency's increment and why is it that increments differ between agencies? These are some of the questions which Williamson (1966) addressed himself to. Drawing from the literature on 'pricing rules of thumb', found in general management economics, Williamson argues that rules such as mark-up pricing are not mere whimsy or accident but must have a rational basis. Incremental budgeting is analogous to mark-up pricing. If we take the basic incremental rule

$$y_t = \alpha_0 y_{t-1} + \mu_t$$

then α_0 can be thought of as the mark-up. What determines the value of α_0? Williamson provides an answer in terms of demand elasticities and by introducing demand as an explanatory factor allows for an explanation in terms of politics. The value of the mark-up will be high for those programmes for which there is a strong pressure of demand, which might be made effective through increases in resources arising from income increases (i.e. a high income elasticity of demand) and those programmes for which there is a strong political resistance to reductions even when prices rise (i.e. low price elasticity of demand). There is, therefore, nothing incompatible between an economic explanation in terms of demand factors and a political explanation in terms of the way in which preferences and the intensity of preferences are articulated through the system.

The role of political forces in determining the size of an agency's (department's) increment or mark-up is aptly illustrated by Taverne (1976, pp. 7–8) who was himself a UK Treasury Minister:

> ... when the time comes for a cut back, when the Treasury gets its stand strengthened, because the Treasury looks at the whole and tries to control the whole, it depends very much upon the personalities of the individual Ministers. Ministers do not in fact ask themselves, 'What is the best for the country as a whole?' No, they want to make their own reputation as strong Ministers in their own departments, by getting more than the average share of the cake. The Treasury, on the other hand, is determined to cut spending back. The Chancellor will look around, consulting with his allies and ask, 'now which Minister is the weakest, whom can we get most out of?' ... The rational question of choosing between programmes is not necessarily done on the merits of different programmes, it is often done on the balance of power in the Cabinet and the personality of individual Ministers.

The way to proceed in this area is to provide a more explicit theoretical framework to budgeting which is sufficiently comprehensive to allow a number of perspectives to come together without necessarily conflicting e.g. politics, organisation theory, public administration and economics. The results reported in Greenwood, Hinings and Ranson (1977) are a step in this direction.

(d) *Non-Incremental Decisions*

Whilst incremental decision making might be appropriate for describing day-to-day decisions, Etzioni (1967) has argued that it is not a suitable framework within which top level 'once for all' decisions on long-range policies are made:

> ... the number and role of fundamental decisions are significantly greater than the incrementalists state. ... while incremental decisions greatly outnumber fundamental ones, the latter's significance for societal decision making is not commensurate with their number; it is thus a mistake to relegate non-incremental decisions to the category of exceptions. Moreover, it is often the fundamental decisions which set the context for the numerous incremental ones. Although fundamental decisions are frequently 'prepared' by incremental ones in order that the final decisions will initiate a less abrupt change, these decisions may still be considered relatively fundamental.
>
> (Etzioni 1967, pp. 387–8)

Etzioni proceeds to argue that incrementalism might indeed be dysfunctional since, because it concentrates upon the short-run, incremental decision making amounts to drifting, 'while an accumulation of small steps could lead to a significant change, there is nothing in that approach to guide the accumulation; the steps may be circular — leading back to where they started — leading in many directions at once but leading nowhere' (p. 387).

There is much of governmental decision making which is non-incremental. Thus, incrementalism can only be a partial model of decision making. What remains unanswered is how does bureaucracy deal with the unexpected, the unusual and the critical? This question was looked at in Chapter 4, where the issue of decision making under conditions of uncertainty was reviewed. These issues are considered again and developed in the remainder of this chapter.

Finally, if an incremental system does 'drift' as Etzioni suggests, what are the cumulative effects of this drifting? Catastrophe theorists, following in the tradition of René Thom (1964) and Christopher Zeeman (1972) would argue that the confluence of small incremental changes in a number of different variables could combine and 'flip' the whole system with catastrophic effects. The application of catastrophe theory has been primarily confined to the biological and psychological sciences. There is, however, scope to apply this kind of analysis to social process (Knoer 1978).

Incrementalism in the UK

One widely quoted study of public sector incremental budgeting in the UK is that which was carried out by Heclo and Wildavsky (1974). Their approach was to examine the process of interaction and bargaining between the Treasury and the central government spending departments. The conclusion of their study was that it is the political forces between departments which are the most important factors determining the outcome pattern of public spending, rather than the dictates of party policy or the demands of pressure groups etc. In common with all incrementalist theories, they emphasise that decision makers/policy makers have very little time to be fully informed and that as a result, changes in expenditure are marginal and upwards and that once a programme is established it becomes difficult to change it, especially if you wish to dispose of it. From their interviews, Heclo and Wildavsky demonstrated that in the UK many Members of Parliament are so pressurised that they have very little time to give careful consideration to their own department's expenditure plans, let alone those of other departments (a point made by Crossman in his diaries). This therefore tends to challenge the idea of collective decision making in Cabinet on expenditure priorities. The Heclo and Wildavsky view of the Treasury is set out very much in the terms of anthropologists' field notes. Conflicts are resolved by the members of the 'expenditure community' who have a well-developed sense of norms and fairplay etc. Peace is maintained at the expense of policy innovation; just add £1 here and take £1 from there. Thus the pattern of public expenditure is in this view very much determined by the Treasury men and not through the interaction of pressure groups and party politics.

Whilst this case study is interesting and has much anecdotal information to offer, it does nevertheless lack rigour. The authors describe a behavioural process rather than presenting a model. Whilst they interviewed many Treasury people, much of their information was second-hand and of course those interviewed are notorious for being careful to let the interviewer know only what they want him to. Because they did not set up a formal model, the role of pressure groups and parliament is left out of the picture. It is, therefore, easy to gain the erroneous view that these institutions have no role to play. Whether or not they have a role and what that role is remains an open question which can only be answered through the testing of an explicit model.

The Political Economy Model of Budgeting: A Resource Dependence Perspective

One of the criticisms of the incremental model of budgeting was that because it focused upon the issues of decision making under uncertainty and complexity, it left out the political reality of competition over scarce resources. The political economy model of organisations, which was introduced in Chapter 3, viewed both inter and intra-organisational behaviour as a constant struggle for autonomy and discretion. Organisations and sub-units were seen as being in continual competition with one another for scarce resources, with competition being heightened as resources became increasingly more scarce. Individuals and groups of individuals vie with one another for those resources that are necessary to satisfy their own particular preferences. Their ability to do so depends upon the amount of discretion which exists over the allocation of intra-organisational resources.

The political economy model can be supplemented by the 'resource dependence' perspective of organisations which has been advocated by Pfeffer and Salancik (1978). The resource dependence perspective, which grows out of the 'contingency theory' of organisations (*op. cit.*), argues that in order to survive organisations require resources and that in order to acquire resources organisations are forced to interact with their environment. To obtain resources organisations are dependent upon their environments (hence the name), but the acquisition of resources is both problematical and uncertain and the organisation's survival is contingent upon its being able to exercise some control over the sources of uncertainty.

Thus, organisations will, through vertical integration, for example, attempt to reduce the uncertainties of supplies and distributional outlets which they face in their environment. Other forms of uncertainty-reducing behaviour include forming coalitions with other organisations and lobbying political decision makers in order to change the laws and rules of the game within which they operate. In these respects the resource dependence model, although it has been developed within the context of organisation theory, has many similarities to the economist's approach which focuses upon interaction and exchanges with the environment i.e. with agents in the environment.

It was also noted in the political economy model that organisations are coalitions of varying interests which are frequently incompatible and which, therefore, come into conflict. Whose interests are to prevail is determined by the final outcome of the conflict, which in turn depends upon the distribution of power and influence amongst the various coalitions within the organisation. This point was recognised early on by Wildavsky (1961, p. 184):

> The crucial aspect of budgeting is whose preferences are to prevail in disputes about which activities are to be carried on and to what degree in the light of limited resources. The problem is not only 'How shall budgetary benefits be maximised?' as if it made no difference who received them, but also, 'who shall receive budgetary benefits and how much?'

Thus, the final allocation and distribution of resources within organisations will depend upon the differences in power between the sub-units, departments and coalitions that comprise the organisation. Such an approach, however, requires a clear understanding of the concept of power. Contingency theorists have focused attention upon non-personal sources of power. In organisations, as in other social systems, power is assumed to be dependent upon control over critical and scarce resources (Hickson *et al.* 1971, Hinnings *et al.* 1974, Perrow 1970 and Thompson 1967). Following Crozier (1964)[15] it is argued that power is held by those sub-units that can cope with critical organisational contingencies. Since many of the uncertainties and contingencies arise within the organisation's environment, it is the environmental context that partially determines the distribution of power within the organisation. Power is defined as potential influence over organisational decisions (Lewin 1951). Thus, to the extent that the interest is in budgetary decisions, a department's power to influence the allocation of resources in its own favour must be incorporated into our theory of budgeting.

One question which was left unanswered in the incremental model of budgeting was, 'what detemines the size of a department's increment?'. Economic factors such as the price and income elasticities of demand were suggested along with political forces. These political forces can now be articulated more clearly in terms of a department's (agency's) relative power, which is assumed to depend upon (a) its capacity to cope with uncertainty and critical contingencies and (b) the centrality of the department to the organisation's workflow, i.e. a measure of the importance of the uncertainty to the organisation. Thus it is now argued that the observed differences in departmental increments can be explained partially in terms of the department's relative power position within the organisation. Moreover, variations in the size of a department's increment over time could be explained (partially) in terms of the dynamics of changing relative power.

The foregoing discussion is nothing other than *a priori* theorising and speculation. It is necessary to subject such a model to empirical testing. This was done in a study of resource allocation (budget decision making) by Salancik and Pfeffer (1974). They set out to test the thesis that, the more powerful sub-units (departments) within an organisation are those which provide resources to the organisation, if resources are critical for survival. The particular organisation which they studied was the State University of Illinois at Urbana, Champaign, which in 1972 had 34,000 students of which 8,000 were graduate students. The specific hypotheses which they set out to test were (a) is a department's relative power within the University a function of the extent to which it generates resources, and (b) is the relative power of a department a good predictor of budget allocations to departments within the University?

In order to proceed with their study Salancik and Pfeffer required measures of relative power and of organisational resources. Conceptual definitions, let alone empirical indices, of power are extremely difficult to pin down (see March 1966). Salancik and Pfeffer tried a number of measures in an attempt to see if they correlated as expected, e.g.:

(a) each department head was interviewed and asked to rank the relative power of each department (including his own) on a 7 point scale,
(b) the department's representation on important University committees (i.e. those committees affecting resource allocation),
(c) membership on the University research board.

Each of the above are standard ideas of what might constitute a measure of power. However, following the contingency theorists' route, the researchers sought to find out whether or not a department's power was a function of its control over resources which are important and crucial to the organisation's survival. The resources which they examined were:

(a) number of graduate students
(b) number of undergraduates
(c) national rank or prestige of the department
(d) administrative and service contribution to the University
(e) amount of outside grants and contracts
(f) public visibility of the department.

Since outside funds bring in overheads etc., they are a useful form of organisational slack. Salancik and Pfeffer concluded:

> ...the most important determinant of sub-unit power was the unit's provision of outside funds to the organisation. Closely following outside funds as a predictor of sub-unit power was the relative proportion of graduate students ... less important ... was the relative proportion of undergraduates taught by the department.

When resources are scarce, especially in a zero growth situation, all competitors for the stock of resources are locked into a zero sum game. If x wins over y, then y will lose resources, but for x to win requires that x must have the power to overcome y's pressures. The more important (scarce) the resource, then the more crucial will power be in determining its allocation as compared to objective criteria:

> ... a sub-unit within an organisation will vie for a resource to the extent that the resource is critical and the sub-unit's probability of obtaining the resource will depend upon its power relative to other sub-units also contending for the resource.
>
> (Salancik and Pfeffer 1974, p. 470)

Power depends upon the extent to which the sub-unit is instrumental in providing those resources which are highly valued by the total organisation:

> ... power derived from acquiring resources is used to obtain more resources, which in turn can be employed to produce more power — the rich get richer.
>
> (Salancik and Pfeffer *op.cit.*)

From interviews with faculty members and heads of departments, the researchers found that departments regarded University graduate fellowships to be especially scarce resources, followed by Research Board Grants for faculty research. Thus it would be expected that a department's relative power would determine its allocation of these scarce resources. They found (p. 468) that:

> ... power is most highly correlated with the allocation of university graduate fellowships, is next most highly correlated with the allocation of grants for faculty research and is least highly correlated with the allocation of summer faculty fellowships.

Over 80% of the variance in the allocation of graduate research fellowships was explained in terms of a department's power, which in turn was a function of its acquisition of outside grants. Thus, they found (p. 470) that those units with the most outside support also tended to obtain the most internal support, because the external resources bring with them discretionary power,

> Instead of compensating for the differential access to outside resources, the internal resource allocation system actually exacerbates resource inequalities (p. 470).

But suppose this was not the case. Suppose there was greater redistribution of resources within the organisation. What would happen then? One possibility might be that it would destroy the incentive for a department to go for external funds. The result of this would be that the total fund for discretionary redistribution (out of overheads) would be smaller and the weaker departments would lose out. Thus there is a balance to be struck between a policy which provides incentives for departments to obtain external resources and a policy of equity.[16]

Salancik and Pfeffer are at pains to emphasise that too much should not be made of this single case study. Whilst in the case that they examined the general thesis appeared to be supported, it will be necessary to carry out a large number of further case studies before generalisations can be made.

Personal Influences in Budget/Resource Allocation Decision Making

In the bureaucratic model of resource allocation, resources are allocated according to objective and universalistic criteria in accordance with formulae, laws/rules, strongly held norms or some external agency. There is no intra-organisational discretion in the allocation of resources and hence no explanatory role for concepts such as relative power or personal influence. The resource dependence version of the political economy model stands in contradistinction to the bureaucratic model, as does the next model that will be considered.

The general thesis of the model, which is reviewed in this section, is that personal influence is important when decisions are made under conditions of uncertainty. This model was empirically tested by Pfeffer, Salancik and Leblebici (1976). They analysed National Science Foundation grant allocations to four social science subjects (economics, social psychology, sociology and political science) over the period 1964–71. They took as their measure of uncertainty the degree of paradigm development within each of the social science subjects.

The argument is as follows:

(a) where there is uncertainty (lack of paradigmatic development) resources will be allocated using particularistic criteria such as friendship relationships and social similarity i.e institutional similarity was thought to be the most critical dimension of social similarity, since individuals identify closely with institutions with which they are affiliated. The indicator of particularism used was, 'the extent to which there was a relationship between an institution's representation on the National Science Foundation Advisory Panel and the receipt of funding'.

(b) where there is less uncertainty, resources will be allocated according to universalistic criteria such as the quality of a particular department (its position on a National ranking of departments), or the size of a department measured in terms of the number of faculty. The argument is that the larger the department, the more funds will be allocated to it, since it will have more faculty members to carry out research and to publish and to engage in professional activities. Thus quality and size of departments are likely to be related to one another and also to NSF advisory panel membership insofar as the NSF will wish high quality persons on its panels.

The results are summarised in table 6.2. The dependent variable in the statistical analysis was the proportion of funds received by each University for each of the subjects each year.

In table 6.2 it can be seen that the researchers found that there is a significant effect of panel membership on grant allocations. However, does the effect differ across subjects depending upon the degree of uncertainty (paradigm development)? Assuming that economics is the subject with the greatest degree of paradigm development and political science is that with the least, it was found that universalistic criteria were relatively more important in explaining grant allocations in economics. Political science had the highest coefficient for panel membership. Clearly, from table 6.2 it is

Table 6.2

Subject	*Constant*	*National Rank*	*Panel Membership*	*Size*
Economics	2.71	–0.0508 (0.0071)	2.48 (0.378)	–0.0009 (0.0078)
Social Psychology	1.41	–0.0192 (0.0057)	2.014 (0.514)	0.0172 (0.0086)
Sociology	2.66	–0.0448 (0.0117)	3.61 (0.568)	–0.009 (0.016)
Political Science	2.57	–0.0356 (0.025)	6.92 (1.50)	–0.014 (0.037)

Notes: (a) figures in brackets refer to the standard errors of the coefficients
(b) the coefficients are the unstandardised regression coefficients
Source: Pfeffer, Salancik and Leblebici (1976), page 236.

seen that panel membership affects the decision in each subject, illustrating the importance of personal influence in resource allocation decisions.

The next question they asked was, 'how stable is the effect?'. To what extent is the probability of receiving a grant allocation a function of having received a grant allocation in a previous period? They found (p. 238) that:

> both previous funding and panel membership are related to current funding and both previous panel membership and previous funding are related to current panel membership. The data certainly indicate a precedence effect.

They also tested the stability of grant allocations to changes in committee composition. As the composition of the committee changes, does the grant allocation change? If allocations were made according to universalistic criteria, then changes would take place over a much longer period of time and would not be so sensitive to changes in committee composition. It was found that grant allocations were more stable in economics and psychology and significantly less stable in political science.

Whilst they have chosen to illustrate their principle in the field of grant allocation, Pfeffer, Salancik and Leblebici argue that the principle is more general and could be applied to other decisions such as hiring, promotion and pay. One other important finding in this study was that the researchers concluded that very little is known about the *criteria* used in organisational decision processes. This is sobering, given that the criteria used and the outcomes associated with resource allocation in organisations have important distributional effects on the wider society.

It follows therefore that the work of Pfeffer and Salancik *et. al.* is only a beginning and a first shot at tackling a much wider and more ambitious set of issues and questions. For example, an alternative approach to that which has been adopted would be a focus upon sources of power and the means through which that power and the criteria used in decision making are legitimised. Take the problem of the allocation of funds (grants) for research; one question not considered in the Pfeffer and Salancik framework is what *kind* of research topics receive funding? Is it projects which support the existing capitalist system which stand the greatest probability of receiving a grant; is it projects which are formulated within the prevailing accepted framework of what constitutes good academic research and if so, how is this framework legitimised and how does it serve to maintain and support the wider socio-economic system? These questions, which must be high on the agenda of future research in this area, are not intended to be destructive of the contingency theory approach. Instead we are suggesting that Pfeffer and Salancik's approach is partial, since although power as a concept (whatever the origins of that power) has an explanatory role to play for the allocation of resources, that power has to be placed in a much wider context, since some sources of power are legitimised whereas others are not. This more general framework will, therefore, seek to explain one allocation of resources rather than another in terms of criteria which serve the wider socio-economic system. To take an extreme example, research projects which are likely to upset or threaten the whole social order are less likely to be funded than those which are more supportive. The interesting question then is who funds such research, especially that which will be instrumental in changing the existing subject paradigm.

Conclusions

In this chapter a number of approaches to budgeting and resource allocation have been considered. Each in its own right provides a partial view and each gives a good deal of insight into the total process of resource allocation and distribution. Taken together, these models flesh out the abstract optimality models which economists frequently use. One future development must be to integrate the vote maximising models of Downs *et al.* and the bureaucratic or budget maximising models of Niskanen *et al.*, with the political economy models outlined in this chapter. This will not be a simple task and complex political games are likely to result in indeterminate outcomes.

Notes

1 Wildavsky (1968), p. 193.

2 Budgets are plans (*ex ante*), whereas the audited accounts show what happened (*ex post*). When looking at the relationship between budgets *ex post* and *ex ante* one asks questions such as: 'were plans realised?'; if not, why not; were the plans too ambitious?' (See Wildavsky 1975, Chapter 1.)

3 Effective power refers to power *de facto* as compared to *de jure*.

4 The term synoptic means a broad and general view and was first used in this context by Braybrooke and Lindblom (1963). The comparison of the incrementalist and synoptic models is delayed until later in this chapter.

5 See Simon (1962).

6 See Wildavsky (1964), pp. 65–98.

7 For an excellent discussion of the sequential nature of budgeting decisions and the problems that follow from this, see Steiner (1974), pp. 300–13

8 It is tempting at this point to draw a number of normative conclusions from the preceding analysis. If the order in which decisions are made and implemented is important, and if decisions are fragmented in practice, should they not be coordinated via some planning system such as in Programme, Planning and Budgeting Systems (PPBS)?

9 Although different actors will portray Shakespeare's Hamlet in different ways, they are nevertheless constrained by the specification imposed by Shakespeare in his writing of the part.

10 Wildavsky (1964), pp. 21–32.

11 Quoted in Downie (1960), p. 281.

12 The criteria used to select whether or not a set of equations was confirmed by the evidence was that of maximum (adjusted) correlation coefficients plus the *d*-statistic test for serial correlation.

13 DDW (1966(b)) were aware of a number of limitations to their analysis; see pp. 539–40.

14 Schumpeter (1954) argues that, 'it is not necessary that the concepts we use in the study of social groups be familiar to the members of these groups themselves ... if, in terms of concepts of our own we formulate the conditions for maximising profits we need not assume that the businessman himself uses those concepts; our 'theory' is perfectly meaningful even if we know that he does not' (*op. cit.*).

15 Crozier's study of organisational behaviour in a French factory is now a classic. He found that power accrued to the plant's maintenance crew, since they possessed the knowledge relevant to repair equipment. Breakdowns of plant was an area of uncertainty affecting the whole set of operations. Uncertainty critical to the organisation's functioning determines a sub-unit's power and the distribution of effective power throughout the whole organisation.

16 This point about the equity/efficiency trade-off is discussed again in Chapter 7.

CHAPTER 7

Efficiency in Bureaucracy

... many of these departments have been gradually evolved in compliance with current needs, and the purposes for which they were called into being have gradually so altered that the later stages of the process have not accorded in principle with those that were reached earlier. In other instances departments appear to have been rapidly established without preliminary insistence or definition of function and precise assignment of responsibility.

(Haldane Report 1918)

Introduction

The rapid growth in the relative size of the public sectors of Western governments has brought along with it voters' disenchantment with government. The fiscal containment movement, which demands restraints upon government spending and taxation, has gained political power in recent years. This is seen clearly in the election of the Thatcher and Reagan administrations, which campaigned, in part, on the fiscal containment ticket, and in the Proposition 13 movement in California during June 1978. Following the voter initiative, which amended the Californian state constitution, 23 other American states passed some form of fiscal limitation.

An important element of the fiscal containment argument is that bureaucracy, which has grown out of all reasonable proportions, is inherently inefficient. There are too many bureaucrats, they are overpaid, they enjoy job security and receive pension rights, which are more favourable than their private sector counterparts. Demands, by the electorate, for reductions in taxation and public spending, have created politicians whose purpose is to eliminate bureaucratic waste and the 'fat' in the budget by disbanding those public services for which there is little demand and by rolling back government and reducing the number of public employees.

The issue of public sector efficiency is nothing new. Journalistic investigation has always sought to expose scandals in the public sector. As government has grown, unfavourable images of bureaucracy have been advanced. It was C. Northcote Parkinson (1957) who advocated that bureaucracies achieve and sustain their height of activity (and size) long after the purpose for which they were originally created has either considerably diminished or disappeared, a view which had been presented many years earlier in the Haldane Report (*op. cit*).

The issue is one of identifying the goals and objectives of the bureaus (see Chapters 3 and 4). Bureaucratic inefficiency and waste in one particular UK central government department was highlighted by Chapman (1978), a retired senior civil servant, in his book, *Your Disobedient Servant*.

There is also the Machiavellian model of bureaucracy, which has been proposed by Tullock (1965). Bureaucracy is described in terms of a number of agents; the chief or 'Sovereign'; the peers, courtiers and barons; the followers, subordinates and inferiors. In the drama of bureaucracy the principal objective governing individual behaviour is to please the sovereign. This is done by providing information to one's superiors which simultaneously evokes the sovereign's pleasure and serves the transmitter's own ends. Serving one's own ends can usefully be achieved by producing information which puts one's peers in a poor light. One of the conclusions of Tullock's political model is that, because a good deal of the energies of the members of the bureaucracy are absorbed by infighting and intrigue, the efficiency of the organisation is reduced.

Modern discussion of the efficiency of public sector bureaucracy is, however, part of an older and broader based debate, namely the comparison of the relative efficiencies of market or centrally administered provision of goods in an economy i.e. the debate between socialist and capitalist forms of economic organisation and between centralised *versus* decentralised planning. This debate raged in the 1930s and 1940s (Hayek 1935, 1940; Lange 1938; Lerner 1944; and Von Mises 1935) and is still played out today in disguised form through discussions of bureaucratic efficiency. Mises and Hayek argued that a centrally controlled economy does not have the institutional means to ensure an efficient allocation of resources. Such an allocation could be secured only through a system of decentralised markets. Lange argued the opposite. Recently, McAuley (1966) has argued that comparisons of the relative efficiencies of different institutions represent an impossible and meaningless exercise. Liberal philosophers have pinned to the mast their *faith* in the merits of decentralisation and the devolution of economic power. They fear the real or imagined spectre of concentrated power and inefficiency in large planned systems of organisations, be they in the public or the private sector. To them, small is beautiful since it is efficient and controllable. But is it? Does smallness, for example, ignore possible economies of scale whilst emphasising the romantic idealisation of illusory control?

Is it necessarily true that large organisations are inefficient? In addition to the arguments of Parkinson and Tullock, it is frequently suggested that as an organisation grows in size there is a 'control loss' i.e. a loss in the accuracy of transmitting information through layers of the organisation's hierarchy. Like the dinosaur, the head and tail of large organisations are far removed, resulting in delays in decision making. Questions of organisational efficiency are indirectly considered in Chapters 2 and 3. There, the scientific management and the classical administrative theories and human relations approaches to organisational analysis were compared. Since each of these schools of thought is concerned with improvements in productivity and organisational efficiency, we will have occasion to refer to them once again throughout this chapter.

The issue of the efficiency of bureaucracy is problematic and is not as clear cut as much of the rhetoric would suggest. First, we need to know more about what it is that people are criticising when they denounce bureaucracies, since questions of waste, bureaucratic constraints on personal freedoms and a dislike of bureaucratic goals frequently become mixed up. Second, much of the antagonism and many of the criticisms of bureaucracy paradoxically arise because bureaucracy *is* efficient. The problem is that in performing their tasks efficiently, bureaucrats do so in an impersonal fashion without recognising the merits and individual characteristics of each case. To treat each individual as a special case would result in efficiency but at a high resource cost, (Blau and Meyer 1971). Third, those who argue strongly for improvements in efficiency have to face and contend with the possibility of 'goal displacement' (Merton 1957). That is, efficiency might become the substantive goal of the bureaucracy, bringing with it a number of undesirable consequences.[1] Furthermore, many of the incentive structures and performance measures which are used to improve efficiency have both unintended and undesirable consequences. Fourth, those who demand improvements in efficiency have culture bound notions of what efficiency is. Often they themselves do not know what the 'best way' of doing things is, since they do not have a sufficient amount of contextual or situational knowledge.

This chapter and the next consider the issue of inefficiency in the public sector and the problems involved in controlling the activities of public sector bureaucracies. Rather than beginning by assuming that bureaucracy is inefficient, the approach adopted will be less positive and more abstract. First, the concept of inefficiency will be taken as problematic. What is meant by inefficiency and what do observers mean when they say bureaucracy is inefficient? Second, what factors contribute to bureaucratic inefficiency? Third, how might public sector efficiency be improved and what are the limits to such improvements?

The Economist's Treatment of Efficiency

One of the apparent achievements of micro-economics is its formal analysis of the concept of efficiency. Whereas accountants, lawyers and management specialists assign to the word efficiency a variety of meanings, the micro-economist has developed a formal framework within which the concept of efficiency can be debated unambiguously. This was certainly the view which was held by almost all economists until the mid 1960s. In 1966, however, Leibenstein (1966) opened up the economists' definition of efficiency to include those ideas of efficiency held by management specialists. Following Leibenstein, we now distinguish between (a) allocative efficiency and (b) *X*-efficiency.

Allocative Efficiency

Allocative efficiency is defined as a by-product of the micro-economists' analysis of perfectly competitive markets. It is therefore derived within the context of the equilibrium paradigm which was discussed in Chapter 3. A general competitive equilibrium is established through a process of competition, in which producers seek to maximise profits, landlords maximise rents, and workers maximise real wages. In this process the commercially fit drive out the commercially weak; as in all competitions some people win whilst others lose. One of the outcomes of the competitive process is that prices are forced down to the lowest costs. The process, however, takes place within constraints which are worthwhile remembering. Each individual maximises his own objectives, subject to the constraints of his own initial endowments i.e. his personal qualities, skills and abilities, his inherited position in society and inherited wealth. Goods and services are produced within the bounds of existing technical knowledge.

The state of a perfectly competitive equilibrium is defined in terms of a set of marginal conditions i.e. when the prices of all products are equal to the marginal costs of producing them and when all factor prices are equal to the values of their marginal products and where all total costs are minimised. Formally we have:[2]

(a) *efficiency in exchange* For all private goods the marginal rates of substitution (MRS) are equal amongst individuals i.e. for products 1 and 2 and for individuals i and j, then
$\text{MRS}_i = \text{MRS}_j = p_1/p_2$.
(where p_1 and p_2 are the prices of the products).

(b) *efficiency in production* This is defined as:
   (i) efficient factor combinations require that for any two factors of production the marginal rates of technical substitution are equal for all products;
   (ii) efficient distribution of a factor within an industry requires that its marginal physical product be identical in all production units;
   (iii) efficient composition of total production requires equality of the marginal rates of transformation (MRT) for any two production units which produce the same products.

(c) *joint efficiency in production and exchange* This defines overall allocative efficiency within an economy and requires that the set of relative prices equal the marginal costs of production, i.e. $\mathrm{MRS}_{12} = \mathrm{MRT}_{12} = p_1/p_2$

In each of the above cases, efficiency is thought of in the following terms; in equilibrium it is impossible by rearranging factors of production to produce an additional unit of output of one good without reducing the output of another; nor is it possible to make any consumer better off by reducing his consumption of one good and increasing his consumption of another; nor can a producer add to his profit by reducing his production of one good and increasing his production of another. At the margin, therefore, all factors of production and all products are *allocated* efficiently. For the economy as a whole, *Pareto efficiency* exists in the sense that it is impossible through a rearrangement of the consumption of final products to make one individual better off without making another worse off. A general competitive equilibrium is, therefore, Pareto efficient.

These properties of the competitive market equilibrium have been used to compare the desirability of different market structures, especially those of monopoly and perfect competition. Since our interests are in the efficiency of the public sector monopoly, a general discussion of the comparative efficiencies of competitive monopoly markets will be of value to our analysis of public sector monopoly in particular.

One of the essential factors leading to the efficiency outcome of competitive markets is the assumption that there is a very large number of producers and consumers, such that no single producer or group of producers can influence the market price by restricting output.[3] If the number of producers is reduced to unity a monopoly problem then arises. The monopolist and perfectly competitive firms both face identical cost conditions.[4] If the market was perfectly competitive, all firms in the industry would be price takers and price would be set equal to marginal costs. In the case of the single producer monopolist, the profit maximising level of output is found where price equals marginal revenue.

Compared to the perfectly competitive outcome, output is lower and prices are higher under monopoly. Consumers lose what the monopolist gains in excess profit, so that not only is there a reallocation of outputs, there is also a redistribution of incomes. For these reasons it is argued that monopoly is allocatively less efficient than perfect competition; first, because consumers get a mix of products that provide less satisfaction and second, because real income is transferred to the monopolist.

As a theoretical exercise, the comparison of market structures always allows perfect competition to win over monopoly since the game is played with dice loaded by tautology. That is, it will always be the case that perfect competition will win by the definition of efficiency we start off with. However, to the analyst concerned with the empirical problems of organisation design, does it necessarily follow that perfectly competitive markets are to be preferred to monopoly, or central planning, or other economic systems?

The technical conditions required to establish a general competitive equilibrium and hence a Pareto efficient allocation of resources are very stringent. In addition to freedom of entry and the requirement of a large number of agents on both sides of the market, all forms of non-convexity such as diminishing returns to scale and externality are ruled out. In practice these conditions do not exist. The real world is characterised by any number of non-convexities, information is not freely available to all agents in the market and as we saw in Chapter 3, firms do not necessarily maximise profits. Instead, they either satisfice or serve the interests of non-owner/managers. Indeed, it would be difficult to validate empirically whether or not profits are maximised. Moreover, there are additional reasons to be considered, but before these can be discussed it is necessary to introduce the concept of *X*-efficiency.

X-Efficiency

In 1966 Harvey Leibenstein, a Harvard University economist, pointed out that as a consequence of the gradual refinement of economic theory, the concept of efficiency had been narrowed to the single meaning of allocative efficiency and nothing more. In traditional micro-economic theory, 'non-allocative' efficiency is an unnecessary concept, since it has by means of definition been assumed away. Schwartzman (1973, p. 763) is forthright in his criticisms of the standard model: '... this is not a model for the analysis of efficiency but one which seeks to avoid such analysis ... price theory is inappropriate when the central question involved efficiency, variations in which are assumed away rather than analysed'. The problem with the standard price theory model was that the *internal* efficiency of firms was not challenged or discussed in great detail by economists, although it was by other disciplines such as business management. It was generally assumed in the standard analysis that one firm was as efficient as another. The monopoly, producing a smaller output and charging a higher price, was assumed to be producing in the least costly way, as was the perfectly competitive firm.

What the standard price theory model or equilibrium paradigm amounts to is a theory of markets, not a theory of intra-organisational behaviour. The managers of the firms are *assumed* to have made the optimal *input decisions* so that the analysis then focuses upon the allocation of goods and services along a production frontier (i.e. allocative efficiency), rather than movements from a less efficient frontier to a more efficient one (X-efficiency). The implicit idea underlying the allocative efficiency view of the firm (organisation) must be that there is some central controller who determines how inputs are to be combined in order to achieve minimum cost. But as Leibenstein (1973, p. 766) points out, this is a very simplistic and naive view of organisational reality. The distortion of reality arises because in traditional micro theory, the behavioural processes within the firm are not considered. However, many of the factors which in practice contribute to inefficiency are due to problems arising from internal organisational processes.

Leibenstein's identification of X-efficiency forms one of the vital links between the economic analysis of organisations and the sociological and management analysis outlined in Chapter 2. Variations in costs between organisations can arise for a number of reasons:

(i) contracts for labour are incomplete;
(ii) the production function is not completely specified or known; and
(iii) not all inputs are marketed, or if marketed are not available on equal terms to all buyers.

Leibenstein's causes of X-inefficiency are sufficiently general for us to incorporate them with the analysis of internal organisation as set out in Chapters 2, 3, and 4 above. First, the lack of specificity of labour contracts means that individuals (management and workers) can to some degree pursue their own goals, rather than the formal goals of the organisation. This lack of specificity can arise, either because the formal goals of the organisation are insufficiently well specified, or because the full set of labour activities which are required to fulfil the goals are unknown. Even if contracts are fully specified, the transactions costs (i.e. costs of monitoring and policing the system) of enforcing the contracts are likely to be high, thereby providing scope for individuals to pursue their own goals. Furthermore, if we assume that the environment within which decision making and productive activities take place is both complex and uncertain, then it becomes clear why contracts cannot be completely specified. A completely specified contract would require a definition and description of the complex situation. As has already been pointed out, not only is there a problem that different individuals will perceive complex realities in different ways, but the costs of analysing and specifying the situation for the purpose of drawing up a contract is likely to outweigh many advantages. Uncertainty compounds the problem, since it requires that we have a set of contracts contingent upon all possible future states of the world. Once again, this would be an unrealistic and costly process.

The lack of specificity of contracts offers scope for discretionary decision making by individuals within organisations. Each individual has, therefore, a degree of freedom to decide upon: 1) the *activities* he will carry out; 2) the *pace* at which he will carry out these activities; 3) the *quality* of the activities; and 4) the *time* spent on the activities. According to Leibenstein, each individual chooses an activity-pace-quality-time (APQT) bundle. The choice of an APQT bundle is a complex process. It will be recalled from the Hawthorne Studies, outlined in Chapter 2 earlier, that an individual's choice of APQT bundle, including his work effort decision, will in a number of instances be made in a group setting with the constraints of social approval or disapproval of workmates influencing that decision. Different individuals will interpret a situation differently and will choose to react differently. Training programmes are designed to impart a common framework which reduces the range of differences in perception and interpretation, but they do not eliminate the differences. The more complex the task the greater is the problem of giving instructions and the greater is the problem of obtaining information about compliance to instructions.

In principle, management could try to specify the nature of every job, which means directing every employee to work in accordance with one specific APQT bundle. This is what the proponents of scientific management advocated, namely the requirement that individuals work in accordance with pre-determined job descriptions and a very high degree of close supervision. Such close supervision is, as was demonstrated by the human relations school of management, resented by employees. Moreover, management seldom has the detailed knowledge to preset APQT bundle for each individual, let alone the resources to ensure that each individual works in accordance with the prescribed bundle.

If the goals of the organisation are not known, or if the organisation has multiple objectives, or if the objectives are frequently changing, then the production function which relates inputs to outputs through a technical relationship will not be fully specified. In many public sector agencies, the technical relationship between inputs and outputs is not known with any amount of precision e.g. the relationship between police activities and the crime rate, or between classroom activities and educational attainment. Should the nationalised industries be thought of in terms of profit making, or in terms of serving wider social welfare objectives? Until this kind of question is sorted out, we cannot judge the efficiency of the nationalised industries' productive operations and decision making in the nationalised industries will be frustrated until it is known with certainty which set of criteria their performance is to be judged against. Empirical studies of the production functions in a variety of industries[5] have shown that the residual or unexplained element is large, relative to the variance which is explained. Factors normally included in the residual are technology, but also management style and organisation structure, inputs which are seldom discussed by economists.[6]

Finally, not all of the inputs of the firm (organisation) are marketed, or even if marketed they are not available to all firms on equal terms. This was examined in Chapter 3 where internal labour and capital markets were examined. One of the consequences which follow from this is that high profits in an industry need not arise from monopoly power, but might instead arise from special advantages enjoyed by certain firms in an industry. Demsetz (1974) has suggested that these special advantages might be a firm's superior organisation. Its superior organisation might lead to growth and concentration, thereby offering an alternative explanation to economies of scale for high concentration ratios and an alternative motive to increased monopoly power to explain mergers.

We could add to Leibenstein's list of causes of *X*-inefficiency differences in management's aspiration levels. Simon argued that managements satisfice rather than maximise. Variations in aspiration levels could then account for differences in the input mixes of the different firms within an industry, i.e. differences in management's APQT bundle.

The introduction of *X*-efficiency allows us to answer, in a more complete way, the question which was introduced above: is perfect competition more efficient than monopoly? The following quotations from Leibenstein illustrate this:

> Within the framework of conventional micro-theory one cannot answer the question of whether monopolies are less *X*-efficient than competitive firms. Despite the fact that the conventional assumptions of micro theory lead to the conclusion that a monopolistic firm and a competitive firm are equally *X*-efficient ... if we are to determine the relative efficiency of monopoly vs. competition from a theoretical view point we must consider a theory of the firm in which the phenomena we are interested in capturing can occur.
>
> (1973, p. 767)

> ... in a great many instances the amount to be gained by increasing allocative efficiency is trivial while the amount to be gained by increasing *X*-efficiency is frequently significant.
>
> (1966, p. 413)

> The level of unit cost depends in some measure on the degree of X-efficiency which in turn depends on the degree of competitive pressure as well as on other motivational factors.
>
> (1966, p. 412)

Thus, the welfare loss from monopoly is frequently much greater than that depicted by the familiar Marshallian triangle. Reductions in competitive pressure increase the scope for discretionary behaviour in all parts of an organisation, which for the reasons already discussed adds to X-inefficiency. According to Crew, Jones-Lee and Rowley (1971), X-inefficiency is a continuously increasing function of discretionary power. Since there is no threat of being driven out of an industry, there is less incentive for a monopolist to reduce costs by eliminating waste and 'padding' within the organisation and by introducing new cost saving technologies and innovations.

The effect of X-inefficiency is shown in Figure 7.1. Here the X-inefficiency is incorporated in the firm's costs which are shown as AC_2 and MC_2.[7] The profit maximising level of output is OQ_3 which is smaller than the X-efficiency monopolist (OQ_2) and much smaller than the perfectly competitive solution (OQ_1). The profit maximising price is OP_3, which is higher than the price charged by the X-efficient monopolist (OP_2). The higher price and lower output do not only indicate a welfare loss to society generally, but reflect a redistribution of income this time from the shareholders of the firm to the labour inputs. In other words, the firm's inputs are enjoying economic rents i.e. rewards over and above those required to keep them in the firm. Leibenstein has recognised that this concept is similar to the notion of *organisational slack* as used by Cyert and March (1963) and by Williamson (1964). Slack consists in payments made to members of a coalition or an organisation in excess of what is required to maintain the organisation. X-efficiency, however, is not uniquely related to side payments, but 'is related to the many motivational facets both within and outside the firm that determine the effort responses of individuals' (Leibenstein 1975, p. 582).

Thus the concept of X-efficiency represents a common meeting ground for the organisation theorists' and the economists' perspectives which were set out in the earlier chapters. The structure of financial incentives set out by the scientific management school and the manipulation of socio-psychological variables as proposed by the human relations school were all representative of attempts to influence the behaviour of organisation members, to improve productivity and thus to increase efficiency i.e. reduce X-inefficiency. Likewise, the earlier classical administrative theorists and the more recent students of organisation structure are interested in seeking out efficient forms of organisational design. Again 'efficient' organisation structures are efficient in terms of reduced X-inefficiency. Hence much of the apparently diverse literature

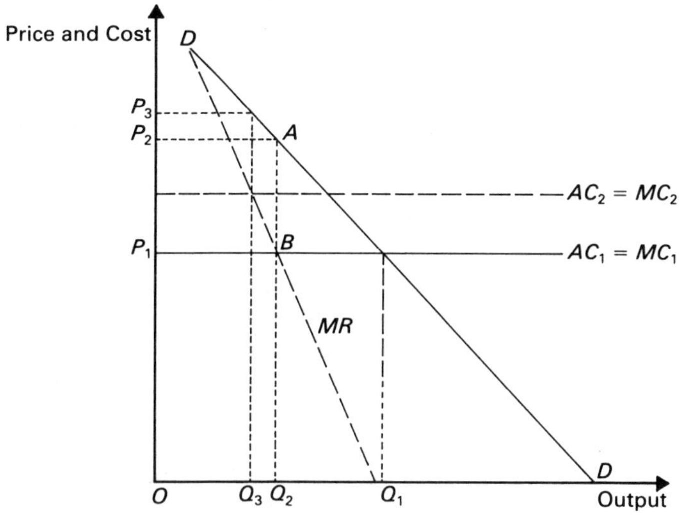

DD = market demand curve
MR = marginal revenue
AC = average costs
MC = marginal costs
AC_1 excludes X-inefficiency
AC_2 includes X-inefficiency

Figure 7.1 *The Effect of X-Inefficiency*

with which this book began comes neatly together through the concept of *X*-efficiency.

Reductions in *X*-inefficiency, therefore, require changes to be made to the supply side of the firm and involve the expenditure of resources. Changes in organisational structure, changes in management/leadership style, the payment of financial incentives to foster cooperation between labour's interests and those of capital and the introduction of control devices are all measures designed to reduce *X*-inefficiency. However, as was suggested in the discussion of the nature of *X*-inefficiency, there are limits to the efficacy of these devices. The transactions or administrative costs limit the power of control devices as too will employees' negative reactions to close supervision. This means that there is a problem involved in designing an *optimal policy* to reduce *X*-inefficiency; not only might the policies have undesirable consequences which result in a further reduction in efficiency (e.g. the lost output following a hostile reception to close supervision), but also the financial benefits (i.e. reductions in efficiency) following from the policy must be weighed up against the costs of implementing it, as in the case of using financial incentives and a costly monitoring system. There is, moreover, another serious limitation to the reduction of *X*-inefficiency. That is, the analyst's limited knowledge of the supply side of the economy, including especially intra-organisational behaviour. Very little is known about the effects of incentives systems, of alternative organisation and administrative systems or the effectiveness of different control devices.

One relatively inexpensive means of partially reducing *X*-inefficiency is to promote competition between firms. As Leibenstein indicated, discretion in the choice of APQT bundles is enhanced by reduced competitiveness. This, however, provides the analyst with a problem. Increased competitiveness requires an increase in the number of producers, which can imply substantially reduced production units. In industries which are characterised by substantial economies of scale, an increase in competition and the reduction in *X*-inefficiency and hence in unit costs has to be weighed up against the *increase* in unit costs arising from the loss in economies of scale. Thus, competition is not necessarily a costless means of reducing inefficiency. Also increasing the number of entrants to an industry does not guarantee maximum *X*-efficiency (Schwartzman 1973). Entry only improves the *average* level of efficiency. In the long run, even under perfect competition, average costs will vary amongst firms of an industry. The conclusion that in the long run average costs are equal among all firms is wrong, because it requires the elimination of all inter-firm efficiency differences. This error reflects the attribution of all variations in factor productivity within a technology to factory quality differences and what is more, it also assumes that such quality differences are completely accounted for by factor prices. The market is supposed to transform all efficiency differences into factor price differences and thus equalise average costs, since the whole system is assumed to be characterised by perfect markets for inputs as well as outputs. Performance, however, depends on individual combinations of factors, operating conditions, history etc., as well as the quality of factors. The market will not, therefore, eliminate cost differences amongst firms. Here we have circularity, since factor quality is not interpreted independently of the performance of firms and so the definition does not permit inter-firm differences.[8]

The concept of *X*-efficiency has undoubtedly contributed much to the efficiency debate, but can we now answer the question, 'is perfect competition more efficient than monopoly?'. The answer must be that the matter remains unresolved. The case for competition has been shown to be deficient in a number of respects. As Schwartzman (1973, p. 762) argues, 'although profit maximisation is likely to promote greater efficiency than other goals such as security within a bureaucracy, it is not a sufficient condition for superiority of efficiency under competition than under central planning and we should not exclude the possibility of its being inferior without investigation'.

This issue will be taken up again in this chapter when alternative means of organising the supply of public sector services are considered.

The Problem of Efficiency in the Public Sector

So far the discussion of efficiency has been general in an attempt to clarify the precise meaning of the concept. Moreover, the analysis has focused upon the relative efficiency of *private sector* monopolies, as compared to firms which face perfectly competitive market conditions. In this section the problems raised by public sector monopolies i.e. bureaucracies, will be reviewed. The distinction between allocative and X-efficiences will be maintained.

The public sector has two broadly defined allocative efficiency problems to solve. First, it has to ensure that resources allocated to the production/provision of public services could not have been put to better use by producing private sector outputs. In other words, is the mix of output between the public and private sectors efficient in the sense that no reallocation of resources from public to private goods will make someone better off whilst everyone else remains no worse off? The second problem refers to the mix of goods within the public sector itself. Is it possible to reallocate resources within the public sector, such that the production of one service is increased without reducing the output of any other?

Allocative inefficiency is almost inherent in public monopoly and arises from the problems involved in demand articulation. There is no simple costless process which will aggregate the diversity of individual preferences into a single collective or social preference ordering over the set of all possible states of the world. Neither is there a simple one to one correspondence between an individual's preferences and the policies offered by politicians, nor is the final outcome simply related to the preferences of the representative politicians. Instead, the outcome is the result of complex political bargaining.[9] Once decisions about taxes and public outputs have been made, the citizen voters are obliged to take these as given and make adjustments in their private spending decisions. This is the public good nature of public sector decisions,[10] although each individual has the potential to adjust his own consumption set by making private sector purchases. For example, an individual who is dissatisfied with the decision pertaining to public sector health provision can, *if* his own resources permit, increase his consumption of health services through private sector purchases.

Allocative inefficiency in bureaucracy arises because public sector decisions are all embracing. There exists a distribution of voter preferences for taxes and public sector outputs around the actual decision outcome. Thus, with the exception of the median voter (if we assume a Downsian world), every other person would have preferred an alternative decision outcome. Consider the following example illustrated by figure 7.2. An individual's demand curve (D_1) for some public good i is shown in figure 7.2. That individual takes as given the public output level OQ_0 and the tax price

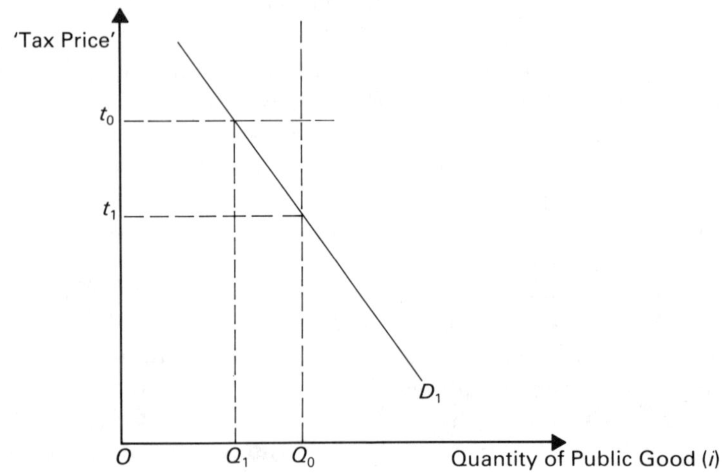

Figure 7.2 *Allocative Inefficiency of Public Sector Output and Price Decisions*

Ot_0. However, if the individual *has* to consume OQ_0 units of the good he would have preferred to pay a price of Ot_1, or put another way, if he has to pay a tax price of Ot_0 he would have preferred to consume OQ_1units of the good. The collective nature of public sector output and price decisions, therefore, results in an allocative inefficiency. Resources are not allocated in accordance with individuals' preferences. The extent of this allocative inefficiency *in aggregate* will depend upon the variance or distribution of preferences around the decision output.[11]

The force of the above arguments is that sources of inefficiency arise because of imperfections on the demand side. In particular, the representativeness of the process through which voter/consumer's demands are articulated is questioned. First, if budget maximising bureaucrats make output decisions, these are unlikely to correspond to the level of output that would have been chosen by, for example, the median voter. Second, even if the role of the bureaucrat were to be minimised to one of producing at minimum cost that level of output demanded by the median voter, there still remains the problem that, whilst that level of public output might be 'efficient' to the median voter, it will not be so for those individuals on either side of his preferences. Thus, on the basis of these arguments, the public sector is inefficient, because the voters' preferences are not sovereign in the decision about what level of output to produce.

It is a well-known result in public sector economics that the rational individual, who realising that the decision to produce the collective good is unlikely to turn on his preferences, will take up a strategic position in which he distorts his preferences in order to pay less for the public good, thereby acting as a free-rider. Not only does the problem of the free-rider impede the use of benefit taxes or prices for public services, but (taken to its logical conclusion) if everyone was to act as a free-rider then the information which this process produces for the decision-maker will in itself lead to inefficiency, since the information is not a true reflection of individual preferences.

The efficiency of the demand articulation process is, therefore, central to any discussion of public sector efficiency. Does the system generate ill-conceived demands, is the political process representative of the interests of the electorate, is the process of representation more heavily weighted towards some interests than others, and do bureaucrats influence the valuation of alternative policies? These questions lie at the heart of the policy analysis debate. To answer them fully is not our present purpose. Rather, the intention is to show the way in which individual/voter preferences are handled in systems which determine where the economy ends up on its efficiency frontier. Those are the same type of questions which economists like Galbraith (1969) have asked about the private sector. Is the consumer sovereign, or is the producer king? It is, however, generally agreed that the problems which surround this question, when asked in the context of the public sector, are more complex because of the nature of public sector output decisions.

There is a potential weak link between the voter and his elected representative and there is a weak link between the decisions of the elected representative and what actually appears as the implementation of these decisions. The act of casting a vote does not permit the voter to express his *intensity of preference* for one policy as compared to another. Also, the system of representative democracy and party politics which exists in the UK, for example, means that a voter when electing a representative has to vote for a vector of policies without being able to express any preferences for policies contained within that vector. It is the Cabinet which makes the final decisions and this raises the question of the relationship which exists between constituency Members of Parliament, the party and the Cabinet when it comes to making decisions. These problems are of course compounded by the role played by bureaucrats in providing information and in guiding policy decisions and also in the implementation of the decision. Thus, the relationship which exists between any single voter's preferences for a particular policy and the final outcome is extremely complex, thereby presenting immense problems for any judgment regarding allocative efficiency.

One aspect of this issue which a number of writers have concentrated upon is the role played by pressure groups and their influence upon output decisions. Buchanan and Tullock (1962), for example, argue that the activities of pressure groups can result in an over-expansion of the size of the public sector. This is equivalent to saying that the public sector is producing too much output and that an improvement in efficiency could be achieved from a re-allocation of resources from the public to the private sector. Pressure groups exist to promote, through lobbying, the interests of one section of the community e.g. to protect the interests of organised labour, or big business, or amenities etc. To the extent that vote maximising politicians can 'buy off' the demands made by each group, public sector output will expand. However, it was Anthony Crosland who always expressed concern about recognising pressure groups and giving in to their demands, because in a large number of instances these groups are totally unrepresentative. The pressure groups which are noticed are those which have the most to gain from the action and, moreover, they are those who are well-organised and have the resources to be organised. At the same time, however, there also exist the weak, the unorganised and those who do not have the resources to be organised. They have to be represented in the system. But if politicians recognise the organised at the expense of the unorganised, not only is there an inefficiency problem, but there is also a moral problem arising from the distribution of the benefits of public services. Problems of distributive justice are discussed later in this chapter.

The Generalised Goal Model of Efficiency

Rational analysis or normative decision models generally formulate the decision process as one in which some well specified objective function is maximised, subject to a given set of physical and technical constraints. The outcome of such decisions is an optimal or an efficient allocation of resources. This approach is well documented in the literature of economics, business and public administration. The early Simon subscribed to such a view, in which efficiency was defined as, 'the ratio of the effects actually obtained with the available resources to the maximum effects possible with the available resources ... In its broadest terms (the concept of efficiency) is scientific method applied to government' (Simon and Ridley 1938, pp. 20–5). They then go on to argue that what is required is a clear specification of the goals of the activity followed by analysis to find out if these goals are achieved. These questions were apparent to Ridley and Simon (1938) when they found problems in calculating the most efficient case loads for social workers. However, what are the problems involved in implementing this framework? Are, for example, goals/objectives as well specified as the rational approach demands?

Discussions of efficiency start with some notion of a performance measure or indicator against which behaviour can be judged. Frequently, especially in economics, univariate performance indicators such as profit or productivity are used (Georgopoulos and Tannenbaum 1957). A question which is frequently asked is, are such univariate measures at all useful in the sense that they encompass what is generally meant by efficiency and effectiveness? In a recent study (Steers 1975), 17 multivariate models of effectiveness were compared and it was found that there was very little consensus on the importance of any specific evaluative criterion. One general view which does, however, emerge from the literature, especially that of the rational choice approach, is that organisations are usefully thought of as goal seeking entities and that efficiency can be discussed in terms of the extent to which organisations achieve their goals (Yuchtman and Seashore 1967, Gross 1969 and Georgiou 1973). Thus efficiency analysis proceeds by examining the reported goals/target variables and the success or otherwise of organisations in achieving these goals.

This approach is not without a number of serious conceptual and operational difficulties. The idea of goal seeking behaviour is, as March and Simon (1958) stressed, problematic. A goal is some future state of the world which the members of the organisation try to bring about by the application of a set of means. A time dependent means–end sequence implies, therefore, the existence of a series of intermediate states which may or may not be emphasised. To the extent that they are, they become themselves goals and might be called intermediate goals, with reference being made to some global or end state which is the primary goal of the system. The efficiency model as set out is a means–ends model. But which ends are achieved? Is it the primary end state, or is it one, or a number of intermediate goals? Whilst the bureaucracy might be successfully achieving one of its intermediate goals and be regarded as being efficient, it might nevertheless be far removed from achieving its primary goal. If sub-optimising is found to be acceptable (satisfactory) by those who control the bureaucracy, there is no incentive for bureaucrats to proceed to a full optimisation. Sub-optimisation and goal displacement (see Merton 1957 and Parsons 1960) are, therefore, related concepts.

A reading of the literature on organisational goals reveals that in study after study there is now general agreement that the official, formally stated goals of the organisation are of little value for judging efficiency and effectiveness (Gouldner 1959, Etzioni 1960, Perrow 1961 and Hall 1972). Each of these and many other studies demonstrate that official or primary goals are too vague and too general to be operational. For example, the primary objectives of many public bureaucracies are found in legislation, but are so general that precise targets are impossible to specify. Thus, the objective of housing policy is to provide 'good housing for the whole populace', whatever that might mean, or education policy is aimed at ensuring that every child receives an 'adequate education'. Precise definitions of what constitutes 'good' or 'adequate' are never set out and become the focus of debate and, in many instances, controversy. In the absence of adequately specified official goals, *operative goals* are used instead. The latter are defined as goals which designate the ends sought through the actual operating policies of the organisation; they tell us what the organisation is actually trying to do, regardless of what the official goals specify as the aims (Perrow 1961, p. 855).

To find out what organisations are doing is itself no simple matter. The collective behaviour of the members of an organisation at any moment in time is a function of the complex interplay of forces and power struggles of the kind described in Chapter 4. Operative goals are, therefore, the objectives of the dominant group or coalition and as the power distribution shifts over time, so too will the specification of the operative goal. It might be thought that goals can be inferred from revealed behaviour; however, the interpretation of the data by the observer means that there is the possibility of bias. Keeley (1978) argues that the activities of organisational participants are not unambiguous and different members of the organisation can give accounts which are inconsistent. 'Since human behaviour is multipurposed and since there is a nearly infinite variety of labels available to describe these purposes, reporting the 'real' purposes of organisation activity is a speculative affair' (Keeley 1978, p. 273). Moreover, the operative goal approach is at best a description of what the organisation is doing. A description severely constrained by the limits of analysis already discussed. There is nothing normative or evaluative in the approach which could lead the analyst to judge the effectiveness or efficiency of the system, let alone compare it to alternative systems.

The achievement of operative goals or intermediate goals is an example of sub-optimisation. It is a second best solution rather than a first best, but given the information constraints on the nature of the primary objectives it is in most cases the best that is available. This is an example of *X*-inefficiency arising from a lack of knowledge of the production function for the organisation's full set of activities. If the primary objective is not unambiguously specified, this is equivalent to saying that the production function is not fully specified.

This is one of the major empirical weaknesses which currently exists in rational policy analysis. Because the production function is so poorly specified, sub-optimisation must often be the rule. The links which specify the relationships between the activities that go on within the organisation and the primary objectives are frequently so ill-defined that improvements in efficiency are almost impossible. For example, if one could take the primary objective of a hospital as one of improvement in patient health and then relate the contributions of all of the various activities to that, then it might be possible to demonstrate that the level of some activities was out of line with what was required. They could be cut back, thereby eliminating waste. However, because such exercises are difficult to carry out, resources tend to be allocated as a result of the budgetary and bargaining games that have already been described throughout this book.

Another source of *X*-inefficiency can arise from the presence of goal conflict. 'A common purpose might be a useful fiction for cementing organisational coalition; but it must be a non-operational goal. Organisational performance depends upon joint purposes'. (Loasby 1976, p. 137). The existence of internal conflict in organisations challenges a number of the often held assumptions about goals in organisations (Selznick 1949 and 1957, Zald 1962, and Perrow 1965). The first point is the one which has already been made. Organisations are not oriented towards a single goal and even in a multiple objective organisation in which the trade-off between the various goals has been negotiated and agreed, these goals are often highly ambiguously specified and not operational. Thus, one is not even sure when these goals have been achieved adequately. The actual goals of the organisation can be found only when the official goal is factored into operational goals (Cyert and March 1963). This process of factorisation increases the number of operational goals and hence raises the chances of goal conflict arising. Many arguments about bureaucratic inefficiency can be reduced to arguments of whether or not the bureaucracy should be performing one set of activities, rather than another i.e. serving one set of goals rather than another. It has already been seen that, given the distribution of preferences within society, this must always be an inherent feature. In this case the goal conflict is interpreted as an allocative inefficiency originating on the demand side. However, inefficiency arising from goal conflict can exist on the supply side also. In this case, active non-cooperation of labour arising from goal conflict (i.e. a clash of interests over whose goals are to be served) will result in *X*-inefficiency.

Examples of goal conflict are found in firms where the sales division's marketing goals do not conform to the production division's production targets or in a university where faculty disapproves of constraints placed upon them by administrators. The goals of treatment and custody are frequently in conflict in prisons and mental hospitals and for those managing the macro-economy the pursuit of full employment, a balance of payments, a low rate of inflation and a high rate of growth are all in conflict. Suppose, for example, that the existing set of operative goals only very partially serves the primary goals of the system and that this set of operative goals is challenged by another set which will, if the challenge is successful, enable the system to move closer to the primary goal. In this case, the outcome of conflict over the operative goals would be functional, provided that the costs of the conflict are outweighted by the present value of the benefits which follow.[12] Second, the progress, growth and development of an organisation depend upon the evolution of new objectives which require the displacement of existing ones. In this case, the conflict is either over primary objectives (i.e. on the demand side) or over operative goals i.e. on the supply side, when the existing means of production are being challenged.

Goal conflict is not, therefore, by definition dysfunctional. But there are other problems to be taken into account. Attempts to reduce goal conflict might in themselves reduce organisational performance. Loasby (1976), following in the tradition of Barnard and Simon, argues that one important set of incentives which face members of an organisation is the nature of the control system and the scope for contributing to joint decision making in formulating the goals of the system. Thus, attempts to align individual and organisational objectives through a formal control system may actually impede the performance of individuals.

There is, however, another aspect to the issue. Cyert and March (1963) have argued that goal conflict can be accommodated if goals are pursued sequentially. However, to do so successfully requires that the organisation's environment is 'benign' i.e. poses few threats such as fierce competition, or that the organisation has a lot of 'slack' i.e. extra resources, money labour and capital. Thus, rather than necessarily causing inefficiency directly, the containment and resolution of goal conflict requires the existence of *X*-inefficiency in the form of organisational slack. Whether or not this is undesirable is arguable, since we would need to know the effects on the organisation's unit costs etc. if that slack was to be eliminated and the goal conflict not contained.

It can be seen, therefore, that simple efficiency rules formulated in terms of the realisation of objectives ignore a number of issues which are encountered when such rules are made operational. This is not to disprove in any sense the prescriptions or conclusions of rational decision analysis. Decisions based upon a fully articulated framework in which goals (objectives) are clearly specified will be more efficient than decisions which are not. What the approach adopted here has demonstrated is that there are in practice a number of limits which are placed upon the realisation of the advantages of rational decision making. The specification of the objectives can in many instances involve real decision costs.

Defining Output

The problems of defining the ouput of public sector services have been stated in at least two different ways. First, in common with many service industries, it is generally difficult to measure the physical outputs of public sector goods. The lack of any suitable physical measure of output is a problem for ensuring productive efficiency and productivity measurement. This follows from the difficulty of specifying a production function as was observed in the previous section. What for example is the output of the education industry? Is it the score on some test, is it the probability of increasing future lifetime earnings, or is it some inherent value placed upon the personal state of being educated? What is the output of the police department? Is it the change in the probability of being involved in a crime, or is it the number of offences cleared up by the police? These are interesting questions which have involved those who study these services in a great deal of imaginative thinking. The points which emerge from arguments of this kind are: 1) physical measures of these output concepts are not readily available; 2) physical measures do not exist because the final outputs of these services are usually thought of as personal states of well being e.g. the state of being educated to some level, or the feeling of being 'safe', or the state of being 'healthy'; and 3) the acts of production and consumption of public services are frequently simultaneous — there is no intermediate *physical* product produced. For example, when doctors and nurses engage in a set of activities which result in the improvement of a patient's state of health there is no clearly identifiable final output which can be measured. Whilst these problems undoubtedly exist, it should, however, be pointed out that identifying and measuring the physical characteristics of final outputs is neither more nor less difficult in the public sector than in the private sector. In either case, the physical characteristics of almost all outputs are exceedingly complex (Schultz 1973, p. 387). For example, it would generally be regarded that the output of the automobile industry is unambiguously the physical output of an automobile. However, there are many different types and styles of automobiles, each embodying a complex amalgam of characteristics. The production function, therefore, is not the relationship between inputs and the output of *an* automobile. It is instead the relationship between a set of inputs and a vector of characteristics which are labelled as an automobile.[14] Thus for each type of automobile there will be a different production function. The identification of these characteristics is just as complex as the identification of the characteristics of some public sector product such as education or health care. Moreover, an automobile is not, as is frequently imagined, a final consumption good. It is an intermediate good. What enters the individual's utility function is miles or hours of motoring, for which an automobile is a means to that end.

The second way of considering the problem of output measurement is that we do not have measures of the *value* of public output. It is this which is important for discussions of efficiency in resource allocation. Physical output measures, it has been seen, are essentially meaningless, whether it be public or private output that is being measured. Dissimilar items can be aggregated, as in the case of the national income accounts, only if they are placed on the same measuring rod. The measuring rod of value (i.e. price × quantity) is a more meaningful measure for such aggregation than physical measures such as volume or weight. Thus, it is the objective of economic policy to maximise the value of the total output of the economy, rather than to maximise its weight! When discussing efficiency the aim is to maximise the value of the output for a given real value of inputs used in the production of that output. This underlies the profit maximisation assumption. The use of value as a measure of output also helps to solve the problem of quality differences like those outlined in the example of the automobile. Quality differences are defined in terms of differences in the vector of characteristics that are embodied in the product. Thus differences in the value of products of differing quality are due to differences in the valuation of the vector of characteristics.[15]

The problem with output measurement in the public sector is not so much a lack of physical output measurement, as an absence of a measure of the value of that output. This arises because the output is not marketed. Cost–benefit analysis, for instance, does make attempts to assign shadow prices to public outputs in order to value them, but there are many technical problems which limit the scope to do so. For example individuals, if asked, might have no idea of how much they would be willing to pay, unless they also knew a lot more about the characteristics of the output they would be receiving. Specification of the output, as already noted, is in practice difficult. It is, however, worthwhile speculating and asking how much the consumers of private sector products know about the characteristics of the goods that they purchase. Every purchase is a gamble and the act of consumption is usually one in which the desirable and undesirable features of the product are discovered and compared against some *a priori* expectation of benefits.[16] Once again, it is found that whilst problems of output valuation are acute in the public sector, similar problems do exist in the private sector, although the private sector is not traditionally thought of in these terms. Another problem which limits the analyst's ability to assign prices to public outputs is that of the 'free-rider'. Because it is rational for individuals to under-represent how much they would be willing to pay for some amount of public output, they are therefore likely to cheat and to lie if asked.[17]

Without some valuation of the output of the service to compare with the costs of production, it is difficult to secure improvements in performance. Lack of knowledge about input and output relationships is central to the issue of public sector efficiency. Olson (1973, p. 363) has put the problem as follows: 'governments generally know only their expenditures, and normally have next to no idea what impact or volume of output these expenditures bring about, if any, and if they did know what they produced they would still have quite a problem to find out what it was worth to its consumers'. For a consumer of public education to know how much education expenditure to vote for, there must be some knowledge of the relation between that expenditure and the outcome. But clearly such technical knowledge about input–output relationships and unit costs are not known to voters — they are not even known to the producers of the service!

What this discussion amounts to saying is, when input–output relationships are incompletely known and when consumers are unable to place a value on the output of the product, the scope for improving the allocative and X-efficiency of the system is severely limited.

Efficiency and Decision Making Costs

In much of the literature, especially the prescriptive management literature, which is aimed at introducing techniques that will improve the efficiency of production and result in cost reductions, the decision costs of acquiring information and implementing cost reducing techniques are seldom discussed. The achievement of cost reductions in many instances involves expenditure of real resources, such as the hiring of consultants to produce a report, the use of experts to implement the policy prescription and the attendant costs of bringing about a more efficient production line, which might involve the organisation in writing-off large amounts of existing capital stock, or making redundancy payments to employees. Thus, in any consideration of efficiency, there exists the following management problem: 'will the present value of the expected benefits gained from the improvements exceed the costs of implementing the policy?' To private firms, the relevant costs and benefits are purely private. This means that society as a whole might forego an improvement in the efficient allocation of resources if that improvement should turn out not to be profitable to the private sector firms. In the case of the public bureaucracy, however, society will benefit from such a calculation to the extent that the public sector decision maker calculates on the basis of social benefits and social costs.

Control Loss and Efficiency

Efficient allocations of resources are based on decisions which are in turn dependent upon information. Information, however, is distributed throughout an organisation and has to be communicated upwards, downwards, and sideways within organisations. March and Simon (1958), Tullock (1965), and Dunsire (1978) argue that information is unintentionally biased and filtered as it passes from one part of the organisation to another. (This was discussed in connection with 'uncertainty absorption' in Chapter 4.) The greater the number of times information is passed from one part of the organisation to another, the greater is the cumulative distortion and bias. Thus, the greater is the potential loss in efficiency. Biased information reduces the chances of an organisation meeting its goals, and a proportion of the organisation's resources are absorbed as unintended inefficiencies (see Down 1967 and Williamson 1967). However, any attempts to obtain compliance and to improve the quality of information, thereby reducing control loss, will involve decision making costs and other transactions costs such as negotiating and implementing, monitoring and control, and coordination procedures. The resource costs of control loss must, therefore, be balanced against the decision costs.

Empirical Studies of Public Sector Productivity

Productivity measurement in the public sector is a relatively new research topic for economists. Given the problems involved in defining the vector of public sector outputs, it is not too surprising that studies of productivity in public sector bureaucracies have faced enormous conceptual as well as measurement difficulties. There are not many studies in this area. However, interesting and useful studies, which also survey the relevant literature and the issues involved, are to be found in Ross and Burkhead (1974), Hayes (1977) and Spann (1977).

What do the studies that have been conducted reveal about public sector productivity? This is not an easy question to answer. Many of the studies are of varying quality and of those which have been carried out in a careful and scientific manner, the majority conclude with the warning that their results are tentative and highly qualified by the assumptions made. The Bradford Malt and Oates (1969) study examined productivity in four US local government services: education, police, fire and hospitals. In each case, they confirmed the existence of low or lagging productivity as compared with other industries in the economy, especially those in the manufacturing sector. Klarman (1964) concluded that one of the most important causes of hospital cost increases was the lag in productivity in the health care sector. Hatry and Fisk (1971) studied productivity in garbage collection in New York and Washington and found that productivity growth in that service had been nil over the period 1960–1968. A study carried out by the Civil Service Commission General Accounting Office and the Office of Management and Budget (1972) estimated the productivity of the Federal government. The results of this study led them to the conclusion that, whilst there had been some productivity gains in federal government activities, nevertheless these gains were less than gains in the private sector.

In each of the studies reviewed, the general approach which has so far been adopted is to measure the trend in the productivity of some public service. This has been done in order to establish whether or not low productivity increases account for the rapid increase in public sector costs (expenditures).[18] However, public sector productivity studies are relatively new in economics and are fraught with difficulties. It is, therefore, not too surprising that progress has been slow and researchers looking for a topic that will provide them with a string of publications have not been eager to rush in!

The next sections to this chapter are therefore of a speculative nature. They are more in the form of a research agenda and consider possible complementary approaches to a fuller discussion of bureaucratic efficiency.

Efficiency and Organisational Structures

X-efficiency refers to the ratio of inputs to outputs and some decisions which relate these inputs to the outputs are said to be relatively more or less efficient than others. Since decisions are made by individuals in an organisational context, it is therefore logical to ask the question, 'how do organisational variables influence input/output decisions and hence the *X*-efficiency of the system?'

In Chapter 2 a number of organisational perspectives were reviewed. Each set of theories was prescriptive and proposed a link between different organisation structures or management (leadership) styles and productivity or efficiency. It was argued by theorists in the scientific management, the classical administration, and the human relations schools that there were certain organisation structures and management styles that were better than others, where 'better' was defined with reference to the single dimension of efficiency. It can now be seen that these approaches were involved in a discussion of *X*-efficiency. They were concerned with the problem of producing some given level of output at a lower unit cost; that is, with movements from some point within the efficiency frontier to some point on its surface.

Two broad organisational structures were identified. These were the mechanistic and the organic forms. Each performed at a level of efficiency relative to a particular specification of the organisation's environment. Thus the mechanistic organisation was characterised by a rigid hierarchical structure of well-specified roles and administrative routines. Such organisations, it was found, performed well in environments which are low in uncertainty, relatively stable and not complex (see Burns and Stalker 1961, Woodward 1958, Emery and Trist 1965, Bennis 1966 and Hunt 1972). Organic organisations, at the other extreme of the continuum, are less structured, more fluid, and thus enable decision makers to be more responsive to the rapid changes brought about by complex, unstable and highly uncertain environments.

This means that to realise efficiency improvements, it will be necessary to think of different organisation structures for different tasks, i.e. for change, for routine activities and for handling complexity. Clearly, there is no single ideal or best organisational structure (Child 1973). There are instead trade-offs which must be made over the set of organisational characteristics. Each structure has advantages and disadvantages relative to a specification of its environment. The appropriate organisation structure depends on the demands made on it by its environment and technology. This was a mistake made by Weber who thought in terms of a single ideal type:

> The decisive reason for the advance of bureaucratic organisation has always been its purely technical superiority over any other form of

> organisation. The fully developed bureaucratic mechanism compares with other organisations as does the machine with the non-mechanical modes of production. Precision, speed, unambiguity, knowledge of the files, continuity, discretion, unity, strict subordination, reduction of efficiency and of personal and material costs — these are raised to an optimum point in the strictly bureaucratic administration and particularly in its monocratic form. As compared with all collegiate, honorific and avocational forms of administration, trained bureaucracy is superior on all these points.
>
> (Weber 1947, p. 214)

Weber's approach was normative rather than positive, which implies that he did not monitor the performance of actual bureaucratic behaviour against the ideal, nor did he discuss the dysfunctions of bureaucracies, such as the limitations that rule-bound behaviour place upon organisational members' ability to deal with new and unprogrammed situations. Moreover, Weber's ideal bureaucracy was compared to the existing organisational forms of his day, which were rife with corruption, nepotism and inefficiency. Bureaucratic or hierarchical organisation structure introduces certainty which is required for efficient decision making of a routine kind. The original use of bureaucracy was to bring stability and control into society. Such structures are not, however, of universal applicability.

The wrong choice of organisation structures will result in inefficiencies. Perrow (1970), when discussing the famous Trist/Bamford study of the Longwall method of coal mining, has pointed out that, 'the rationalisation attempt broke up the existing system of interpersonal relations and mutual support and promoted expensive competition between shifts for the best seams. In general it lowered the level of cooperation and morale'. The set of relationships which had grown up amongst the workers assisted in overcoming their own uncertainty (a similar finding was made by Gouldner (1952) in his study).

There is no doubt that the voluminous literature on management styles and organisational structures has much to teach if the objective of the exercise is to reduce *X*-inefficiency. Downs (1967) recognised this in his early economic study of bureaucracy. The efficiency of the internal communication system, the information gathering (intelligence) system, the internal separation of functions, the ability to motivate members of the organisation to think creatively, the degree of specialisation and the span of control all in some way or another contribute to the ability of decision makers in the organisation to make efficient decisions. Whereas in the past the subscribers to the scientific management school or the classical administration school were highly normative and prescriptive in their approach, today a more positive approach predominates. The focus of attention now concentrates upon searching out how organisational behaviour and efficiency are affected by these factors.

The same conclusion applies to the leadership studies of the human relations school. Undoubtedly, management style can be important to an individual's choice of APQT bundle (see Chapter 4) and hence *X*-efficiency, but just how important leadership style is as compared for example to economic incentives and material rewards remains an open question. To what extent does the presence of restrictive practices, active non-cooperation by labour (e.g. goal conflict)and passive non-cooperation (i.e. insufficient work effort) arise from a desire by workers to enjoy some of the perks, privileges and rents enjoyed by management? To what extent is it part of a class conflict which spills over from the wider society into organisational interactions and exchanges, so that a management style which is seen by workers to be highly rewarded for little effort is met by a low effort performance by workers? But this is entering into the realm of speculation. A good deal more empirical work is required before we know why workers choose the APQT bundles that they do.

Williamson's (1970) distinction between *U*- and *M*-forms of organisation structure, which were discussed earlier in Chapter 3, demonstrated that the *U*-form ran into problems of control and hence efficiency as the organisation grew in size. The *U*-form can grow only by expanding further hierarchical levels which results in control loss (see above) i.e. difficulties in the transmission of information for efficient decision making. On the other hand, the *M*-form 'favours goal pursuit and least-cost behaviour' (Williamson 1970, p. 134).

The message which comes out of these studies is that the particular form of organisation structure influences behaviour within the organisation and that these influences are of relevance to any discussion of *X*-inefficiency. Many of the 'proverbs' of the earlier classical writers in the management sciences might at the end of the day contain many grains of truth. However, whilst the management science and organisation sociology literature give clues about some of the relevant questions to ask about organisation structure, we still remain some considerable distance away from possessing a well-articulated theory of the efficiency properties of alternative organisational structures and even further away from a set of empirically tested propositions. Clearly, this is an area which deserves much greater attention from economists.

Efficiency, Complexity and Uncertainty

Decision makers in organisations face environments which vary in their degree of complexity and uncertainty. Following on from the logic that *X*-efficiency is in part determined by the quality of input/output decisions, we now enquire how such decisions might be affected by the complexity and uncertainty of the environment faced by the decision maker? Clearly, this is related to the previous distinction made between mechanistic and organic organisation structures. In this section, however, other aspects of the problem are considered.

Decision making, it will be recalled, can either be thought of as a purely rational and objective set of responses which result in an optimal choice from a set of alternatives, or it can be viewed as a series of subjective reponses by the decision maker. This latter view proceeds on the assumptions of methodological individualism (i.e. that all economic phenomena should be related to the decisions of individual human actors) and subjectivism, that individuals do not make choices based upon some objectively correct state of the world, but rather upon their own subjective and generally imperfect knowledge of their environment (see Littlechild 1978a and b, Wiseman 1957 and Loasby 1976). This approach, which Littlechild (1978a) has termed 'Austrian', is from the same stable as the behavioural models of Simon and Cyert and March, since each is concerned with the following types of question: what agents are involved in the various stages of the decision making process, what knowledge do they have, what incentives exist to acquire knowledge, what opportunities are open to them (i.e. what are the constraints) and what motivation do they have?[19] This is a positive approach to decision making which searches out the real limitations on the operationalisation of the rational or objective approach, which is prescriptive.

Clearly the questions asked by organisation theorists do fit into this line of reasoning. To what extent do different organisational structures influence the generation and transmission (communication) of information around the system? Is the distribution of rights and functions throughout the organisation the appropriate one for efficient decision making? To what extent do individuals bear responsibility for the consequences (intended or unintended) of their actions? Is there an appropriate set of incentives which will induce individuals to acquire information for decision making? Asking questions in terms of how various features of the organisation affect the perceptions and decisions of individuals, rather than how they affect the behaviour of organisations, is first, more meaningful and second, allows the discussion of a wider set of issues including that of efficiency.

The subjective nature of decision making has been emphasised which in turn implies that there can be no complete or objectively correct procedure or solution to a decision problem. Each individual proceeds as he thinks best and chooses that course of action which he finds satisfies his current set of aspirations. This allows us to examine another kind of statement which is frequently made about efficiency.

Post mortems or post evaluation exercises carried out on major decisions often make the judgment that the decision was poor and could have been better. In making such a judgment the outcome of the decision is set against some measure of performance (e.g. profitability) and if it falls short, the conclusion is that the outcome was an inefficient one. However, there are a number of problems involved in such an exercise. If the environment which the individual faces is both complex and highly uncertain, and this is the kind of environment which typifies most major decisions, then it follows that the individual cannot know at the time of making the decision his mistakes of commission and omission (Littlechild 1978a). Individuals who face different information structures, and this includes their own perceptions which generate that information, are likely to make different decisions. Could the decision have been better? Decision makers are unlikely to know the answer to this question, nor are those who criticise the outcome of the decision *ex post* (i.e. with the benefit of hindsight). The possession of information *ex post* changes the information structure and reduces a situation of uncertainty to one of certainty. All the intended and unintended consequences are then known, whereas previously, when the original decision was taken, they were either nothing more than guesses or completely undreamt of. To decide upon whether or not a decision could have been better would require finding out whether the information available was deficient in some respect, whether the computations and assessments made about the problem were the correct ones and so on. This comes back to finding out more about the organisational context within which the decision was taken, especially the flows of information and their communication and the way in which the problem was structured and perceived. It would, however, be a mistake to assume that this is an easy task. As Loasby (1976, p. 138) points out, '... the degree of ignorance about possible future states and of the impact of particular decisions on future results, may make it difficult to assess the correctness of the choice made. If, for example, that choice is made according to the precepts of decision theory, then assessment of the decision becomes assessment of the subjective probabilities used; and even after the event, that is not easy'.

What has this observation to teach those who carry out post evaluative studies? One thing is that unless these problems are appreciated, then a harsh or a severe treatment of decision makers in the post evaluative report might produce some unintended consequences. If every time the outcome of a decision, which does not meet some target, is subjected to severe criticism, or if the threat of such criticism always exists, then disincentives are likely to be created and those making the decision will always tend to play safe and not take risks. This opens up another set of interesting questions about the nature of the incentives which decision makers face.

Incentives and Efficiency

We have already said a great deal about this in previous chapters. Barnard (1938) and Simon (1965) saw management's problem as one of administering the incentive structure of the organisation in order to establish consensus and harmony and thereby reduce conflict which was assumed to be dysfunctional.

The empirical relationship which exists between alternative incentives and the individual's choice of an APQT bundle, including work effort, remains in dispute. Thus, the manipulation of incentives in order to reduce X-inefficiency in this field remains a grey area.

Incentives, however, do not only relate to choices made by members of the organisation over a set of alternative APQT bundles. There is also the question of the incentives for individuals to reveal their preferences for public services[20] and there are also the incentives for decision makers to choose one set of activities rather than another. For example, what incentives exist for a decision maker to ask for information in order to make a decision and what incentives exist for him to take risks?

Consider a budget maximising bureaucrat of the Niskanen type. When undertaking the appraisal of a new project, it would be in the interests of the budget maximising bureaucrat to understate the costs and to overstate the benefits of the project and at the same time to use a low rate of discount when calculating expected net benefits to the community. This kind of strategy increases the chances of the project being approved and the continued existence of the bureau. Because of the command that the bureaucrat has over specialist information regarding benefits and costs, there is very little control available to the political decision maker, unless he is willing to incur the expenses of obtaining an independent appraisal.

Contractual incentive functions and performance incentive functions abound in the management literature (see Berhold 1971, Baumol 1975 and Weitzman 1976). These are discussed in the context of the mechanisms and rules which relate monetary rewards to performance (such as profit sharing), the motivation of agents in the hierarchy, the problems of obtaining compliance with organisational goals, and methods of reducing decision making discretion. All of these mechanisms are designed with one objective in mind — to meet production commitments with the minimum of X-inefficiency.

But the design and management of incentive systems are fraught with difficulties. First, there is the problem of contract specification. If contracts are poorly specified, X-inefficiency arises because it becomes difficult to decide whether or not an individual's performance fails to fulfil the requirements of the contract. Thus, low levels of performance can be deemed to satisfy the contract. Second, even if contracts were tightly specified, there would be high transactions costs involved in policing and monitoring the system to ensure that the conditions of the contract were being satisfied. Also, as has already been indicated, tight monitoring and close supervision can have the unintended consequences of producing a hostile reaction from those being supervised, which could then result in a reduction in performance. It would, however, be a mistake to assume that all incentive schemes are contractual. Weitzman (1976) describes the new Soviet incentive model. The agents implementing the plan are rewarded according to the degree to which the plan's targets are achieved. These targets are not agreed contractually by the planners and the enterprise managers. Rather, the state unilaterally chooses indicators and rewards and enterprise managers are expected to comply out of self-interest. Third, individuals might engage in search activity in order to find ways of beating the system i.e. to conform to the incentives whilst continuing to maximise their own rents and *X*-inefficiency. Fourth, when uncertainty exists, is it possible to decide whether or not an individual's poor performance, as measured by some outcome, is due to his incompetence, or to events that lie outside his control? If the latter is the case, should they be penalised by losing bonus etc.? This relates back to the problems of specifying contracts. How should contracts be specified for differing risks? Fifth, different incentives might produce unexpected and undesirable consequences. Grove (1973, pp. 394–5) gives the illustration of the body count in the Vietnamese war, 'When first instituted the body count system doubtless had much logic (of a sort) in the back of it. What better measure could there be of a soldier's work performance? But inevitably after a while it no longer mattered what "bodies" were being counted and the GI and his officers were given a bad time if bodies were not produced'. The second example is the incentive system introduced to the police service in the town of Orange, California.[21] The policemen there obtained a 1% increase in their salaries for every 3% reduction in rape, robbery, burglary and auto-thefts. Doubtless the reader is able to work out the undesirable consequences which these incentive systems are likely to produce.

The career structure within the organisation is another source of incentives. It will be recalled from the discussion of the economics of internal labour markets in Chapter 3 that the operation of the career system can produce some unexpected consequences for efficiency. For example, if promotion depends purely upon performance, this can result in a withholding of information by older people who have accumulated knowledge and experience about the job for a number of years. Barriers to the dissemination of information to younger persons, who are seen as a threat, can reduce the average level of performance of the system. Similarly, if promotion is based purely upon a seniority basis, which is not related to performance achievement, there is no incentive within the career system to improve upon performance. The Fulton Report (1968) argued that for the UK Civil Service, 'career planning ... is not sufficiently purposive or properly conceived: civil servants are moved too frequently between unrelated jobs, often with scant regard to personal preference or aptitude. Nor is there enough encouragment and reward for individual initiative and objectively measured performance ...'.

Managerial Risks and Rewards in Public Bureaucracies

The question of how to induce appropriate attitudes by public enterprise and bureaucracy managers towards risks has long been discussed (von Mises 1935, Lange 1938 and Hayek 1948) and continues to be discussed today (Bergson 1978b). These questions of whether or not efficiency exists and whether or not managers are willing to take risks in bureaucracy and public enterprise are in many respects similar to the kind of discussions which surrounded the great debate on the merits of socialism during the inter-war years i.e. the relative efficiency and performances of different economic systems. Mises doubted that public enterprise managers would be willing to take risks, because their rewards for doing so would be constrained under socialist planning. Hayek argued that they would prefer the safe to the risky enterprise, so that they would not lose their job if the risky venture failed. Innovation would, therefore, be hindered under socialist planning because of the burdens of planning and the general aversion of managers to risk. Lange on the other hand argued that socialist planning provided a solution to the tendency of monopoly restrictionism and interventionism which limited the introduction of new technologies under capitalism. Moreover, Dickenson (1939) argued that with suitable incentives, public enterprise managers would experiment and improve the service. His suggestion was to provide bonuses of between 50%–100% of base salary.

More recently, Bergson (1966 and 1978a) has pointed out that if there exists a reasonable minded and fair system with regard to rewards and dismissal, then it should be possible to create a climate in which managers evaluate risk in whatever is considered to be the appropriate manner. Given the assumption of fairness, there is then no reason to suppose that managers will be either too venturesome or too cautious.

The problem of managerial incentives can be stated more precisely in the following terms. The decision maker (i.e. public enterprise manager, bureaucrat or politician) has to make choices between alternative policies. At the time the decision is made, there exists a diversity of social states which may prevail with different probabilities attached to each. The manager's choice of policy not only yields net benefits to the community, but will yield benefits to the manager also. The actual outcome of the decision is, however, uncertain, since it will depend upon the social state which actually prevails. The problem is then to find some means which will ensure that expected community benefit is maximised. Will it necessarily be true that if managerial expected utility is maximised, then expected community net benefit is also maximised? Is it possible to devise a set of incentives to ensure this?

Clearly there are all kinds of problems involved in operationalising such formulations of the problem. It is difficult in practice to measure any activity's net benefit to the community. Nevertheless, this means of proceeding allows us to identify the problem as that of ensuring that public enterprise managers/bureaucrats will take attitudes towards risk which are appropriate from the standpoint of the community. This keys the question back into the issue of allocative efficiency and the representativeness of the demand system. For example, are public enterprise managers' attitudes towards the risks of technological hazard and environmental pollution lower or higher than those that would be tolerated by the general public? If the controllers of an atomic energy plant or a genetic engineering research station are risk lovers, they could be placing the society at a greater risk than the members of society would be willing to accept voluntarily. On the other hand, if public enterprise managers/bureaucrats are risk averse, the average productivity of public investment will be lower than it would be if the investment had been made on the general public's assessment of risks.

Empirically however, very little is known about bureaucrats' attitudes towards risk, nor is there much known about the risks which society would be willing to undertake collectively. The Arrow/Lind theorem shows that, as the size of the population approaches infinity, then the social cost of the risk of a public project tends to zero (Arrow and Lind 1970). However, this theorem is based upon a number of highly restrictive assumptions.[22]

A large number of questions remain unanswered. Do bureaucrats take risks and if so, what kind of risks are they and what is the nature of the likely consequences of these risks? Are bureaucrats adequately rewarded for the taking of risks? How are innovations introduced into public bureaucracies? What incentives exist to innovate? Who are the innovators? Using a Burns and Stalker (1961) framework, is it true that innovations are stifled by rigid hierarchical structures which characterise much of bureaucracy? These questions remain to be answered.

Efficiency and Decentralisation

It is frequently argued that large, highly centralised bureaucracies are inefficient because they are too far removed from the grass roots and have lost control over the implementation of policies. That is, allocative ineffeciency arises because the lines of communication from the electorate have been extended. Moreover, the lines of central control over the production of public services at the local level can become so stretched, that a loss of control allows local bureaucratic discretion and *X*-inefficiency to prevail. These are familiar problems which arise in any highly centralised planning system.

One suggested way of dealing with this problem is to decentralise the system into a large number of autonomous local governments. This has the potential advantages that it will improve allocative efficiency, since each local government will adjust its output decisions, bringing them closer to the preferences of the local electorate, and being a smaller production and distribution unit the prospects for managerial control are improved. The allocative efficiency or welfare gains which arise from a system of decentralised governments were identified by Tiebout (1956). The nature of public services means that individuals are public service output takers. Individuals are assumed to adjust their consumption of public services and the prices that they pay for them by migrating ('voting with their feet') to those local jurisdictions whose tax and public output decisions conform closest to their preferences.

The welfare gains from decentralised public choice are shown in figure 7.3. In this simple illustrative example, the population is divided into two groups. All members within each group have identical demand curves, but the demands for public services differ as between the groups. It is also assumed that the public service is supplied at constant costs. The preferred output for those in group 1 (whose demand curve is D_1) is Q_1 and for group 2 is Q_2.

In a system of centralised government a simple uniform level of public output Q_3 would have been provided. Given this level of output, the welfare loss to individuals in group 1 is shown as the shaded area *ABC*. This represents the excess costs to each individual over his valuation of the excessive units of consumption Q_1 Q_3. The welfare loss to group 2 individuals is given as the area *CDE*. This is the essence of *Oates' decentralisation theorem* (Oates 1972).

However, a number of qualifications have to be made to this result. First, in practice preferences will not be homogeneous within groups such as a local government. It is not feasible to have as many jurisdictions as there are individual preferences for public service outputs. Therefore, within any single local community there will be a distribution of voters' preferences around the actual output level, implying the continued existence of allocative inefficiency although now arguably on a smaller scale, since the

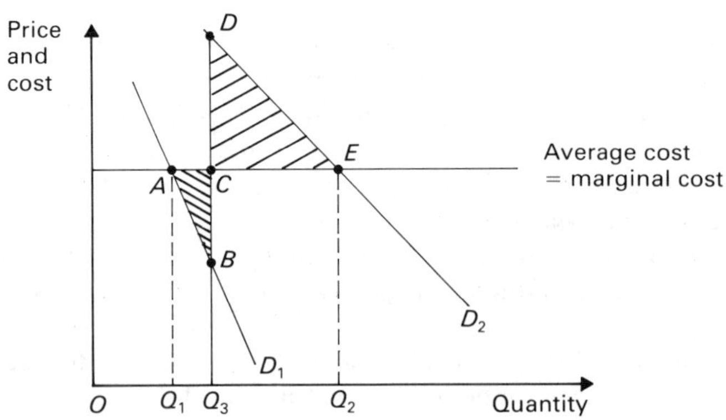

Figure 7.3 *Welfare Gains from Decentralised Public Choice*

local electorate might have greater control over output decisions which should then reflect local conditions and local needs. This, however, leads to the second qualification. The decentralisation of decision making does not of itself guarantee an improvement in the representativeness of voters' demands. Secret and unrepresentative local government is just as undesirable as secret and unrepresentative centralised government. However, the decentralisation of the decision centre does offer greater scope for the control of the decision making system by the local electorate, but that can only be secured by instituting controls and safeguards into the system.

The third qualification refers to the cost side. Decentralisation of itself will not eliminate X-inefficiency and will not necessarily reduce the power of bureaucrats in the decision making system. Fourth, a set of decentralised local governments could result in a loss of economies of scale. This is often referred to as the conflict between the size of political unit required to increase allocative efficiency and the optimum scale of operation necessary to achieve economies of scale. The optimum scale of operation for government produced goods may be greater than or smaller than the political unit and these conflicts have to be weighed up somehow. It is interesting to consider the views of Stanyer (1978) on the advantages of devolution '... devolution is often presented as a simplifying operation — of reducing centralisation and delays in government. The truth is the opposite; devolution makes government more complicated, by forcing the creation of special machinery to overcome its obvious defects, and this in turn takes on a life of its own, leading to yet more modifications of the system of government. There is no way in which government can be simplified whilst society makes complicated demands on it'.

Once again the conclusions are not clear cut. Empirically we know very little about the relative size of the allocative efficiency gains or the size of economies of scale which might exist for different services. Whilst the coordination problem and the decision costs facing the centralised govenment are reduced by having a smaller number of local governments to deal with, these local governments are likely to be sufficiently large to present a central coordinator with problems of establishing some mutually acceptable solution through a process of bargaining and negotiation. A very large number of smaller, decentralised units would be less powerful (assuming no coalitions are formed), but again this advantage would have to be weighed up against the loss in economies of scale and the costs of coordinating large numbers.

Efficiency and Social Justice

The performance of an organisation is generally judged in terms of its contribution to some index like productivity, profitability, or net social benefit. This is the efficiency objective. However, the efficient performance of an organisation is only one dimension in which organisational behaviour is judged. There are others, including those of distributive justice and the morality of the behaviour which exists within an organisation.

Organisations are not reified entities, a point which has been emphasised throughout this book. Rather, organisations are social structures within which some individuals benefit whilst others do not. The central question then becomes, 'whose interests are served in these social structures?' Is it the ruling elites', the clients' (consumers or voters), is it labour's or is it capital's? This question was raised by Barnard (1938) and by those who have, in the Marxian tradition, examined the issue of the exploitation and alienation of labour (Blauner 1964). The prescriptions of the human relations school were as much ethical statements as they were guides for improving efficiency. Whilst Barnard's 'inducements-contribution' approach to management concentrated upon the issue of balancing satisfactions and rewards amongst members of the organisation in order to achieve cooperation and harmony, and hence efficiency, he completely ignored the question of the distribution of these rewards (Krupp 1961). In other words, whilst there might exist a number of alternative distributions of rewards which would bring about harmony and the continued participation of the members of the organisation, some distributions will be more just than others. Moreover, Barnard assumed that satisfactions were generated by modern organisations in excess of those required to maintain the participation of its members. That is, there is organisational slack, X-inefficiency, or rent within the system. In these cases the essential question is, how should the rewards, rents and slack be distributed?

This is a normative question and has to be answered by reference to some notion of distributive justice. A utilitarian would advocate the greatest good for the greatest number, thus ignoring the question of distribution. A Paretian would argue for the maximisation of social welfare, provided that those who were made better off by the action compensated those who are made worse off. But that approach, like the utilitarian, ignores the initial inequalities which exist amongst individuals. Rawls' (1971) 'maximin' principle of distributive justice recognises the problems of the unequal distribution of initial endowments. He argues (p. 62) that, 'all social values — liberty and opportunity, income and wealth, and the loss of all self respect — are to be distributed equally unless an unequal distribution of any or all, of these values is to everyone's advantage'. Rawls argues that inequalities must be justified in terms of the promotion of social welfare. From a benchmark of equality, non-egalitarian social arrangements would be ranked in order of increasing benefits to the least advantaged members of society i.e. the maximin principle maximises the welfare of the least well-off in society. This is akin to minimising regret or suffering to the most regretful participants when different social states are compared. It has been argued by Popper (1966) that the minimisation of regret or suffering is a better moral position to take than that of the promotion of happiness. Satisfaction based principles of justice like those of utilitarianism can sanction both morally repugnant wants and the means of satisfying these wants.

It is well beyond the scope of this book to deal fully with all of the issues which are raised by a proper treatment of distributive justice. This is admirably carried out by Miller (1976). The force of our present argument is that in the final analysis the performance of an organisation is not unidimensional. Efficiency and distributive justice have to be traded-off against one another and the point on that trade-off which different individuals choose will depend upon the particular notion of distributive justice to which they subscribe. Thus different means of organising the supply of output (bureaucracy *versus* the market) are not simply resolved in terms of efficiency criteria; distributive justice is also highly relevant. Consultants' reports and other judgments made about the performance of an organisation which concentrate purely upon efficiency leave out of the picture a whole dimension.

Questions of distributive justice or discussions of the moral element in the behaviour of an organisation's members are seldom presented. The works of Bradley and Wilkie (1974) and Keeley (1978) are notable exceptions which have paved the way for further developments. 'To study organisational behaviour demands a language which is sensitive to the moral dimension of that behaviour' (Bradley and Wilkie 1974, p. 89). Authority and power relations contain moral questions, as too do the distribution of rights and privileges within the organisation. What kind of behaviour is rewarded, what kind punished? What underlying principles of justice and 'fair play' does this reward/punishment system imply?

An examination of the moral behaviour of an organisation's members would seek to find out in what way the incentive structure influences individual moral behaviour. Are profits made at the cost of exploitation of individuals such as black workers in South Africa, or by endangering lives through lack of regard to safety or pollution control requirements? Who benefits from the deals struck between the multi-national corporations and the rulers of less developed countries? But it is not only the means of achieving goals which need to be examined — the goals themselves deserve closer scrutiny. 'An organisation's goals are sometimes defined in terms of society's dominant value system when not only is the content of this value system never specified, but it is also at least arguable that it is a travesty of the facts to assume that a coherent, integrated and popularly agreed upon set of values exists which adequately defines the relationship between an organisation's goals and society' (Bradley and Wilkie 1974, p. 89).

Conclusions

That there exists inefficency and waste in public sector bureaucracies, just as there does in private sector organisations, is an inescapable fact. That private sector organisations, because of the discipline imposed upon them by the market place, are less inefficient than public bureaucracies, is more an article of faith in the allocative superiority of the market system, than a well articulated empirical statement. The idea that private sector inefficiency, passed on in higher prices to the consumer, is more justified than public sector inefficiency, passed on in higher taxes, is equally questionable. This chapter has set out to identify the principal elements in any discussion about public sector efficiency. Issues such as the unrepresentativeness of the demands for public services, the role of bureaucrats in the decision process, the problems of identifying outputs and goals and the questions of designing the appropriate set of incentives have all been reviewed. The use of decentralised local governments and markets were considered as possible alternative means of organising the supply of public services in an attempt to improve efficiency. Finally, the search for a socially optimal organisational performance was examined. Here, the problem was regarded as that of weighing up efficiency gains and losses against alternative amounts of distributive justice.

It should be clear from this discussion that there is nothing straightforward about the concept of public sector efficiency and those who believe that the efficiency of the bureaucracy can be improved through simple-minded tinkering should take special note. Furthermore, much of this discussion about public sector efficiency applies with equal force to the private sector of any economy.

The question of public sector efficiency raises many important issues, such as where does and where should control over the decisions surrounding the allocation and distribution of public services lie in a modern democracy? These are some of the problems which are considered in the next chapter.

Notes

1 Parsons argued that organisations are inefficient when too much attention is paid to integration and latency rather than to adaptation and goal achievement.

2 To the non-economist, some of the formal language used in this section might appear to be daunting. An introduction to the vocabulary can be found in most intermediate micro-economic texts such as Hirshleifer (1975) or Koutsoyiannis (1979).

3 It is also assumed that there is complete freedom of entry and exit from the industry and that firms have complete knowledge of available techniques and the associated costs.

4 This assumes that the production functions are identical (in this case of constant returns to scale) and that there is no monopolistic power in the factor markets. Hence factor prices are indentical in both cases.

5 Empirical studies of the production function are summarised in Brown (1967).

6 The importance of internal organisational factors had been recognised by earlier economists such as Schumpeter (1954, p. 106) and Hayek (1945, p. 523).

7 It is clear from the shape of the AC_2 curve which incorporates X-inefficiency that it assumes such inefficiencies are to be regarded as fixed rather than variable costs. There is no strong empirical justification for such a view and future research must decide whether or not it is tenable.

8 See Schwartzman (1973, p. 761); also the 'Farrell' measure of efficiency recognises this point (Farrell 1957). Clearly, the general equilibrium theorist would define away this problem by assuming 'management' as one of the factors of production. Differences in factor combinations arise because of differences in the *quality* of management.

9 These results are summarised in Brown and Jackson (1978) and Mueller (1979).

10 Note that the decision process has public good qualities, in the simple sense that individuals cannot be excluded from the outcomes of these decisions.

11 A similar point is made by Olson (1973).

12 Included in the costs of conflict are all ethical issues, so that the ends cannot be used to justify the means.

13 An interesting analysis of some of the problems involved in measuring output is to be found in Froomkin, Jamison and Radner (1976) and Williams and Anderson (1975).

14 Some readers will readily recognise this as the 'new' theory of consumer demand as set out by Lancaster (1966). Thus some good or service X_i is defined as:–
$X_i = (X_{1i}, X_{2i}, \dots X_{ni})$, where the elements $X_{1i} \dots$ are the characteristics which are embodied in the final product and which define it.

15 That is, $P_i X_i \equiv (P_1 X_{1i} + P_2 X_{2i} + \dots + P_n X_{ni})$, where P_i is the aggregate price level made up of the individual relative prices $P_1, P_2 \dots P_n$.

16 Because consumption is a gamble, issues surrounding the drawing up of guarantees and product liability present fascinating problems for analysis.

17 Empirical evidence on the free-rider problem is very limited and that which does exist has been carried out under artificial and contrived conditions. The interested reader should consult Bohm (1972), Sweeney (1973), Kurz (1974) and Johansen (1977).

18 See Baumol's (1967) unbalanced productivity model.

19 The equilibrium paradigm is brought into line with these approaches when the following question is asked — 'how are the individual plans or decisions by the various agents made compatible?'

20 The problems of preference revelation were reviewed above. A thorough treatment of these issues at an abstract level is to be found in Green and Laffont (1979).

21 Quoted in Hildebrandt and Tyson (1976a) from *Trenton Times*, Sunday 15 December 1974.

22 It is assumed that all individuals have identical von Neumann–Morgenstern utility functions, that all individuals share equally in the public enterprise gains/losses, and that all the public enterprises gains/losses are statistically independent from other sources of income. For a critique, see Foldes and Rees (1977).

CHAPTER 8

Accountability and Control of Bureaucracy

[Parliament is] ... a representative assembly ... to watch and control the government; to throw the light of publicity on its acts; to compel a full exposition and justification of all of them which anyone considers questionable.
J.S. Mills (1861, p. 239)

Few would dispute that we now live in conditions in which it is difficult to say precisely what we mean in practice by 'accountability' in administration, and even more difficult to assert with confidence that we know how to enforce it.
N. Johnson (1974, p. 3)

Introduction

In the previous chapter a number of the conceptual problems relating to the issue of efficiency in public sector bureaucracies were considered. Allocative and X-inefficiencies were identified. However, there was no discussion of the administrative or procedural institutions which might be used to make bureaucracy more representative and more X-efficient. These questions are taken up in this chapter. After a review of the question, 'why do we need to control bureaucracy and make it accountable?' the concepts of accountability and control will be explored. This is then followed by an examination of the functions and limitations of the institutions of bureaucratic control which have evolved during the recent past. Finally, possible developments in these means of control will be discussed.

The Need for Control and Accountability

On a number of occasions in previous chapters reference has been made to bureaucrats' discretionary powers, the lack of constraints on their actions, their pursuit of their own self-interest, and therefore their possible non-representativeness. In other words, do the activities pursued by bureaucrats reflect the pursuit of the 'public interest' or the bureaucrats' own self-interests; is there allocative inefficiency in the system? Many of the central issues raised by questions of this kind are discussed by Reich (1970) and the following selection of quotations[1] from his book, *The Greening of America*, help to place the issues in perspective.

> Poverty, distorted priorities and law making by private power ... are not the accidents of a free economy, they are intentionally and rigidly built into the laws of our society by those with powerful influence ...
>
> What the New Deal did was to create ... to carry out its reforms a new public state, matching in size and power the private corporate state ... The dominating concept was that all private activity, individual or corporate was subject to restriction, licensing, or regulation 'in the public interest'.
>
> What the theory neglected was the possibility that the two kinds of power might join. And this is what did happen ... to form the inhuman structure in which we now live — the American Corporate State. Activist political radicals ... fail to recognise that bureaucratic socialism or communism presents many of the same evils as America and that in America capitalism is now only a subordinate aspect of the larger evil of the controlled technological state.
>
> Marcuse ... recognised that excess repression was the central fact of our society and that it led inevitably to the state which must seek to dominate both those who live within it and those beyond its borders ...
>
> The plan, the program, the grand strategy is this; resist the state when you must; avoid it when you can.

Reich's final statement could be taken to represent the banner headlines either of those to the right of the political spectrum who, like Thomas Jefferson, fear the spread of Leviathan and the attendant erosion of personal freedoms and liberties and are, therefore, opposed to government intervention; or of those on the left who oppose the 'system maintenance' functions of the State.

The first of these views is representative of the liberal tradition in the political and social sciences, which is based upon an inherent distrust of large aggregations of authority and wealth, whether they are located in the public or the private sector. Their emphasis is upon economic atomism (i.e. perfectly competitive markets) and political democracy. The operation of the price system is assumed to guarantee coordination in the economy among the vast numbers of independent small decision units. Also, democratically based voting systems are assumed to protect society from the force of arbitrary governmental authority.[2] Thus the growth of large-scale business organisations is viewed as a source of concentrated power (monopoly power). Galbraith (1967) has drawn attention to the growing political power of big business and the deals that they do with governments, thereby combining the concentrations of power which exist in the public and the private sectors. Large multi-national corporations operating in developed and developing economies are on many occasions seen as using their market power and political influence to further their own interests, often at the expense of the wider public interest. In these instances the large corporation is viewed as obstructing the free working of the competitive system and as providing a threat to political democracy. This was the position taken by Berle and Means (1934, p. 18) in their classic study of large scale business organisations:

> 'there exists a centripetal attraction which draws wealth together into aggregations of constantly increasing size, at the same time throwing control into the hands of fewer and fewer men'.

In more recent times the liberal tradition has turned its attention to the growth of bureaucracy and state monopoly power. Here the argument is that power is continuously concentrated in the hands of fewer and fewer bureaucrats which results in a breakdown of the representation process. The paradox is that demands to control the power of large-scale private sector organisation resulted in governmental regulatory agencies. But what has happened is that government has replaced one kind of concentration of power with another.

The left-wing view has been treated in depth in the works of O'Conner (1973), Miliband (1969) and Gough (1975). The growth of the state sector, it is argued, is indispensable to the expansion of private industry, especially monopoly industries (state capitalism) and in particular the defence industries which depend upon the state for contracts. This feature of modern societies has a number of undesirable consequences to which these authors draw attention. In particular, the power of the state and private sector monopoly combine in order to promote interests which need not be synonymous with the 'public interest'. Moreover, public (expenditures) activities can be seen as an investment in social control (system maintenance) made necessary by the disruptive impact of capitalism.

For different reasons the state and the bureaucracy come under attack from all sides of the political spectrum. Thus any discussion of accountability and control must, from the outset, make clear why the activities and powers of the state are to be controlled, which activities are to be controlled and how.

These are modern day expressions of older ideas. Michels (1911) and Mosca (1958) both argued that the concentration of power was inevitable and that it would become increasingly difficult to control those at the centre. For Michels, power in popular political parties becomes concentrated amongst the few. Full-time officials in socialist parties and trade unions are strong professionals compared to the challenges from amateurs in the rank and file. Recently these earlier ideas, which related to the concentration of political power, have been developed and extended to the question of whether or not there has taken place a shift in power from the elected political representatives to the non-elected career bureaucrats who have specialist knowledge (control over information) and can use this to their own advantage (see Marcuse 1964). Djilas' (1957) study of the communist system revealed that the communist society had created a new class of technocrats who ran the state and who had more power than others. Tullock (1976), discussing the role played by bureaucrats, whose function it is to regulate the activities of the market, argues that 'the principal beneficiaries of the regulation ... are the technical specialists in the regulation themselves who gain a rent on their specialised knowledge and abilities'.[3]

Bottomore (1966) argues that managers and bureaucrats represent a new class. Recruits to civil service upper grades are drawn from the upper middle class and in promoting their own interests will be promoting the interests of bourgeois values. (See also Hill's (1969) study of recruitment to the UK civil service.) There is, however, an argument against the importance of elitist groups which comes from those who believe in a more pluralistic system (see Dahl 1961 and Dahrendorf 1959). They argue that there are many sources of power in society, e.g. bureaucracy, the state, political parties, pressure groups, trades unions and formal administrative procedures of control, all of which counterbalance the power of the state, the power of bureaucracy and the power of capitalism. The interaction of these countervailing forces, it is assumed, has the effect of levelling power differentials in society. However, it should be recognised that the resolution of this issue is an empirical question rather than one which can be settled *a priori*.[4]

Take, for example, the question of whether or not pressure groups counteract the power of bureaucrats. Clearly they will not if it is bureaucratic pressure groups that are being considered or if bureaucrats are members of, or indeed the leaders of, some of the more powerful pressure groups in society generally. Some of the most powerful pressure groups in the UK against public expenditure cuts are the public sector unions. A similar point has been made by Fox (1974, p. 13):

> employees of professional agencies today are in fact the chief supporters of structural bureau autonomy. Attempts to consolidate all line agencies under his (the governor's) control are met by criticism from bureaus and their interest group allies, who accuse him of treating their programmes in a 'political' manner and who may launch campaigns to enlist opposition ... According to the bureaucrats, the only safeguard against political interference is a guarantee of structural autonomy.

Thus, any arguments about the countervailing forces of pressure groups must recognise the relationships that exist between the memberships of the various groups in society. Who belongs to the more powerful and persuasive pressure groups?[5] Whose interests are being served? To answer these questions is to attempt to study the distribution of power and influence in society and to find out who has the power and the influence over public sector decisions.[6]

The issues then are these: what influence do bureaucrats have over public sector decision making, what is the source of this power, what private values and interests do bureaucrats have? These are distinct questions, but they are obviously inter-related. Simon (1965) and Wildavsky (1964) along with many others have emphasised the basic facts of life which exist in the realm of practical decision making (see Chapters 4 and 6 above). Decision makers, in this case the elected political representatives, do not have the time or the resources to evaluate a large set of options before arriving at a final decision. Practical decision making is characterised by bounded rationality. The options which are presented to politicians and the back-up information relating to these options more often than not originate within the bureaucracy. Bureaucrats have power and influence over public sector decision making because they have control over information. Statements of this kind should, however, be interpreted with care since they can lead to wild conclusions which are difficult to support. First, it need not be the case that there is some grand conspiracy on the part of senior bureaucrats to filter and bias information in an attempt to further their own aims by deceiving their political masters. Such a conspiracy, in the absence of other checks and balances, could exist; but most would regard any actual biasing of information in the majority of cases to be unintended. Second, politicians do have access to alternative sources of information which can act as a countervailing force. In some instances they have their own expert advisers and research staff. A move in this direction was started by the British Labour government during the 1970s, and is a feature of the political systems of Australia, Canada and the USA. It would be a mistake, however, to overemphasise the strength of this countervailing force, since the limited resources available to political advisers and research staffs make it impossible to check more than a small proportion of the major policy decisions.

Evidence of bureaucratic power originating from a monopoly of information is found in Meyer's (1969) study of bureaucracy and policy formation in Sweden. He found that the Swedish commissions have played an increasingly active role in the policy formation process. Similar evidence for Japan is found in Pempel (1974).

These issues bring into the arena, once again, the well worn debate about the distinction between policy formation and policy execution. The position of classical public administration on this issue originates in Woodrow Wilson's (1887) distinction that politics is the practice of policy formation, whereas administration is purely that of policy execution. According to this view, the bureaucrat is passive and does not enter into the policy formation process. This is, however, a normative and extremely romantic and idealised view of the bureaucrat and the bureaucratic process. The bureaucrat, like any other individual, brings to his role a complex set of values, beliefs and personal interests, which will influence his perception and the way in which he sees issues, structures problems and interprets data.[7]

It is no longer debated whether or not senior bureaucrats have power and promote their own self-interests. Such influence is now widely recognised and accepted. After studying the political attitudes of senior civil servants in Western European countries, Putnam (1973) concludes: 'can there really be much doubt who governs our complex modern societies? ... the modern political system is essentially bureaucratic — characterised by the rules of officials'.

Who are the senior bureaucrats, what values do they have, and how are they recruited? These questions have been the subject of much empirical analysis; see Bendix's (1949) study of higher civil servants in American society, and Krislov's (1974) examination of the ethnic and religious backgrounds of bureaucrats and the limitations these place upon bureaucratic representativeness. Krislov (p. 7) argues that, '... broad social groups have spokesmen and office holders in administrative as well as political positions' — a point which dovetails into the discussion above of bureaucrats' membership of pressure groups. Hill's (1969) study of recruitment to the British Civil Service has been updated by the recent analysis carried out by the UK House of Commons Expenditure Committee (HMSO 1977). In his evidence to the Expenditure Committee[8] Lord Crowther-Hunt pointed to three biases which he saw as currently existing in the recruitment of administrative trainees[9] who then go on to become senior civil servants. First, there exists a preference for graduates from Oxford and Cambridge. Over the period 1971–75, 21.6% of the applicants were Oxford and Cambridge graduates, but they provided 50% of the appointees (in 1975 and 1976 it was 60%).[10] Second, there is a preference for former pupils of fee-paying independent schools.[11] For the period 1973–75 ex-independent schoolboys constituted 29.2% of Oxford and Cambridge educated applicants and 34.6% of Oxford or Cambridge educated civil service recruits. This bias increased in the case of civil service recruits from other universities where the figures are: 8.6% of ex-independent schoolboy applicants as compared with 21.3% of recruits. Thus it looks as if the Civil Service Commission not only reinforces an Oxford/Cambridge bias, but also creates a bias which either does not exist in other universities or is much smaller there. The third bias was in favour of arts and humanities graduates rather than physical science and social science applicants. The 1971–75 figures are: 42.5% of applicants were arts and humanities graduates as against 56.7% of recruits.

Doubtless these statistics can be debated, but they tend to draw attention to the similarity of background of many recruits to the bureaucracy. But the answers to the questions about recruitment are by themselves insufficient to support a strong theory of consolidated bureaucratic power and influence. There are a sufficient number of differences in social backgrounds to argue the case for a heterogeneous group of top civil servants which would weaken the influence of social backgrounds. If, however, secondary socialisation *within* the bureaucracy exists to promote and enforce a dominant set of values, then differences in social backgrounds are levelled off. Heclo and Wildavsky (1974) seem to place emphasis upon the power of secondary socialisation in their behavioural study of the upper echelons in the British civil service. Their analysis is presented in terms of a kinship system in which there exists a set of supportive relationships which are maintained throughout, despite changes in the membership of the group. Any analysis of secondary socialisation comes down to questions of the nature of the incentives within the system; what kind of behaviour (values) is rewarded and what kind of behaviour is punished; what is the origin of the incentive system and who applies it? Behaviour is sanctioned officially according to formal procedures and informally according to the norms held by peers within a social setting.

The power and influence of bureaucrats does, therefore, have many sources: (a) social background (b) a monopoly of technical skills and (c) a weak political system. This last point is discussed by Debbasch (1969), who argues that the weakness of the Fifth Republic in France allowed an increase in the power of the bureaucracy. Whilst questions of the power and influence of bureaucrats have occupied a good deal of the American literature, there is, as Gordon (1971) points out, a lack of critical literature on the British civil service.

So far the discussion has focused upon the issue of representative bureaucracy (see Kingsley 1944 and Hyneman 1950) and the need to make bureaucrats accountable. There is, however, another aspect which is frequently debated. That is the question of the size of the bureaucracy, the number of government agencies and the number of bureaucrats. Those who fear the spread of Leviathan place particular emphasis upon this aspect of the argument. As the absolute and the relative size of the bureaucracy grows then, it is argued, the problems of an unrepresentative bureaucracy become a greater threat to personal freedoms. One popular view of the bureaucracy is that government agencies seldom die off or fade away. Once established, they go on forever, whether or not they are needed, whether or not they are wanted or useful. They tend to enjoy a natural immunity or gory immortality. Most agencies are created by statute and statutes tend to be enduring. Clearly this is an example of X-inefficiency. This problem has been analysed by Kaufman (1976) for the USA. Kaufman found that once an agency is granted an appropriation it tends to be borne along by the momentum of the budgetary process (incrementalism). Agencies, if their existence is threatened, in order to stay alive cultivate and draw support from other agencies and from pressure groups, the media etc. There is, however, a price to be paid for such 'insurances'; (a) some agencies are unable to adapt quickly to changing conditions because the laws that created them are rigid and inflexible and (b) protection from allies implies that these allies be given the right to be consulted on issues and if bargains and agreements are to be sought, this limits flexibility. Kaufman found that the main causes of the death of an agency were obsolescence resulting from adherence to past methods, completion of mission and changes in policies resulting from changes in government.

A more recent concern both in American and British society has been the rapid expansion which has taken place in the *contract state*[12] — that is, the widespread delegation of administrative authority to semi-official and private institutions. These institutions of the contract state have been given a number of labels, but generally they are popularly referred to either as 'intermediate government' or *QUANGOS*[13] (quasi non-governmental organisations). As increasingly more complex demands have been placed on modern governments to provide goods and services, one reaction has been to rely upon more decentralised structures and upon a growing range of extra-departmental and extra-governmental agencies. This 'hiving off' of certain activities from departments to autonomous boards and agencies of the State was advocated by the Fulton Report (1968; see Volume 1, Chapter 5).[14] During the 1960s and 1970s in the UK, the boundaries of the public sector became increasingly fuzzy with the emergence of a wide range of agencies such as the Arts Council, White Fish Authority, Port Authorities, English Tourist Board, Price Commission, Area and Regional Health Authorities and the Research Councils. These agencies use public funds and are headed by non-elected executives whose lines of responsibility and accountability are never at all clear from the point of view of controlling their activities, although the Minister whose department funds them is of course technically accountable to Parliament for the use of these funds. In addition to the emergence of quangos, more and more activities were devolved to local government and nationalised industry undertakings were expanded. At the same time, Crowther-Hunt and Peacock (1973) have referred to the growth of an *intermediate layer of government* which is comprised of *ad hoc* bodies of the kind described above. Whilst statutes have authorised many quangos, these statutes have been worded so vaguely that it is not clear that *ultra vires* acts have been committed (Davies 1979, p. 22). This observation reinforces the point made in the previous chapter that in the absence of well specified objectives, analysis and judgment of the efficiency and performance of government agencies become very difficult. The result of this 'diffusion of sovereignty' has been to weaken the traditional means of control over state and bureaucratic activities.

In the USA, fears of the growth of the contract state have been bound up with the growth of the military industrial complex. That is, the procurement practices employed by government, it is argued, give too much power and influence over government defence policy to the non-elected industrial contractors. In this case the demand is again for the need to re-assert the integrity of the formal institutions of government. One important difference between the post-war experiences of the UK and the USA has been that whereas in the UK the hiving off of departmental responsiblities was to public boards etc., in the USA the Federal government devolved responsibilities to private sector organisations on a contractual basis.

The control of these dispersed agents of government does, however, have to be balanced against the effectiveness and efficiency which comes from their autonomy. The need to create the institutional arrangements that will enable government to maintain a strong central policy directive over quangos, nationalised industries, local governments and private institutions performing services for the government has to be set against providing these organisations with enough independence of operation to produce the maximum incentives for providing an efficient service (Smith 1971). This trade-off between independence and control has been central in the UK to many of the policy debates about the appropriate relationship which should exist between central and local government and government and the nationalised industries.

Accountability and Control

The basic questions asked about democratic decision making are these: what is to be the character of the institutions, rules, and procedures of the democracy, what are to be the guarantees that these institutions will be representative, and how are the rights of the individual to be protected, i.e. what is to be the scope of political decision making (Cornford 1972)? These questions summarise the issues raised in the previous section. The state and its bureaucracy needs to be made accountable and requires to be controlled, because there exist tendencies for it to become unrepresentative if left unchecked. But before concepts such as accountability and control are made operational it is necessary to know what they mean.[15]

Basically, accountability involves explaining or justifying what has been done, what is currently being done and what is planned. Accountability arises from a set of established procedures and relationships of varying formality. Thus, one party is accountable to another in the sense that one of the parties has the right to call upon the other to give an account of his activities. Accountability involves, therefore, the giving of information. The questions which then follow are: (a) how can information be called for, what are the formal channels and procedures; (b) who has the right to call for information, from whom and about what; (c) the answer to the previous question can then be set against the answer to the normative question, is the distribution of these rights optimal; and (d) what is the quality of the information provided?

In giving an account, its form and substance depend upon the values, beliefs and perceptions of the person giving the account. One of the inherent limitations in any system of accountability is, therefore, found in one of the principal reasons that gives rise to the need for accountability in the first place — namely that the accountee (in this case the bureaucrat) can control the information which is used both for decision making and in providing an account of the activities leading up to decisions.

There are a number of facets to the concept of accountability. Traditionally in the public administration literature it refers to financial, political and legal accountability. In recent years efficiency and effectiveness accountability have been added. Thus, in addition to asking the question why does it cost £x to perform some activity y, efficiency accounting seeks to answer the question, is the activity y the most X-efficient way of achieving some overall objective z and, moreover, is y the most effective means of achieving z? These latter questions of efficiency and effectiveness attempt to evaluate the set of activities performed in the public sector in terms of their 'value for money'. The problems involved in defining such concepts were explored in the previous chapter.

The traditional model of accountability was aimed at ensuring that departments operated within their specific powers and within the broader legal framework. It was concerned with financial rectitude; to ensure that each department spent its allocation of resources in the way in which parliament had voted them and to ensure that each department presented a set of properly audited financial accounts. Thus if parliament voted £xm. to Department Y to be spent on capital programmes, it was not an option open to the department to transfer these resources to wages and salaries. Embodied within the audit and legal dimensions of the traditional model of accountability is the concept of ministerial accountability and responsibility.

Accountability is a relationship intended to enhance the responsiveness of administrative agents to those whom they are expected to serve and to provide a means by which complaints and grievances may be raised and redressed. In this sense accountability attempts to ensure the maintenance of, or improvements in, allocative efficiency. If the activities of any department should step out of line from the general view of what is demanded, or if it should jeopardise the fulfilment of the public interest, then the system of accountability enables complaints to be aired and a redress to be obtained. One channel through which complaints are aired is parliament where, by means of written and oral questions, Members of Parliament can call a Minister to account for the performance and activities of his department. Political accountability is, therefore, to judge the performance of those in political office and to apply sanctions where necessary, including the demand for the removal of a Minister from office.[16] In this respect the Minister is assumed to 'carry the can' for what goes on in his department. Ministerial responsibility and accountability are to be compared with a system which would hold the civil servants accountable. In the UK a permanent civil service exists. The idea of a permanent civil service originated in the Northcote Trevelyan Report of 1854, in which it was argued that government could not be carried out efficiently without the assistance of a group of permanent officers who were responsible to ministers who in turn were responsible to the Crown and to Parliament. Senior bureaucrats are not elected to office. It, therefore, follows that bureaucrats cannot be removed from office for matters of public censure, although obviously they can be removed from office for other reasons such as professional misconduct. Because political accountability in the UK takes the form of ministerial responsibility, bureaucrats have 'retreated steadily into the mists of non-accountability' (Johnson 1974, p. 6).

Is ministerial accountability effective as a means of ensuring allocative and X-efficiency, or is it an obsolete concept inappropriate to the problems of controlling the complex tasks of modern governments? Sir John Hunt's (1976) view on this is expressed in his evidence to the Expenditure Committee of the House of Commons on 'The Civil Service'. 'The concept that, because somebody whom the Minister has never heard of has made a mistake, means that the Minister should resign, is out of date and rightly so' (para 95). Johnson (1974, p. 7) argues:

> we cannot expect to find solutions by maintaining our traditional obsessions with the political accountability of elected representatives ... there is more prospect of achieving some of the objectives of accountability in government if we look at the problem in terms of achieving control over the activities of public authorities rather than in terms of rendering them accountable.

In that passage Johnson makes the distinction between accountability and control. Rather than simply ensuring that departments (bureaus) have kept within their legal constraints and have disbursed their funds appropriately, it is necessary to direct attention to what goes on within the bureaucracy and to control these activities.

This view was also taken up by the Expenditure Committee's investigation into the Civil Service (see *Eleventh Report of the Expenditure Committee*, HC 535, 1976–7). It regards the present system of accountability of the Civil Service through its Ministers as totally inoperative. What the members of that Committee would prefer to see instituted would be a system in which civil servants were held directly accountable to parliament. This, it is argued, would make parliament more effective and would allow it to ensure that the bureaucracy was more efficient.

The functions of the state have changed. The state is now a purveyor of goods and services and not simply a regulatory agent as in earlier times. Control issues now centre around questions about the scale and quality of the services provided (allocative efficiency) and how demands are fed into the politico-bureaucratic machine. In this case the legal/accounting model of accountability is not so relevant. What is now needed is a means of (a) monitoring the performance of bureaus (b) ensuring that clients' changing demands/needs/attitudes are registered and taken into account when decisions are taken and (c) ensuring that there is a channel to register new needs.

The extended time scale of many projects and programmes makes nonsense of ministerial accountability. Many public sector projects such as the building of a hospital, a bridge, or an urban motorway system are spread over the lifetime of so many different governments that at any one moment in time it would be inappropriate to hold any single Minister accountable and responsible for the accumulation of commitments which his predecessors entered into.

Complexity of the task and structure of modern government likewise limit the usefulness of the idea of ministerial accountability. The things modern governments are expected to do are complex, as too are the organisational structures through which these tasks are carried out. It, therefore, becomes difficult to hold someone (such as the Minister) accountable for the whole, when he is only responsible for a part and does not necessarily understand the whole. Also, in complex organisations where many parts are interdependent with each contributing to the overall output, the 'buck' is passed whenever anything goes wrong, since each part of the organisation is only willing to claim partial responsibility. In complex interdependent organisations it becomes difficult to locate points of control.

The location of points of control is pertinent not only to the issue of control within a department; it applies also to the broader question of locating centres of control within the structure of modern government, which is characterised by decentralisation, diffusion and dispersal, i.e. local government, quangos, non-departmental public agencies and nationalised industries etc. The pursuit of efficiency via administrative rationalisation, economies of scale, integrated corporate management and the organisational and governmental structures, that have grown up embodying these concepts, nowadays makes it difficult to decide who is accountable to whom. To what extent is ministerial responsibility to parliament relevant in cases like this? The answer is very little as the present structures stand. But if the objective is to obtain greater control over these decentralised agencies of government, then it becomes important to understand the problems which these agencies create.

The analysis of accountability and control in a system of decentralised government is an underdeveloped subject in the UK. It does, however, give rise to a number of interesting problems. To whom should the decentralised agency be accountable? In the case of local government, should local elected politicians and bureaucrats be accountable to the local electorate or to the central govenment (i.e. national electorate)? Should quangos and nationalised industries be responsible to parliament or to their clients? On most issues there is likely to be a difference in the values, beliefs and perceptions of problems as viewed by those at the centre and the local area. These differences form the basis of conflicts between central and local interests. How then should such conflicts be resolved? If a solution cannot be found through the standard procedures of bargaining, should the centre have the power to impose *its* solution or should there instead be some council which will arbitrate; if there should be, what guidelines should it have? Whilst it is easy to raise such questions, it is more difficult to provide answers. We shall not attempt to do so here, since the purpose of this analysis is to identify the nature of the problems.

What we have identified above is the classic trade-off between local autonomy and central control. The basis of local autonomy is clear, but that for central control is not. Local autonomy is derived from the efficiency aguments set out above, in which decentralisation follows from demands to allow each local area to adapt service provision to local conditions and needs. However, complete autonomy does not exist because central government might place requirements and constraints on the scope of local government, e.g. to provide minimum levels of service or not to increase local expenditure, taxes or borrowing above some prescribed levels. In these instances local government's freedom to pursue allocative efficiency is constrained by demands placed on central governments to redistribute incomes (welfare) and to manage the economy (i.e. through tax policy, public expenditure control and debt management). What this comes down to saying is that there should be a recognition that it is the *functions* of governments (i.e. the efficient allocation of resources, the redistribution of welfare and the management/stabilisation of the economy) which comes into conflict, and to the extent that different parts of government are responsible for these functions then they will come into conflict also. If central govenment is the regulator of the whole system it has to decide which of the goals are to be given priority: efficiency, distribution or stabilisation. Insofar as it places the control of the economy, through public spending cuts, above the achievement of social policy objectives, which require the expenditure of resources, then central and local governments will come into conflict. This conflict will be exacerbated if the controlling party in central government is of a different political persuasion from that in local government.

Central control in these cases does not simply arise from the needs of financial rectitude. It arises from the demands of any system which faces the problem of balancing mutually incompatible objectives of the kind outlined above. The existence of decentralised units poses a problem for central government in terms of *how* it is to exercise control.

One means would be simply to lay down a set of constraints which the decentralised units would be expected to observe and which would be compatible with the centre's overall plan with regard to its social and economic policies. The decentralised unit would then be free to operate within these centrally determined constraints. This is essentially the way in which things are currently carried out in the UK. An alternative means of central control would be to get the decentralised units to agree to the central plan. This would be achieved through bargaining and negotiation in which the central government would be required to 'purchase' agreement through a number of fiscal exchanges etc. Such a method is likely to be expensive to implement, both in terms of the bargains struck by central government and in terms of decision costs. It is unlikely that an agreed solution could be found quickly, which limits the method as a useful or flexible means of dealing with short-run problems which require rapid solutions. Moreover, there is also the problem of ensuring that all local governments will honour the agreements and bargains which are made. In the terminology of the previous chapter, the system would incur high transactions costs including policy costs. Irrespective of which means is chosen (i.e. the centralised constraint model or the bargaining model), the central government still faces a dilemma. In order to decide upon an optimal set of constraints or to enter into efficient bargains, it requires information about local conditions, demands, needs and the activities of the decentralised units. The central government does have at its disposal inspectors, public enquiries and the enforced collection of local statistics, but that only provides fragmentary information of varying quality. To obtain a great deal of the information required for planning purposes, the centre must rely upon the local area. Clearly the local area has control over what information is provided and has an incentive to filter it.

The Agency Relationship and the Professional Bureaucrat

Information lies at the centre of another problem which faces those who wish to control modern bureaucracies. The classical accountability/control model of public administration assumed a neutral bureaucracy. But applying the economist's model of bureaucracy, as we have done throughout this book, we have argued that bureaucrats have self-interests which can come into conflict with 'the public interest'. This problem can be illustrated using the example of the role played by professional specialists employed by the agencies of modern governments.[17]

The 'expertise' component of policy making has increased and along with this there has been an increase in the number of scientists, technologists, economists, social scientists, lawyers and medics employed by the bureaucracy. The groups are employed for the specific specialist skills that they possess, rather than as occupants of some more general administrative role. This raises the issue of the need for control over expertise which has been recognised in the writings of Downs (1957) and Wildavsky (1964).

Government's relationships with professional specialists is very similar to the *agency relationship* which Arrow (1970) has defined to exist between the patient and his doctor. The patient does not have the specialist knowledge which is required to make decisions about the diagnosis of his illness or its treatment, e.g. what pills to take, whether hospitalisation is required and whether or not surgery is necessary. The agency relationship is one based upon trust and faith, in which the patient devolves the power to make decisions on his behalf to the doctor — or at least if making his own decision, the patient will rely upon the advice given to him by the medical specialist. In a situation of this kind, to whom is the doctor accountable? What control does the patient have over the set of activities which are used to effect a cure etc.?

These are similar questions to those which lie at the centre of the issue about specialist information and advice given to political decision makers by their economic advisers, political advisers etc. Of course, it is usually possible to seek a second opinion and the Labour government's use of specialist advisers was a move in that direction. However, the issue of the accountability of and the control over specialist advisers remains. The problems of making specialist advisers accountable and having control over their activities can be illustrated by continuing the medical example with an analysis of the control which exists over the actions of doctors in the British National Health Service (see Klein 1974).

The present system of accountability and control which exists in the NHS can be set out as follows:

(a) the Department of Health and Social Security's (DHSS) Regional Medical Officers can apply pressure on general practitioners (GPs) who are over generous when prescribing drugs etc. Any final sanctions, however, if it is necessary to apply them, are left to the GP's Local Medical Committee which is made up of medics. In this case, it is the GP's professional peers who judge the case on professional standards;

(b) hospital consultants can be starved of additional resources if it is considered they are misusing existing ones;

(c) the Health Service Commissioner (HSC) can deal with *administrative* failures and performs the role of calling health administrators to account;

(d) the Hospital Advisory Service (HAS) is like an NHS inspectorate and inspects all hospitals for the mentally ill, for geriatric patients and for the chronically sick. It produces an audit of the quality of care. Although the HAS has found gaps in the quality of care, parliament has not seemed interested in making use of its findings.

Whilst it might seem from the above list that there does exist a large measure of accountability and control, nevertheless the HSC and the HAS can look only at the quality of care provided. They cannot examine the quality of professional judgment, even if the two are related. Professionals such as doctors, generally regard themselves accountable to their peers for the maintenance of professional standards. Thus, there is the strong probability that on many occasions there will exist a conflict between their need to be held accountable to their professional group and to the members of society (their clients) whom they serve. This can manifest itself as a conflict between professional standards and Ministerial intentions, when the performance of professionally run services such as the health service (but also education, administration of the law, personal social services etc.) are judged according to professional standards. These professional standards can safeguard individual discretion and professional judgment and can run counter to other indicators of service performance such as public dissatisfaction with the quality and mix of the services provided. The dilemma here is that professional standards are being maintained at the expense of allocative and *X*-efficiency in service provision, whilst at the same time it has to be recognised that professional specialist advice is necessary in order to make allocatively efficient decisions in the first place. This dilemma is resolved if the specialist's role in providing information for decision making is separated from the subsequent performance of specialists in providing the services. In the latter case, society must examine more closely than it has done in the past the criteria and standards which professional groups use to judge the performance of their members. Having done so, it must then decide whose interests are being served by these criteria and proceed to make those changes which are required to safeguard the 'public interest'.

The role of the professional in government again illustrates that ministerial accountability and responsibility need to be thought about more carefully. Whilst DHSS has broad control over the direction of resources, at the point of service delivery its control ceases. This is clearly demonstrated in evidence given to the House of Commons Expenditure Committee (1971):

> ... it is important to note that the existence of clinical freedom substantially reduces the ability of the central authorities to determine objectives and priorities and to control individual facets of expenditure.

In concluding this section on the current problems of accountability and control, we return to Johnson (1974, p. 3) whose remarks were used to introduce this chapter:

> The apparent simplicity of the political and administrative geography in which our traditional notions of accountability were shaped and put to work has been supplanted by a map of administrative life of appalling complexity and uncertainty: we have literally lost the capacity to provide even a reasonably complete and accurate map of the public and quasi-public sector, let alone to describe with precision the conditions under which many of the bodies in it are operating and the extent to which they find themselves in relationships of accountability.

The complexity of the tasks of modern governments and the complexity of their structures create problems for traditional methods of control over the activities of modern governments and their bureaucracies. The preceding sections have set out the nature of some of the control problems faced by modern governments. In the next sections some of the institutions used to exercise such control are examined for the UK.

Institutions of Accountabiity and Control: the Experience of the UK

There exist a number of alternative approaches to the analysis of the institutions of accountability and control. For example, a legal based approach would be interested in the legal relationship which exists between the citizen and the agencies of the state. In this respect it is of interest to note that the UK has (a) no satisfactory body of public law (b) no effective judicial control of administrative bodies and (c) no recognition of the concept of the 'state' in its laws. These problems have led to much discussion and suggestions such that the UK should establish something akin to the *Conseil d'Etat* which is a body that works out legal principles to govern conflicts between the citizen and the state in France (see also Street 1975). There has also been a good deal of discussion about the effectiveness of the Parliamentary Commissioner (Ombudsman). The original intention of setting up the Parliamentary Commission[18] was to provide some degree of parliamentary control over administrative action. However, his activities are restricted to 52 departments and as Street (1975) has pointed out, his office is weak.

Interesting and important as the legal aspects of the issue undoubtedly are, we will instead use the economist's perspective of accountability and control. In that respect we are interested in the control of public expenditures etc. in attempts to achieve macro-economic stabilisation and efficiency within the public sector.

Financial Accountability

Financial accountability is frequently contrasted with the political and legal dimensions to accountability; however it should be clear that there is a strong interdependence between these concepts and that differences are due to the emphasis placed on certain concepts. The idea of financial accountability to Parliament is concerned with the evaluation of past performance. It is an *ex post* exercise, of limited scope, which is directed at ensuring that public funds have been spent properly (Chubb 1952, Normanton 1966, 1975 and Johnson 1975).

Public Accounts Committee

The PAC is a high prestige committee of the House of Commons which attracts senior MPs for its membership. Set up by Gladstone in 1861 and serviced by the Exchequer and Audit Department, which is headed by the Comptroller and Auditor General (CAG), the PAC exercises *post facto* control on behalf of Parliament through its scrutiny of public expenditures. Its functions are to ensure that departmental funds have been spent according to Parliament's original intentions when it voted the funds (i.e. an audit function) and moreover, that departments carry out their activities giving due regard to providing value for money (i.e. an efficiency function). As an *ex post* exercise the work of the PAC is to provide information for Parliament. It has no control over the size or the composition of public expenditures. These annual exercises are carried out by the PAC on a small number of government departments[19] and arise from points raised by the CAG in his reports on the audited accounts of departments. These efficiency audits of the PAC are published in the reports from the PAC and are presented to Parliament for debate. The work of the PAC is directed towards judging the adequacy of a department's financial control, systems of planning and costing of projects. It performs this task by calling witnesses from departments and subjecting them to cross examination in order to account for and thereby explain the existing set of departmental procedures. The advantages claimed by the PAC are:

(i) it draws attention to certain undesirable bureaucratic practices and speeds up the introduction of improvements which are suggested by the PAC and usually adopted by departments. For example, in the past it drew attention to lack of control over the drawing up of government contracts which had led to public scandals such as the Ferranti affair and the costings of the Bristol Siddeley aero-engine contract (see Clayton 1971);

(ii) the PAC is a powerful reminder to permanent secretaries that funds voted by Parliament must be accounted for to Parliament. Thus permanent secretaries' decisions do not have to be explained only to their own Ministers, they might also have to be *justified* to the PAC. No permanent secretary wishes to be publicly found negligent or incompetent and will, therefore, choose to do things in such a way as not to be a candidate for a PAC investigation;

(iii) in the past, the PAC has drawn attention to certain problem areas e.g. it raised questions about the taxation of North Sea Oil (1972–73 *1st Report*) and the activities of the Housing Corporation (1977–78 *9th Report*).

The PAC, however, suffers from a number of limitations;

(i) Only about 60% of total public expenditure is open for scrutiny by the PAC.[20] The expenditures of local government, the nationalised industries and agencies such as the National Enterprise Board and quangos are not covered by the activities of the PAC (see note 19). Despite this incomplete coverage of public expenditure programmes' success, CAGs have provided the PAC with a representative sample of public expenditure programmes for examination (Flegmann 1979).

(ii) The turnout of MPs to debate the PAC reports in Parliament is never high (Johnson 1975 and Flegmann 1979). Unless the reports of the PAC are of current political interest, the House does not generally find them to be suitable material for debate. Since the PAC exercise is *post facto* (shutting the stable door once the horse has bolted) and it takes time to prepare the report, the performance to which the reports refer is often well out of date by the time it is presented to Parliament. Flegmann found that the number of MPs who took part in the debate was about 4% and of them about half were members of the PAC. Despite the power of the PAC in making senior bureaucrats publicly accountable for their performance, it is surprising that Parliament takes so little notice of PAC reports.

(iii) The PAC is serviced by a very small staff provided by the Exchequer and Audit Department. This severely limits the number of subjects that the PAC can study and the type of exercise it can undertake. For example, it is impossible for it to contemplate a full efficiency audit for a single department. This is compared to similar institutions in other countries such as the Government Accounting Office in the USA which has an enormous staff to carry out efficiency audits. Moreover, a number of commentators, especially Mackintosh (1972), have criticised the range of skills which are available through the Audit Department to the PAC. These skills tend to be concentrated in accountancy and law. To assess the performance of modern government, skills in engineering, technology, science and computing should be readily available to the PAC, but are not.

(iv) The PAC does not carry out a full efficiency study. Finding out about the efficiency of a department by cross examining witnesses is not the best way of proceeding. However, the lack of staff prevents the PAC carrying out detailed O & M work studies, or detailed analysis of manpower utilisation. Moreover, it does not get down to details of organisation and management that would pick up a number of issues relating to cost effectiveness. Also, the work of the PAC is more limited to questions of *X*-inefficiency, rather than allocative efficiency and does not, therefore, tend to take a close look at objectives. This is often referred to as the need to extend the work of the PAC into 'effectiveness auditing'. Whilst the terminology can be confusing, what this criticism amounts to is, rather than just picking upon a set of activities and judging whether or not these activities could be performed using less resources (i.e. elimination of *X*-inefficiency), the PAC might also consider whether or not the set of activities is the most appropriate set for achieving the department's objectives. This, however, opens up a hornet's nest, since the PAC would then be judging government policies rather than bureaucratic procedures. For example, in a broader based efficiency exercise which would take in allocative efficiency, would the PAC be expected to report upon the appropriateness of the choice of objectives? Even if we ignore that problem for a moment there are others. The PAC in a full efficiency audit would judge whether or not it would be less costly to use vouchers or student loans as a means of financing education. However, surely the choice of the means of financing is a matter of government policy. There is no doubt that questions of this kind should be debated and if the PAC were to report on them then it might be a means of improving the turnout to debate PAC reports. However, the questions which remain are: (a) does this destroy the present function of the PAC and (b) would it not be better to set up a new committee to report on such issues?

(v) Does the threat of a permanent secretary and his department being publicly censured by the PAC result in an over-cautious attitude towards the taking of risks which might not best serve the public interest? Does the behaviour which is rewarded and that which is punished promote the most appropriate form of decision making when bureaucracies are confronted by complex ambiguous and uncertain environments? Evidence on this issue is partial, since a full scale study of bureaucrats' attitudes to risk has not been carried out. However, Sir Derek Rayner in his evidence to the Expenditure Committee's report on the Civil Service (HC 535) argued:

> I often do not believe that they (civil servants) are encouraged to take the calculated risk — and it is not much of a risk — that a businessman will take in dealing with certain problems. How do we encourage it? I think that we have to reward people ... by acknowledging their success. I have never heard of the Committee of Public Accounts sending for someone who did an excellent job. I have certainly heard of a board of directors sending for someone who has done an excellent job ... I think that you have to recognise success from time to time in a public way. (11/Q1513)

(vi) Finally the CAG, which guides the work of the PAC and provides it with information, has been criticised for being too closely tied in with the Treasury, thereby reducing its effective independence (Normanton 1975). It is the Treasury which decides which accounts will be brought before the CAG. This is compared to the operation of the State auditors of other countries, who in addition to being independent are also more concerned with effectiveness auditing (see (iv) above). Finally, those who staff the CAG's department are themselves civil servants. Also, the CAG, although a servant of Parliament, is chosen by the government without any need for Parliamentary approval.

The Estimates Committee and the Expenditure Committee

Another set of institutions which have been available to the UK Parliament for the scrutiny and control of public expenditure were the Estimates Committee set up in 1912 and the Expenditure Committee which replaced it in 1971. The Expenditure Committee was abandoned in 1979 and was replaced by a set of special committees which shadow the activities of each of the major spending departments.

The purpose of the Estimates Committee was to consider public expenditure estimates before they received Parliamentary approval (see Johnson (1966) for a study of the work of this committee). It had, however, to exclude policy questions, since these were the area of responsibility of government. Thus the Committee made statements about possible economies that might be made *within* policies. Post-1945, the Estimates Committee concentrated upon reporting on: (a) possibilities of financial savings and (b) administrative and management questions, such as Treasury control of establishments and recruitment to the civil service. Whilst like the PAC it became a *post facto* accountability committee, it retained the power to ask questions about the implications of past performance for future action.

The Estimates Committee had a number of inherent weaknesses which severely limited its effectiveness as a means of Parliamentary control over public expenditure. Its reports were superficial and discursive, covering a wide range of topics without formulating sufficiently precise recommendations. As time passed the reports became more and more divorced from the current estimates passing through Parliament for approval. Only a few days were set aside to debate the Estimates Committee's reports and as such, the topics debated like those of the PAC reports did not arouse much interest. Finally, the Estimates Committee suffered from problems of inadequate staffing. Apart from clerks provided by the House and the very occasional external adviser, the Committee had no full-time staff.

The Expenditure Committee was set up in 1971 to replace the Estimates Committee. The origins of the Expenditure Committee have been set out by Robinson (1978). During the 1960s a number of moves were made to restore, to the House of Commons, power which many MPs had thought had been lost to the Executive (including the bureaucracy).[21] Following the House of Commons' Procedure Committee Report *The Control of Public Expenditure and Administration*, (Session 1968–9, HC 410), the Conservative government of 1970 decided to set up an Expenditure Committee along the lines suggested in HC 410. The new Expenditure Committee consisted of a General Sub-Committee and five specialist sub-committees (Defence; Trade and Industry; Environment; Social Services and Employment; Education, Arts and the Home Office).

The original vision of the Committe on Procedure was that the Expenditure Committee through the specialist sub-committees would scrutinise the assumption upon which the public expenditure plans, as embodied in the Public Expenditure White Papers, were based. Thus it was envisaged that the Expenditure Committee would provide information that would enable Parliament to consider in detail the public expenditure proposals. The General Sub-Committee would analyse in detail the projections of total public expenditure and the general medium-term assessments of the economy upon which the expenditure projections were based, whereas the specialist sub-committees would analyse in detail the expenditure projections for the departments for which they were responsible.

The original intentions for the Expenditure Committee were not altogether realised. The work of each of the sub-committees was never coordinated. Whilst the General Sub-Committee pursued the original intentions of scrutinising the figures contained in the Public Expenditure White Papers and the bases of the medium-term assessments of the economy, the sub-committees failed to become involved in the details of expenditure projection. Instead, they considered a wide and disparate range of topics which had very little to do with expenditure plans.[22] Rather than operating as a finance committee concerned with the scrutiny of public expenditure, the Expenditure Committee functioned more like a set of specialist Select Committees (Robinson 1979). However, it seems that following the public expenditure crisis of 1976, the Expenditure Committee did begin to work in a more coordinated fashion with greater attention being paid to the scrutiny of the White Paper public expenditure projections. This activity increased in intensity following the IMF loan, with the demands that public expenditure and the public sector borrowing requirement be brought under stricter control (Robinson 1979).

The effectiveness of the Expenditure Committee as a means of promoting Parliamentary control over public expenditure, and hence the bureaucratic activities which lie behind these expenditures, has been limited by a number of factors. The recurrent comment about the staff which service Select Committees applies in the case of the Expenditure Committee also. The problem is best illustrated by the following quotation from John Boyd Carpenter[23] during the debate on the 1970 Green Paper on Select Committee reform;

> If the new Committee is to work efficiently, this is not just a question of giving it one or two extra clerks ... It involves equipping it with a real investigating staff of its own. We are kidding ourselves if we think that an assembly of very busy members of this House with, as we know, many other commitments and obligations sitting perhaps twice a week for a couple of hours, can possibly get at what is referred to in the Green Paper as .. 'the reasons and policies behind the figures', unless there is a staff.

This emphasises a point which has been developed throughout this book and which was highlighted a long time ago by Wildavsky (1964), — the quality of decisions depends upon good luck, but it also depends upon good judgment and the information upon which the decisions are made. Politicians are very busy people who find it extremely difficult to allocate sufficient time to the process of being informed. They do not have the specialist knowledge to understand the subjects that they are dealing with, nor do they have the time to carry out the research and analysis which will help them to be informed. Thus, when a busy MP, who is a member of an Expenditure Sub-Committee is cross examining expert witnesses on a highly specialist subject about which he has little expertise, it is not surprising that the type of question he asks is superficial and does not get to the heart of the issue. Much of the relevant information never comes forward in the deliberations of the Expenditure Committee, because the appropriate question which would have elicited it was not asked. In that event the information is retained by the bureaucracy.

This is not to suggest for a moment that the quality of all the questions asked by members of the Expenditure Committee were of a superficial character. Far from it. Many of the cross examinations revealed much. However, those sub-committees such as the General Sub-Committee who had the services of specialist advisers got much further and much deeper into the workings of the bureaucracy, because the specialist adviser was able to prompt the members to ask the appropriate questions. Not all of the sub-committees had specialist advisers, but it is interesting to note that the quality of the work carried out by the Social Services and Employment Sub-Committee improved for the short period for which it did have a specialist adviser.

For the work of Select Committees to be an efficient method of obtaining information and an understanding of the policy process (formulation and execution), it is necessary for the Committees to be adequately staffed with experts along the lines of the American Congressional Budget Office. There is, however, a paradox which Robinson (1979) points out; ' ... the Committee *as a whole* has devoted so little of its time to the sort of studies of expenditure that would require the services of an expert staff. Most of its time has been taken up with long detailed studies of administration. And so the pressure from Committee members to obtain the necessary back up staff to enable them to perform adequately an Expenditure scrutiny role, has not been strong enough for this reform to be enacted'.

One of the principal objectives of the Expenditure Commmittee was to give Parliament the information necessary to have a full and meaningful debate of the government's public expenditure projections as contained in the annual Public Expenditure White Papers. However, this debate failed and never became a key occasion or event on a parliamentarian's calendar on the same scale as, for example, the annual budget debate. This has disappointed those who had come to realise that much of the budget had already been settled in the Public Expenditure White Paper and all the Chancellor was doing each year on budget day as he presented the financial statement was a tidying-up job in which he announced how the expenditure plans were to be financed. This is not wholly due to the failure of the Expenditure Committee who have faced real resource constraints (see above). It is in part due to the way in which the extremely complex technical content of the expenditure plans are presented in the White Paper.[24] These do not make easy or exciting reading and so a busy parliamentarian is unlikely to prepare himself for the debate and in all probability is unlikely to attend it.[25] It could be argued, however, that if the Expenditure Committee had done its job properly (and had been adequately staffed), then the contents of the White Paper would have been more easily understood and a proper debate carried out. Parliament's inability to discuss the government's expenditure plans amounted to an abdication, a giving away of its powers to control public expenditure *ex ante* rather than *ex post* as in the case of the PAC. Walkland (1977) has argued that the work of the Expenditure Committee has in all probability not resulted in public expenditure being allocated differently or budgetary policy being modified in any way.

The work of the Expenditure Committee has on a number of occasions been frustrated by the activities of the government and senior officials in departments. The government has delayed in replying to Expenditure Committee reports and has refused to provide information when it has been asked for by the Committee. Senior bureaucrats when being cross examined by members of the Expenditure Committee refuse to give information that will politically embarrass their Minister. In that event, the Committee has to call for the Minister to answer the question. However, on one infamous occasion, Harold Wilson, then Prime Minister, refused to allow Harold Lever MP to appear before the Expenditure Committee to be cross examined. This problem of the free flow of information has been emphasised on many previous occasions throughout this book and is usefully highlighted in this context by Ian Mikardo MP (1979):

> In considering the relative powers of the Front Bench and the Back Benches, the basic fact is that knowledge is power. My Right Honourable Friend the Lord President ... is more powerful than I am because he knows a lot more than I do, and the reason is that he has a lot of people to tell him what is going on, and I have not. The reason why he knows a lot more than I do is that he has access to the books and I have not. It is this which has made the ability of Parliament to exercise control over the Executive grow dimmer and dimmer with every year that has passed.

Without access to the books, without access to information about what is going on within the Executive arm of government, and with access only to information that is in an indigestible form, Parliament is impotent and is unable to provide anything other than the most superficial control of public spending.

Select Committee on Nationalised Industries

In addition to the Expenditure Committee, Parliament had at its disposal the Select Committee on nationalised industries to look after the activities of these public enterprises. Many of the criticisms levelled at the Expenditure Committee apply with equal force to this Committee also. It has long been argued that Parliament has an insufficient amount of control over the activities of the nationalised industries to ensure accountability for their performance (Robson 1960). The Committee examined the reports and the accounts of the nationalised industries, but the information contained in these data sources was for audit purposes and was not useful for forming judgments about performance or commenting on management and efficiency. The lack of staff to service the Committee implied that the Committee could only examine one industry about every eight years. Given the resources at its disposal, including data, the Committee tended not to consider financial questions and issues relating to the nationalised industries' contribution to public expenditure. Instead, it concentrated on management and organisational issues such as, how are economic objectives relating to these industries defined and how are policy decisions taken? Through its examination of the organisational, administrative and political constraints which face the nationalised industries, the Committee made a very important contribution to policy debates.[26]

The Select Committee on Nationalised Industries was instructive in drawing attention to many of the dilemmas which such state controlled industries faced. On the one hand, there was the need for these industries to provide value for money, to be efficient and to pay heed to the demands of their customers, whilst at the same time there was the need for them to be accountable to Parliament and to serve as one of the instruments of the government's social policy, especially with regard to pricing of the nationalised industries' products. The results of the tension of these interests is that the management of the nationalised industries are drawn in all directions as they try to satisfy mutually incompatible objectives. This dilemma could be greatly reduced if the functions of the nationalised industries were to be spelt out. Are they part of the 'commanding heights' of the economy whose investment plans need to be carefully coordinated with those of other key industrial sectors? Here in particular we are thinking of the strategic position occupied by transport, British Steel, and the energy producing industries. Should their prices be controlled in an attempt by government to further its distribution of incomes policy? How does price control square up with the establishment of incentives for the pursuit of efficiency?

This discussion of the work of the Estimates Committee and the Expenditure Committee has emphasised some of the problems and limitations of Parliamentary control of public expenditure and the performance of the executive branch of government. There are, however, other limitations which are relevant to our discussion. One such limitation is the incentive structure which faces MPs. The UK has a strong party system and the strength of the party is in no small measure due to the discipline of its MPs.[27] This greatly reduces the power of the individual MP who, through his questions in the House, could embarrass the government. If an MP wishes to enhance the probability of holding political office, he will avoid asking embarrassing questions relating to the provision and delivery of services, about taxation and about public expenditure control. Thus, when a government which has a working majority, is presenting its Bills to the House it expects those Bills to pass without anything other than minor amendments, because it does not expect its own backbench MPs to suggest major changes. Robinson (1978) has emphasised the power of the party in the UK and argues that the whole party system in the UK works against the spirit of all party Select Committes which might consider and evaluate alternatives to the Government's plans. In this respect one is left wondering to what extent Parliament is, in the UK, usefully viewed as a representative assembly which watches over and controls the government, or to what extent such a view is simply an idealised one.

In summarising this section what can we conclude? Parliament formally approves expenditure but does not play any *effective* role in providing such approval. Instead, it scrutinises public expenditure as part of the ritual of deference by the executive to elected members. This is one of its main weaknesses. Parliament has not shown, through its actions in the past, an ability to perform its traditional role of control over the purse strings with any conviction. With the recent exception of the Rooker/Wise amendment to the 1978 Finance Bill, there have never been significant changes made to the public expenditure plans of any government. Parliament's discussion of the Public Expenditure White Paper has been likened to 'flogging a dead mouse' — it's a farce.

To understand why this is so, one has not only to look at the functioning of the Expenditure Committees, it is also necessary to examine carefully the role of the MP, his attitudes to public spending and taxation and his relationship to his party. The point has already been made that to the majority of MPs, there are formidable intellectual problems in giving the public expenditure figures any real meaning. Public expenditure control is very boring and it requires a great deal of time and energy for MPs to come to grips with the issues involved. This is the real significance of the concept of bounded rationality which was used in Chapter 4. Rather than spend time on the issue of public expenditure control, the average MP would regard the time as better spent looking after his constituents' problems, since there are votes in that activity and few in the former. Also, there are few votes in controlling public expenditure, especially if that expenditure falls in the MP's own constituency. Rather than arguing for reductions in public expenditure, it is found from an examination of the business of Parliament that MPs are more likely to argue for increases in public expenditure, especially in their own constituencies (Robinson 1978).

There is no indication that major reforms of Parliament are on the immediate horizon. In 1979 the Expenditure Committees were disbanded and were replaced by a set of Select Committees which allow backbench MPs to 'shadow' government departments. Whether or not this change will weaken or strengthen Parliament's powers of control remains to be seen. An organisational change of this kind is, however, unlikely to overcome the kinds of limitations which were encountered by previous Parliamentary committees. One of the essential elements in future discussions of Parliamentary control of the executive must be a consideration of the kind of information which is required to make control effective. The work of the Expenditure Committee has shown time and again that information is not always available in a form that makes it useful for accountability. There is a good deal of information for auditing purposes but not for appraisal. This point is taken up again in the last sections of this chapter.

Public Expenditure: The Crisis of Control

The procedural limitations on the UK Parliament's ability to control public expenditure, which were reviewed in the previous section, were dramatically thrown into relief during the mid-1970s when the question of government's ability to exercise control over the machinery of public expenditure planning was severely tested and shown to be wanting. The problem arose when the economy was thrown into reverse, following the industrial relations problems encountered by the Heath administration, the quadrupling of the world price of oil by OPEC, and a rapid expansion in the money supply. These events compounded the problems faced by an economy which had for most of the post-war period lagged behind its foreign competitors on any index of performance that might be chosen. Given the low rates of economic growth, the very high rates of inflation and the massive increase in the public sector borrowing requirement, it was decided by the government that its public expenditure plans must be cut back. The financial crisis of 1976 which culminated in the UK receiving a large loan from the IMF, brought with it demands from the IMF to cut back on public expenditure. Within the period of the 1970s, key institutions in the UK which included the Treasury, the Bank of England and latterly, the government, gradually turned towards many aspects of the monetarist philosophy.[28] Those particular aspects that they adopted were a need to set realistic monetary targets, which in turn implied a tighter control over the PSBR and hence over public expenditure itself.[29]

At a time when there were increasing demands for public expenditure control, there was a growing uneasiness about the ability of the current machinery of control to perform its task. Attention had been drawn to inherent weaknesses of the system by financial commentators such as Sam Brittan of *The Financial Times* and Peter Jay of *The Times* and also by academic economists, especially Wynne Godley of Cambridge. Another important source of information about the weaknesses of the system was that produced by the Expenditure Committee's General Sub-Comittee.

However, it was the no growth plus rapid inflation conditions of the 1970s which placed the machinery of public expenditure planning and control under its greatest strain and found it lacking in many respects (for an extended analysis of these issues see Klein 1979, Wright 1977 and Jackson 1979).

The machinery of public expenditure planning in the UK had evolved from the recommendations contained in the Plowden Committee Report of 1961 which had reviewed the then existing system of public expenditure control. The Plowden Committee had been set up following the 1958 Report by the Select Committee on Estimates, *Treasury Control of Expenditure*. That report had presented the weaknesses of the pre-Plowden system of public expenditure planning which concentrated too much attention on the expenditure proposals of the coming financial year (as presented in the Supply Estimates), with too little regard to the commitments and consequences of these expenditure plans for future years. In the words of the Select Committee (para. 23):

> If both the total and the balance of expenditure are to be effectively controlled, it is essential that policy decisions should be taken with full knowledge of what the policy will cost, not only next year, but if possible, the following year and the year after that ... Money must be voted and allocated annually but an obsession with annual expenditure can stultify forward planning.

The Plowden Committee was an internal review committee which had access to Treasury papers etc., was under the control of the Chancellor of the Exchequer and which gave away few secrets. The central philosophy upon which the post-Plowden machinery of public expenditure planning was to be founded is to be contained in paragraphs 7 and 12 of Cmnd. 1432. Essentially, what Plowden advocated was that, 'decisions involving substantial future expenditures should always be taken in the light of surveys of public expenditure as a whole over a period of years and in relation to the prospective resources' (para. 7). Out of this grew the annual exercise of public expenditure planning, in which central government departments prepared estimates of their spending over the next five years based on the assumption of unchanged policies and constant prices.[30] These estimates of *real* public expenditure growth were then compared to estimates of the growth of real resources in the economy as a whole.[31] Such a comparison showed the probable course of the public sector's share of the economy's resources. This exercise recognised that any changes in public expenditure plans had to be made several years in advance for them to be effective.[32]

The planning exercise is coordinated by PESC, the Public Expenditure Survey Committee, which is an inter-departmental committee of officials chaired by the Treasury. The procedures adopted for preparing the annual public expenditure review (i.e. the PESC report which is now published annually as the Public Expenditure White Paper) varies from year to year according to circumstances. However, the essential cycle is as follows:[33]

(a) The Treasury issues instructions to each department giving the basis and working assumptions on which the forecasts will be made;
(b) On the basis of these instructions departments send their estimates of their expenditure for the next 5 years;
(c) The Treasury discusses the estimates with each department. During these discussions they agree the policies and statistical assumptions on which the estimates should be based. The figures in the estimates are then agreed. These discussions ensure that all departments are working to a similar set of assumptions so that the overall plan fits together;
(d) A draft report, on the basis of the departmental estimates, is drawn up by the Treasury and agreed by the PESC. Included in the report, along with the public expenditure estimates, is the medium-term assessment for the economy;
(e) This report is then submitted to Ministers who, during the summer recess, debate the public expenditure plans and then take decisions on the aggregate of public expenditure and its allocation to the various programmes;
(f) The White Paper is then published and contains the PESC report. The White Paper is usually published around November, but in recent years it had been delayed until January or February, and is now published in March along with the Budget Statement.

It is worthwhile considering the kinds of questions that the PESC report is designed to answer for Ministers taking expenditure decisions:

(i) What is the existing state of the expenditure plans?
(ii) What amendments or additions to the existing plans are proposed by departments, and why?
(iii) Where could reductions be made if necessary?

There are a number of inherent weaknesses in the PESC system of public expenditure planning. These are examined under the following headings:

(a) *The Planning Paradox* If public expenditure is planned in relation to available resources, as Plowden suggested, and if the estimate of the medium-term growth of the economy turns out to be wrong, then public expenditure as a share of GNP will turn out to be different from that planned. For example, if GNP is forecast to grow at 4% p.a. in real terms and public expenditure is geared up to grow in line with GNP at 4% p.a. also, then if the actual growth in GNP is only 2% p.a., cumulatively over a number of years the relative size of the public sector (as measured by the ratio of public expenditure to GNP) will grow. The medium-term forecast is, therefore, a crucial element in the whole exercise and the paradox lies in tying the growth in expenditure to the growth in resources. Get the economic forecast wrong and you actually end up promoting an expansion in the *relative* size of the public sector! Bearing in mind that it takes some time to bring public expenditure under control, then this can have serious consequences for the stabilisation and management of the economy.

Many of the reports produced by the Cambridge Economic Policy Group and the Expenditure General Sub-Committee draw attention to the Treasury's persistent failure to get the medium-term assessment right. They show the failure of the economy to grow at rates sufficiently high to sustain the planned growth in public expenditure. There are some who would, of course, argue that the rapid growth in the relative size of the public sector caused the slow growth in GNP and herein lies a possible second paradox!

(b) *The Price Basis of the Estimates* Public expenditure is planned in real terms at constant prices. The whole exercise is concerned with resource planning rather than financial planning. Given the relative price effect, (i.e. that the rate of inflation of unit costs in the public sector exceeds that for the economy as a whole) rapid rates of inflation, as were experienced during the post-1973 period, present problems for the financing of these public expenditure plans as they roll forward. What this implies is that public sector activities were indexed for inflation, whereas most other sectors in the economy were not. This problem spilled over into rapid increases in the tax bill and the Public Sector Borrowing Requirement.

Since 1979, with the introduction of the Conservative administration, a greater degree of financial planning has been introduced into public expenditure decisions. Public expenditure plans and the implied public sector borrowing requirement have now to be compatible with the government's financial strategy and money supply targets.

(c) *Costed Options are Not Presented* The PESC exercise is essentially one of 'incrementalism' (see Chapter 6 above) i.e. the bulk of public expenditure is already committed. What the White Paper shows are the increments to the plans from one year to the next. However, these increments are not related in an easily identifiable way to new policies or extensions of existing ones, so that there is no way that Parliament can unscramble the omelette of the public expenditure figures and discuss policy options. Also, the public expenditure plans are often presented at a different moment in time from the government's taxation proposals, so that the two sides of the equation cannot be discussed by Parliament.[34]

(d) *Lack of Monitoring* Prior to 1976–77, the public expenditure plans were not monitored against outturn. To do so would have required an elaborate statistical exercise, since outturn public expenditure valued at current prices would have had to be linked via some index to planned public expenditure at constant prices. The result was that control over the *volume* of public expenditure was non-existent, because it was difficult to distinguish between public expenditure increases which originated from unauthorised volume increases and those due to price increases.

In 1976, following the IMF loan, a system of cash limits was introduced in an attempt to strengthen the control over public expenditure. Cash limits had been introduced in 1974–75 on certain building programmes, but it was in April 1976 that a fuller system of cash controls on public expenditure was announced in the White Paper, *Cash Limits on Public Expenditure* (Cmnd. 6440). The cash limits are derived from the volume plans set out in the public expenditure White Paper. These volume estimates are multiplied by an appropriate set of figures to produce cash figures. Real resource planning and financial planning are brought together through this exercise.

Not all public expenditure programmes are subject to cash limits. The principal elements of central government spending that are excluded are social security benefits, such as unemployment benefits and pensions. The rate support grant payment to the local authorities is subject to cash control, but the remainder of local government expenditure which is financed by the local property tax is not. About 66% of the public expenditure which is voted by Parliament is subject to cash limit control.

Along with the introduction of cash limits, the government also introduced a more sophisticated system for monitoring public expenditure called the financial information system (FIS). Effective control requires up-to-date information on the cash flow of public spending. At the start of each financial year, departments prepare a forecast of the time profile of cash flows (expenditures) for each quarter. As the cash is spent, the actual flow is compared to the forecast. The cash expenditure figures are analysed to show expenditure at the constant prices of the public expenditure survey and pay and price increases. This enables a distinction to be made between volume and price changes. The whole monitoring system is computerised and can rapidly show how actual spending compares with the Parliamentary Estimates, cash limits, and the figures in the White Paper. The comparison of these data provides the necessary management information required for adjusting public expenditure programmes, so as to keep them within the plan (real and financial).

It is too early yet to provide a full appraisal of the new system of cash limit control. The evidence which does exist shows that over the period 1976–79, departments did manage to operate within the cash limits set. Indeed, for the financial year 1977–78 there was an increase in the 'shortfall', which means that public expenditure in real and financial terms was well below target. Whilst some might regard this as an achievement, it should be remembered that a massive underspending of public expenditure is just as problematical as an overspend. If the government's overall economic strategy is based on the assumption that the public expenditure plans will be met, but in the event they are not, the result is likely to have a deflationary effect upon the level of economic activity.

Post-Fulton Developments

The Fulton Committee which reported in 1968 stimulated concern with problems of management control and techniques for the efficient allocation of resources. The aim of Fulton was to identify a new structure for the executive and management functions that exist in departments. It also attempted to identify responsibilities and to allocate these to units which were to be held accountable to Ministers and Parliament for their performance. Fulton's analysis found that the element of accountability for carrying out government programmes was missing and this led to one of the basic proposals of Fulton, namely that there should be a 'hiving off' of activities to separate accountable management units, such as sub-departments and independent extra-departmental and extra-governmental agencies (see quangos above). This 'hiving off' exercise was carried out, but instead of Ministers retaining control over these decentralised units, control was lost and as these agencies proliferated they increasingly escaped the net of accountability (see above).

Another set of recommendations made by Fulton was that the management information required to improve the efficiency of resource allocation and the reduction in X-inefficiency was not readily available and should be. The thinking surrounding public expenditure management which followed from the Plowden Report was essentially macro-economic. It was directed at resource planning in the aggregate i.e. ensuring the total amount of public spending was optimal and that the balance of spending between programmes was about right. Fulton in comparison was more concerned with the allocation of resources within departments and within programmes. In this respect it was promoting the micro-economic efficiency dimension of public sector management.

To fulfil the micro-economic efficiency objective required a complete revolution in the type of information provided about public programmes. The audit type of information, or the public expenditure aggregates published in the Supply Estimates and the public expenditure White Papers, were not appropriate for the micro questions of internal management and resource allocation. Instead, what was required was an information system that would produce data on the unit costs of key public sector activities, answers to questions such as who are the beneficiaries from public expenditure programmes, and how much does it cost to do *X*. In other words, what was being requested was some kind of rational decision making models of budgeting along the lines of those discussed in Chapters 4 and 6 above. Despite the scorn and cold water poured on such approaches, a number of essential questions remain to be answered.

These questions are: (a) what is it that departments are currently doing and why are they doing it; (b) what does it cost to do what they are doing; (c) can they fulfil their objectives or provide their service by means of an alternative set of activities; (d) what would the alternative set of activities cost; and (e) if we compare (b) and (d) and then take into account the distribution questions, who benefits under the different schemes? Only by answering these questions can alternative means of supplying public outputs at reduced costs and increased efficiency be found.

To what extent have such information systems been introduced following Fulton? The simple answer is, to all intents and purposes no such information system exists. The Department of Education and Science made an attempt at introducing output budgeting in the early 1970s and the Department of Health and Social Security operates a skeletal PPB system. About the only department which produces micro-economic management data on the scale envisaged by Fulton is the Ministry of Defence. Programme Analysis and Review (PAR) exercises do take place but, since these are internal exercises, very little is known about them, how often they take place and with what effect. The Central Policy Review Staff (CPRS) provide some data on a one off basis in their reports on specific government programmes, but there is nothing like a comprehensive information system within departments providing micro-management data necessary for the efficient allocation of resources.

Evidence that most of the efficiency questions raised by Fulton remain unanswered is found in the most recent review of the Civil Service produced as the Eleventh Report of the Expenditure Committee (HC 535, 1976–77). The principal interest of the committee was to find out to what extent government departments effectively and efficiently achieved their objectives. The report raised all the issues presented already in this chapter and lots more. It raised questions about the political position of civil servants, the traditional concept of the neutrality and objectivity of the Civil Service and examined recruitment and training policies (*op. cit.*). The Expenditure Committee also suggested that government should provide to Parliament much more information than it presently does on the cost implications of policy. In their response[35] to the Select Committee's report, the government replied that whether or not such cost information should be provided must be left to the discretion of individual Ministers. Thus, it would seem that immediate reforms, by way of providing Parliament with more information on the costs of public programmes, are unlikely.

Beyond Plowden and Fulton

Questions of accountability and control should not be separated from the more fundamental questions about the whole rationale of the public sector, its existence and continuation. For example, the work of Ivan Illich (1971, 1976) in this respect strikes hard at many of the cherished beliefs surrounding the education and health sectors (both public and private). What benefits do these services in practice provide? These are the fundamental questions of accountability and control.

Information is the essential lubricant of any system of accountability and control. This point has been emphasised time and again. One striking feature of UK government compared, for example, with that of the USA, is the lack of freedom to have access to official information originating from within the bureaucracy. This severely limits the system of Parliamentary control. Good government requires public access to information at low cost. The White Paper on official information does not offer an opening up of the provision of such information. Instead, it has concentrated upon the report of the Franks Committee (1966) and limited its attention to Section 2 of the 1911 Official Secrets Act which covers the unauthorised disclosure of official information.

What advantages arise from an improvement in the public's access to information? This is answered in a recent report published by the Outer Circle Policy Unit (p. 5):

> ... it would have a salutory effect upon ministers if they knew that the impartial balanced and well informed advice of the civil servant was shortly to be available to the public; and salutory for the civil servants to know that what may sometimes be partial, incomplete and ill informed advice would be made public too.

Given this greater flow of information, Parliament would be better placed and better equipped to hold Ministers to account than it is now. The point of increased public access to information would be to shift the balance between an enormously expanded permanent civil service, the small number of politicians who are supposed to be in charge of it and Parliament to which they in turn are supposed to be answerable. The OCPU report goes further than simply suggesting greater access to information. It also wishes the rules of the game to be made public via the publication of manuals, rules and codes used in administration. This action, it is hoped, would 'do something to mitigate the widespread frustration and resentment that many people feel at the arbitrary, secretive and insensitive ways in which government schemes are administered' (p. 5).

There is no doubt that the production of information and the carrying out of PAR exercises etc. would be costly. These costs, however, need to be balanced up against the gains in both allocative and *X*-efficiency which would result. In this respect the OCPU report (p. 4) makes the valid point that, '... the government already spends large sums on its information services whose function it is to tell people what the Government wants them to know. We think it more important that these resources should be used to enable people to find out for themselves what they want to know'. In other words, by redirecting existing resources the final costs of producing the increased information might not be as great as many of the critics of the idea suggest.

The Official Information Bill does *not* suggest complete access to all information. That would be a naive suggestion and would endanger the success of reform in this area. Public access would be limited and information about defence, security, foreign relations and personal privacy would be subject to stricter regulation and control. Other aspects of government activities (as with private sector activities also) must remain confidential and closed (a) if the security of the nation is placed at risk and (b) *during* negotiations in certain areas e.g. economic policy, foreign relations etc. However, after such negotiations have been completed, there is no reason why information relating to the particular bargains struck and the deals and trades made to effect such bargains should not be made public in order that it might be judged whether or not the 'public interest' was adequately served.

Information is not only required for external accountability and control and hence the pursuit of allocative efficiency, it is also required for internal management control purposes in order to secure improvements in X-efficiency. The example of an increase in the number of PAR type exercises has been given. These exercises must be a regular feature in all areas of government: central, local, nationalised industries and extra-departmental agencies (quangos). This is a part of the Fulton Report which has not been followed up properly. It is not being suggested that X-inefficiency can be eliminated by the use of such techniques. Previous chapters have shown that there are severe organisational limits to the implementation of efficiency techniques. However, there surely exists scope for additional gains to be derived from an examination of the system of public supply, from gaining more information about how things work, how much certain activities cost and for considering alternative means of supply.

Finally, there might be a role for the bureaucrat to supply some of the necessary information. This idea was mooted by Ralph Nader (1965) as 'insider control'. It is frequently suggested (as above) that improvements in efficiency and greater control over bureaucratic activities require more information about what is going on. This takes the form of a greater supply of information from the bureaucracy to the outside and an improvement of the flow of information within the bureaucracy as between departments etc. However, Nader is extending the idea of supplying information to the outsider by going beyond the normally understood boundaries. Because it is difficult for outsiders to monitor what is going on in the bureaucracy (they need to know what should be monitored and then they need to be able to interpret technical information), significant improvements in the flow of information depend upon insiders taking considerable responsibility in not keeping their activities secret when they know that such information is required for control and accountability.

This idea of insider control dissolves the basic tenet that bureaucrats should not place their Minister in an embarrassing situation *vis-à-vis* Parliament and the public. In other words, the possibility that bureaucrats can voluntarily supply information reduces the chance of there being 'cover ups'. But of course, the problem facing dissenters is that they place their careers in jeopardy. Hence, there would need to be some means of protecting these careers and at the same time allowing justice to prevail.

Conclusion

Any system of accountability and control must ensure that: (a) public agencies are responsive to the needs and demands of the electorate, especially in a changing environment; (b) decisions which are made are 'fair' i.e. that they conform to the general climate of ethical opinion; and (c) performance of the bureaucracy is monitored and evaluated with a view to cutting back waste and providing value for money. In this chapter we have done nothing other than to explore a limited number of the issues involved in an attempt to clarify rather than prescribe. The gaps which exist in the present system of control are clear and future developments will undoubtedly take the form of designing institutions which will make such gaps narrower. However, the speed at which these developments are introduced, the direction they take and their success all remain unknown.

Notes

1 These quotations from Reich (1970) are drawn from many different sections of the book and were assembled and presented in Olson and Clague (1971).

2 Not all Liberals made this assumption: e.g. J.S. Mill, following Tocqueville's analysis, was aware of the dangers inherent in democracy: '[in a democracy] the 'people' who exercise the power are not always the same people with those over whom it is exercised; and the "self government" spoken of is not the government of each by himself, but of each by all the rest, ... the people consequently may desire to oppress a part of their number and precautions are as much needed against this as against any other abuse of power' (*On Liberty*, Chapter 1).

3 This general statement could be extended to many different groups (apart from bureaucrats) including doctors, accountants, lawyers etc.

4 *A priori* argument will help to make the issue clearer for empirical investigation.

5 It will be recalled that there are decision, information and other costs involved in organising pressure groups. Thus, it is those who can afford such costs who will mobilise the resources for protest and put themselves into a powerful and influential position. Again this raises questions about the normative distribution of such influence.

6 Fiorina and Noll (1978) argue that politicians and bureaucrats together conspire to produce a jungle of red tape. Voters are unable to penetrate the jungle and bureaucrats can continue to pursue their wasteful activities. It should be noted that this 'conspiracy theory' is not supported by empirical testing.

7 It might be countered that training and professionalisation will overcome these personal qualities. Two things have to be said in reply to that argument; first, training will not change the individual's perceptions or values completely; second, professionalism reinforces certain values and will force bureaucrats to see problems in a particular and specialised way. It is therefore necessary to analyse the nature of that bias and ask if the serving of professional interests/standards/values is in the public interest.

8 See HMSO (1977) Q 1051–1065, Appendix 47.

9 About 200 administrative trainees were recruited in 1976 out of a total of 10,000 persons recruited by the Civil Service Commission (including all executive, scientific and professional recruits). This places the numbers in perspective, but it should be remembered that it is this small group of administrative trainees who have the better chances of internal promotion to top posts in the civil service.

10 Crowther-Hunt and the Committee did, however, suggest that this might simply reflect biases in the education system, '... if the civil service is seeking to recruit the most able people it is hardly surprising that Oxbridge supplies a higher proportion than other universities'.

11 Lord Franks Committee (1966) demonstrated a bias in the selection of undergraduates by the Oxford colleges in favour of the independent schools. Two fifths of undergraduates came from independent schools in 1966.

12 For an excellent review of the issues involved see Smith and Hague (1971), especially the introductory essays; the first by Smith and the second by Hague.

13 The first person to use this phrase was Alan Pifer (see Hague, Mackenzie and Barker 1975). There is no simple definition of a quango; however, it is generally thought of as a non-departmental non-judicial body which has a degree of autonomy to perform some function on behalf of central government (see Chester 1979 and Davies 1979). However, as Davies reports, quango is an unsatisfactory label since it covers a number of types of organisations, 'fringe bodies', public bodies and non-departmental organisations. See Davies (1979, pp. 8 *et seq.*) for a useful survey of the problems of defining quangos and also Hague, Mackenzie and Barker (1975).

14 The Fulton Report reviewed the structure, recruitment, management and organisation of the UK civil service.

15 In this section I am indebted to Nevil Johnson (1974) whose paper on *Defining Accountability* has helped me to clarify my thoughts.

16 This has not happened in the UK for many years.

17 It is not being suggested that bureaucrats and professional specialists are synonymous. We are using the problem of controlling the specialist to illustrate a more general issue which includes the control over bureaucrats' activities.

18 See Street (1975) for a full discussion.

19 The PAC is dependent upon the CAG for information. However, the CAG today only audits abut 60% of public expenditure; see *Evidence to the Expenditure Committee*, 11th Report 1976–77, HC 535–11, p. 588. The areas that lie outside his control include local authorities, nationalised industries, the National Enterprise Board etc. See du-Cann (*Select Committee on Procedure*, 1st Report 1978).

20 The Eleventh Report of the Expenditure Committee *The Civil Service* (HC 535 1976–77) recommended that the CAG be given powers to audit local authority accounts, which are presently audited by the Department of Environment's District Audit, and the accounts of those agencies which use public funds but which are not currently subjected to CAG audit. See also *Select Committee on Procedure*, 1st Report 1977–78.

21 See Fourth Report from the Select Committee on Procedure, *Specialist Committees*, Session 1964–65, HC 303, and Robinson (1977).

22 Topics which were covered included, *Wages and Conditions of African Workers Employed by British Firms in South Africa*, the *Children and Young Persons Act (1969)*, *National Health Service Facilities for Private Patients, The Fishing Industry, Charity Commissioners their Accountability, New Towns, Planning Procedures, Preventative Medicine*, etc. For a more complete listing, see Robinson (1978).

23 The quotation is originally found in H.C. Debates, 12th November 1970, Col. 632 and was presented in Robinson (1979).

24 For an insight into the ambiguities contained in the White Paper and alternative interpretations that can be placed on its contents, see the varying views of the expert witnesses in 2nd Report from the Expenditure Committee, *The Government's Expenditure Plans 1978–79 to 1981–82*, HMSO Cmnd 7049, Session 1977–78, HC 257.

25 Robinson (1978) gives details of the attendance at Public Expenditure White Paper debates.

26 For example, see, *First Report of the Nationalised Industry Committee 1967–68, Ministerial Control of the Nationalised Industries* (HC 351–1).

27 Some would argue that it is not simply a question of the strength of the party. Within the party the power is concentrated in the office of the Prime Minister — see Mackintosh (1972). Such a view was recently expressed by Tony Benn in his criticism of the Labour Party. Those who do not hold such a view, counter it by arguing that pressure groups weaken the power of parties and the Prime Minister and that the 'office' of the PM is too ambiguous a term without a discussion of the characteristics of the role occupant. The debate continues!

28 Of course, they did not accept all the elements of the monetarist creed.

29 A very useful and interesting account of this period is found in Blackaby (1978).

30 There had been earlier experiments with forward planning of expenditure carried out in some departments. In 1955 Selwyn Lloyd had produced an unpublished 5-year rolling programme for defence and in 1956 Sir David Eccles produced a 5-year plan for technical education.

31 Pre-1965, only public expenditure forecasts were produced. Post-1965, with the establishment of the Department of Economic Affairs, which was concerned with the medium-term assessment of the economy, the public expenditure forecasts were compared with medium-term economic assessment.

32 The momentum of public expenditure has frequently been compared to that of an express train. In order to bring it to a halt or to slow it down, the brakes must be applied well in advance.

33 For greater detail, see *Planning and the Control of Public Spending*, Memorandum submitted by the Treasury, October 1976, Thirteenth Report from Expenditure Committee 1975–76 (HC 718) HMSO.

34 Since the Conservative government's Budget of 1980, public expenditure and taxation proposals have been considered alongside one another. This is a move in the desired direction.

35 Response to the White Paper on the Civil Service (HC 374, 1977/78) HMSO.

CHAPTER 9

Organisational Limits: The Problems of Implementation

Ko-Ko:
When your Majesty says, 'Let a thing be done', it's as good as done — practically it is done — because your Majesty's will is law. Your Majesty says 'Kill a gentleman', and a gentleman is told off to be killed. Consequently that gentleman is as good as dead — and if he is dead why not say so?

The Mikado:
'I see. Nothing could possibly be more satisfactory'.
(Gilbert and Sullivan: *The Mikado*)

A Choice is not effective without implementation, which may be far from simple, and often imperfectly accomplished. It is dangerous to assume, either that what has been decided will be achieved, or that what happens is what was intended.
(Loasby 1976, p. 89)

Introduction

During the past two decades economists, social policy makers, and political scientists have all become increasingly disillusioned and disappointed by the effectiveness of legislation and policies designed to bring into reality the vision of the 'Great Society'. Great expectations, held at the beginning of the 1960s, about the delivery of social services, that economic growth could be engineered and that full employment could be guaranteed have been dashed and frustrated on a large number of occasions. We have slowly come to learn that in many situations in which we know *what* to do we frequently do not know *how* to do it. The problem is one of implementation. The issue is of differences between ambition and accomplishment, legislation and execution, promise and performance. Whilst the shortfalls between our expectations and accomplishments are plain to see, the problems of implementation have only recently started to occupy the mind of the policy analyst (see Crozier 1976, Etzioni 1975, Pressman and Wildavsky 1973, van Meter and van Horn 1975, King 1975, 1976 and Hood 1976).

To what extent is the bureaucracy's inability to deliver the goods a result of the executive and the legislature having inappropriate and unrealistic ambitions and expectations, or to what extent is it due to internal organisational problems? That is to say, are there *limits* to an organisation's ability and effectiveness to deliver the goods and services which politicians and voters demand? Are many policies non-implementable? For example, what seems to be feasible on a blue print or in a small scale model frequently presents the engineer with technical problems when the blue print is implemented.[1] Should we, therefore, blame administrators for the practical failures and problems of policy implementation and also for the unanticipated undesirable consequences of policies? What are the critical institutional factors which make a project succeed or fail? Is it leadership and managerial style, coordination and control, or information flows? If such limits to policy implementation do exist, what are they, what are the appropriate means of discussing them, and is it possible to design organisations in order to improve the implementation process?

These questions have formed the basis of much of the material which was discussed in the earlier chapters. In this chapter we will draw some of these threads together.

In the earlier chapters it was seen that organisations are characterised in part by the division of labour and by specialisation. The environment is frequently complex, changing and uncertain. Personnel have their own goals and values and differ from one another in terms of their abilities. To manage this situation organisations are bounded by rules, routines and procedures which necessarily make them inflexible, undemonstrative and slow to change. However, it is often argued that such aspects of organisational life are necessary in order to control the behaviour of personnel, to cope with a hostile and changing environment and to coordinate a diversity of activities. Whilst hierarchy, rules, and specialisation are means of dealing with these problems, they carry with them their own costs. Controls are in practice difficult to operate, objectives are not clearly specified, there are attendant costs of policing and monitoring any system, information is difficult and expensive to process and the political reality of organisational life is that there are competing power points in the system. All of these taken separately or combined can paralyse an organisation and result in impaired action. It is the constraints placed upon the behaviour of an organisation's members which are of interest in this chapter. The following example from Bradley and Wilkie (1974, p. 60) illustrates vividly the nature of the implementation problem:

> The story has been told of a Soviet citizen taking a rifle into Red Square and firing a number of shots into Mikoyan's car. Red Square at that time was saturated with security guards, but they did not dare to act immediately without orders, because they could not be sure that the attempted assassination was not sanctioned by an even higher authority than Mikoyan. The guards were effectively paralysed until higher clearance was obtained to shoot the offender. Political complexity, size and centralisation all combine to paralyse the organisation just at the point where the need for swift action is greatest.

Economists and the Implementation Process

Economists have in the main tended to ignore the problems of implementing policies. They tend to be stronger on prescription than upon understanding the policy execution process. The charge of lack of attention to the problems of implementation cannot, however, be levelled against some of the earlier economists. Thus, for example, in the writings of Schumpeter (1964), von Mises (1920) and Hayek (1935) there is a strong feeling that implementation problems under socialist planning systems render them inferior to the price mechanism (markets). More recently, the problems of implementation have been taken up by writers in the fields of economic/socialist planning and development economics; see Liberman (1950), Kornai (1959), Bergson (1964) and Hirschman (1967). Niskanen's analysis of bureaucracy had very little to say about policy implementation, although by recognising the possible discretionary behaviour of bureaucrats who pursue their own objectives, he had introduced one of the basic problems of policy implementation. The many volumes written by economists on the topics of cost–benefit analysis and programme budgeting are purely prescriptive and are devoid of considerations of the problems which will occur once the decisions are implemented. What has been left out of the picture is the reality of the processes of administration, i.e. the persuading, manipulating, or coercing of people to act in accordance with the policy decisions. A good number of economic policy prescriptions are based upon the results of analysis derived from models that rely upon highly restrictive assumptions such as perfect competition and perfect knowledge etc. These results are then often applied with very little care or attention to situations which are far removed from the assumptions of the model. In the case of policy implementation, the policy outputs and prescriptions assume perfect frictionless organisations which will implement the policy according to the dictates and expectations of the designers of the policy. Seldom is there any question that organisations are not perfect, that they will, through the actions of their members, either wittingly or unwittingly, distort and change the policy out of all recognition. What are these organisational processes which play havoc with the best laid policy blueprints? What are the limits which are placed upon the realisation of the expected policy outcome? Tullock (1965) talks in terms of, '... the inherent limitations that organisational and administrative constraints placed upon the choice of policies'.

Perrow (1972, p. 161) says, '... organisations are tools in the hands of their masters, but they are imperfect, not completely controlled tools and it is a struggle to maintain control over them'.

Just as markets are not perfect, neither are organisations. The problems of ineffective implementation can be thought of in terms of administrative limits or administrative frictions. Consider the following statements of contemporary writers on this issue:

> There are ... two aspects of the nature of the managerial limit on the rate of expansion of the firm. First, the services available from the existing managerial group limit the amount of expansion that can be planned at any time because all plans for expansion absorb some of the services available from this group and the larger and more complex the plans, the more services will be required to digest and approve them on behalf of the firm ... Secondly, the amount of activity that can be planned at a given time limits the amount of new personnel that can profitably be absorbed in the next period.
>
> (Penrose 1959, p. 49)

> ... in the contemporary world, there seems to be an obvious tendency for the political demands which are generated by mass democracy to push administration to its limits, both by pursuing incompatible goals simultaneously and by stretching administrative resources too far ... governments are easily pushed into promising things which they cannot possibly deliver.
>
> (Hood 1976, p. 205)

> The central problem facing most administrators is that of maximising the number of decisions taken by subordinates that do, in fact, carry out the general policy of the whole organisation.
>
> (Tullock 1965, p. 205)

> Neither strategies nor tactics, however superior, may bring victory except through the way they deploy troops and armour and their equivalents in other services; what troops and armour are capable of is a *given*, within very narrow limits.
>
> (Dunsire 1978a, p. 125)

> ... the power of the firm's higher officers to enforce a decision is severely restricted by middle management's ability to delay or to act only with limited drive and enthusiasm. The mayor of a large city once remarked at his shock on learning how things work when he first assumed office. 'On Friday I would announce that beginning on Monday things will change in such and such a way and on Monday absolutely nothing happened.'
>
> (Baumol and Stewart 1971, p. 139)

Each of these statements illustrate the statement which the Iron Czar Nicholas I is reported to have said: 'I do not rule Russia; ten thousand clerks do'. At the same time they highlight the artificiality of Woodrow Wilson's separation of policy making from the implementation, execution and administration processes. For too long attention has been focused upon policy making at the expense of a realisation that implementation problems are equally, if not more, important.

Each of the above statements illustrate different elements of the problem. Implementation failures can arise because of: the inelastic supply of managerial skills; the limitations of managerial skills relative to the size and complexity of the problems to be solved; the tendency for subordinates to pursue activities which primarily serve their own interests rather than the objectives of the plan; and because of management's inability to allocate resources optimally in order to achieve the targets of the plan. The list is not exhaustive but instead suggests where we need to look for an explanation of the limits to organisation in the implementation of policy.

A Framework: Organisational Failure

The remarks outlined in the above section have simply served to identify the problem. To understand the issues involved it is necessary to place the problem into a framework which will enable us to identify more clearly the characteristics and the dimensions of the implementation process and then to analyse the administrative or organisational limits.

The concept which will serve our purpose is that of *organisational failure*.[2] In comparison the ideal type of the 'perfect market' plays a central role in much of economic analysis. However, perfect markets fail to exist for a variety of reasons and the sources of market failure or market imperfections become of interest.[3] A number of different factors cause markets to fail and to deviate from the ideal of perfect competition, e.g. imperfectly specified contracts, transactions costs, imperfect information, monopoly elements, externalities and uncertainty.

The presence of market failures has caused a number of economists to use the concept as a basis for replacing the market with internal organisation. This was discussed in greater detail in Chapter 3 above. The substitution of internal organisation for market exchange occurs, not because of technological economies associated with production, but because of transactional failures.[4] For example, Williamson (1971, 1973) and Arrow (1975) explain the vertical integration of firms as an 'internalisation' of market exchanges which attempts to reap economies gained through the firm's greater control over these activities. Williamson's argument is that the firm (i.e. internal organisation as compared to the market) has a greater number of incentives than does the market e.g. selective use of employment, promotion, remuneration and internal resource allocation processes. The firm's reward and penalty instruments are more refined. Moreover, the firm has a superior control system, since it has access to low cost information which will permit it to carry out more precise 'own performance' evaluations. Finally, there are economies to be gained in information exchange. Communication with respect to complex matters is facilitated by a common training and experience through repeated inter-personal interactions.

Market failures and the presence of consumption externalities and public goods have also been employed by economists to account for the existence of a public sector. For cases of complete market failure (as in the case of pure public goods[5]) when the market fails to exist, public collective provision of these goods is necessary if the goods and services are to be made available for consumption. In other words, certain goods and services are made available for consumption through non-market institutions i.e. in the case of public goods and services they are supplied through public sector bureaucracies and public budgets. For cases where market failure is less complete, the public sector has a regulatory role to play as in the cases of the control of monopoly and environmental protection.

Thus in each case of extreme market failure the market is replaced by a non-market institution i.e. internal organisation. Furthermore, in each example, where the market is replaced by internal organisation, analysts have made assertions about the superiority of internal organisation, either in terms of its allocative efficiency, its control structure, its incentives or generally its inherent structural advantages. However, such assertions cannot be permitted to resolve issues which are essentially empirical matters. The presupposition in many instances is that imperfect markets are being replaced by perfect, frictionless, internal organisations.

As soon as we recognise the possibility of organisational failure, the problem becomes an empirical question of balancing up the relative imperfections of two different allocative mechanisms. Tullock (1970, p. vi) has argued:

> The injuries that externalities may inflict on individuals if everything is left to the market and the injuries that government may inflict on individuals through the inherent nature of its decision process are the two basic factors in selecting the proper institutions to deal with any given problem. We must always weigh the specific advantages and disadvantages of these two imperfect instrumentalities.

This approach breaks the ideological clashes which exist between those who advocate the extension of market mechanisms and those who wish an increased scope for the public sector.

In an interesting and stimulating contribution to the discussion of organisational failure, Hood (1976) analyses the limits to administration by setting down a model of perfect administration against the imperfections of actual administrative systems. Hood's preconditions for perfect administration/implementation can be summarised as [6]:

(a) circumstances external to the implementing agency do not impose crippling constraints. That is, some obstacles to implementation are outside the control of the agency e.g. overseas events, as in the case of the OPEC group increasing the world price of oil;

(b) adequate time and sufficient resources are made available to the programme; e.g. frequently too much is expected too soon. Also key resources are often not available;

(c) the policy to be implemented is based upon a valid theory of cause and effect. Pressman and Wildavsky (1973) point out that any policy is 'a hypothesis containing initial conditions and predicted consequences'. The controversy between Keynesian and monetarist theories of economic policy is a clear example of this problem. Also, there is the question of the precise nature of the cause/effect relationship i.e. the transmission mechanism or process. Is the relationship between cause and effect, for example, direct or are there many intervening links? Pressman and Wildavsky (*op. cit.*) point out that policies based on a long sequence of cause and effect have a particular tendency to break down, since the longer the chain of causality the more numerous are the reciprocal relationships among the links and hence the more complex does implementation become. The greater the number of links, the greater are the number of bargains and negotiations that have to be struck; the greater are the transactions costs not only of negotiation but also of coordination and control; and the greater is the chance that the policy will be badly executed;

(d) there should be a single implementation agency — if there is to be more than one, then the dependency relationships should be minimal in number and importance. King (1976) argues that in the UK the number of dependency relationships has increased over time, thereby making implementation more difficult. These problems exist in Federal countries where the cooperation of a large number of different government departments at a number of different levels of government has to be secured in order to implement the policy. The same issue caused the failure of the PPBS experiment;

(e) complete understanding of an agreement upon objectives. It was seen in a previous chapter that the neoclassical rationality decision making model was based upon the assumption of clearly specified objectives. However, goals are not, in practice, clearly specified which means that they are defined in the process of implementation. Furthermore, over time there is the problem of goal conflict and goal displacement. Combined, these problems complicate the implementation process and tend to reduce its success;

(f) it is possible to specify in complete detail and perfect sequence the tasks to be performed by each participant. The nature of sequential decision making, however, emphasises the interdependences between stages of the implementation process over time. One small mistake at an early phase can become cumulative. There are also the dysfunctional effects of providing tightly specified contracts and rules for individuals to work under. Apart from the inflexibility that rigid rules introduce, there is also the cost of alienation felt by those who are asked to implement the task according to the rules. Discretion is, therefore, inevitable and desirable, otherwise there will be no improvisation, no responsibility taken and no flexibility, but instead a climate of hostile alienation;

(g) there is perfect communication and coordination and also those in authority can demand and obtain perfect obedience. Again this ignores the costs of obtaining and processing information and the costs of operating communication channels within an organisation. Moreover, it fails to recognise the strategic role played by information in the political games carried out within the organisation, where information is used to serve the interests of the members of the organisation rather than the objectives of the primary task. Coordination is not a costless process and as was seen above, tight policing of the system can be dysfunctional.

The 'ideal type' of the perfect organisation or the perfect administrative system is a myth of the theorist. It is a frictionless entity which does not contain the frictions or imperfections of real world organisations. Whilst it is an ideal type or blueprint for administrative *efficiency*, it must be realised that it is not an organisational form which those who design organisations should totally aim for. Such perfect organisations are only efficient if they are peopled by mindless automata. As soon as real individuals, who have their own value systems, aspirations and human limitations are introduced into organisations, then the interaction between individuals and organisation structures means that we have to modify our ideas of what constitutes an ideal. The same is also true when we place organisations into complex, rapidly changing and uncertain environments. The prescriptions of the classical school of administration are then modified as we have seen in the previous chapters.

Allocative efficiency is not the sole objective in the design of organisations. Other considerations such as the distribution of the benefits obtained by individuals joining together in association must be taken into account, as too must the ethics of expected and actual behaviour within an organisation. Many administrative tangles involve legal complexities such as the question of the ownership of property rights and the equitable or socially desirable distribution of rights and net benefits. Whether or not one subscribes to a Marxist interpretation of social events, it is clear that administrative structures are not independent of general social class structures. Administrative tinkering and changes at the margin will be futile if to bring about the 'New Society' requires more radical structural changes to class structure and the access to rights. Thus administrative action will fail and so too will those policies required to bring about substantial changes within the social milieu.

Models of the Implementation Process

One useful way of approaching the analysis of the implementation process is to view it as a decision making problem and as an extension to the problem of planning. The recent literature in central planning (see Nove 1973) has evolved the concept of 'taut-planning'. In this framework it is recognised that whilst plans can deal with macro-aggregates, they are generally incapable of dealing with detail. Thus, a plan is often held up because of the shortage of some essential material for which detailed material balance planning is often impossible. The problem of planning is, therefore, one of specifying the details of the implementation process and of coordinating the elements of that process. But the paradox of planning is that 'if you try to plan everything you end up planning nothing'. This would seem to suggest that a pre-requisite of central planning is to leave alone as much as possible.

The fundamental problems seem to be: (i) the specification of the objectives of plans; (ii) the appraisal of the alternative means of achieving the objectives; but now most especially (iii) a specification of how to implement the plan. Lest it be thought that the implementation problem is trivial, it should be emphasised that there are often severe costs associated with imperfect implementation processes. For example, scarce resources can become frozen or locked into uncompleted projects, because a plan was implemented in such a way that too many projects were started in relation to the flow of investment funds. The mistakes of implementation can be cumulative and are, therefore, not costless. This means that the famous phrase of Jevons that 'by-gones are by-gones' must be reinterpreted by those economists who frequently use it to excuse the muddles and the mistakes of the past.

The idea that implementation is a *process* which takes place in real time and that earlier mistakes and muddles in the implementation of a plan can be cumulative brings us back to the question of how we should view the decision making process.

It will be recalled that decision making models can be divided broadly into those which either view the decision process as a simultaneous act, or as a logical sequence of actions which take place in real time. The former are associated with the standard view of decision making as portrayed in the economist's equilibrium paradigm, whereas the latter represents a more pragmatic or behavioural approach to how decisions are actually made.

Within the broad class of sequential decision models there exist a number of competing sub-categories. For example, there are the organic or development models[7] which are associated with the works of Barnard, the early Simon, and Tullock. Whilst any decision process is seen as a sequence of actions, any succeeding step in the sequence is assumed to be *uniquely* determined by the preceding step. This view of decision making leaves out of the picture totally the act of individual choice. Every action is assumed to be fully programmed and pre-determined. These models are based upon biological analogies such as that of the growth of a cell. In any sequence of events, the preceding event is both a necessary and a sufficient condition for the succeeding event to take place.

The organic model of sequential decision making can be compared to one which allows the decision maker greater scope for discretion and choice:

> Getting something done is seen as a matter of putting together a number of discrete units — making a chain, each part of which will contribute some necessary operation or make some necessary transformation of the raw material, each unit accepting as its input the preceding unit's output and the various types of work culminating to the desired change. (Dunsire 1978d, p. 125)

Given the units, there are many different alternative chains that can be constructed and hence there exists the potential for many different sequences. Since each unit has its own specialist function, skill and knowledge etc., the implementation problem is one of designing (choosing) the sequencing of units. In the organic model there is no implementation or execution problem, since the ordering of sequences is assumed to be pre-determined. Consider the following simple example. Assuming a closed system with 7 elements, each connected to every other element by a channel in each direction with a single on/off switch on each channel, then such a system generates 2^{42} different states! 'The greater a system's variety the more ways it has of transforming an input to the system into an output from the system'. It is this variety which forces the policy executors to make choices between alternative implementation paths.

Whilst this model of the implementation process is better than the organic model, it is nevertheless incomplete as it stands. Before it is possible to make choices between the alternative 'states' of the system, it is necessary to know something about the constraints on these choices. For example, it would be necessary to know how many of the linkages are allowable, how many are technically and budget feasible and how many are desirable, and with reference to what set of criteria?

The implementation process is a sequence and can be thought of as such in at least three ways. First, there is the dynamic or time path sequence. This aspect is familiar enough to the economist who is concerned to know how long it takes to implement policy (the 'implementation lag'). However, what the economist seldom asks is 'what factors determine the length of the implementation lag?'. This question is answered, in part, by considering the other dimensions of the implementation process, the second being its logical sequence. That is, if *X* has to be done, then it must be preceded by *Y*. The third aspect is the organisational sequence of implementation. It is generally assumed that the implementation process is a linear progression through the hierarchy. However, in practice, whilst decisions go from top to bottom in an organisation and then from bottom to top, they also move sideways.

Organisational Limits to Implementation

It is the intra-organisational up and down and side to side communications and interactions which contain so much of the frictions and limitations of the implementation process. For writers such as March and Simon (1958), the design of various organisational activities, such as that of the implementation process, is an exercise in finding a logical sequence of operations in organisational space, such that the dynamic path of the process, *de facto*, joins the units of the sequence together, laterally across specialisms and vertically across ranks. The programming or logical sequence of the process is the primary concern, whereas the authority structure within the organisation is secondary and is tailored to suit. As was seen in Chapter 2, this structural functionalist approach ignores the reality of organisational life, especially the political economy dimension. This point is taken up by Pressman and Wildavsky (1973) who do not see the set of organisational relationships in terms of authority, but see them rather as a set of political relationships such that the success and failure of implementation depends upon securing the cooperation of the various intra-organisational units: '... good or bad, efficient or inefficient, administration is beyond the control of the designer of the formal structure' (Tullock 1965, p. 21).

The implementation process thus draws us back to the politics of intra-organisational behaviour, the nature of decision making within the organisation, and the complexity of the environment which the decision maker faces. Any 'machine theory' of implementation, such as that of March and Simon (*op. cit.*), is doomed to failure because it is incomplete. Unfortunately, it is such an approach which is usually found in economics i.e. a clearly formulated and internally coherent plan is assumed to be easily implemented. This naive view is deficient in a large number of respects.

Politicians are assumed to make decisions about competing objectives and to leave it to the bureaucrats to recommend alternative means.[8] Whilst it is true that in a large number of instances the objectives of the plan/policy will be imprecisely stated, it is not tenable to assume that the objectives of plans are set by politicians, while bureaucrats (planners) are the professional technicians who implement the activities of the plan in a neutral fashion.[9] The success of a plan will, in part, depend upon its effective integration into the political process (see Ashford 1965, Benveniste 1970 and Caiden and Wildavsky 1974). In practice, goal formation is situational, fluctuating, and means-oriented and is not a disembodied exercise in rational decision making. Vote maximising politicians will look for those problems in most need of solution and will search for those strategies that will produce perceptible results in a short time (Rondinelli 1976). Bureaucrats for their part will tend to choose those means which, whilst serving their own interests, will also be found acceptable to politicians and which do not, therefore, require major restructuring of society. To illustrate this point consider the following example provided by Warwick (1979, p. 5). '... a Peruvian planner who recommended the return to Standard Oil of the government's nationalised petroleum holdings would be widely regarded as irrational, however sound the proposal might be on economic grounds'.

Thus, the implementation of a plan or policy is an integral part of the political economy of the organisation. Those at the top of the organisation might agree a plan, but they might not have the *de facto* power to execute it. Instead, each agency or bureau might have a great deal of discretion and whilst the Minister has titular control, he might not in practice have much political control.

Managerial discretion will, therefore, play an important role in the implementation process. 'Decisions cannot be delegated without giving the decision maker the power to make organisationally perverse choices' (Loasby 1968, p. 357). Whether or not the formal objectives of the policy or the plan are served does not only depend upon how clearly they are specified, but also depends upon the jointness between the policy objectives and those of the management. The amount of discretion available to managers/bureaucrats depends upon the behavioural contraints that they face. In particular, the degree of managerial discretion is a function of the effectiveness of management control systems.

Managerial discretion is inevitable when information is imperfect. The imprecision and ambiguity of policy objectives has already been repeatedly emphasised, but so too should the issue of the problem of measuring managerial performance. What is meant by good (satisfactory) performance and can it be measured? By serving professional codes of conduct are managers/bureaucrats serving the objectives of the plan/policy? These questions become even more complex once uncertainty is introduced into the analysis. Management decisions are not independent of the information which is available. Judgment about whether or not a decision was appropriate must be made with reference to the information which was available at the time, not with reference to the knowledge of hindsight.

Enhanced scope for managerial discretion due to weakness in the management control system is, therefore, an imperfection in the implementation process and represents a limit to the extent to which the intentions of the original plan might be served. A response to this limit, however, might involve the tightening up of the control system and the introduction of rigid bureaucratic rules, but as has been repeatedly emphasised, this runs the risk of back-firing by raising feelings of alienation and introducing unnecessary inflexibility. Limits to the implementation process must, instead, be relaxed through negotiation and bargaining, rather than a solution being imposed.

Rushing's (1962) study of deference in a psychiatric hospital serves as a partial illustration of these points. It was found that on occasions the psychiatric nurses would disagree with the treatment which was prescribed by the doctors. The vital question from the point of view of implementation is, did the nurses accede to the doctor's sapiential authority and carry out the treatment as prescribed? What Rushing found was that the nurses used a variety of means to limit the implementation of treatments that they disagreed with. They would either go to the chief resident physician in order to persuade him to change the treatment, or they would report patient observations which were contrary to the doctors' expectations. This would in all probability result in a change in prescribed treatment more in line with what the nurses thought appropriate. On other occasions the nurses would ask questions claiming that they did not fully understand the order. The doctors' explanation would lead to new questions and would again increase the probability of ordering treatment more in line with the nurses' views of the patient's illness.

In the above example the barrier to implementation is obvious. The sapiential power of the physician is challenged, but his ability to make subsequent decisions following the challenge is based upon the availability and quality of information which is controlled by others, and moreover he is influenced by the complexity and uncertainty of the decision environment and the risks involved in making a wrong decision.

Organisational Limits and the Distribution of Information

It is a trivial observation that one of the problems of decision making is that information is not equally distributed within an organisation and hence power groups, which have access to that information, are set up. Crozier (1973) asks the question, 'why do individuals in organisations create and recreate barriers to two way communication?' Driggers (1977, p. 156) answers, 'to give up information control is to reduce one's influence on situational objects and relationships'.

Despite the importance of information systems within organisations, all social scientists (economists, sociologists and organisation theorists) have tended to ignore their importance (Zald 1970, p. 253). The signals generated by the internal accounting and information systems act like a price mechanism which influences the final allocation and distribution of resources within the organisation and hence the distribution of net benefits to organisational members. The distribution of rights of access to information and the ability to influence information signals within the organisation is a major element of the political economy model and is a principal determinant of the limits of implementation. The accounting/information system signals performance, efficiency, effectiveness and serves to guide resources.

The allocation of resources to intra-organisational activities establishes the linkages of the implementation process and, therefore, determines the organisational sequence i.e. in what order things get done in the organisation. It follows, therefore, that the timing, efficiency and effectiveness of the impact and the distributional consequences of the implementation of policy are in large measure determined as the outcomes to the resolution of the political games which are played within the organisation. Central to the conduct of these games is the distribution of information.

Not only is there a question of the distribution of information within the organisation, there is also the issue, do those who have *de jure* control of the organisation (bureaucracy) have insufficient information about its activities to make any control effective? Thus, as was seen in Chapter 8 above, Parliamentary control is weakened as departments and bureaus take on the appearance of semi-autonomous fiefdoms over which the Minister has very little effective control. This, of course was recognised by Weber (1947, p. 339):

> ... bureaucratic organisations ... have the tendency to increase their power still further by the knowledge growing out of experience in the service. For they acquire through the conduct of office a special knowledge of facts and have available a store of documentary material particular to themselves.

Clearly there are benefits arising from the exclusive use of knowledge. But possession of knowledge is not enough; it must be augmented by control over the application of knowledge. It is control over the application of knowledge which probably represents the greatest barrier to the implementation of policy.

Having made these observations, is there anything that can be done to improve the distribution of information and to re-distribute power over the application of knowledge? To answer this question requires a more detailed understanding of the communication process within organisations.

Consider first of all differences in the levels of comprehension possessed by various individuals within the organisation. This was analysed in Chapter 6 when the basis of incremental budgeting was discussed. Those who occupy roles in the upper levels of the organisation do not wish to be lumbered or hindered with the trivia and detail of organisational processes:

> The view from the top is exhilarating. Divorced from problems of implementation, federal bureau heads, leaders of international agencies and prime ministers in poor countries think great thoughts together. But they have trouble imagining the sequence of events that will bring their ideas to fruition.
>
> (Pressman and Wildavsky, 1973)

There are severe constraints on the time of those in higher roles to become informed of organisational details but there is also the constraint that in many instances they do not have the capacity to comprehend the technical details of what goes on during the implementation stage. Whilst the upper echelons of the organisation have a broad view, the lower levels have a narrower but more detailed view. Thus, those who create policies, but only confine themselves to taking a broad view without paying proper regard to the probable consequences of their decisions, are abdicating responsibility and are weakening any constraints which might exist on the behaviour of the executors by increasing the discretionary powers of the latter.

The issues of vertical communication within organisations have long been recognised and understood (Simon, Smithburg and Thompson 1950, Tullock 1965 and Downs 1967). Status differences and the nature of the incentive system can hinder communication, leading subordinates to filter upcoming information so that superiors will receive that information which places the subordinate in the best light. Moreover, information will be filtered and distorted in ways that will best serve the interests of the various groups within the organisation.

Whilst the problems of vertical communication are discussed, often horizontal problems, which are of equal importance, are not. Horizontal communication problems arise from important differences between individuals that occupy the same horizontal status position within the organisation. Differences in the language of specialised groups, different perspectives and frames of reference all contribute to communications failures within the organisation,

> To some extent, communication between individuals is always subject to 'cognitive gaps': none of us can make effective use of information we do not fully understand; we cannot understand something we cannot recognise and classify; and our means of recognising and classifying derive from our personal stock of knowledge and experience which of course is different from individual to individual.
>
> (Dunsire 1978a, p. 159)

There are strong similarities between this position and that of Weber as quoted above. In this case, however, the emphasis is shifted away from the information *per se* to the problems of the communication of information. A failure to understand, a failure to communicate because of cognitive gaps between the different groups within the organisation, result in a breakdown in coordination and a break in the logical and organisational sequence. This breakdown of sequences results in a failure of the implementation process. Those further down the hierarchy do not always fully understand the nature of the decisions at the top, or how their activities relate to the overall objectives. Thus there is a tendency towards sub-optimisation as each sub-group sets out to meet its own achievement target. In addition, there can be feelings of alienation (Blauner 1964). Those at the upper levels of the organisation do not always understand the problems which exist further down — not unless they have worked their way up through the organisation. Individuals in organisations only know what is going on in those other parts with which they have some contact and yet even then there can exist severe cognitive barriers to their understanding about what actually goes on in these other parts. As Dunsire (*op. cit.*) has pointed out, a visitor taken on a tour of the organisation probably knows more about the total set of operations than do many of the members of the organisation. This leads Dunsire (1978a, p. 176) to propose the interesting idea of the *Babel House Model*:

> ... a different tongue (concepts and vocabulary) is talked on each floor — amounting to a considerable linguistic disparity between top floor speech and ground floor speech — and differing jargons and dialects are spoken on any one floor, in each of the corners and other areas. As between one floor and the next or as between one office and its neighbour on the same floor, differences in language and habitual style of doing business can usually be noted, though it is quite easy for adjacent ranks and denizens of adjacent offices, to understand one another. Messages from distant locations in any direction — from a far-away corner or from a much higher or a much lower floor — do not, by contrast, make much sense on first hearing or reading: the more distant the less intelligible.

The cognitive gaps and communications failures have another important consequence for the implementation process. In part they reduce uncertainty. On each successive phase of the communication process, information which started off at one point in the organisation as an educated *guess* ends up elsewhere within the organisation as a working fact. The more distant, the less intelligible is the communication signal likely to be and the more probable will the degree of uncertainty be suppressed.

The cognitive gaps in the communication process, therefore, result in the filtering out of important messages and information content and introduce ignorance: 'no kind of ignorance can be more dangerous than ignorance regarding the limits and limitations of one's knowledge...' (Hutchison 1977, p. 5). Ignorance and the limits to knowledge place severe restrictions upon what can be achieved and widen the gap between what is intended by policy makers and that which the executors produce. To close these gaps, resources have to be invested in an attempt to remove the cognitive barriers internal to the organisation. Thus individuals within an organisation receive training in a large number of different functional areas and in some organisations, such as the British Civil Service, administrators are moved around frequently from one part of the organisation to another. The costs of these procedures are, however, that there is a loss of continuity and generalist knowledge replaces the deeper knowledge of the specialist.

Apart from the cognitive gaps that might emerge, information can also be distorted as it is transmitted throughout the organisation. Such distortions can be deliberate or unconscious, but generally they refer to the skewing of data rather than selective perception and communication. In most of the literature it is generally assumed that distortions take place up and down in the organisation, but it can also occur from side to side. Competing groups within the organisation might withhold information from others if it is to their group's political advantage to do so. For one reason or another, information is screened and condensed as it is transmitted throughout the organisation. Moreover, the degree of uncertainty associated with pieces of data is suppressed as they journey through the organisation, so that higher levels or distant units (as in the case of lateral communication) 'accept as working fact what is always to some extent an educated guess'. Data are compressed and factorised as they are transmitted. Orders or instructions issued by level A to level B are interpreted by level B and reissued to level C and so on. Between each interpretation there is a discretionary gap.

Lack of information, ignorance and uncertainty bound and limit any organisation's ability to fulfil its objectives. Uncertainty exists both inside and outside an organisation, although boundaries between internal and external environments tend to be arbitrarily drawn. There are many sources of ignorance and uncertainty. Understanding of the technical relationships between cause and effect is frequently incomplete and often non-existent. Modern Man's ability to improve his condition through social policy action is severely constrained by his lack of knowledge about the means necessary to bring about desired ends. Socio-economic life is extremely complex and as yet we are insufficiently aware of the nature of the panoply of interdependencies that will enable the social policy maker to bring about desired changes. *Ad hoc* partial adjustments, whilst making local improvements, can worsen the situation for the system as a whole.[10] But decomposition of any complex system, even for the purpose of sub-optimisation, is frequently beyond the capabilities of the analyst:

> It is no easy task for the designer to predict ... the outcome of such dynamic and complex processes ... The system is so complex that it thoroughly defies analysis by means of even the most complex models ... It must be approached through what has come to be known as 'scenario writing'... (which) is an art. It requires imagination and intuition ... It forces the designer to think seriously about the obvious design problems, particularly the financial costs ...
>
> (Bardach 1977, pp. 254–55, 262–63)

To design the whole system and to specify completely the entire plan is, for most systems, an impossible task. Environmental constraints and contingencies are rarely, if ever, specifiable since they are seldom known in advance. This implies, therefore, that it is not possible to specify every possible organisational procedure to implement organisational activities which are dependent upon each contingency which might arise. Organisations cope with ignorance and uncertainty by being fluid and not mechanistic. 'The most advanced organisations, because they now feel capable of integrating areas of uncertainty in their economic calculus, are beginning to understand that the illusion of perfect rationality has too long persisted, weakening the possibilities of action by insisting on rigorous logic and immediate coherence' (Crozier 1964, p. 159).

Implementation, Efficiency and Control

Individuals, singly or collectively, make plans. Because most plans cannot be realised through individual action, collectivities or organisations emerge in order to implement plans via the concerted actions of a number of individuals, each a specialist and each in need of coordination if the plan is to be realised. The implementation process is, therefore, the key element in the set of organisational processes and coordination is the principal act necessary to ensure that implementation takes place smoothly and effectively.

In order to discuss the implementation process adequately it is necessary to draw upon the discussions of the earlier chapters. How are decisions made; who are the principal actors in the decision making process; is the distribution of rights to decision making the appropriate one; is the implementation process efficient; could be it be improved upon and if so, how could it be improved upon; what controls exist to constrain the implementation process; do those who implement policies serve their own interests or some higher order notion such as the 'public interest'? Until we understand the features of the policy implementation process, our knowledge of the supply of public services and public policies will be partial and incomplete. Without this knowledge it will be meaningless to discuss issues such as the coordination of policy initiatives, nor will it be possible to design control systems in any but a crude fashion.

But this realisation will be slow to take effect. Grand plans for the design of a new society will continue to emerge from the top of all the organisations which go to make up that society. Individuals will have their own private plans and taken together all of these plans may or may not be compatible. Incompatibility will result in adjustments being made to each plan, whilst each individual uses the resources at his disposal to ensure that his plan is dominant and that his interests are served. The cool rational coordination of plans in a highly synoptic system is a myth. The reality is that of keen competition, as each individual or group of individuals, vies for dominance in the area of political economy.

The competition of non-market decision making is more overt than that which occurs in the market place. Who wins the struggle in the implementation process will, in large measure, determine the policy outcome. Hence the need for control. But control can never be complete. Areas of ignorance, the presence of uncertainty and the dysfunctions of the control mechanisms themselves will always ensure that there are areas of discretion for those who implement policies. Even if control were complete, it need not sustain a political equilibrium. The means of control will be held by a ruling elite. Only in the most romantic vision of society can it be thought that such an elite will serve the 'public interest'. In practice, the goals, prejudices and perspectives of the elite are challenged through continual political action. To change these might mean to change the whole structure of society and the goals of all organisations which support that structure. It is, therefore, naive to assume that improvements in the delivery of public services and policies are simply a matter of improving the information supplied to policy makers, improving communication within the organisation, and enhancing existing control mechanisms. Changing the structure of organisations by reducing the levels of hierarchy and eliminating the 'pathologies' of bureaucracy is nothing other than tinkering within the existing power structure. It escapes answering questions such as: for whom does this represent an improvement in the delivery of public services; for whom *should* it represent an improvement; against what criteria is an improvement to be judged? In the face of awkward questions of this kind, elites are likely to hold on to their power. Thus, the system of control is most likely to be used to maintain and protect existing vested interests. The distribution of information within an organisation is closely associated with the distribution of power. Attempts to change these distributions, in the name of improvements in the implementation process, will not go unchallenged.

It is because of the political reality of organisational life that the economist's rational or synoptic model of the planning, budgetary and implementation processes has come under ridicule from political scientists and decision making theorists, (see Self 1975 and Wildavsky 1969).[11] Typically, the economist conceives a plan or a budget as an interconnected logical structure, a set of technical instruments and targets. These plans are, however, given their dynamic and reality through the implementation process. It is this link which the economist usually ignores. The concept of the implementation process, and the political behaviour contained therein, must in future form a central focus to the planning debate. No longer should the economist think of drawing up fully consistent, let alone optimal plans, in sufficient detail to make them operational. Individuals' rationality is bounded; there is inherent uncertainty about the outcome of any real-time action; information (which is continually changing) must be dispersed; each individual (and group of individuals) is self interested. The role of any plan can only be to define broad objectives and to place broad based constraints upon the types of behaviour that can be pursued. The plan establishes a set of initial conditions (property rights) from which actual behaviour (allocations) is realised through a complex set of political exchanges. To understand the outcome of any plan is to know the nature of these exchanges. To modify the outcome of any plan it is necessary to change the power structure of the implementation system.

The limits of organisation are the limits of the individual as a decision maker, i.e. bounded rationality, selective perception, ignorance, uncertainty, the inability to cope with complexity and the lack of resources to improve his computational abilities (i.e. information costs). 'There are moments of history when we simply must act, but to retain our full rationality we must sustain the burden of action without certitude, and we must always keep open the possibility of recognising past errors and changing course' (Arrow 1974, p. 29).

Conclusion

'Administration is too specific an activity that grand programmes are particularly vulnerable to the banana skin or to the small piece of grit which immobilises the whole machine' (Hood 1976, p. 20). In this book we have examined a number of the banana skins which catch the unwary as they journey through any complex organisation. The institutions of the market place and the non-market organisation are imperfect and yet they are the institutions of the real world through which social policy is transformed into action. Unless the analyst places greater emphasis upon understanding the imperfections of the policy transmission mechanism, rather than designing blueprints for a grand new society, policy outcomes will continue to fall short of expectations and resources will be inefficiently allocated and distributed.

> If to do were as easy as to know what were good to do, chapels had been churches, and from men's cottages princes' palaces ... I can teach twenty what were good to be done, than one of the twenty to follow mine own teaching.'
>
> (*The Merchant of Venice*, Act I, Scene II)

Notes

1 This problem is well-known to chemical engineers. One interesting example of the problem was related to the author by Victoria Chick. A planner was commissioned with the task of designing a car park such that the number of parking spaces be maximised. Having (supposedly) successfully completed his task the planner revealed his plan whereupon it soon became clear that, whilst it was possible to *lift* the cars on and off the scale model, it would in practice be impossible for anyone to *drive* their car into the parking spaces!

2 The term 'organisational failure' was first used by Williamson (1971, p. 113).

3 See Bator (1958) for a major contribution to this literature.

4 This was discussed earlier in Chapter 3 under the heading of the Coasian theory of the firm.

5 It is impossible to go into a discussion of the theory of pure public goods here. The interested reader should consult Brown and Jackson (1978).

6 This summary is found in L.A. Gunn, *Why is Implementation So Difficult?*

7 Much of what follows in the next few pages was influenced by Dunsire (1978a).

8 This is the Woodrow Wilson dichotomy between policy formulation and implementation.

9 See the Niskanen model of bureaucracy in Chapter 5 above.

10 This will be recognised as the economist's theory of the second best.

11 Lest it be thought that I am abdicating totally to their views, I am not. The debate is muddled primarily because the political scientists have failed to distinguish clearly enough between the economists' equilibrium and behavioural paradigms (*op. cit.*).

Bibliography

Akerloff, G.A. (1970) The market for lemons: quality uncertainty and the market mechanism, *Quarterly Journal of Economics*, Vol. 84, pp.488–500.

Albrow, M. (1970) *Bureaucracy*, Macmillan.

Alchian, A.A. (1950) Uncertainty, evolution, and economic theory, *Journal of Political Economy*, Vol. 58, pp. 211–21.

Alchian, A. and Demsetz, H. (1972) Production, information costs and economic organisation, *American Economic Review*, Vol. 62, December, pp. 777–95.

Allison, G.T. (1971) *The Essence of Decision*, Little, Brown & Co.

Ando, A. (1979) On the contributions of Herbert A. Simon to economics, *The Scandinavian Journal of Economics*, Vol. 81, No. 1.

Andrews, P.W.S. (1949) *Manufacturing Business*, Macmillan.

Andrews, P.W.S. (1949) *On Competition in Economic Theory*, Macmillan.

Applewhite, P.B. (1965) *Organisational Behaviour*, Prentice – Hall.

Argyris, C. (1957) *Personality and Organisation*, Harper and Row

Argyris, C. (1960) *Understanding Organisational Behaviour*, Dorsey, Homewood, Illinois.

Argyris, C. (1964) *Integrating the Individual and the Organisation*, John Wiley.

Argyris, C. (1972) *The Applicability of Organisational Sociology*, Cambridge University Press.

Argyris, C. (1973) Some limits of rational man organisation theory, *Public Administration Review*, pp. 253–267

Armstrong, Lord (1976) A hardly noticed transition from Whitehall to the City, *The Times*, London, 15th November.

Arrow, K.J. (1951) *Social Choice and Individual Values*, John Wiley (2nd edn 1963).

Arrow, K.J. (1959) Rational choice functions and orderings, *Economica*, (NS) Vol. 26, pp. 121–7.

Arrow, K.J. (1963) *Social Choice and Individual Values*, Yale University Press.

Arrow, K.J. (1969) The organisation of economic activity: issues pertinent to the choice of market vs. non-market allocation, in Joint Economic Committee, , *The Analysis and Evaluation of Public Expenditures. The PPB System*, Washington Government Printing Office.

Arrow, K.J. (1970) The organisation of economic activity: issues pertinent to the choice of market vs. non-market forces, in R. Haveman and J. Margolis (eds), *Public Expenditures and Policy Analysis*, Markham, Chicago.

Arrow, K.J. (1971), *Essays in the Theory of Risk Bearing*, Markham, Chicago.

Arrow, K.J. (1971) The firm in general equilibrium theory, in R. Marris and A. Wood (eds), *The Corporate Economy; Growth, Competition and Innovative Potential*, Macmillan.

Arrow, K.J. (1974) *The Limits of Organisation*, Norton.
Arrow, K.J. (1974) On the agenda of organisations, in R. Marris (ed.) *The Corporate Society*, Macmillan.
Arrow, K.J. (1975) Vertical integration and communications, *Bell Journal of Economics*, Vol. 6, No. 1, pp. 173–83
Arrow, K.J. and Hahn, F. (1971) *General Competitive Analysis*, Oliver and Boyd.
Arrow, K.J. and Hurwicz, L. (1962) Decentralisation, and computation in resource allocation, in R.W. Phoutts (ed.), *Studies in Mathematical Economics and Econometrics*, University of North Carolina Press.
Arrow, K.J., Hurwicz, L. and Uzawa, H. (1958) *Studies in Linear and Non-Linear Programming*, Stanford University Press.
Arrow, K.J. and Lind, R.C. (1970) Uncertainty and the evaluation of public investments, *American Economic Review*, June.
Ashford, D.E. (1965) *Morocco–Tunisia: Politics and Planning*, Syracuse University Press.
Bachrach, P. (1969) *The Theory of Democratic Elitism*, University of London Press.
Bailey, J.J. and O'Connor, R.J. (1975) Operationalising incrementalism: measuring the muddles, *Public Administration Review*, Vol. 35, No. 1, pp. 60–66.
Baker, R.J.S. (1972) *Administrative Theory and Public Administration*, Hutchinson.
Bardach, E. (1977) *The Implementation Game*, MIT Press.
Barnard, C. (1938) *Functions of the Executive*, Harvard University Press.
Barry, B.M. (1970)*Sociologists, Economists and Democracy*, Collier Macmillan.
Bator, F.M. (1958) The anatomy of market failure, *Quarterly Journal of Economics*, Vol. 72, August.
Baumol, W.J. (1959)*Business Behaviour, Value and Growth*, Macmillan.
Baumol, W.J. (1967) Macro-economics of unbalanced growth, *American Economic Review*, Vol. 57, pp. 415–26.
Baumol, W.J. (1975) Payments by performance in rail passenger transportation: an innovation in Amtrak's operations, *The Bell Journal of Economics*, Spring, pp. 281–99.
Baumol, W.J. and Quandt, R.E. (1964) Rules of thumb and optimally imperfect decisions, *American Economic Review*, Vol. 54, March, pp. 23–46.
Baumol, W.J. and Stewart, M. (1971) On the behavioural theory of the firm, in R. Marris and A. Wood (eds.), *The Corporate Economy*, Macmillan.
Becker, S.W. and Gordon, G. (1960) An entrepreneurial theory of formal organisations, 1: patterns of formal organisations, *Administrative Science Quarterly*, Vol. 11, pp. 315–44.
Bendix, R. (1945) Bureaucracy and the problem of power, *Public Administration Review*, Vol. 5, pp. 194–209.
Bendix, R. (1949) *Higher Civil Servants in American Society*, University of Colorado Press.
Beneviste, G. (1970) *Bureaucracy and National Planning. A Sociological Case Study of Mexico*, Praeger.
Bennis, W.G. (1966) *Changing Organisations*, McGraw-Hill.
Benson, K.J. (1977)Organisations: a dialectical view, *Administrative Science Quarterly*, Vol. 22, No. 1, March.
Bergson, A. (1964) *The Economics of Soviet Planning*, Yale University Press.
Bergson, A. (1966)*Essays in Normative Economics*, Harvard University Press.
Bergson, A. (1978a) *Productivity and the Social System — The USSR and the West*, Harvard University Press.
Bergson, A. (1978b) Managerial risks and rewards in public bureaucracies, *Journal of Comparative Economics*, Vol. 2, No. 3, September, pp. 211–26.

Bernhold, M. (1971) Theory of linear profit sharing incentives, *Quarterly Journal of Economics*, pp. 460–82.
Berle, A.A. and Means, G.C. (1934) *The Modern Corporation and Private Property*, Macmillan.
Bird, R.M. (1976) *Charging for Public Services: A New Look at an Old Idea*, L'Association Canadienne d'Etudes Fiscalles, Toronto.
Black, D. (1948) On the rationale of group decision-making, *Journal of Political Economy*, Vol. 56, pp. 23–34.
Black, D. (1958) *The Theory of Committees and Elections*, Cambridge University Press.
Blackaby, F.T. (1978) *British Economic Policy 1960–1974*, Cambridge University Press.
Blau, P.M. (1963) *The Dynamics of Bureaucracy*, Chicago University Press.
Blau, P.M. (1974) *On the Nature of Organisation*, John Wiley.
Blau, P.M. and Meyer, M.N. (1971) *Bureaucracy in Modern Society*, 2nd edn, Random House.
Blau, P.M. and Scott, W.R. (1963) *Formal Organisations*, Routledge & Kegan Paul.
Blauner, R. (1964) *Alienation, Freedom and Technology*, Phoenix Books, Chicago.
Blumberg, P. (1968)*Industrial Democracy*, Constable.
Boffey, P.M. (1976) Nader and the scientists: a call for responsibility, *Science*, Vol. 171, pp. 549–51.
Bohm, P. (1972) Estimating the demand for public goods: an experiment, *European Economic Review*, Vol. 3, pp. 111–30.
Boreham, P.R. *et al.* (eds) (1976) *The Professions in Australia: A Critical Appraisal*, University of Queensland Press.
Boreham, P.R. (1979) Capitalist crisis and the labour process: the dialectics of theory and control, University of Queensland (unpublished paper).
Boreham, P.R. and Dow, G. (1979) Work, control and ideology, *Social alternatives*, Vol.1, No. 4.
Bottomore, T.B. (1966) *Elites and Society*, Penguin Books (1974 reprint, Pelican Books).
Boulding, K.E. (1953) *The Organisational Revolution*, Harper & Row.
Bower, J.L. (1965) The role of conflict in economic decision making groups, *Quarterly Journal of Economics*, Vol. 70, pp. 253–77.
Bradford, D.F., Malt, R.A. and Oates, W.E. (1969) The rising costs of local public services: some evidence and reflections, *National Tax Journal*, Vol. 22, June, pp. 185–202.
Bradley, D. and Wilkie, R. (1974) *The Concept of Organisation*, Blackie.
Bradley, D. and Wilkie, R. (1979) *The Radical Attack on Organisation Theory: An Assessment*, Department of Administration, University of Strathclyde (unpublished paper).
Braybrooke, D., and Lindblom, C.E. (1963) *A Strategy of Decision: Policy Evaluation as a Social Process*, Free Press, Glencoe, Illinois and Collier Macmillan, London.
Breton, A. (1974) *The Economic Theory of Representative Government*, Aldine, Chicago.
Breton, A. (1978) Accountability, bureaucracy and representative government, in H.C. Recktenwald (ed.), *Secular Trends of the Public Sector*, Editions Cujas, Paris.
Breton, A. and Wintrobe, R. (1975) The equilibrium size of a budget-maximizing bureau, *Journal of Political Economy*, Vol. 83, pp. 195–207.
Brown, M. (1967) *The Theory and Empirical Analysis of Production*, National Bureau of Economic Research, Studies in Income and Wealth, No. 31, Columbia University Press.

Brown, R.G.S. (1970) *The Administrative Process in Britain,* Methuen.

Buchanan, J.M. (1979) *What Should Economists Do?*, Liberty Press, Indianapolis.

Buchanan, J.M. and Tullock, G. (1965) *The Calculus of Consent,* University of Michigan Press.

Burns, T. and Stalker, G.M. (1961) *The Management of Innovation*, Tavistock Publications.

Burrell, G. (1979) *Radical Organisation Theory,* Department of Behaviour in Organisations, Lancaster University (unpublished paper).

Caiden, N. and Wildavsky, A. (1974) *Planning and Budgeting in Poor Countries,* John Wiley.

Carey, A. (1967) The Hawthorne studies: a radical criticism, *American Sociological Review,* Vol. 32, pp. 403–16.

Carey, A. (1976) Industrial psychology and sociology in Australia, in P.R. Boreham *et al.* (eds), *The Professions in Australia: A Critical Appraisal*, University of Queensland Press.

Cartwright, D. & Zander, A. (eds) (1960) *Groups Dynamics: Research and Theory,* (2nd. Edn.) Row, Peterson, Evanston, Illinois.

Castle, B. (1973) Mandarin power: an attack on civil service methods and how they stifle true political decisions, *The Sunday Times,* 10th June.

Chamberlin, E.H. (1933) *The Theory of Monopolistic Competition,* Harvard University Press.

Chapman, L. (1978) *Your Disobedient Servant,* Chatto and Windus.

Chester, N. (1979) Fringe bodies, quangos and all that, *Public Administration*, Vol. 51, Spring.

Child, J. (1972) Organisational structure, environment and performance, *Sociology*, Vol. 6, No. 1, pp. 1–22.

Child, J. (1973) Organisation: a choice for man, in J. Child (ed.), *Man and Organisation*, Allen & Unwin.

Child, J. (1973) Managerial and organisational sectors associated with company performance, *The Universtiy of Aston Management Centre, Working Paper Series,* No. 4.

Chubb, B. (1952) *The Control of Public Expenditure,* Oxford University Press.

Civil Service Commission, General Accounting Office and Office of Management and Budget (1972) *Measuring and Enhancing Productivity in the Federal Government,* prepared for the Joint Economic Committee of the Congress of the United States, Washington DC, US Government Printing Office.

Clapham, J.H. (1922) Of empty economic boxes, *Economic Journal,* Vol. 32, pp. 305–14. (Reprinted in G.J. Stigler and K.E. Boulding, *Readings in Price Theory* (1952) Allen & Unwin.)

Clayton, P. (1971)Accountability in government expenditure, *National Westminster Bank Quarterly Review,* November.

Clegg, S. and Dunkerly, D. (eds)(1977) *Critical Issues in Organsations,* Routledge & Kegan Paul.

Clegg, S. (1979) *The Theory of Power and Organisation*, Routledge & Kegan Paul.

Coase, R. (1937) The nature of the firm, *Economica*, (NS) pp. 386–405. (Reprinted in G.J. Stigler and K.E. Boulding, *Readings in Price Theory* (1952).)

Coase, R.H. (1960) The problem of social cost, *Journal of Law and Economics,* October.

Cohn, M.L. (1971) Bureaucratic man, *American Sociological Review,* Vol. 36, pp. 461–74.

Collard, D. (1978) *Altruism and Economy,* Martin Robertson.

Coleman, J.S. (1974) *Power and the Structure of Society,* Norton.

Connell, R.W. (1977) *Ruling Class, Ruling Culture*, Cambridge University Press.

Cornford, J. (1972) The political theory of scarcity, in P. Laslett, W.G. Runciman and Q. Skinner (eds), *Philosophy, Politics and Society*, Basil Blackwell.

Cornford, J. (1974) The illusion of decision, *British Journal of Political Science*, Vol. 4.

Crecine, J.P. (1967) *Governmental Problem Solving*, Rand McNally. (Also published by Markham, Chicago (1969).)

Crecine, J.P. (1970) A simulation model of municipal budgeting: the impact of problem environment, in I. Sharkansky (ed.), *Policy Analysis in Political Science*, Markham, Chicago.

Crew, M.A., Jones-Lee, M.W. and Rowley, C.K. (1971) *X*-theory versus management discretion theory, *Southern Economic Journal*, Autumn, pp. 19–34.

Crossman, R.H.S. (1972) *Inside View*, Jonathan Cape.

Crossman, R.H.S. (1975) *Diaries of a Cabinet Minister*, Vol. 1, Hamilton and Cape.

Crossman, R.H.S. (1976) *Diaries of a Cabinet Minister*, Vol. 2, Hamilton and Cape.

Crowther-Hunt, Lord, (1973) *Memorandum of Dissent to the Report of the Royal Commission on the Constitution* (Kilbrandon Commission), Cmnd 5460, HMSO.

Crozier, M. (1964) *The Bureaucratic Phenomenon*, Chicago University Press.

Crozier, M. (1970) *La Société Bloquée*, Editions du Seuil, Paris.

Crozier, M. (1973a) The problem of power, *Social Research*, Vol. 40, No. 2, pp. 211–28.

Crozier, M. (1973b) *The Stalled Society*, Viking, New York.

Culyer, A.J. (1970) A utility maximizing view of universities, *Scottish Journal of Political Economy*, Vol. 17, November.

Culyer, A.J., Lavers, R.J. and Williams, A. (1972) Health indicators, in Shonfield, A. and Shaw, S. (eds), *Social Indicators and Social Policy*, Heinemann.

Cyert, R.M., Dill, W.R. and March, J.G. (1958) The role of expectations in business decision making, *Administrative Science Quarterly*, Vol. 3, pp. 307–40.

Cyert, R.M. and Hedrick, C.L. (1972) The theory of the firm: past, present and future, *Journal of Economic Literature*, June, Vol. 10, No. 2.

Cyert, R.M. and March, J.G. (1963) *A Behavioural Theory of the Firm*, Prentice-Hall.

Cyert, R.M., Simon, H.A. and Trow, D.B. (1956) Observations of business decision, *Journal of Business*, Vol. 29, pp. 237–48.

Dahl, R.A. (1957) The concept of power, *Behavioural Science*, Vol. 2, pp. 201–15.

Dahl, R.A. (1961) *Who Governs*, Yale University Press.

Dahrendorf, R. (1959) *Class and Conflict in Industrial Society*, Routledge & Kegan Paul.

Danziger, J.N. (1976) Assessing incrementalism in British municipal budgeting, *British Journal of Political Science*, Vol. 6, Part 3, pp. 335–50.

Davies, A. (1979) *What's Wrong With Quangos?*, The Outer Circle Policy Unit, London.

Davis, O.A., Dempster, M.A.H. and Wildavsky, A. (1966a) A theory of the budgetary process, *American Political Science Review*, Vol. 60, September, pp. 529–47.

Davis, O.A., Dempster, M.A.H. and Wildavsky, A. (1966b), On the process of budgeting: an empirical study of Congressional appropriations, in G. Tullock (ed.) *Papers in Non-Market Decision Making*, Thomas Jefferson Center for Political Economy, Charlottesville, Virginia

Davis, O.A., Dempster, M.A.H. and Wildavsky, A. (1974) Towards a predictive theory of government, *British Journal of Political Science*, Vol. 4, Part 4, pp. 419–52.

Day, R.H. (1964) Review of behavioural theory of the firm, *Econometrica*, Vol. 32, July, pp. 461–4.

Day, R.H. (1967) Profits, learning and the convergence of satisficing to marginalism, *Quarterly Journal of Economics*, Vol. 81, May, pp. 302–11.
Day, R.H. and Tinney, E.H. (1968) How to cooperate in business without really trying: a learning model of decentralised decision making, *Journal of Political Economy*, Vol. 76, July, pp. 583–600.
Dearborn, D.C. and Simon, H.A. (1958) Selective perception: a note on the departmental identification of executives, *Sociometry*, Vol. 21, pp. 140–44.
Debbasch, C. (1969), *L'Administration au Pouvoir, Fonctionnaires et Politiques sous la Ve République*, Calmann-Levy, Paris.
Debreu, G. (1959) *Theory of Value*, John Wiley.
Demsetz, H. (1974) Concentration and rates of return, *Journal of Law and Economics*, Vol. 17.
Deutsch, K. (1966) *The Nerves of Government*, Free Press, New York.
Dewey, J. (1933) *How We Think*, D.C. Heath, Boston.
Dickenson, H.D. (1939) *Economics of Socialism*, Oxford University Press.
Dill, W.R. (1958) Environment as an influence on managerial autonomy, *Administrative Science Quarterly*, Vol. 2, pp. 409–43.
Djilas, M. (1957) *The New Class: An Analysis of The Communist System*, Praeger.
Downie, J., (1960) Statistics and the economist, *Proceedings of the Royal Statistical Society*, Part 3.
Downs, A. (1957) *An Economic Theory of Democracy*, Harper and Row.
Downs, A. (1967) *Inside Bureaucracy*, Little, Brown & Co.
Driggers, P.F. (1977) Theoretical blockage: a strategy for the development of organisational theory, *The Sociological Quarterly*, Vol. 18, Winter, pp. 143–59.
Dror, Y. (1964) Muddling through: science or intertia, *Public Administration Review*, pp. 153–7.
Drucker, P.F. (1954) *The Practice of Management*, Harper and Row.
Dunphy, D. (1978) Bureaucracies, *The University of New South Wales, Occasional Paper*, No. 3.
Dunsire, A. (1973) *Administration: The Word and the Science*, Martin Robertson.
Dunsire, A. (1978a) *Implementation in a Bureaucracy: The Execution Process: Volume 1*, Martin Robertson.
Dunsire, A. (1978b) *Control in a Bureaucracy: The Execution Process: Volume 2*, Martin Robertson.
Dye, T.R. (1966) *Political Economics and the Public*, Rand McNally.
Dye, E. (1972) *Understanding Public Policy*, Prentice-Hall.
Easton, D. (1965) *A Framework for Political Analysis*, Prentice-Hall.
Einstein, A. (1950) *Out of My Later Years*, Princeton University Press.
Emery, F.E. (ed.) (1969) *Systems Thinking*, Penguin Books.
Emery, F.E. and Trist, E.L. (1965) The causal texture of organisational environment, *Human Relations*, Vol. 18.
Emery, F.E. and Trist, E.L. (1969) Socio-technical systems, in F.E. Emery (ed.) *Systems Thinking*, Penguin Books.
Etzioni, A. (1958) Industrial sociology: the study of economic organisations, *Social Research*, Vol. 25, pp. 303–24.
Etzioni, A. (1960) Two approaches to organisational analysis: a critique and a suggestion, Administrative Science Quarterly, Vol. 5, pp. 257–78.
Etzioni, A. (1960) New directions in the study of organisation and society, *Social Research*, vol. 27, pp. 223–8.
Etzioni, A. (1961) *A Comparative Analysis of Complex Organisations*, Free Press, New York.
Etzioni, A. (1964) *Modern Organisations*, Prentice-Hall.

Etzioni, A. (1967) Mixed scanning: a third approach to decision making, *Public Administration Review*, December, Vol. XXVII.

Etzioni, A. (1975) *Social Problems*, Prentice-Hall.

Farrell, M.S. (1957) The measurement of productive efficiency, *Journal of the Royal Statistical Society*, Series A, pp. 253–90.

Fayol, H. (1917) *Administration industrielle et générale: prévoyance, organisation, commandement, co-ordination, contrôle*, Dunod & Pinat, Paris. (English translation by C. Stours, *General and Industrial Management*, 1949, Pitman.)

Feldman, J. and Kantner, H.E. (1965) Organisation decision making, in J.G. March (ed.), *Handbook of Organsations*, Rand McNally.

Feldstein, M. (1967) *Economic Analysis for Health Service Efficiency*, North-Holland Publishing Co.

Fenno, R.F. (1959) *The Presidents's Cabinet*, Harvard University Press.

Fenno, R. (1966) *The Power of the Purse: Appropriations Politics in Congress*, Little, Brown & Co.

Fiorina, M.P. and Noll, R.G. (1978) Voters, legistators and bureaucracy. Institutional design in the public sector, *American Economic Review*, May.

Firth, R. (1964) *Essays on Social Organisation and Values*, Athlone Press.

Flegman, V. (1979) Parliamentary Control of Public Expenditure: The Public Accounts Committee, paper presented to a *Conference on the Control of Public Expenditure*, Bath University Centre for Fiscal Studies, July.

Foldes, L.P. and Rees, R. (1977) A note on the Arrow–Lind theorem, *American Economic Review*, March.

Follett, M.P. (1918) *The New State: Group Organisation the Solution of Popular Government*, Longmans, Green & Co.

Fox, D.M. (1974) *The Politics of City and State Bureaucracy*, Goodyear, Pacific Palisades, California.

Franks Committee (1966) *Report of Commission of Inquiry into Oxford University*.

Friedman, M. (1953) *Essays in Positive Economics*, Chicago University Press.

Frohlich, N. and Oppenheimer, J.A. (1978) *Modern Political Economy*, Prentice-Hall.

Froomkin, J.T., Jamison, D.T. and Radner, R. (1976) *Education as an Industry*, National Bureau of Economic Research, Ballinger.

Fulton Committee (1968) *The Civil Servant*, HMSO.

Furubotn, E. and Pejovich, B. (1972) Property rights and economic theory, *Journal of Economic Literature*, Vol. X, No. 4, December.

Galbraith, J.K. (1967) *The New Industrial State*, New American Library, Mentor Books.

Galbraith, J.K. (1969) *The Affluent Society*, 2nd edn. revised, Houghton Mifflin.

Galbraith, J.K. (1973) *Economics and the Public Purpose*, Houghton Mifflin.

Georgiou, P. (1973) The goal paradigm and notes toward a counter paradigm, *Administrative Science Quarterly*, Vol. 18, pp. 291–310.

Georgopoulos, B.S. and Tannenbaum, A.S. (1957) A study of organisational effectivenes, *American Sociological Review*, Vol. 22, pp. 534–40.

Gerth, H.H. and Mills, C.W. (eds. & translators) (1946) *From Max Weber*, Oxford University Press, New York.

Gilbreth, F.B. and Gilbreth, L.M. (1917) *Applied Motion Study*, Sturgis and Walton, New York.

Goffman, E. (1956) The nature of deference and demeanor, *American Anthropologist*, Vol. 58, pp. 473–502.

Goffman, E. (1961) *Asylums*, Penguin Books.

Gordon, M.R. (1971) Civil Servants, politicans and parties, *Comparative Politics*, Vol. 4, October.

Gough, I. (1975) State expenditure in advanced capitalism, *New Left Review*, Vol. 92.

Gouldner, A.W. (1952) *Patterns of Industrial Bureaucracy*, The Free Press of Glencoe, Glencoe, Illinois. (Also 1954 and 1955 editions.)

Gouldner, A.W. (1955) Metaphysical pathos and the theory of bureaucracy, *American Political Science Review*, Vol. 49, pp. 493–507.

Gouldner, A.W. (1959) Organisational analysis, in R.K. Merton, L. Broom, and L.S. Cottrell Jr. (eds) *Sociology Today*, Basic Books.

Graiounas, V. (1937) Relationship in organisation, in L. Gulick and L. Urwick (eds), *Papers on the Science of Administration*, Institute of Public Administration, Columbia University, pp. 181–7.

Green, J.J. and Laffont, J. (1979) *Individual Incentives in Public Decision-Making*, North-Holland Publishing Co.

Greenwood, R. and Hinings, C.R. (1977)The study of local government: towards an organisational analysis, *Public Administration Bulletin*, No. 23, April.

Greenwood, R., Hinings, C.R. and Ranson, S. (1977) Budgetary process in English local government, *Political Studies*, Vol. XXV, No. 1.

Gross, E. (1969) The definition of organisational goals, *British Journal of Sociology*, Vol. 20, pp. 277–94.

Grove, E.W. (1973) Comment on Olson's paper, in M. Moss (ed.) *The Measurement of Economic and Social Performance*, Columbia University Press for the National Bureau of Economic Research (NBER), Washington DC.

Gulick, L. and Urwick, L. (eds) (1937)*Papers in the Science of Administration*, Institute of Public Administration, Columbia University.

Hague, D.C., Mackenzie, W.J.M. and Barker, D. (1975) *Public Policy and Private Interests*, Macmillan.

Hahn, F.H. (1973)*On the Notion of Equilibrium in Economics*, Cambridge University Press.

Haldane Report (1918) *Machinery of Government Report*, Vol. 12, Cmnd 9230, HMSO.

Hall, R. and Peter, L.J. (1969) *The Peter Principle*, Morrow, New York.

Hall, R.H. (1972) *Organisations: Structure and Process*, Prentice-Hall.

Hall, R.L. and Hitch, C.J. (1939) Price theory and business behaviour, *Oxford Economic Papers*, May, pp. 12–45.

Hartley, K. (1974) Programme budgeting and the economics of defence, *Public Administration*, Vol. 52.

Hatry, H.P. and Fisk, D.M. (1971) *Improving Productivity and Productivity Measurement in Government*, prepared for the National Commission on Productivity, The Urban Institute, Washington DC.

Hayek, F.A. (1935)The present state of the debate, in Hayek (ed.), *Collectivist Economic Planning*, Macmillan.

Hayek, F.A. (1940) Socialist calculation: the competitive solution, *Economica*, May.

Hayek, F.A. (1945)The use of knowledge in society, *American Economic Review*, Vol. 35, No. 4, September, pp. 519–30.

Hayek, F.A. (1948) *Individualism and Economic Order*, Chicago University Press.

Hayes, F.O'R. (1977)*Productivity in Local Government*, D.C. Heath, Boston.

Hazelhurst, C.H. and Nethercote, J.R. (1977)*Reforming Australian Government, The Coombes Report and Beyond*, Australian National University Press.

Heclo, H. and Wildavsky, A. (1974) *The Private Government of Public Money*, Macmillan.

Heller, W.W. (1975) What's right with economics, *American Economic Review*, Vol. 65, No. 1, March, pp. 1–26.

Herzberg, F. *et al.* (1959)*The Motivation to Work*, John Wiley.
Herzberg, F. (1968)*Work and the Nature of Man*, Staples, London.
Hettich, W. (1975) Bureaucrats and public goods, *P-ublic Choice*, pp. 15–25.
Hickson, D.J., Hinings, C.R., Lee, C.A., Schneck, R.E., and Pennings, J.M. (1971) A strategic contingencies theory of intra-organisational power, *Administrative Science Quarterly*, Vol. 16, pp. 216–29.
Hildebrandt, G. and Tyson, L. D'A. (1976a) Performance incentives and planning under uncertainty, *Econometric Research Progress Memorandum*, University of Princeton, No. 201, July.
Hildebrandt, G., and Tyson, L.D'A. (1976b) Performance incentives vs. prices vs. quantities, *Econometric Research Progress Memorandum*, University of Princeton, No. 204, October.
Hill, M.J. (1969) The exercise of discretion in the national assistance board, *Public Administration*, Vol. 47, Spring.
Hill, M.J. (1972) *The Sociology of Public Administration*, Weidenfeld and Nicolson.
Hinings, C.R., Hickson, D.J., Pennings, J.M. and Schneck, R.E., (1974) Structural conditions of inter-organisational power, *Administrative Science Quarterly*, Vol. 19, pp. 22–44.
Hirschman, A.E. and Lindblom, C.E. (1961) Economic development, research and development policy-making: some converging views, *Behavioural Science*, Vol. 7, No. 2, pp. 211–22.
Hirschman, A.O. (1967) The principle of the hiding hand, *The Public Interest*, Vol. 6, pp. 10–23.
Hirshleifer, J. (1975)*Price Theory and Applications*, Prentice-Hall.
HMSO (1977)*The Civil Service*, Eleventh Report From the Expenditure Committee, Session 1976/77 HC 535.
Homans, G.C. (1950) *The Human Group*, Harcourt Brace Jovanovich.
Homans, G.C. (1961)*Social Behaviour Its Elementary Forms*, Harcourt Brace Jovanovich.
Hood, C. (1976)The Limits of Administration, John Wiley.
Hunt, Sir John (1976) *Evidence presented to Eleventh Report of the Expenditure Committee*, Civil Service, HC 535, 1976–77, HMSO.
Hunt, J.W. (1972) *The Restless Organisation*, John Wiley.
Hutchison, T.W. (1977) *Knowledge and Ignorance in Economics*, Basil Blackwell.
Hyneman, C. (1950) *Bureaucracy in a Democracy*, Harper and Row.
Illich, I. (1976) *Limits to Medicine*, Marion Boyars, London.
Illich, I. (1971) *Deschooling Society*, Calder and Boyars, London.
Imerschein, A.W. (1977) Organisational change as a paradigm shift, *The Sociological Quarterly*, Vol. 18, No. 1.
Jackson, P.M. (1979) *Public Expenditure Planning and Control in the U.K.*, Unit 15, Political Economy and Taxation Course D323, Open University.
Jacoby, H. (1973) *The Bureaucratization of the World*, University of California Press.
Johansen, L. (1977) The theory of public goods: misplaced emphasis?, *Journal of Public Economics*, Vol. 7, pp. 147–52.
Johnson, N. (1966) *Parliament and Administration: The Estimates Committee, 1945–65*, Allen & Unwin.
Johnson, N. (1971) Financial accountability to parliament, in L. Smith and D.C. Hague (eds), *The Dilemmas of Accountability in Modern Government*, Macmillan.
Johnson, N. (1974) Defining accountability, *Public Administration Bulletin*, No. 17, December, pp. 3–13.

Johnson, N. (1975) *Financial Accountability To Parliament*, in D.C. Hague, W.J.M. Mackenzie and D. Barker, *op. cit.*

Kahn, R.L. and Boulding E. (eds) (1964) *Power and Conflict in Organisations*, Basic Books.

Kaldor, N. (1938)Professor Chamberlin on monopolistic and imperfect competition, *Quarterly Journal of Economics*, Vol. 52, May, pp. 513–29.

Kaldor, N. (1972)The irrelevance of equilibrium economics, *Economic Journal*, Vol. 82, December, pp. 1237–55.

Kapp, K.W. (1976) The nature and significance of economics, *Kyklos*, Vol. 29.

Kassem, M.S. (1976) Organisation theory: American and European styles, *International Management and Organisation*, Vol. 3, pp. 46–59.

Katz, D. and Kahn, R.L. (1966) *The Social Psychology of Organisations*, John Wiley.

Kaufman, H. (1976) *Are Government Agencies Immortal?*, The Brookings Institution, Washington DC.

Keeley, M. (1978) A social justice approach to organisational evaluation, *Administrative Science Quarterly*, Vol. 23, 272–92.

King, A. (1975) Overload: problems of governing in the 1970's, *Political Studies*, Vol. 23.

King, A. (1976) The problem of overload, in King (ed.) *Why is Britain Becoming Harder to Govern?*, BBC Publications.

Kingsley, J.D. (1944) *Representative Bureaucracy*, The Antioch Press, Yellow Springs, Ohio.

Klarman, H. (1964) *The Economics of Health and Medical Care*, University of Michigan Press.

Klein, R. (1974) The doctor's dilemma for accountability, *Public Administration Bulletin*, No. 17, December, pp. 31–43.

Klein, R. (1979) Issues in the control of public expenditure. Paper presented at a *Conference on the Control of Public Expenditure*, Bath University, Centre for Fiscal Studies, July.

Knight, F.H. (1921) *Risk Uncertainty and Profits*, Chicago University Press.

Knoer, E. (1978) Catastrophe theory, tax exportation and public good spillovers, in W. Loehr and T. Sandler (eds) *Public Goods and Public Policy*, Sage, London.

Kogan, M. (1973) *Comment on Niskanen's 'Bureaucracy Servant or Master?'* Institute of Economic Affairs, London.

Koontz, H. and O'Donnell, C. (1972) *Principles of Management*, 5th edn, McGraw-Hill.

Kornai, J. (1971) *Anti-Equilibrium: On Economic Systems Theory and the Task of Research*, North-Holland Publishing Co.

Koutsoyiannis, A. (1979) *Modern Microeconomics*, 2nd edn, Macmillan.

Krislov, S. (1974) *Representative Bureaucracy*, Prentice-Hall.

Krupp, S. (1961) *Pattern in Organisational Analysis*, Holt, Rinehart and Winston.

Kurz, M. (1974) Experimental approach to the determination of the demand for public goods, *Journal of Public Economics*, Vol. 3, pp. 329–48.

Lancaster, K.J. (1966) A new approach to consumer theory, *Journal of Political Economy*, Vol. 74, pp. 132–57.

Lange, O. (1938) On the economic theory of socialism, in B.E. Lippincott (ed.), *On the Economic Theory of Socialism*, Minn, Minneapolis.

La Porte, T. (1975) *Organisational Complexity: The Challenge to Politics and Policy*, Princeton University Press.

Lasswell, H.D. (1936) *Politics: Who Gets What, When, How?* McGraw-Hill.

Lawrence, P.R. and Lorsch, J.W. (1967) *Organisation and Environment*, Division of Research, Graduate School of Economics, Harvard University.

Layard, R. (1972) *Cost Benefit Analysis*, Penguin Books.
Leibenstein, H. (1966) Allocative efficiency vs. X-efficiency, *American Economic Review*, Vol. 56, June, pp. 392–415.
Leibenstein, H. (1973) Competition and X-efficiency: reply, *Journal of Political Economy*, Vol. 81.
Leibenstein, H. (1975) Aspects of the X-efficiency theory of the firm, *The Bell Journal of Economics*, Vol. 6, No. 2.
Leontieff, W. (1971) Theoretical assumptions and non-observed facts, *American Economic Review*, Vol. 61, March pp. 1–7.
Lerner, A.P. (1944) *The Economics of Control*, Macmillan.
Lewin, K. (1951) *Field Theory in Social Science*, Harper and Row.
Liberman, E.G. (1950)*Khozyaistvennyi Raschet Mashinostroitel 'nogozovoda.*
Likert, R. (1961) *New Patterns of Management*, McGraw-Hill.
Likert, R. (1967) *The Human Organisation*, McGraw-Hill.
Lindblom, C.E. (1959) The science of muddling through, *Public Administration Review*, Vol.19.
Lindblom, C.E. (1965)*The Intelligence of Democracy: Decision Making Through Mutual Adjustment*, Free Press, Glencoe, Illinois.
Litterer, J.A. (1963)*Organisations: Structure and Behaviour*, John Wiley.
Litterer, J.A. (ed.) (1969) *Organisations: Systems, Control and Adaptation*, 2nd edn, Vol. 2.
Litterer, J.A. (1973)*The Analysis of Organisations*, 2nd edn, John Wiley.
Little, I.M.D. and Mirrlees, J.A. (1974) *Project Appraisal and Planning for Developing Countries*, Heinemann.
Littlechild, S. (1978a) The use of cost benefit analysis, in M.J. Artis and A.R. Nobay (eds), *Contemporary Economic Analysis*, Croom Helm.
Littlechild, S. (1978b) Comment, in *The Economics of Politics*, Institute of Economic Affairs Readings, 18, London, p. 90.
Loasby, B.J. (1967)Management economics and the theory of the firm, *The Journal of Industrial Economics*, Vol. XV, No. 3.
Loasby, B.J. (1968) The decision maker in the organisation, *Journal of Management Studies*, Vol. 5, No. 3.
Loasby, B.J. (1971) Hypothesis and paradigm in the theory of the firm, *Economic Journal*, Vol. 81 (324), December, pp. 863–85.
Loasby, B.J. (1976) *Choice, Complexity and Ignorance*, Cambridge University Press.
Lodahl, J. and Gordon, G. (1972) The structure of scientific fields and the functioning of university graduate departments, *American Sociological Review*, pp. 57–72.
MacDougall, D. (1974) In praise of economics, *Economic Journal*, Vol. 84, December, pp. 773–86.
Mackintosh, J.P. (1968)*The Devolution of Power*, Penguin Books.
Mackintosh, J.P. (1971) The House of Commons and taxation, *Political Quarterly*, Vol. 42, pp. 75–86. (Reprinted in B. Crick and W.A. Robson (eds), *Taxation Policy* (1972) Pelican Books.)
Maclup, F. (1967) Theories of the firm, *American Economic Review*, Vol. 57, March, pp. 1–33.
Maclup, F. (1969) The universal bogey, in E. Streissler (ed.), *Roads to Freedom: Essays in Honour of Friedrich A. von Hayek*, Routledge & Kegan Paul.
Malngren, H.B. (1961) Information, expectations and the theory of the firm, *Quarterly Journal of Economics*, Vol. 75, pp. 399–421.
March, J.G. (1965) *Handbook of Organisations*, Rand McNally.

March, J.G. (1965) The power of power, in D. Easton (ed.) *Varieties of Political Theory*, Prentice-Hall.

March, J.G. and Olsen, J.P. *et al.* (1976) *Ambiguity and Choice in Organisations*, Universitetsforlaget, Bergen.

March, J.G. and Simon, H.A. (1958) *Organisations*, John Wiley.

Marcuse, H. (1964) *One Dimensional Man, Studies in the Ideology of Advanced Industrial Society*, Routledge & Kegan Paul. (Reprinted 1968.)

Marglin, S.A. (1974/75), What do bosses do? The origins and functions of hierarchy in capitalist production, *The Review of Radical Political Economics*, Vol. 6, pp. 60–112.

Margolis, J. (1958) The analysis of the firm: rationalism, conventionalism and behaviourism, *Journal of Business*, Vol. 31, pp. 187–99.

Marris, R. (1963) A model of the managerial enterprise, *Quarterly Journal of Economics*, Vol. 77, No. 2, pp. 185–209.

Marris, R. (1966) *The Economic Theory of Managerial Capitalism*, Macmillan.

Marris, R. (ed.) (1974) *The Corporate Society*, Macmillan.

Marris, R. and Wood, A. (eds.) (1971) *The Corporate Economy*, Macmillan.

Marschak, J. (1955) Elements for a theory of teams, *Management Science*, Vol. 1, January, pp. 127–37.

Marschak, T.A. (1965) Economic theories of organisation, in J.G. March (ed.) *Handbook of Organisations*, Rand McNally.

Marschak, J. and Radner, R. (1972) *Economic Theory of Teams*, Yale University Press.

Marx, K. (1970) Critique of Hegel's philosophy of right, in A.J. O'Malley (ed.) *Karl Marx Critique Hegel*, Cambridge University Press.

Maslow, A.H. (1954) *Motivation and Personality*, Harper and Row.

Massie, J.L. (1965) Management theory, in J.G. March, (ed.) *Handbook of Organisations*, Rand McNally.

Mayo, E. (1933) *The Human Problems of an Industrial Civilisation*, Macmillan, New York.

Mayo, E. (1945) *The Social Problems of an Industrial Civilisation*, Division of Research, Graduate School of Business Administration, Harvard University.

Mayston, D.J. (1974) *The Idea of Social Choice*, Macmillan.

Merton, R.K. (1957) Bureaucratic structure and personality, in R.K. Merton, *Social Theory and Social Structure*, revised edn. Free Press, Glencoe, Illinois. (First published in *Social Forces* (1940), pp. 560–68.)

Merton, R.K. (ed.) (1963) *Reader in Bureaucracy*, Free Press, Glencoe, Illinois.

Meter, van D.S. and Horn, van C.E. (1975), The policy implementation process: a conceptual framework, *Administration and Society*, Vol. 6, No. 4.

Meyer, H. (1969) Bureaucracy and policy formation in Sweden, *Scandinavian Political Studies*, Vol. 4, pp. 103–6.

Michels, R. (1911) *Zur Soziologie des Parteiwesens in der modernen Demokratie*, Leipzig. (English translation by E. and C. Paul, *Political Parties. A Sociological Study of the Oligarchical Tendencies of Modern Democracy* (1959), Dover, New York.

Migue, J.L. and Belanger, G. (1974) Towards a general theory of managerial discretion, *Public Choice*, 17, Spring.

Mikardo, I. (1979) *House of Commons Official Report*, HMSO, 19th February.

Miliband, R. (1969) *The State in Capitalist Society*, Weidenfeld and Nicolson.

Mill, J.S. (1861), *On Representative Government*, Everyman edition, London (1948).

Miller, D. (1976) *Social Justice*, Clarendon Press.

Mills, C.W. (1959) *The Sociological Imagination*, Pelican Books.

Mirrlees, J.A. (1976) The optimal structure of incentives and authority within an organisation, *Bell Journal of Economics,* Spring, pp. 105–31.

Mises, L. von (1920), Economic calculation in the socialist commonwealth, in Hayek (ed.), *Collectivist Economic Planning* (1935), Routledge & Kegan Paul.

Mises, L.V. (1944) *Bureaucracy,* Yale University Press.

Mommsen, W.J. (1974) *Perspectives on the Political Sociology of Max Weber,* Basil Blackwell.

Mooney, J. (1947) *The Principles of Organisation*, Harper and Row.

Mosca, G. (1958) *The Myth of the Ruling Class,* McGraw-Hill.

Mouzelis, N.P. (1967) *Organisation and Bureaucracy*, Routledge & Kegan Paul.

Mueller, D.C. (1979), *Public Choice,* Cambridge University Press.

Mushkin, S. (ed.) (1972) *Public Prices for Public Products,* The Urban Institute, Washington DC.

Myrdal, G. (1957) *Economic Theory and Underdeveloped Regions,* Duckworth & Co.

Myrdal, G. (1968) *Asian Drama,* Pantheon Books.

Myrdal, G. (1978) Institutional economics, *Journal of Economic Issues,* December.

McAuley, A.N.D. (1966) Rationality and central planning, *Society Studies, Vol. XVIII.*

McGregor, D. (1960) *The Human Side of Enterprise,* McGraw-Hill.

McGuire, C.B. and Radner, R. (1972) *Decision and Organisation*, North-Holland Publishing Co.

McManus, J.C. (1975) The costs of alternative economic organisations, *Canadian Journal of Economics,* August.

McNeil, K. (1978) Understanding organisational power: building on the Weberian legacy, *Administrative Science Quarterly,* Vol. 23, pp. 65–90.

Nader, R. (1965) *Unsafe at Any Speed*, Grossman, New York.

Nash, C., Parce, D.W. and Stanley, J. (1975), An evaluation of cost benefit analysis criteria, *Scottish Journal of Political Economy,* June.

Natchez, P.B. and Bupp, I.C. (1973), Policy and priority in the budgetary process, *American Political Science Review,* Vol. LXVII, pp. 951–63.

Nelson, R.R. (1977), *The Moon and the Ghetto,* Norton.

Neustadt, R.E. (1960) *Presidential Power,* John Wiley.

Newhouse, J.P. (1970) Towards a theory of non-profit institutions: an economic model of a hospital, *American Economic Review,* Vol. 60, March, pp. 64–74.

Newman, G. (1974) Review of 'Epistemico and economics: a critique of economic doctrines', *Philosophy of the Social Sciences,* Vol. 4, pp. 409–17.

Niskanen, W. (1968) Non-market decision making: the peculiar economics of bureaucracy, *American Economic Review,* May, Vol. 58, pp. 293–305.

Niskanen, W. (1971) *Bureaucracy and Representative Government,* Aldine, Chicago.

Niskanen, W.A. (1973) *Bureaucracy: Servant or Master?* Hobart Paperback 5, Institute of Economic Affairs, London.

Normanton, E.L. (1966) *The Accountability and Audit of Governments,* Manchester University Press.

Normanton, E.L. (1975) Public accountability and audit: a reconnaisance in public policy and private interests, in D.C. Hague, W.J.M. Mackenzie and D. Barker (eds.) *Public and Private Interests,* Macmillan.

Normanton, E.L. (1977) *Memorandum to Select Committee on Procedure,* First Report, HMSO, 1977–78.

Nove, A. (1973) *Effiiency Criteria for the Nationalised Industries,* Allen & Unwin.

Oates, W.E. (1972) *Fiscal Federalism,* Harcourt, Brace Javonovitch.

Oates, W.E. and Strassmann, D.L. (1978) The use of effluent fees to regulate public sector sources of pollution, *Journal of Environmental Economics and Management*, Vol. 5, No. 3, September, pp. 283–91.

O'Conner, J. (1973) *The Fiscal Crisis of the State*, St. Martin's Press.

Olson, M. (1965) *The Logic of Collective Action*, Harvard University Press.

Olson, (1973) Evaluating performance in the public sector, in M. Moss (ed.) *The Measurement of Economic and Social Performance*, Columbia University Press for the National Bureau of Economic Research.

Olson, M. and Clague, C.K. (1971) Dissent in economics: the convergence of extremes, *Social Research*, Vol. 38, Winter, pp. 751–76.

Oppenheim, F.E. (1953) Rational choice, *The Journal of Philosophy*, Vol. 50, No. 2.

Ostrom, V. (1971) *The Intellectual Crises in Public Administration*, University Alabama Press.

Papandreou, A.G. (1955) Full costs, cost changes and prices: a comment, in B.F. Haley (ed.), *Business Concentration and Price Policy*, Princeton University Press.

Parker, R.S. (1976) The meaning of responsible government, *Politics*, Vol. 11, No. 2.

Parkinson, C.N. (1957) *Parkinson's Law or the Pursuit of Progress*, Penguin Books.

Parsons, T. (1951) *The Social System*, Free Press, Glencoe, Illinois.

Parsons, T. (1956) Suggestions for a sociological approach to the theory of organisations, *Administrative Science Quarterly*, Vol. 1, No. 1 and 2. (Reprinted in A. Etzioni (ed.) *A Sociological Reader on Complex Organisations* (1961), Holt Rinehart and Winston.)

Parsons, T. (1960) *Structure and Process in Modern Societies*, Free Press, Glencoe, Illinois.

Pateman, C. (1970) *Participation and Democratic Thought*, Cambridge University Press.

Pauly, M.V. and Redisch, M. (1973) The not-for-profit hospital as a physician's cooperative, *American Economic Review*, Vol. 63, March, pp. 87–100.

Peacock, A.T. (1973) *Memorandum of Dissent*, to the Report of the Royal Commission on the Constitution (Kilbrandon Commission), Cmnd. 5460, HMSO.

Peacock, A.T. (1973) Cost benefit analysis and the political control of public investment, in J.N. Wolfe (ed.) *Cost Benefit and Cost Effectiveness*, Allen & Unwin.

Peacock, A.T. (1978) The economics of bureaucracy: an inside view, in *The Economics of Politics*, Institute of Economic Affairs Readings, No. 18, London.

Pempel, T.J. (1974) The bureaucratisation of policy making in post-war Japan, *Midwest (American) Journal of Political Science*, Vol. 18, November.

Pennings, J.M. (1975) The relevance of the structural contingency model of organisational effectiveness, *Administrative Science Quarterly*, Vol. 20, September.

Penrose, E. (1959) *The Theory of the Growth of the Firm*, Basil Blackwell.

Perrow, C. (1961) The analysis of goals in complex organisations, *American Sociological Review*, Vol. 26, pp. 854–66.

Perrow, C. (1965) Hospitals, technology, structure and goals, in J.G. March, *Handbook of Organisations*, Rand McNally.

Perrow, C. (1967) A framework for the comparative analysis of organisations, *American Sociological Review*, April.

Perrow, C. (1970) Departmental power and perspective in industrial firms, in M. Zald (ed.) *Power in Organisations*, Vanderbilt University Press, pp. 59–89.

Perrow, C. (1972) *Complex Organisations: A Critical Essay,* Scott Foresman, Glenview.

Pfeffer, J. and Leblebici, H. (1973) The effect of competition on some dimensions of organisational structure, *Social Forces,* Vol. 52, pp. 268–79.

Pfeffer, J. and Salancik, G.R. (1974) Organisational decision-making as a political process: the case study of a university budget, *Administrative Science Quarterly,* Vol. 19.

Pfeffer, J. and Salancik, G.R. (1978) *The External Control of Organisations: A Resource Dependence Perspective,* Harper and Row.

Pfeffer, J. Salancik, G.R. and Leblebici, H. (1976) Personal influence in organisational decision-making, *Administrative Science Quarterly,* Vol. 21, pp. 227–45.

Pifer, A. (1967) The quasi non-governmental organisation, in *Annual Report,* Carnegie Corporation, New York.

Pigou, A.C. (1922) Empty economic boxes: a reply, *Economic Journal,* Vol. XXXII, pp. 458–65. (Reprinted in G.J. Stigler and K.E. Boulding, *Readings in Price Theory,* 1953, Allen & Unwin.)

Plowden Committee Report, (1961) *Control of Public Expenditure,* 1432, HMSO, July.

Pondy, L.R. (1970) Towards a theory of internal resource-allocation, in M. Zald (ed.), *Power in Organisations,* Vanderbilt University Press.

Popper, K. (1966) *The Open Society and Its Enemies,* 5th edn., Princeton University Press.

Pressman, J. and Wildavsky, A. (1973) *Implementation,* University of California Press.

Presthus, R. (1962) *The Organisational Society,* Knopf.

Putnam, R.D. (1973) The political attitudes of senior civil servants in Western Europe, *British Journal of Political Science,* Vol. 3, No. 3, July.

Radner, R. (1961) The evaluation of information in organisations, in J. Neyman (ed.) *Proceedings of the Fourth Berkeley Symposium on Mathematics, Statistics and Probability,* Vol. 1, University of California Press.

Radner, R. (1962) Team decision problems, *Annals Mathematics and Statistics,* Vol. 33, pp. 857–81.

Radner, R. (1968) Competitive equilibrium under uncertainty, *Econometrica,* Vol. 36, No. 1, pp. 31–58.

Radner, R. (1970) Problems in the theory of markets under uncertainty, *American Economic Review,* May, Vol. 60, No. 2, pp. 454–60.

Radner, R. (1974) Market equilibrium and uncertainty: concepts and problems, in M.D. Intrilligator and D.A. Kendrick (eds), *Frontiers of Quantitative Economics,* Vol. II, North Holland Publishing Co.

Radner, R. (1975) A behavioural model of cost reduction, *The Bell Journal of Economics,* Vol. 6, No. 1.

Rawls, J. (1971) *A Theory of Social Justice,* Harvard University Press.

Reder, M. (1965) Some problems in the economics of hospitals, *American Economic Review,* Vol. 56, May, pp. 472–80.

Reich, C. (1970) *The Greening of America,* Random House.

Ridley, C.E. and Simon, H.A. (1938) *Measuring Municipal Activities,* The International City Managers Association, Chicago.

Robinson, A. (1977) The House of Commons and public expenditure, in S.A. Walkland and M. Ryle (eds), *The Commons in the Seventies,* Fontana Books.

Robinson, A. (1978) *Parliament and Public Spending: The Expenditure Committee of the House of Commons 1970–76,* Heinemann.

Robinson, A. (1979) Parliamentary Control of Public Expenditure: The Experience of the Expenditure Committee of the House of Commons 1971–79. Paper presented to a *Conference on the Control of Public Expenditure*, Bath University Centre for Fiscal Studies, July.

Robinson, J. (1933) *The Economics of Imperfect Competition*, Macmillan,

Robson, W.A. (1960) *Nationalised Industry and Public Ownership*, Allen & Unwin.

Roethlisberger, F. and Dickson, W. (1939) *Management and the Worker*, John Wiley.

Rondinelli, D.A. (1976) Public planning and political strategy, *Long Range Planning*, Vol. 9, No. 2, pp. 75–82.

Rose, M. (1975)*Industrial Behaviour: Theoretical Development Since Taylor*, Allen Lane.

Rose, J.P. and Burkhead, J. (1974) *Productivity in the Local Government Sector*, Lexington Books.

Rothenburg, N. (1964) Efficiency in the government sector, *American Economic Review*, May.

Rushing, W.A. (1962) Social influence and the social psychological function of deference: a study of psychiatric nursing, *Social Forces*, Vol. 41, pp. 142–8.

Salaman, G. (1978) Towards a sociology of organisational structure, *Sociological Review*, Vol. 28, No. 3, August.

Salancik, G.R. and Pfeffer, J. (1974) The basis and use of power in organisational decision-making: the case of a university, *Administrative Science Quarterly*, Vol. 19.

Samuelson, P.A. (1953) *The Foundations of Economics*, Harvard University Press.

Sayre, W.S. and Kaufman, H. (1960), *Governing New York City: Politics in the Metropolis*, Russell Sage Foundation.

Savage, L.J. (1954) *The Foundations of Statistics*, John Wiley.

Savage, P. (1974) Dismantling the administrative state, *Political Studies*, Vol. 22.

Scarf, H. (1967) On the computation of equilibrium prices, in W. Fellner *et al.*, *Ten Economic Studies in the Tradition of Irving Fisher*, John Wiley.

Scherr, B.A. and Babb, E.M. (1975) Pricing public goods: an experiment with two proposed pricing systems, *Public Choice*, Vol. 23, pp. 35–48.

Schultze, C.L. (1968) *The Politics and Economics of Public Spending*, Brookings Institution, Washington DC.

Schultze, C.L. (1973) Comment, in M. Moss (ed.) *The Measurement of Economic and Social Performance*, National Bureau of Economic Research, Columbia University Press.

Schumpeter, J.A. (1954) *Capitalism, Socialism, and Democracy*, Harper and Row.

Schwartzman, D. (1973) Competition and efficiency, *Journal of Political Economy*, pp. 756–814.

Seers, D. and Faber, M. (eds) (1972) *Crisis in Planning*, Chatto and Windus.

Seldon, A. (1977) *Charge*, Temple Smith.

Self, P.O. (1975) *Econocrats and The Policy Process*, Macmillan.

Sen, A.K. (1970) *Collective Choice and Social Welfare*, Oliver and Boyd.

Sen, A.K. (1976) Rational fools: a critique of the behavioural foundations of economic theory, *Philosophy and Public Affairs*, Vol. 6.

Selznick, P. (1948) Foundations of the theory of organisation, *American Sociological Review*, Vol. 13, pp. 25–35.

Selznick, P. (1949) *TVA and the Grass Roots*, University of California Press.

Selznick, P. (1957) *Leadership and Administration*, Harper and Row.

Selznick, P. (1969) Foundations of the theory of organisations, in A. Etzioni, *A Sociological Reader on Complex Organisations*, Holt Rinehart and Winston, pp. 19–32.

Shackle, G.L.S. (1972) *Epistemics and Economics: a Critique of Economic Doctrines*, Cambridge University Press.

Shackle, G L.S. (1974) Decision: the human predicament, *The Annals of the American Academy of Political and Social Science*, Vol. 412, March, pp. 1–10.

Sharkansky, I. and Hofferbert, R.L. (1969) Dimensions of state politics, economics and public policy, *American Political Science Review*, Vol. 63, No. 3, pp. 867–79.

Shubik, M. (1970) On different methods for allocating resources, *Kyklos*, Vol. 23.

Sills, D.L. (1957) *The Volunteers: Means and Ends in a National Organisation*, Free Press, Glencoe, Illinois.

Silverman, D. (1970) *The Theory of Organisations*, Heinemann.

Simon, H.A. (1957) *Models of Man*, Harper and Row.

Simon, H.A. (1960) *The New Science of Management Decision*, Harper and Row.

Simon, H.A. (1962) The architecture of complexity, *Proceedings of the American Philosophical Society*, Vol. 106, No. 6, pp. 467–82.

Simon, H.A. (1964) On the concept of organisational goal, *Administrative Science Quarterly*, Vol. 9, pp. 1–22.

Simon, H.A. (1965) *Administrative Behaviour: A Study of Decision-Making Processes in Administration Organisation*, 2nd edn, Free Press, Glencoe, Illinois (1st edn 1947).

Simon, H.A. (1969) *The Sciences of the Artificial*, MIT Press.

Simon, H.A. (1978) Rationality as a process and as a product of thought, *American Economic Review*, May, Vol. 68, No. 2.

Simon, H.A., Cyert, R.M. and Trow, D.B. (1956) Observation of a business decision, *Journal of Business*, Vol. 29, pp. 237–48.

Simon, H.A. and Ridley, C. (1938) The criterion of efficiency, *The Annals of the American Academy of Political and Social Science*, September, pp. 20–25.

Simon, H.A., Smithburg, D.W. and Thompson, V.A. (1950) *Public Administration*, Knopf.

Sisson, C. (1966) *The Spirit of British Administration*, Faber & Faber.

Smith, B.C. (1971) Reform and change in British central administration, *Political Studies*, Vol. XIX, No. 2, June.

Smith, B.L.R. and Hague, D.C. (eds) (1971)*The Dilemma of Accountability in Modern Government*, Macmillan.

Solow, R.M. (1971) Some implications of alternative criteria for the firm, in R. Marris and A. Wood, (eds) *The Corporate Economy*, Macmillan.

Spann, R. (1977) Rates of productivity change and the growth of state and local government, in T.E. Borcherding (ed.), *Budgets and Bureaucrats*, Duke University Press.

Spence, M. (1974) *Market Signaling: Information Transfer in Hiring and Related Screening Processes*, Harvard University Press.

Spence, A.M. (1975) The economics of internal organisation: an introduction, *The Bell Journal of Economics*, Vol. 6, No. 1.

Stanyer, J. (1978) Divided responsibilities: accountability in decentralised government, *Public Administration Bulletin*, No. 17, pp. 14–30.

Starbuck, W.H. (1965) Organisational growth and development, in J.G. March (ed.) *Handbook of Organisations*, Rand McNally.

Steers, R.M. (1975) Problems in the measurement of organisational effectivenesss, *Administrative Science Quarterly*, Vol, 20, p. 546–58.

Steiner, P.O. (1974) Public expenditure and budgeting, in A.S. Blinder and R.M. Solow *et al.*, *The Economics of Public Finance*, Brookings Institution, Washington DC.

Sterne, R.S., Rabushka, A. and Scott, A.A. (1972) Serving the elderly — an illustration of the Niskanen effect, *Public Choice*, Vol. 13, pp. 81–90.

Stewart, M. (1933) *The Jekyll and Hyde Years,* Dent.
Stigler, G.J. (1961) The economics of information, *Journal of Political Economy,* Vol. 69, pp. 213–25.
Stiglitz, J.E. (1975) Incentives, risk and information: notes towards a theory of hierarchy, *Bell Journal of Economics,* Vol. 6, No. 2, pp. 552–79.
Storing, H.J. (1962) The science of administration: Herbert A. Simon, in H.J. Storing, (ed.), *Essays on the Scientific Study of Politics,* Holt, Rinehart and Winston.
Street, H. (1975) *Justice in the Welfare State,* Hamlyn Lectures, 20th Series.
Sugden, R. and Williams, A. (1970) *The Principles of Practical Cost Benefit Analysis,* Oxford University Press.
Sweeney, J.W. Jr. (1973) An experimental investigation of the free-rider problem, *Social Science Research,* Vol. 2, pp. 277–92.
Tannenbaum, A.S. (1966) *Social Psychology of the Work Organisation,* Tavistock Publications.
Taverne, D. (1976) *The Control of Public Spending,* Institute for Fiscal Studies, London.
Taylor, F.W. (1911) *The Principles of Scientific Management,* Harper and Row.
Thom, René (1964) Local topological properties of differential mappings, in *Bombay Coloquium on Differential Analysis,* Oxford University Press.
Thompson, E.A. (1973) Review of Niskanen's bureaucracy and representative government, *Journal of Economic Literature,* September, pp. 950–53.
Thompson, J.D. (1967) *Organistions in Action.* McGraw-Hill.
Thompson, J.D. and Bates, F.L. (1957) Technology organisation and administration, *Administative Science Quarterly,* pp. 325–42.
Tiebout, C.M. (1956) A pure theory of local expenditures, *Journal of Political Economy,* Vol. 64, pp. 416–24.
Tinter, G. (1941a) Theory of choice under subject risk and uncertainty, *Econometrica,* October, pp. 298–304.
Tinter, G. (1941b) The pure theory of production under technological risk and uncertainty, *Econometrica,* October, pp. 645–67.
Tisdell, C. (1975) Concepts of rationality in economics, *Philosophy of the Social Sciences,* Vol. 5.
Tisdell, C. (1976) Rational behaviour as a basis for economic theory, in G. Mortimore and S. Benn (eds), *Rationality in the Social Sciences,* Macmillan.
Trist, G.L. and Bamforth, K.W. (1951) Some social and psychological consequences of the Longwall method of goal getting, *Human Relations,* Vol. 4, pp. 3–38.
Trist, G.L. (1959) *Socio-Technical Systems.* Lecture given at University of Cambridge (unpublished).
Tullock, G. (1965) *The Politics of Bureaucracy,* Public Affairs Press, Washington DC.
Tullock, G. (1970) *Private Wants, Public Means: An Economic Analysis of the Desirable Scope of Government,* Basic Books.
Tullock, G. (1976) Regulating the regulates, in S. Pejovich, *Government Controls and the Free Market,* A and M Press, Texas.
Urwick, L.F. (1943) *The Elements of Administration*, Harper and Row.
Urwick, L.F. (1956) The manager's span of control, *Harvard Business Review,* 34.
Urwick, L. (1957) Public administration and business management, *Public Administration Review,* XVII, Spring, pp. 77–82.
Vroom, V.H. (1964) *Work and Motivation,* John Wiley.
Waldo, D. (1971) *Public Administration in a Time of Turbulence,* Chandler, New York.

Walkland, S.A. (ed.) (1977) *The Commons in the Seventies*, Collins for the Study of Policy Group.

Warwick, D. (1979) Integrating planning and implementation: a transactional approach, *Harvard Institute for International Development, Discussion Paper* No. 63, June.

Watson, G.B. (1945) Bureaucracy as citizens see it, *Journal of Social Issues*, Vol. 1, No. 4.

Weber, M. (1947) *The Theory of Social and Economic Organisation*, Free Press, New York.

Weitzman, M. (1976) The new soviet incentive model, *Bell Journal of Economics*, Spring.

Wheeler, H.J. (1967) Alternative voting rules and local expenditure, in G. Tullock (ed.), *Papers in Non-Market Decision-Making*, Vol. 2, pp. 61–70, Thomas Jefferson Center for Political Economy, Charlottesville, Virginia.

Wildavsky, A. (1961) Political implications of budgetary reform, *Public Administration Review*, Vol. 21, pp. 183–90.

Wildavsky, A. (1964) *The Politics of The Budgetary Process*, Little, Brown & Co.

Wildavsky, A. (1966) Towards a radical incrementalism, in A. de Grazia (ed.), *Congress the First Branch of Government*, American Enterprise Institute, Washington DC.

Wildavsky, A. (1968) Budgeting as a political process, *International Encyclopaedia of the Social Sciences*, Collier Macmillan.

Wildavsky, A. (1969) The political economy of efficiency: CBA, *Public Administration Review*, Vol. 29, No. 2.

Wildavsky, A. (1973) Does planning work? *The Public Interest*, No. 33.

Wildavsky, A. (1975) *Budgeting: A Comparative Theory of Budgetary Processes*, Little, Brown & Co.

Wiles, P.J.D. (1956) *Price Cost and Output*, Basil Blackwell.

Williams, A. (1973) Cost benefit analysis: bastard science? and/or insidious poison in the body politick?, in J.N. Wolfe (ed.), *Cost Benefit and Cost Effectiveness*, Allen & Unwin.

Williams, A. and Anderson, R. (1975) *Efficiency in the Social Services*, Basil Blackwell and Martin Robertson.

Williamson, O.E. (1963) Managerial discretion and business behaviour, *American Economic Review*, Vol. 53, December, pp. 1032–57.

Williamson, O.E. (1964) *The Economics of Discretionary Behaviour, Managerial Objectives in a Theory of the Firm*, Prentice-Hall.

Williamson, O.E. (1966) A rational theory of the federal budgeting process, in G. Tullock (ed.), *Papers in Non-Market Decision-Making*, Vol. 2, Thomas Jefferson Center for Political Economy, Charlottesville, Virginia.

Williamson, O.E. (1967) Hierarchical control and optimum firm size, *Journal of Political Economy*, Vol. 75, No. 2, pp. 123–38.

Williamson, O.E. (1970) *Corporate Control and Business Behaviour*, Prentice-Hall.

Williamson, O.E. (1971) The vertical integration of production: market failure considerations, *American Economic Review, Papers and Proceedings*, Vol. 27, pp. 112–23.

Williamson, O.E. (1971) Managerial discretion, organisation form and the multi-division hypothesis, in R. Marris and A. Wood (eds), *The Corporate Economy*, Macmillan.

Williamson, O.E. (1973) Markets and hierarchies: some elementary considerations, *American Economic Review*, Vol. 63, No. 2, May.

Williamson, O.E. (1975) *Markets and Hierarchies: Analysis and Anti-Trust Implications*, Free Press, New York.

Williamson, O.E. (1976) *The Evolution of Hierarchy: An Essay on the Organisation of Work,* The Fels Lecture on Public Policy Analysis, Norton.

Williamson, O.E., Wachter, M.L. and Harris, J.E. (1975) Understanding the employment relation: the analysis of idiosyncratic exchange, *The Bell Journal of Economics,* Vol. 6, No. 1.

Wilson, R. (1975) Informational economics of scale, *The Bell Journal of Economics,* Vol. 6, No. 1, Spring.

Wilson, Woodrow (1887) The study of administration, *Political Science Quarterly,* Vol. 2, pp. 197–222. (Reprinted Vol. 56 (1941), pp. 481–506.)

Wiseman, J. (1957) The theory of public utility pricing — an empty box, *Oxford Economic Papers,* NS, Vol. 9.

Wiseman, J. (1978) Some reflections on the economics of group behaviour, in P. Caroni, B. Dafflon and G. Enderlie (eds), *Nur Oekonomie ist keine Oekonomie,* (*Festschrift für Professor Buicchi*), Paul Haupt.

Woodward, J. (1958) *Management and Technology,* HMSO.

Worswick, G.D.N. (1972) Is progress in economic science possible?, *Economic Journal,* Vol. 82, March, pp. 73–86.

Wright, M. (1977) Public expenditure in Britain: the crisis of control, *Public Administation,* Vol. 55, Summer.

Wright, R. (1972) *The Day the Pigs Refused to be Driven to Market,* Hart-Davis MacGibbon.

Yuchtman, E. and Seashore, S.E. (1967) A system resource approach to organisational effectiveness, *American Sociological Review,* Vol. 32, pp. 891–903.

Zald, M. (1962) Power balance and staff conflict in correctional institutions, *Administrative Science Quarterly,* 7, June, pp. 22–49.

Zald, M.N. (1970) *Organisational Change: The Political Economy of the YMCA,* University of Chicago Press.

Zald, M.N. (1970) *Power in Organisations,* Vanderbilt University Press.

Zeeman, E.C. (1972) Some models from catastrophe theory in the social sciences, in E.C. Zeeman (ed.), *Catastrophe Theory: Selected Papers* (1977), Addison-Wesley.

Index

Accountability,
  and control, 220–5
  and decentralisation, 224
  UK institutions of, 228
Adaptive behaviour, 103
Agency relationships, 225–8
Algorithmic search (*see* Search procedures)
Allocative efficiency, 176–8
Arrow's Possibility Theorem, 109
Aspiration levels, 79

Budgeting and politics, 145–6
Bureau,
  budget–output function, 126–7
  cost function, 128
  equilibrium, 126–31
  power, 8–9
Bureaucracy,
  definitions, 4 ff.
  economist's approach, 112
  growth of, 135
  Marx's analysis, 6
  Michel's analysis, 7
  Mosca's analysis, 6
  Weber's analysis, 5–6

Cash limits, 243
Classical administrative theories, 21–4
Collective choice (*see* Decision making)
Complexity, 114–7
Compliance, 40,44
Constitutions, 75
Contingency theory, 34–6, 113–4, 164–70
Contract state, 219
Control loss, 195 ff.
Cyclical majorities, 109–10

Decentralisation, 205–7
Decision making, 88 ff.
  bounded rationality model, 95–101
  collective, 108–12
  costs, 115–16
  unbounded rationality model, 88–95
  and uncertainty, 112–18
Disjointed incrementalism, 147–8

Efficiency, 36, 173–5
  allocative, 176–8
  and decision costs, 195
  economist's analysis of, 176–84
  and goals, 188–92
  and incentives, 201–3
  and organisation structures, 197–9
  public sector, 185–8
  and risk, 204–5
  and uncertainty, 199–201
  X-efficiency, 178–185
Estimates Committee, 232–3
Exception principle, 22
Expenditure Committee, 233–6
Experiential budgeting, 150

Firms,
  behavioural theories, 77–82
  existence of, 50–53
  managerial theories, 53–6
  traditional theories, 48–50
Franks Committee, 246
Free rider, 100, 194
Fulton Committee, 246 ff.

Garbage-can model of choice, 119
Goal paradigm, 38–9
Goals, 79, 105–8

Hawthorne Studies, 25–6
Heuristic search (*see* Search procedures)
Human relations approach, 24–30

Implementation, 91, 252–72
Incentives, 201–3
Incommensurability, 67
Incrementalism, 146–64
Indecomposability, 67
Internal organisation, economics of, 56–60

Leadership, 25–6

Majority voting (*see* Voting)
Maximum principle, 208
Mechanistic model, 36
Monitoring, 91

Nationalised industries, Select Committee, 236–9
Niskanen, model of bureaucracy, 123

Oates' decentralisation theorem, 206
Organic model, 36
Organisation,
  action approach to, 39–40
  classical theories, 21–4
  contingency theory, 34–7
  definition, 16–17
  human relations school, 24–30
  M-form, 68
  radical critique, 39–40
  rational model, 38
  U-form, 66–7
Organisational,
  failure, 256–60
  limits, 260–62
  slack, 80, 182

Paradigm, 69–71
Pareto efficiency, 177
Partisan mutual adjustment, 147
PESC (Public Expenditure Survey Committee), 152, 241
Planning paradox (*see* Public expenditure planning)
Plowden Report, 240
Political economy model, 40–41, 73–5
  of budgeting, 164–70
Power, 40–42, 62–5, 76–7, 166–70
Public Accounts Committee (PAC), 229–32
Public choice school, 2
Public expenditure planning, 240–44
  costed options, 242–3
  planning paradox, 241–2
  price basis, 242
Public sector employment, 13

QUANGOs, 3, 219 ff.

Rational model of organisations, 38–9
Rationality, 91–5
  bounded, 95–101
  selective, 104–5
  unbounded, 88–91
Resource allocation systems, 10–12
Resource dependency theory, 41, 164–70

Satisficing, 99–101
Scalar principle, 22
Scientific management, 19–21
Search procedures,
  algorithmic, 101–2
  heuristic, 102
Selective rationality (*see* Rationality)
Simon's certainty equivalent theorem, 101–2
Slack, 182
Social justice, 207–9
Socio-technical system, 34–8
Span of control, 22
Strategic contingencies theory, 41
Structural functionalism, 33
Supply-side economics, 12
Sure thing principle, 92–3

Taut planning, 260
Teams, 60–62, 179–80
Transactions costs, 51–2, 83, 115–16

Uncertainty, 36, 112–18
Uncertainty absorption, 116–17
Unity of command, 22

Vote trading, 110
Voting, 108–11
  majority, 109

X-efficiency, 178–84

Zero base budgeting, 151